The Christian Schism in Jewish History and Jewish Memory

How did Jews perceive the first Christians? By what means did they come to appreciate Christianity as a religion distinct from their own? In *The Christian Schism in Jewish History and Jewish Memory*, Professor Joshua Ezra Burns addresses those questions by describing the birth of Christianity as a function of the Jewish past. Surveying a range of ancient evidences, he examines how the authors of Judaism's earliest surviving memories of Christianity speak to the perspectives of rabbinic observers conditioned by the unique circumstances of their encounters with Christianity to recognize its adherents as fellow Jews. Only upon the decline of the Church's Jewish demographic were their successors compelled to see Christianity as something other than a variation of Jewish cultural expression. The evolution of thought in the classical Jewish literary record thus offers a dynamic account of Christianity's separation from Judaism counterbalancing the abrupt schism attested in contemporary Christian texts.

Joshua Ezra Burns is an Assistant Professor in the Department of Theology at Marquette University specializing in Judaism and Christianity in antiquity. He earned his doctorate in Religious Studies and Judaic Studies from Yale University.

The Christian Schism in Jewish History and Jewish Memory

JOSHUA EZRA BURNS

Marquette University, Milwaukee, Wisconsin

CAMBRIDGE
UNIVERSITY PRESS

CAMBRIDGE
UNIVERSITY PRESS

32 Avenue of the Americas, New York, NY 10013-2473, USA

Cambridge University Press is part of the University of Cambridge.

It furthers the University's mission by disseminating knowledge in the pursuit of education, learning, and research at the highest international levels of excellence.

www.cambridge.org
Information on this title: www.cambridge.org/9781107120471

First published 2016

Printed in the United Kingdom by Clays, St Ives plc

A catalog record for this publication is available from the British Library.

Library of Congress Cataloging in Publication Data
Names: Burns, Joshua Ezra, author.
Title: The Christian schism in Jewish history and Jewish memory / Joshua Ezra Burns.
Description: New York, NY : Cambridge University Press, 2016. |
Includes bibliographical references and index.
Identifiers: LCCN 2015043649 | ISBN 9781107120471 (hardback)
Subjects: LCSH: Judaism – Relations – Christianity. | Christianity and other religions – Judaism. | Jews – Identity.
Classification: LCC BM535.B87 2016 | DDC 296.3/9609–dc23
LC record available at http://lccn.loc.gov/2015043649

ISBN 978-1-107-12047-1 Hardback

Contents

Acknowledgments

This book began its life as doctoral dissertation submitted to the Department of Religious Studies of Yale University in 2010. Although the project has evolved considerably since then, I should like first and foremost to thank those of my professors who served as my mentors during my time in New Haven. My principal advisor Steven Fraade was a tremendous source of support throughout my career as a graduate student and an attentive guide as I produced my dissertation. Harold Attridge honored me by serving alongside Steven as codirector of the dissertation. Christine Hayes offered careful and constructive feedback as a member of my dissertation review board. John Collins was a constant dialogue partner and unfailing supporter of my work. I am fortunate to call Steven, Harry, Chris, and John my mentors and friends. I thus offer the present book as a token of my abiding gratitude to each of them.

Many others deserve credit for helping me along my path. I would not be the scholar I am today without the lessons of all my cherished teachers at Yale and during my undergraduate days at New York University. I also thank those of my fellow students with whom I shared the joys and frustrations of life among the dregs of academic society, particularly Alan Appelbaum, Dylan Burns, Tracy Lemos, Matthew Neujahr, Brent Nongbri, and Michael Peppard.

The second life of my project to which the present book attests could not have been without the help of my dear friends in the Department of Theology at Marquette University. My former department chairperson Susan Wood, SCL, was a stalwart supporter. As the interim dean of Marquette's College of Arts and Sciences, Rev. Philip Rossi, S.J., was instrumental in helping me to procure the means needed to complete my work in a timely fashion. My current department chair Robert Masson mercifully kept my workload manageable as I put the finishing touches on the manuscript. Of my many colleagues who found time to discuss my revisions, I give special thanks to Michel Barnes, Julian Hills, and Rev. Joseph Mueller, S.J., for their expert advices on all things ancient and Christian. I also thank my student Nathan Thiel for his editorial assistance as I readied the revised manuscript for submission.

Lewis Bateman, my editor at Cambridge University Press, was generous to accept my work for publication and exceptionally patient in seeing the manuscripts through its transition from unwieldy thesis into what I hope is now its more easily palatable state. Elda Granata and Rachel Cox were of great help overseeing that transition and guiding me through the process of becoming an author. I benefitted greatly from the comments of the anonymous colleagues who reviewed my work on behalf of the press. I am grateful to all of these men and women for their support of my scholarship and professional development.

Finally, I would like to thank my family. My parents, Edward and Chaya Burns, have shown me nothing but love and support since I decided to test my mettle in the uncertain world of academia. I therefore dedicate this book to them as I did the dissertation on which it is based. I furthermore express gratitude to my brothers and sisters, Judah and Aliza Burns, Ari and Ariella Burns, and Israel and Estie Rose, along with all of their wonderful children. Spending time with my family has provided much gladness and respite over the roughly ten years it took to see this project through its course. I could not have done it without them.

Abbreviations

The reader is advised of the following abbreviations utilized in reference to rabbinic texts.

b.   Babylonian Talmud (*Talmud Bavli*)
m.   Mishnah
t.   Tosefta
y.   Palestinian Talmud (*Talmud Yerushalmi*)

Titles of biblical and other ancient books are abbreviated per the stylistic guidelines of *The SBL Handbook of Style*, ed. B.J. Collins et al. (2nd edn.; Atlanta, GA: SBL Press, 2014).

Introduction

A PRELUDE: PARIS, 1240

In the summer of 1240, the city of Paris witnessed an unusual trial.[1] The lead prosecutor was Nicholas Donin, an apostate Jew turned Franciscan friar. The defendant, however, was not a person but a set of books. Since converting to Christianity several years earlier, Donin had worked tirelessly to prove his Catholic bona fides by exposing his former coreligionists as enemies of the Church. Having already denounced the Jews for their alleged blasphemies, Donin now set his sights on what he believed was their source. His target was the Babylonian Talmud, the great repository of classical rabbinic learning that stood second only to the Hebrew Scriptures in Judaism's sacred canon.[2] For months Donin had petitioned Pope Gregory IX to investigate the Talmud's rumored crimes against the Christian faith. The trial in Paris was to be a vindication of his efforts, a public exhibition of the guilt of those who conducted their lives in accord with the Talmud's perfidious teachings.

In submitting the Talmud as a work offensive to Christian doctrine, Nicholas Donin took advantage of the Church's habit of disavowing all manner of sacred knowledge alien to the Christian intellectual tradition. That the Talmud belonged to that order was hardly a novel observation on Donin's part. Generations of Christian theologians had traded in rumors of its treachery. Yet the Talmud's contents had remained largely unknown outside of the Jewish academies, its vast pages of Hebrew and Aramaic script forbidding even to the most seasoned Christian readers. Only with the aid of former Jews trained in

---

[1] For the following, compare Robert Chazan's detailed account of the trial in Friedman et al. (2012: 31–80). A summary overview with extensive bibliography appears in Krauss and Horbury (1995: 153–61).

[2] On perceptions of the Talmud's authority in medieval Jewish culture, see Fishman (2011), especially ibid. (121–54), on the proliferation of Talmudic knowledge in northern Europe during the High Middle Ages.

its study were its mysteries now being brought to light. Fueled by the zeal of the convert, Friar Nicholas was incensed by what he had come to see as the Talmud's stultifying ritual precepts and naked theological falsehoods. Insofar the Jews professed to live by the Talmud's wisdom, Donin now believed, their mere presence in Christian society undermined its ethical constitution.[3]

The unenviable task of defending the Jewish position fell to a panel of four distinguished French rabbis summoned to the court of King Louis IX at the Franciscan's behest. Leading the cause was Rabbi Yehiel ben Joseph of Paris, a noted scholar who had known Donin prior to his conversion.

Unfortunately for Yehiel and his associates, the trial was a farce. Surviving records of the affair suggest that the rabbis were allowed little more than to entertain Nicholas' audience, to exemplify the disbelief of which he had already persuaded the local ecclesial authorities.[4] Consequently, despite the capable efforts of the venerable Jewish sages to deflect Donin's allegations, theirs was a losing cause from the outset.

While his initial report of its alleged blasphemies certainly misrepresented the whole of the Talmud, Donin's grasp of its content was formidable enough to paint the rabbis into a corner. The friar seized upon Talmudic legislation involving gentiles and heretics, accusing the Jews of using such laws as pretexts for disparaging Christians. He expounded on ancient rabbinic doctrines seemingly at odds with the Catholic catechism. He exulted in the Talmud's rare but damning instances of polemical rhetoric overtly targeting Jesus and his followers. Donin, in short, knew precisely where to strike to exact the greatest damage against his opponents.

Given the effectiveness of their adversary's technique, Rabbi Yehiel and his colleagues could not simply deny Donin's charges. The friar had already provided the royal adjudicators a detailed catalogue of the unflattering Talmudic passages at issue.[5] The rabbis had recourse only to argue that those textual selections did not actually mean what Donin claimed they meant, and that the Talmud's polemics in fact were not directed against Christianity.

[3] The foregoing account follows Chazan (1988), who argues that Donin based his charges on controversies current among the Talmud's Jewish readers. Compare, however, J. Cohen (1982: 60–77), who contends that the friar drew chiefly upon traditional Christian polemics against the Talmud. With respect to Cohen, the Talmud's notoriety among certain Christians did not always speak to secure knowledge of its contents; cf. Fishman (2011: 167–74).

[4] Perhaps the best known of these is an elaborate Hebrew account written by Rabbi Yehiel several years after the fact. We also have a number of Latin court documents drafted by Donin and his associates. Forgiving the embellishments of each party to the affair, their reports agree with one another frequently enough to permit a fair degree of confidence as to the actualities of the trial. See Krauss and Horbury (1995: 153, n. 18), for the primary sources. For the sake of simplicity, I shall refer to the English translations of the major documents provided in Friedman et al. (2012).

[5] Although the only surviving record of Donin's initial charges was produced several years after the trial, its correspondence with Rabbi Yehiel's account of the Talmudic passages cited by the prosecution suggests its general accuracy; see Chazan in Friedman et al. (2012: 16–21).

Yet while this strategy might have worked in some cases, it would not work in all. What of those passages taking direct aim at Jesus? What of the notorious story casting the Christian Messiah as the illegitimate offspring of a Roman soldier?[6] What of the passage condemning Jesus to a hellish eternity submerged in a caul-dron of boiling excrement?[7] How, Donin begged his audience, could the rabbis deny the libelous nature of these passages? How, moreover, could Jewish readers who believed the Talmud's lies be permitted to commit such sacrilege?

The rabbis were up against the wall. Even if they had regarded the Talmud as a reliable record of Jesus' life, they could not uphold that position in court. Forced, therefore, to defend their sacred tradition against the indefensible, Yeḥiel and his associates devised a daring rebuttal.[8] The Jesus of the Talmud, they asserted, was not the Jesus of the New Testament. He was, rather, an oth-erwise unknown Jewish miscreant who happened to share the name of the Christian Messiah. In fact, Yeḥiel submitted, the ancient Jewish sages who authored the Talmud knew of several such Jesuses of no consequence to the Christian faith. He even produced the following Talmudic passage as evidence:

When King Yannai was putting the rabbis to death, Joshua ben Peraḥiah and Jesus fled to Alexandria in Egypt. When there was peace, Shimon ben Shetaḥ wrote to him, "From me, the Holy City, to you, Alexandria in Egypt: Oh sister of mine, my husband dwells with you while I sit abandoned!" So Rabbi Joshua arose to return. He happened upon a certain inn where they showed him great honor. "What a fine inn/innkeeper this is," he proclaimed.[9] "But rabbi," Jesus replied, "her eyes are narrow." "You wretch," Joshua cried, "Is this how you behave?" So he dispatched four hundred trumpets and excommunicated him. Jesus returned to him several times, saying, "Take me back!" But Joshua paid him no mind. One day Jesus approached Joshua while he was reciting the *Shema* prayer. Joshua considered taking Jesus back, and so made a gesture to him with his hand. But Jesus thought he was rebuffing him.[10] So he went and set up a brick and

---

[6] The passage appears in uncensored manuscripts of *b.Shabbat* 104b and *b.Sanhedrin* 67a, on which see Schäfer (2007: 15–18). It is cited by Yeḥiel (Friedman et al. 2012: 136–37) and the court recorder (ibid., 122).

[7] The passage appears in uncensored manuscripts of *b.Gittin* 56b–57a, on which see Schäfer (2007: 82–90). It is cited by Yeḥiel (Friedman et al. 2012: 135) and the court recorder (ibid., 122).

[8] For the following, see Yeḥiel's account in Friedman et al. (2012: 138–39), and compare the court recorder's account (ibid., 122). Although the Latin document does not explicitly assign the follow-ing stratagem to Yeḥiel, its account of the proceeding testimony of his colleague Rabbi Judah ben David of Melun suggests that the latter alluded to a Talmudic passage impugning Jesus "because he derided the words of the wise" (Ms. Paris Lat. 16558, fol. 231c: *quia derridebat verba sapien-cium* [sic]; cf. ibid., 124.). Per Chazan (1999: 88–90), it is possible that Yeḥiel collapsed the testi-monies of all the Jewish defendants into a singular dialogue for the sake of clarity. I shall proceed to refer to Yeḥiel as the author of the stratagem for lack of a more secure identification.

[9] The Aramaic term *akhsania* typically connotes an inn or a guest house (cf. Greek *xenia*), although the same lexical form is used elsewhere in the Babylonian Talmud to refer to a female innkeeper (e.g., *b.Bava Metzi'a* 87a). Hence, Jesus appears to misinterpret his teacher's compli-ment as referring not to the inn but to its proprietor.

[10] Rabbinic custom dictates that one should avoid interruption while reciting the *Shema* prayer; see *m.Berakhot* 2.1–2; *t.Berakhot* 2.2. The unfortunate timing of Jesus' arrival is thereby implied to

began to worship it. Joshua called to him, "Come back!" But Jesus replied, "So have I learned from you: Anyone who sins and causes others to sin is incapable of repentance." That is why the master said that Jesus the Nazarene practiced magic, deceiving Israel and leading them astray.[11]

At first glance, a story depicting Jesus as a lecherous idolater appears to be an odd choice for the defense. Evidently, moreover, this was not among the incriminating Talmudic passages on which Friar Nicholas predicated his charges.[12] Yeḥiel's decision to adduce the story appears to speak to his appreciation of its chronological confusion. The Hasmonean king Alexander Jannaeus, here dubbed Yannai, reigned over Judea from 103 to 76 BCE, that is, significantly earlier than the lifetime of Jesus of Nazareth. The Pharisaic sages Joshua ben Peraḥiah and Shimon ben Shetaḥ were active during roughly the same era. Rabbi Yeḥiel knew this, and he suspected that Nicholas Donin knew it too.[13] Donin would therefore have had to concede that the subject of the Talmud's condemnation could not possibly have been the Jesus of Christian devotion. Extending that logic to all of its indictments of persons named Jesus, Yeḥiel asserted that not one of them could be proven to refer to their hallowed Christian namesake.

From a contemporary standpoint, the rabbi's gambit seems fairly transparent. Clearly, the author of the Talmudic story meant to caricature the reputed founder of Christianity as an apostate Jew. Yet even if disingenuous, Yeḥiel's argument was no less resourceful. Friar Nicholas had aimed to indict the Talmud for what he perceived as its libelous claims about the Christian Messiah. To the faithful Christians who attended the trial, the Talmud's disparaging remarks about Jesus substantiated the very worst of Donin's accusations. If, as the prosecution contended, the Christian likeness of Jesus was true, the Jewish likeness must be false. Yeḥiel, of course, could not well have denied the truth professed by his opponent. But neither could he debase the Talmud by denying its historicity. He therefore asserted that the Talmud contained truths more numerous and more obscure than Donin had led his audience to believe.

prohibit Joshua from greeting his disciple upon his arrival. Instead, the rabbi manually gestures for Jesus to wait until he finishes reciting the prayer. Jesus, however, misinterprets his teacher's gesture as a signal to shove off.

[11] Excerpted from *b.Sanhedrin* 107b and *b.Sotah* 47a, uncensored manuscripts, on which see Schäfer (2007: 34–36). My translation is based on the text of *Sanhedrin* in Ms. Munich Cod. Hebr. 95 as recorded in Rabbinovicz (1868–1897: 9.339–40) with orthographical emendations supplied by the *Sotah* version.

[12] The Latin report does not include this passage amidst its list of the Talmud's blasphemies against Jesus (cf. Friedman et al. 2012: 117). Perhaps Donin knew of its potential to confound his case.

[13] While it is unclear whether Yeḥiel would have known the precise dates of Jannaeus' reign, he likely reasoned that Donin would have known that the Hasmonean king was no longer in power during first century CE. For further notices of Jannaeus' reign in Talmudic texts, see *b.Berakhot* 48a and *b.Qiddushin* 66a, with discussion in Kalmin (1999: 61–67). See also *m.Avot* 1.6–9, on the relatively early dates of Joshua ben Peraḥiah and Shimon ben Shetaḥ.

That the ancient Jewish sages who authored the Talmud were less preoccupied than Friar Nicholas with biography of Jesus Christ was, in theory, a
plausible defense. Yet, needless to say, Yehiel's ploy did not help win his case.
The official court record indicates that Donin simply dismissed Yehiel's logical
subterfuge as the very height of his Talmudic sophistry.[14] And so, following the
testimonies of the other Jewish luminaries forced to partake in the charade,
the trial was brought to an unceremonious close. It would take until May of
1248 for the Vatican to issue its first formal condemnation of the Babylonian
Talmud. But by that point the verdict was inconsequential. The intervening
years had seen copies of the Talmud and other classical Jewish texts confiscated
and burned by the cartload in Paris and throughout the dominion of King
Louis. The once thriving rabbinic academies of France were left desolate. With
no books at their disposal, their teachers and students had no reason to stay
there. Rabbi Yehiel was one of many who would decamp for the Holy Land
in the wake of the Paris trial.[15] In the end, Nicholas Donin did not succeed in
his mission to purge France of its Jews. But he did manage to extinguish their
intellectual fire for what would prove a long time to follow.

A JEWISH GOSPEL?

The Paris trial exposed a fault in traditional Jewish discourse of the Christian
other. At one time, the Jews of medieval Christendom could take heart in the
belief that the faith of their subjugators was nothing more than a base corruption of their own. Where Christians subscribed to the truth of the gospels,
Jews professed what they believed was the superior truth of their own sacred
books. The legends of the Talmud provided solace to an oppressed minority
who needed to know Jesus as a degenerate Jew in order to cope with their
abusive existence at the hands of those self-righteous gentiles who professed
his teachings. Jews both ignorant and educated circulated these and other such
condescending biographical fictions in the *Toledot Yeshu*, or the "Chronicles of
Jesus," a wildly popular Hebrew parody of the Christian gospels.[16] In a sense,
they had to. Satirizing the Christian majority by undermining their collective
sense of self was a crucial, if sometimes crass, mechanism of Jewish survival.[17]

---

[14] Friedman et al. (2012: 122). Yehiel's triumphant account records no such rejoinder.
[15] On these developments, see Chazan in Friedman et al. (2012: 80–92); Krauss and Horbury
(1995: 160–61).
[16] On the origin and function of the *Toledot Yeshu* literature in medieval Jewish culture, see
Meerson and Schäfer (2014: 1.3–18). The basic form of the composition is first attested in a
ca. 826/827 polemical treatise by Archbishop Agobard of Lyon (*De iudaicis superstitionibus et
erroribus* 10), on whose account see ibid. (1.3–5). Allusions to Jesus' supposed apprenticeship
under Joshua ben Perahiah appear in several surviving versions of the text, on which see ibid.
(1.58–59).
[17] For the characterization of the *Toledot Yeshu* as a polemical counterpoint to the canonical gospels, see Biale (1999: 132–37), and cf. Funkenstein (1993: 39–40).

Nicholas Donin understood the psychology of the Jews. In exposing their secrets to their Christian neighbors, Donin laid bare the discomfiting fact that the Jews, despite their self-assurances to the contrary, actually knew very little about Christianity. Some years earlier, the Spanish Jewish chronographer Abraham ibn Daud could assert with confidence the reliability of the Talmudic narratives involving Jesus, dismissing "the historical works of the gentiles" while hailing the "authentic tradition from the Mishnah and the Talmud, which did not distort anything."[18] Donin defied that conceit. Having joined Christian camp, Friar Nicholas was able to force the Jews to accept the superior truth of the gospels, and to falsify their own in the process. Indeed, one might discern in his elaborate trial a desire to reenact for the sake of his former rabbinic acquaintances the process of discovery whereby Donin himself came to realize that everything he thought he knew about Christianity was wrong.

What Donin did not know was that the Jews' supposed knowledge of Christianity was no less contrived than Rabbi Yeḥiel's defensive stratagem. Recent research has shown that the Babylonian Talmud is far from a reliable witness to the life of Jesus.[19] Originating during the late ancient period, the scandalous tales invoked during the Paris trial reflect the sensibilities of Jewish scribes who apparently knew very little about Christianity. The critical reader must therefore acknowledge that the Talmud's commentaries on Jesus were colored by the already centuries-old conflict between Christian and Jew that was just beginning to make its way into the Mesopotamian cultural sphere during the age of the Talmud's composition. The incentive of the Talmud's authors to denigrate the man whom they believed had incited the conflict naturally casts doubt over the sincerity of their portrait of the Christian Messiah.

The passage cited by Rabbi Yeḥiel is a case in point. On the surface, the strange tale of Jesus' apostasy seems to evoke elements of the gospel tradition preserved in the New Testament.[20] The flight from Judea to Egypt recalls the report in the Gospel of Matthew of a similar journey during Jesus' infancy.[21] Jesus' lascivious remark about the innkeeper might allude to his reputation for having shown compassion to his female disciples.[22] Perhaps most tellingly, his miscommunication with his master recalls Jesus' reported disputes with the

---

[18] G.D. Cohen (1967: 20–21), with discussion, ibid. (171–72, 229–30). As noted by Cohen (ibid., 114, n. 100), a corresponding claim appears in the work of ibn Daud's contemporary Judah Halevi (*Kuzari* 3.65).

[19] For the following, compare Schäfer (2007: 36–40), whose account of the story's composite nature are in general agreement with my own. See also Rubenstein (2010: 116–49), for a detailed analysis stressing the story's function as a warning for rabbinic masters to maintain cordial relationships with their disciples.

[20] This was long the premise Jewish scholars apt to treat the Talmud's allusions to Jesus as authentic, on which see Catchpole (1971: 11–69). For a recent proponent of this outdated approach, see Basser (2000: 73–74).

[21] Cf. Matt 2.13–18. For this identification, see, e.g., Laible (1893: 43); Klausner (1925: 26); Goldstein (1950: 77).

[22] Laible (1893: 44); Klausner (1925: 26).

Pharisees.[23] The Talmudic tale might therefore be read as an attempt to challenge the dominant Christian narrative by recasting it in negative terms.[24]

Yet closer examination reveals that its affinities with the Christian gospels are merely superficial. In fact, nearly every one of its components can be traced to elsewhere. The motif involving a flight to Egypt evidently was lifted from a similar passage in the Palestinian Talmud in which the roles of Joshua ben Peraḥiah and Jesus are played by the Pharisaic sage Judah ben Tabbai and an unnamed disciple.[25] The report of Jesus' excommunication echoes an unrelated procedural discussion elsewhere in the Babylonian Talmud of the rabbinic ordinance of *niddui*, or temporary excommunication from the Jewish community.[26] Joshua's failed reconciliation with his disciple is mirrored in the Palestinian Talmud's report of the prophet Elisha's relationship with his own insubordinate disciple Geḥazi.[27] Finally, the allegation that Jesus corrupted his fellow Jews appears verbatim in an unrelated Talmudic passage confirming the legality of his execution in view of later rabbinic teachings on capital punishment.[28] In other words, none of these elements of the story appears to reflect sound knowledge of the Christian gospels. At best, one might surmise that its author synthesized and embellished his Jewish source materials using the gospel narrative as a structural template.

The story's characterization of Jesus is no more compelling. That Jesus had possessed magical capabilities was a commonplace belief among early

---

[23] For similar assessments, see Bammel (1966–1967: 320–24); P.S. Alexander (1992: 17–18); Schäfer (2007: 39–40).

[24] So Lauterbach (1951: 488–89), and compare more recently Jaffé (2003). In a similar vein, Boyarin (1999: 25–26), likens the author's brusque rhetoric to that of early Christian thinkers who likewise presumed to trace the origins of alleged Christian heresies to the moral failings of their reputed authors.

[25] See *y.Ḥagigah* 2.2 (77d), and cf. *y.Sanhedrin* 6.6 (23c). Both Palestinian versions portray Judah ben Tabbai as a contemporary of Shimon ben Shetaḥ, who is cited elsewhere as a contemporary of Alexander Jannaeus (*y.Berakhot* 7.2 [11b]; *y.Nazir* 5.3 [54b]). On the literary relationship between the Palestinian and Babylonian stories, see Maier (1978: 114–16), and more extensively, Rubenstein (2010: 128–42). I follow Rubenstein (ibid., 124–27), in dating the Babylonian story to a relatively late stage in the Talmud's composition, i.e., the late sixth or seventh century. Cf. Kalmin (1999: 101–09), who estimates its date closer to that of its Palestinian prototype.

[26] The Babylonian sage Ulla is twice credited for the opinion that this temporary ban was to be enacted by sounding four hundred trumpets, i.e., the procedure whereby the Israelite Judge Barak cursed the Canaanite city of Meroz (*b.Mo'ed Qatan* 17b; *b.Shevu'ot* 36a; cf. Judg 5.23). The sounding of a horn also figured in the Babylonian procedure for *ḥerem*, the more permanent rite of excommunication implicitly applied to Jesus in the Talmudic account of his apostasy; cf. *b.Sanhedrin* 7b, and see Horbury (1985: 34–37).

[27] The Palestinian version of the Geḥazi story appears in *y.Sanhedrin* 10.2 (29b) (cf. 2 Kgs 6.1), while more elaborate Babylonian versions accompany the Jesus story in *b.Sanhedrin* 107b and *b.Sotah* 47a. See also *b.Berakhot* 17b; *b.Sanhedrin* 103b.

[28] I allude to a passage appearing in uncensored manuscripts of *b.Sanhedrin* 43a, where Rabbi Ulla asserts that Jesus was justly indicted as a *mesit*, an Israelite who entices others to idolatry (cf. Deut 13.6–11), on which see Schäfer (2007: 64–65). Specifically, Ulla accuses Jesus of having practiced sorcery and having led Israel astray, allegations echoed in the story of Jesus' apostasy.

Christians.²⁹ His reputation for having performed miraculous feats of healing seems to explain his anachronistic pairing with Joshua ben Peraḥiah,
whom Babylonian Jews likewise knew as a master sorcerer.³⁰ The verbal mis-
understanding whereby Jesus insults the homely innkeeper appears to reflect
a folkloric motif attested in a pair of Christian hagiographic texts predating
the Talmud's composition.³¹ Finally, the story's allegation that Jesus realized
his apostasy by worshipping a brick seems to refer to an obscure cultic rite
described in similar terms elsewhere in the Talmud itself.³² These assorted
effects of Mesopotamian popular culture perhaps were woven into the story to
bolster its credibility before the eyes of the Talmud's target readership. In any
case, they clearly speak to its fabrication by an irreverent rabbinic scribe possessing no reliable knowledge of the life of Jesus, much less of his significance
to Christian believers.³³

   Although Rabbi Yeḥiel likely did not appreciate the extent of its forgery, that
he doubted the story's integrity is sufficiently clear. He evidently knew enough
about the New Testament to recognize that the Talmud's portrait of Jesus was
nothing more than a distorted mirror image of the real Jesus of Nazareth. One
might therefore surmise that Yeḥiel chose to produce his unexpected Talmudic
witness precisely because he knew that he could deny its historicity without
compromising the integrity of its source. But Yeḥiel's ingenuity came with a
price. His confession that Jews trained on the Talmud actually knew very little
about Christianity's origins exposed a lapse in his people's collective memory.

²⁹ The use of Jesus' name as a magical talisman is widely attested in literary and epigraphic materials of the late ancient period, on which see M. Smith (1978: 45–67). On the currency of this
  practice in late ancient Mesopotamia, see Geller (1977). Evidently, even local Jewish sorcerers
  were not averse to invoking Jesus' name in service of their craft; see Levene (2003: 120–38)
  (no. M163).
³⁰ Although not noted as a sorcerer in classical rabbinic texts, Joshua ben Peraḥiah is assigned
  magical capabilities in a number of Babylonian incantation formulas; for examples, see Naveh
  and Shaked (1998: 158–160) (no. 5), with discussion, ibid. (162–63); Levene (2003: 31–35)
  (nos. M50 and M59). See also Reiner (1998: 255–60), who posits that the Pharisaic sage was
  posthumously reinvented as a magician by Jews in search of a functional talismanic alternative
  to Joshua's Christian namesake.
³¹ See Gero (1994), followed by Rubenstein (2010: 146–48). For the Christian texts, see Garsoïan
  (1989: 207); Price (1991: 147).
³² The Aramaic term *binta*, conventionally translated as "brick" or "tile," has stymied commentators wishing to find specific Christian connotations in the object of Jesus' worship.
  Alternative readings have thus described the article as an icon, a fish, and the moon; see Maier
  (1978: 122–25). Most recently, Murcia (2011) has inferred that the brick was molded in the
  shape of a cross. Per Maier, (ibid., 122), the Talmud elsewhere cites the veneration of bricks as
  a common Mesopotamian cultic rite (cf. *b.Avodah Zarah* 46a; *b.Avodah Zarah* 53b). Although
  not obvious to the modern reader, its intended heathen symbolism presumably would have res-
  onated with the ancient reader. For similar comments, see Schäfer (2007: 37).
³³ Rubenstein (2010: 142–46) is probably correct to note that the Babylonian story was meant to
  function primarily not as an indictment of Christianity but to underscore the lesson of the earlier morality tale involving Gehazi. That said, its author's presumption to cast Jesus in similarly
  unflattering terms must be understood to connote a distinct polemical intentionality on his part.

The evidence put forth at the trial suggests that the Jewish sages who lived through Christianity's birth presumed to document it only centuries after the fact, and even then upon no sound evidentiary basis. The knowledge of the Christian other thereby inscribed upon the Jewish imagination was no less flawed than the polemical fictions upon which it was founded.[34]

Ironically, the Paris trial marked a turning point in the classical Jewish discourse on Christianity. Against all reasonable expectations, Rabbi Yeḥiel's counterintuitive reasoning was adopted by learned Jews eager to protect their sacred books from the bonfire. In time, the *Toledot Yeshu* fell into disrepute, its credibility compromised by its readers' loss of innocence regarding its counterfeit quality.[35] Outright denial of the Talmud's familiarity with the Christian Messiah became the norm among its devoted readers.[36] When, in the sixteenth century, the advent of Hebrew printing promised to open the secrets of the Talmud to a wider audience than ever before, its antagonistic allusions to Jesus and his followers were excised by Jewish editors eager to appease the Catholic censors then overseeing the production of their books.[37] Few of its Jewish readers mourned the loss. As far as they were concerned, a sanitized Talmud was better than no Talmud at all.

In view of these looming developments, one might infer that the unraveling of the ancient Jewish polemic against Christianity was inevitable. As the Christian argument against Judaism evolved to integrate genuine Jewish knowledge, the Jewish counterargument needed to evolve as well. Forced to accept the truth of the gospels against that of the Talmud, Rabbi Yeḥiel and his colleagues challenged their fellow Jews to rethink their received wisdom as to how the difference between Christian and Jew came to be. Not since the days of the Babylonian sages had the Jewish people been obliged to ponder that question. No longer could the critical thinker afford to imagine the Christian as nothing more than a Jewish antitype. The Paris trial thereby set in motion a search for Jewish meaning in the Christian schism that continues to this day.

---

[34] See Chazan (2004: 72–76), who attributes this void in common Jewish knowledge to the populist *Toledet Yeshu* as opposed to its more obscure Talmudic sources.

[35] Ironically, the covert Jewish transmission of the *Toledot Yeshu* after the High Middle Ages is best attested by the number of Christian authors who sought to expose its secrets; see Deutsch (2011). The fractured channels of the book's transmission likely account for the wide variety of forms in which the *Toledot Yeshu* has survived, on which see Meerson and Schäfer (2014: 1.28–39).

[36] Among those who adopted Yeḥiel's strategy was the famed Spanish rabbi Moses ben Naḥman, or Naḥmanides, who utilized the same argument in a 1263 disputation in Barcelona. For further comments to this effect, see Berger (1998: 25–39), with reference to Rabbi Yeḥiel's ploy, ibid. (33–34). For a modern adaptation of the same apologetic technique, see Maier (1978: 268–75), who rather dubiously argues that all of the Talmud's alleged allusions to Jesus of Nazareth are medieval interpolations drawn from the *Toledot Yeshu*.

[37] See Raz-Krakotzin (2007), especially ibid. (135–40), on the preemptive Jewish censorship of some of the earliest printed editions of the Talmud.

READING THE CHRISTIAN SCHISM AS JEWISH HISTORY

The purpose of this study is, in one sense, to fill the gap exploited by both the Christian and Jewish parties to the Paris trial. Why is the classical Jewish literary record, though replete with detailed information on all manner of Jewish subjects, virtually silent on Christianity's break from Judaism? What caused the memory lapse whereby the Jewish sages failed to document as it unfolded a development that would prove tremendously significant to their people and to the world at large? In the chapters to follow, I shall show that those questions demand a number of assumptions regarding the nature of the Christian schism difficult for the contemporary historian of Judaism to defend. In another sense, therefore, the object of this study is to reframe the question prompted by the Paris trial regarding the deficiency of the Jew's knowledge of the Christian other. I aim to pose that question from the perspective of a classical Jewish tradition that knows not of Christianity per se but, rather, of a movement of Christians from within the boundaries of ancient Jewish society to without.

My objective will not be to probe the Talmudic texts purporting to tell of Jesus' life as a Jew. Rabbi Yeḥiel and generations of scholars since have shown the feebleness of that approach. Nor shall I produce new evidence drawn from hitherto untapped sources. Rather, I shall attempt to configure previously acknowledged Jewish and Christian evidences within a new analytical framework. Tracing the Jewish encounter with Christianity from its inception through its earliest remembrances in the classical Jewish literary record, I shall attempt to explain how and why the rabbinic sages who authored that record responded to Christianity as they did. My aim, in other words, is not to retrieve a lost Jewish history of Christian origins to replace the discredited stories of the Talmud and the *Toledot Yeshu*.[38] I intend merely to account for how the memories informing those counterfeit histories might productively be read as witnesses to collective cognitive process whereby ancient Jews came to distinguish the Christian schism as such.

In order to demonstrate the empirical advantage of my approach, a few definitions of terms are in order.[39] What does it take to produce history? The concept of history is often confused with the past it is meant to document. Personalities and events are deemed "historical" in the sense that they are of the past, or, more simply, that they are no longer. But the discourse of history is far more complex than many of its casual consumers tend to recognize. To write history is to compose a narrative of the past tailored to advance the historian's agenda in documenting it.[40] To serve that agenda invariably compels

[38] Cf. Horbury (2010a: 358–66), who speculates that these sources, though admittedly flawed, might preserve elements of a lost Jewish narrative of Christian origins stemming from contemporary witnesses to the events in question. While that might well be the case, Horbury's thesis is too conjectural to offer significant guidance for my project.

[39] The following comments are informed by Jenkins (1991), particularly ibid. (6–32).

[40] Cf. Jenkins (1991: 40): "It is never really a matter of the facts per se but the weight, position, combination and significance they carry vis-à-vis each other in the construction of explanations."

the historian to submit certain persons and events as more meaningful than others. In other words, the historian must choose which elements of the past to preserve and which to omit for the sake of relating the past to his or her present narratalogical objective. History, therefore, is not simply a record of what happened in the past. It is the product of an intentional literary design, a subjective impression of the past conditioned by what the historian wishes his or her readers to know about it.

The will of the historian to streamline the past in view of his or her discursive need might be likened to an exercise in the orchestration of memory.[41] That an individual will remember certain facts about the past while forgetting others is only natural. One will recall, for instance, being involved in an automobile accident while casually forgetting the many occasions upon which he or she traveled without incident. Because the accident is atypical of the subject's normal routine, the circumstances of its occurrence are deemed more significant by comparison. The task of the historian is to remind his or her readers of the proverbial accidents that helped to shape the world in which they live. By drawing attention to specific persons and events ostensibly of consequence to the reader's experience or worldview, the disciplined historian can help the reader retrieve meaningful memories from an otherwise useless file of facts about times gone by. History therefore serves not only to remind the reader about which elements of the past are consequential but also to purge the reader's memory of its less meaningful effect by way of omission.

The conceptual distance between the abstract past and its concrete historical representation has elicited wariness among some cultural critics regarding the precision of historiography as a scientific discourse. To choose one notable example, Hayden White has argued that written history must be received not as an impartial record of the past but as a deliberate effort of the historian to represent that past in view of the subjective realities governing his or her interpretation thereof.[42] The historical narrative, White contends, inevitably entails a metahistorical subtext, an unstated guiding narrative that serves to render its host narrative no more trustworthy than the fictive literary form it is made to emulate.[43] The historian, in other words, forces the reader to consent to his or her interpretive biases by presenting only those facts pertinent to his or her narratalogical agenda. The result is a past that exists only insofar as the historian wills it into existence. Historiography, therefore, is by its very nature resistant to empirical inquiry. It is an ever-shifting discourse of cultural relativism at hopelessly odds with its own positivist assumptions.[44]

While critics of White have defended the ability of the historian to write without prejudice, the lesson of his critique has been well taken.[45] Despite its

---

[41] See Ricoeur (2004: 135–40).
[42] For the following, see H. White (1978: 51–100), and cf. Ricoeur (2004: 234–80).
[43] H. White (1978: 81–82).
[44] For comments to this effect, see Iggers (1997: 118–33).
[45] Cf. Iggers (1997: 134–40).

customary pretensions of objectivity, the writing of history is not an exact science. Simply to acknowledge the historian's authorial prerogative is to question whether he or she has allowed a subjective construction of reality to guide his or her work to insincere effect. The clash of Christian and Jewish narratives exposed during the Paris trial well illustrates that ethical pitfall. Nicholas Donin's knowledge of the Christian schism was conditioned by metahistorical data prioritizing the truth of the gospels over that of the Talmud. Rabbi Yeḥiel's sense of the same event was conditioned by his prioritization of the Talmud's truth. Each of their assumptions regarding the reliability of the other's knowledge was conditioned by their respective social realities, Donin's as a Christian and Yeḥiel's as a Jew. But the idea of alternative realities did not exist in their medieval minds, at least not in the antagonistic theater of their debate. Only one of their histories could speak the truth, only one account of the past deemed real. Only when individuals such as Nicholas Donin opted to trade their Jewish realities for Christian realities did the inconsistencies of their historical memories threaten the Jew's confidence in his truth.[46]

Donin's ability to impose his reality on Rabbi Yeḥiel was a function of his superior social standing. His rhetoric of persuasion worked only because Yeḥiel could not possibly have questioned the objective truth of the gospels in the setting of their dispute. Thankfully, that is no longer the case. To heed White's critique is to recognize the right of the historian to acknowledge that no one narrative of the past can represent the entirety of its truth. It therefore stands to reason that contemporary historians possess the right to pursue histories of the Christian schism informed by Jewish sensibilities. Still, the socially responsible interpreter of Jewish history must forgo the ugliness of the past in favor of respectful and accountable engagement with the Christian historical record. As Nicholas Donin knew, no viable account of the Christian schism can function solely on the basis of Judaism's defective memory of that event.

That brings me back to the aim of this study. My purpose is not to write a history of the schism between Judaism and Christianity. It is, rather, to write a Jewish history of the Christian schism. By that I mean to interrogate the earliest surviving Jewish memories of the Christian other in order to determine what their authors thought they knew about Christianity and why. My principal subjects of interest are the fairly rare notices on Christians and Christianity preserved in the writings of the rabbinic sages of Roman Palestine between the first and third centuries of the Common Era.[47] I shall draw those evidences from the Mishnah and

---

[46] For like considerations, see Funkenstein (1993: 206–08).

[47] Note that I will not be dealing with the testimonies of the first-century CE Greco-Jewish historian Flavius Josephus to the lives of Jesus (*Ant.* 18.63–64), his brother James (*Ant.* 20.199–203), and John the Baptist (*Ant.* 18.116–19). As the works of Josephus survive only in Christian manuscripts, suspicion of their embellishment by pious redactors renders these testimonies problematic. On these passages and the difficulties concerning their interpretation, see Carleton Paget (2001), especially ibid. (554–606), on Josephus' unlikely allusion to Jesus as the Messiah (*Ant.* 20.200). As Carleton Paget, ibid. (606–19), concludes, Josephus exhibits meager knowledge

the Tosefta, anthologies of legal and narrative materials traditionally ascribed to the sages of that era, also known as the *Tannaim*. I shall also call upon rabbinic documents originating in Byzantine Palestine and Sasanian Babylonia, and preserving traditions of the *Amoraim*, that is, the rabbinic sages of roughly the third through fifth centuries.[48]

Extracting legitimate historical data from classical rabbinic texts requires great care. A full exposition of the analytical assumptions and techniques to be utilized in the chapters to follow need not be articulated here.[49] For now, I offer the following analogy. My proposed method of interpretation evokes the process of epistemological inquiry described by Michel Foucault as the archeology of knowledge.[50] The archeologist excavates relics from the neutral context of the earth, later to determine the historical significance of those items with the aid of corresponding forensic data culled from elsewhere. The bits of bone and pottery, of no diagnostic quality on their own, are thereby imbued with historical meaning by virtue of their contextualization in a more secure analytical framework. In a similar fashion, I intend to mine the archival memories of the ancient rabbis for abstract historical data pertinent to my investigation.[51] At times, I shall have to read the data against the designs of their creators, in effect, forcing their authors to say what they did not mean to say. Often, moreover, I shall have to cut through the rhetorical misdirection inscribed upon the surfaces of the evidences at issue in order to unearth the realities hidden beneath.

But discussion of those texts will occupy only part of my study. The greater share will be devoted to discussing the ideological and social contexts of the rabbinic record in view of contemporaneous historical developments pertinent to its interpretation. My intention in these discussions will be to demonstrate that the faulty Jewish knowledge of Christianity exposed by Nicholas Donin was not the result of a mass memory lapse, but, rather, was the effect of a unique social reality that conditioned the early rabbinic sages to describe the Christian's alterity or otherness primarily in reference to their own experiences as Jews. This technique of reflexive construction created the illusion that the rabbinic sages failed to appreciate the Christian schism as it happened. In fact, I shall contend, their failure was merely to account for what they saw

of the activities of Jesus' followers after the death of James. This suggests that he knew not of Christianity per se but merely of certain individuals instrumental to its early history. In any case, Josephus was largely unknown to Jewish readers until the modern age, which makes his testimonies to the proto-Christian figures in questions largely inconsequential to my investigation.

[48] On the parameters of these conventional rabbinic classifications, see Rubenstein (2007: 59–65).

[49] For a recent discussion of the pertinent methodological issues, see P.S. Alexander (2010). I shall offer more substantial methodological comments as I introduce the rabbinic texts in question.

[50] Foucault (1972: 190–92), describes the foremost object of historical inquiry as the ability of the reader to uncover the discursive practices that gave rise to the development of a given body of knowledge, and thereby to distinguish the dynamic relationship between its factual and its interpretive elements.

[51] I elaborate upon this methodological analogy in greater detail in Burns (2007: 403–11).

as a schism. Only when their subjective reality was challenged by the opposing reality of Christians self-identifying as non-Jews did the rabbinic collective reevaluate its received understanding of the Christian other in order to
acknowledge that a decisive rupture had taken place.

In choosing to set my investigation amidst the twin discourses of Jewish
history and Jewish memory, I take my cues from others who have examined
the interplay of those phenomena. In his classic 1982 study *Zakhor*, Yosef
Hayim Yerushalmi submitted the concept of collective memory as a key to
understanding the historical mindset of the Jewish people.[52] The term collective memory was coined by sociologist Maurice Halbwachs, who observed that
the memory of the individual is controlled by the social framework in which
that individual operates. The memory of a collective thus constitutes an objective reality created through the conscious efforts of that group to sustain its
defining ideologies and social practices.[53] Applying Halbwach's theory to the
Jewish collective, Yerushalmi demonstrated the tendency of premodern Jewish
authors to shape their readers' memories of the past by representing the Jewish
experience in cyclical terms. As the passage of time brought the Jews alternating prosperity and suffering, their efforts to make sense of the past have hinged
on their distant recollections of God's covenantal promises to the children of
Israel. These ancient scriptural promises were burned into the minds of faithful
Jews conditioned to believe that God rewards his chosen nation when they follow his will and, conversely, punishes them when they go astray. The meaning
of a given event of the past was therefore weighed by the Jewish collective in
reference to that divine equation. Only, they believed, when their merits were
completely to offset their sins would the repetitious sequence of reward and
punishment be broken by the arrival of a Messiah, who would render God's
final judgment in Israel's favor.[54]

As Yerushalmi observed, classical Judaism's sense of history is at variance with a tradition of western historicism typically objectifying the present
rather than the past as the culmination of the human experience. Of course,
the dominant tradition was tempered by a triumphalist Christian mentality
generally not obliging to the Jewish experience. In any event, Yerushalmi's
theory helps to explain why the authors of the earliest surviving Jewish testaments to Christianity's birth subordinated its significance toward Jews. To
their minds, Christianity mattered only insofar as the new religious initiative
stood to affect the salvation of Israel, that is, the Jewish Israel. But their initial indifference toward Christianity does not necessarily indicate their ignorance thereof.

---

[52] Yerushalmi (1982).
[53] Yerushalmi (1982: xxxiv–xxxv). Cf. Halbwachs (1992), especially his comments on religious
memory, ibid. (84–119).
[54] Yerushalmi (1982: 5–26).

Nevertheless, that rabbinic authors of the late ancient period drew upon earlier traditions when finally forced to account for the Christian schism suggests that their lack of formal records of that event did not deter them from drawing history from the memories of their predecessors. Those memories furnished the raw data from which the authors of the Talmud and the *Toledot Yeshu* adduced their own records of the history in question. Consequently, one might argue, all of what the early sages produced during the early centuries of the Common Era constitutes a record of how they experienced the Christian schism. It is an incomplete record, to be sure, but useful one nonetheless.

On such grounds did Amos Funkenstein challenge Yerushalmi's theory of early Judaism's limited historical imagination.[55] According to Funkenstein, the meagerness of premodern Jewish historiography was the effect not of a cyclical collective memory but, rather, of psychological conditioning. The trials of Jewish experience, he acknowledges, at times have yielded perspectives on the past colored by the prospect of future salvation. But in order to reach that future, the Jews had first to survive the present. In this respect, the Jews were not unique. Every collective seeking to preserve its communal identity must use the past to justify its continued existence. Inasmuch, therefore, as the past bears meaning only in the present, it was not static memories that informed the Jewish historical mind but an ever-evolving set of perceptions regarding the continuity between Judaism's past and its present. The effect of this dynamic objective, Funkenstein posits, was an acute and pervasive historical consciousness. Although Jews typically did not mimic the exultant historiography practiced by their Christian contemporaries, their diverse literary legacies nonetheless are endowed with meaningful reflections on the past. One therefore can seek legitimate historical data in all manner of classical Jewish texts and cultural artifacts not meant to function as archival records.

Although I find value in both Yerushalmi's and Funkenstein's definitions of what constitutes Jewish history in the ancient frame of reference, I am wedded to neither. I prefer to uphold Yerushalmi's inference of distance between Jewish history and Jewish memory, even if, per Funkenstein, they did always function independently of one another. To my mind, that both acknowledge the impact of psychosocial conditioning upon the Jewish historical imagination validates my methodology. For my purpose, simply to recognize the historical alignment of classical Jewish thought is to widen the pool of textual evidences plausibly to be read as witnesses to the Christian schism. Even if it took centuries for the rabbinic sages to see the schism for what it was, it stands to reason that their reexamination of the Christian other took its cues from the initial encounter documented in their earliest surviving traditions. It simply takes a discerning eye to see how that process of converting memory to history took place.

---

[55] For the following, see Funkenstein (1993: 1–21).

My inquiry will proceed as follows. Chapter 1 will address contemporary
scholarship on the Christian schism as it relates to the experiences of the Jews.
At issue will be a popular critical narrative of the schism known as the parting of the ways between Judaism and Christianity. After commenting on the
empirical validity of that narrative, I shall identify those of its critical assumptions that I believe render it incompatible with the Jewish evidences I intend to
examine. By demonstrating the weaknesses of the "parting" model as a key to
experiences of the early rabbinic sages, I aim to demonstrate the usefulness of
my own historical project as well as to establish methodological guidelines for
its pursuit in the pages to follow.

Chapter 2 will focus on the idea of Jewish identity during the early centuries of the Common Era. My goal will be to establish the existence of certain
discernible standards of thought and behavior commonly, if not universally,
understood to have defined the Jew during Christianity's formative age. Probing
the ancient idea of Jewish identity from several theoretical perspectives, I shall
argue that its practical application at the site of the initial encounter between
Christian and Jew was predicated on a widely recognized program of cultural
affiliation resistant to simple description or classification. Nevertheless, I shall
submit that that program was distinctive enough to provoke debate amidst an
early Christian collective at odds with itself regarding how best to relate to the
Jewish collective whence it derived.

Chapter 3 will examine precisely how the idea of Jewish identity came to
be problematized within the Christian collective. Focusing first on Paul's letters to the Galatians and the Romans, I shall describe a conflict of missionary
priorities among the earliest followers of Jesus ultimately to define the difference between Christian and Jew outside the rabbinic frame of reference. I shall
then demonstrate how those Christians still given to traditional Jewish ways
of life came to populate the areas where the early rabbinic sages operated.
I thus intend to describe the uniquely Jewish character of Christian life in the
environments where the initial rabbinic encounter with the Christian other
took place.

Chapter 4 will focus on a series of early rabbinic texts attesting to that
encounter. Mining these texts for historical data, I shall demonstrate their varied functions as fabricated memories testifying to their respective authors' perceptions of the Christians operating in their midst. I thereby shall explain why
the authors of those ancient notices cast the followers of Jesus as fellow Jews
rather than subscribers to a cultural system foreign to their own. The resulting
perception of Jewish commonality with the Christian other, I therefore shall
argue, left a unique impression of Christianity on the writings of the Jewish
sages distinct from that assumed by most Christians of their age.

Chapter 5, the final chapter, will trace the evolution of the rabbinic polemic
against Christianity through the Christianization of the Roman Empire, a complex and multifaceted process that began in the early fourth century. Utilizing a
range of Jewish and Christian texts, I shall demonstrate how the initial rabbinic

impression of the Christian as Jew gave way to a more fully realized sense of difference as the Jewish population of Palestine began to sustain the effects of Christian imperialism. I thereby aim to show how the rabbinic sages who lived through that transition adjusted their received rhetoric of Christian otherness to reflect their own newly realized sense of Jewish otherness relative to their Christian neighbors.

Finally, I should say a few words about how I hope my study will be received. I will begin by offering the reader some insight into my own interpretive agendas and metahistorical assumptions. Although I am a theologian by avocation, I conceived this book as a study in Jewish history. As such, my principal objective is to document a misunderstood chapter of the Jewish experience in antiquity. I do not mean to offer a comprehensive survey of the many and diverse Jewish sources of early Christian life and thought. Scholarship of that variety is available in abundance.[56] Nor do I mean to consider the extent to which Jewish ideas continued to influence the evolution of Christianity during the centuries following its birth.[57] I shall leave it to the reader to apply my findings to future critical explorations of those subjects.

Bearing that in mind, I should say that I also write as a Jew committed to my religion and to the collective welfare of my people. To my mind, the well-being of the Jews depends on our ability to engage in honest communication across cultural lines. In that respect, I consider theological dialogue between Christian and Jew a matter of paramount importance to both. To be clear, I make no claim to engage in constructive Jewish theology vis-à-vis Christianity, much less in constructive Christian theology vis-à-vis Judaism.[58] I nevertheless hope that my work will help to improve the foundation of knowledge informing those vital conciliatory efforts. For Christian and Jew, to recognize our many ideological and cultural commonalities is a vital first step in that process. But in order to realize what Emmanuel Lévinas aptly described as the ethical encounter, we must also assume the more challenging assignment of validating one another's differences.[59] Genuine reconciliation demands that each party to the negotiation assume responsibility for

---

[56] To name but a few helpful guides to this labyrinthine subject, see Fredriksen and Reinhartz (2002); Nickelsburg (2003); Levine and Brettler (2011).

[57] On this question, see Boyarin (2012a), who offers an inventive interpretation of the Jewish dimensions of early Christian Messianism, although cf. Schäfer (2012), who demonstrates that much of the Jewish evidence submitted by Boyarin postdates the New Testament and must therefore be read as responding to Christianity rather than vice versa. Although I tend to favor Schäfer's approach over Boyarin's, to consider the relative merits of their respective treatments would be beyond the scope of this study.

[58] For studies of the former variety, see, e.g., Frymer-Kensky et al. (2000); Ben-Chorin (2001); Kogan (2008). For studies of the latter variety, see, e.g., Reuther (1974); Boys (2000); Yoder (2003).

[59] I refer to the dialogical objective described in Lévinas (1969: 197–201; and 1998: 45–51). For a recent application of Lévinas' theory to the arena of interreligious dialogue, see Urbano (2012).

the needs of the other. Consequently, both parties must do away with those dialogical pretenses liable to elicit mistrust. To that end, we must dare to confront the inadequacies of what we think we know about the other even if at risk of revealing discomfiting truths about ourselves. I hope that readers on both sides of the contemporary meeting of Christian and Jew will find my work obliging to that task.

I

The Parting of the Ways in Contemporary Perspective

Today, scholars assaying the schism between Judaism and Christianity often speak of a parting of the ways between the two religions. In contemporary English usage, the language of "parting ways" indicates an amicable taking of leave between persons or parties minded to choose different courses of thought or action.[1] To part ways, in other words, is to pursue one's preferred path in distinction to another's. Applied to the ancient schism between Christian and Jew, the parting metaphor euphemistically describes the choice of the ancient devotee of God to follow either of the two ways leading to the terminal points of Christianity and Judaism.

The dominant historical account whereby that choice came to the attention of persons as yet unaware of the difference between the two religions originated in a 1934 study by James Parkes titled *The Conflict of the Church and the Synagogue*.[2] An Anglican clergyman and Church historian, Parkes affixed the "parting of the ways" within a more comprehensive narrative laying bare the origins and subsequent ills of anti-Semitism, a timely project in a world soon to bear the tragic denouement of that ancient prejudice.[3] After the Holocaust, Parkes' take on the circumstances that first pitted Christian and Jew against one another was to prove an almost prophetic call for reconciliation, his work facilitating the reinvention of a tradition of scholarship on Christian origins rife with bigotry and hatred. No longer could the conscientious Christian historian afford to blame the Jews for rejecting the Christian mission, much less

[1] The earliest known instance of the language appears in the King James Bible, which reads for Ezek 21.2, "For the king of Babylon stood at the parting of the way, at the head of the two ways, to use divination." Ironically, Nebuchadnezzar's choice of paths was invariably to lead to destruction, whether of Jerusalem or of Rabbath-Ammon. So much for the peaceable metaphor.
[2] Parkes (1934). Parkes' metaphor, although not his historical reconstruction, was preceded by Foakes Jackson (1912).
[3] For general insight on Parkes and his scholarly formation, see Richmond (2005).

for the centuries of Christian resentment that followed. Nor could the Jewish scholar pass on the opportunity for rapprochement. In short time, therefore, Parkes' evenhanded explanation of the schism that separated Christianity from Judaism would become de rigueur for scholars both Christian and Jewish seeking to recount that event in similarly conciliatory terms.

Yet despite serving a vital need in its time, Parkes' narrative has not aged gracefully. In recent years, scholars of early Judaism and Christianity have grown wary of his sources, his methodology, and his critical assumptions. Before attempting my own reading of the evidence, it will be helpful to weigh the merits and drawbacks of Parkes' theory. In what follows, I shall attempt to show that the now conventional parting of the ways narrative does not adequately serve the needs of the interpreter of Jewish history. I shall argue that it incorporates elements of two distinct critical narratives current to the age of its composition, one Christian and the other Jewish, entailing irreconcilable theological discourses steeped in mutual suspicion. I thereby aim to clear the field of inquiry for my own project, demonstrating the need for the uniquely Jewish perspective on the history in question that I shall pursue in the chapters to follow.

THE PARTING OF THE WAYS NARRATIVE

Let us begin with a summary of Parkes' narrative.[4] Following the conventional wisdom of his day, Parkes begins by recounting Judaism's initial "clash with Christianity" represented in the conflict stories of the New Testament pitting Jesus, Paul, and other apostles against Jewish persons and parties unsympathetic to their causes.[5] Acknowledging that Christianity remained a characteristically Jewish phenomenon throughout these controversies, Parkes submits that the decisive split between Judaism and Christianity had yet to occur during Paul's lifetime and the concomitant end of the apostolic mission, that despite the success of Paul's mission to the gentiles and the resulting eclipse of the Church's original Jewish demographic. Rather, he contends, Christianity's departure from its parent religion hinged on the movement of the Judeo-Christians, or, in today's preferred terminology, the Jewish Christians.[6] Operating in the Jewish environs of Palestine and its surrounding region, those individuals distinguished themselves from the rest of their Christian brethren by eschewing Paul's gentile-oriented antinomian gospel. They preferred their gospel Jewish, believing that the teachings of Jesus complemented the laws

---

[4] For the following, see Parkes (1934: 77–120), especially ibid. (77–79). I have revised the language and orthography of some of Parkes' terms for the sake of coherence with my discussion to follow.

[5] On this prelude to the schism, see Parkes (1934: 27–70).

[6] Although he does not discuss their origins at length, Parkes evidently assumes that the Jewish Christians originated among Jesus' original disciples; cf. Parkes (1934: 56).

of the Torah.[7] Even, therefore, as the greater part of the Church espoused a Pauline Christianity removed from Judaism's orbit, the Jewish Christians chose to think and to act otherwise.

But the Jewish Christians managed to sustain their dual theologies only as long as their circumstance allowed. According to Parkes, a rapidly deteriorating state of social relations between Jews and gentiles in Palestine during the late first and early second centuries drove a wedge between Christian and Jew that ultimately would drive the Jewish Christians toward the gentile camp. That process began with the first Jewish revolt against Rome of 66 to 73 CE. When the rebels overran Jerusalem, both the leaders of mainstream Judaism and of the Jewish Christians fled for more secure locales. The mainstream Jewish leadership, represented by the Pharisaic sages, regrouped at the coastal city of Jamnia or, in Hebrew, Yavneh, where they would reinvent themselves as rabbis. Meanwhile, the Jewish Christians sought refuge in the predominantly gentile city of Pella in the Transjordan.[8] Both groups thus managed to survive the war, witnessing from afar the destruction of Jerusalem in 70 CE and the fall of her Temple, the central cultic institution of the Jewish religion.

Yet where the rabbis perceived the fall of the Temple as a catastrophe, the Jewish Christians saw it as a prophetic fulfillment. Jesus had warned of apocalyptic doom for the Jews unless they were to purge their society of sin and serve God in moral perfection. The gentile Christians, fueled by Paul's critique of his fellow Jews, had since taken Jesus' prophecy to denote God's total rejection of the Jewish cult and his impending judgment of the Jewish people. That belief now seemed vindicated by signs too clear for the Jewish Christians to deny. The outcome of the war thus compromised their ideological platform, making it difficult for them to believe that God still supported the Jews per the covenantal theology of the Torah. As a result, while some returned to Jerusalem, most Christians still living as Jews opted to join the gentile Churches, ultimately to embrace Paul's gospel and relinquish their Judaism accordingly.

But the Jewish Christians were not the only Jews seeking answers from God in the wake of their national tragedy. The rabbis and their supporters were reeling in agony. Without a functioning Temple cult, they feared that other of their fellow Jews would be drawn to Christianity, trading their ancestral faith for one predicated in part on the notion that God had left his chosen people for another. The rabbis of Yavneh therefore devised a preemptive strategy that would root out those Christians in their midst who stood to entice their fellow Jews toward apostasy. The result was the notorious liturgical formula known as the *birkat ha-minim*, literally "the blessing of the heretics."[9] Assuming that Jewish Christians would not wish to confess their gentile sympathies before their fellow Jews, the sages inserted this blessing-cum-curse in the daily prayer

---

[7] Parkes (1934: 68–70).
[8] Parkes (1934: 77), referring to Eusebius, *Hist. eccl.* 3.5.3.
[9] Parkes (1934: 77–80), referring to the Talmudic account in *b.Berakhot* (28b–29a).

known as the *Amidah*. Asked to lead a Jewish assembly in worship, the suspected Christian would be forced to decline unless he wished to imprecate
himself as a heretic. His refusal, of course, would be just as incriminatory.
So, Parkes contends, did the rabbis instruct their constituents in Palestine and
abroad, declaring their categorical rejection of the Christian religion that they
believed had already rejected their own.

The Yavnean reform, Parkes posits, aggravated an already strained relationship between Christians and Jews outside of Palestine. The Christian population of the wider Mediterranean world was already predominantly gentile in
its ethnic makeup. By the time Jerusalem fell, the apostolic mission to the Jews
had stagnated and Paul's promised return of the Messiah seemed delayed indefinitely. Growing suspicions about the legality of the Christian enterprise had
seen to the start of what would become a large-scale clampdown by the Roman
authorities. All the while, Jews throughout the Roman Empire remained free to
practice their religion as members of a protected cult. Embattled Christian theologians had recourse only to affirm their convictions that God had revoked his
covenant with the Jews in favor of a new covenant with the disciples of Jesus.
They triumphantly assured their flocks that God had used the Romans to discipline the Jews, confirming Paul's promise that the future of the world's salvation lay with the nations. The Christian polemic against Judaism thereby came
to function differently than it had in Paul's hands, now serving as an avowal
of irreconcilable difference rather than a call for Jewish ethical renewal.[10] The
Christians therefore responded to *birkat ha-minim* in kind, citing the decree of
the rabbis as proof that the bond between Christian and Jew had been broken.

The pressures from the Jewish and Christian sides naturally attenuated the
positions of the few Jewish Christians remaining in Palestine and its vicinity.
Their final blow, Parkes submits, arrived in the person of Simon bar Kosiba,
popularly known as Bar Kokhba, the leader of the second Jewish revolt against
Rome of 132 to 135 CE. A capable and dynamic military strategist, Bar Kokhba
also was endorsed by the renowned sage Rabbi Akiva as the Messiah, the long
foretold savior of Israel.[11] Under Akiva's influence, the entire Jewish nation
threw their support behind the rebellion in the hope of seeing their Temple
rebuilt and Jerusalem restored to her former glory. But the Jewish Christians
already had a Messiah. They therefore refused to take up arms in support of
Bar Kokhba. That aroused the ire of the Jewish rebels, who persecuted the
Jewish Christians even as they engaged the Romans in battle.[12] In the end,
another Roman victory compelled the emperor Hadrian to punish the Jews
with heavy disciplinary measures including the closure of Jerusalem to Jewish

---

[10] Parkes (1934: 81–85), referring to various expressions of hostility toward the Jews in the Gospel
of John and the letters of Ignatius of Antioch.

[11] Parkes (1934: 78–79), referring to the Talmudic account in *y. Ta'anit* 4.8 (68d) (cf. *Lamentations
Rabbah* 2.4).

[12] Parkes (1934: 93), referring to Justin Martyr, *1 Apol.* 31.6.

habitation. Having already given up hope of converting their fellow Jews, the last remaining Jewish Christians now faced banishment from the city that had been their base of operations for nearly a century. They therefore appointed a gentile bishop to lead their congregation, committing as a group no longer to live according to Jewish custom.[13]

Following these developments, Christian theologians attentive to their religion's Jewish past began to write Judaism out of its history. Instrumental to this effort was Justin Martyr, who in his *Dialogue with Trypho* asserted the Church's exclusive claim to the legacy of ancient Israel.[14] Justin cast the Jews as Christian heretics, miscreants whom God once again had shown unfit for his covenantal promises in view of their most recent military defeat. He thereby sought to efface the historical pretext whereby the Jew might claim an advantage to the Christian by virtue of his Israelite lineage. Thenceforth, to the minds of the Christian faithful the Church was to be considered the true Israel and the Jews illegitimate pretenders.

Meanwhile, the defection of the Jewish Christians left the Jews with little investment in the continuing development of Christianity. The rabbinic sages were duly alarmed by the new Christian approach to reading the Hebrew Scriptures and ever wary of the Church's potential to attract their Jewish clientele. They therefore joined the Romans in maligning Jesus and his followers.[15] For the most part, however, the rabbis simply ignored the Christians. As gentiles, they were no longer consequential to a rabbinic agenda predicated on serving the needs of a nation of Israel constituted exclusively by Jews. Despite stray evidences of continued operation of Jewish Christians after the Bar Kokhba rebellion, their reduced numbers no longer posed a substantial threat to the Jewish or Christian establishments.[16] The Jewish revolts against Rome had prompted most of their respective adherents in Palestine and throughout the Mediterranean world to know Judaism and Christianity as discrete categories of religious expression. And while the conceptual space shared by their respective theologies would remain contested in the years to follow, Parkes concludes, the parting of the ways was more-or-less a fait accompli by the middle of the second century.

Writing on the eve of the Second World War, James Parkes devised his history at a time when the world needed his conciliatory perspective. Since the Middle Ages, Christian theologians had plotted their polemics against Judaism on the pretext that the Jews had rejected Jesus as the Christ, the Messianic king of the Jewish prophetic tradition. Jewish thinkers had responded by embracing

---

[13] Parkes (1934: 93), referring to Justin Martyr, *1 Apol.* 47.5–6, and Eusebius, *Hist. eccl.* 4.6.3–4. Parkes here mistakes Hadrian for his predecessor Trajan.

[14] Parkes (1934: 95–101).

[15] Parkes (1934: 108–10).

[16] Parkes (1934: 92–95), on Christian evidences for the continued occurrence of Jewish Christians, and ibid. (110), on Jewish evidences.

that accusation. But the nineteenth century had seen scholars in both camps move past that insoluble doctrinal dispute to cast the object of Christianity's principal debate with Judaism as the mutability of God's covenant with Israel.[17] Fixing their attention on Paul's gospel, they reframed the question of how his mission to the gentiles served to strain relations between Christian and Jew. Yet assigning the schism to Paul incurred an equally intractable theological impasse over the significance of Jesus' crucifixion toward the status of God's law in the eschatological age.[18] Forgoing such doctrinal conceits, Parkes aimed to show that the seminal division between Christian and Jew was not a clash of exclusive theological truths. Their separation, he argued, was neither ordained by Jesus' death on the cross nor confirmed by Paul's sense of its significance. It was, rather, the net effect of a lengthy process of mutual alienation driven by devout Jewish and Christian agents who wished only to shield their respective communities from the perils of war and persecution.

Living in Europe at a time when state-sanctioned anti-Semitism was on the rise, Parkes designed his history to help debase what he perceived as that grave social ill.[19] Though all but ignored by mainstream scholarship upon its publication, his study would find its readership after the war among scholars newly sensitized to the need for Parkes' evenhanded perspective. Not surprisingly, scholars of early Christianity were among the first to validate his work. The years leading up to the war had seen their academic discipline infected by the worst heuristic impulses, their studies marred by senseless and vengeful rhetoric against the reputed killers of Jesus and falsifiers of his gospel.[20] Where they once described the Christian schism as a great humanistic liberation from Judaism and its brutal culture of spiritual degeneration, Christian theologians now sought to reevaluate Christianity's Jewish roots to positive effect. Scholarship on Christian origins was thus primed to engage the Jewish people both as subjects of genuine historical interest and as contemporary partners

---

[17] I refer on the first count to the work of F.C. Baur and his followers in the so-called Tübingen school of New Testament scholarship, on which see H. Harris (1975: 1–8), and on the second count to the attempted engagement of said scholarship by Abraham Geiger and other progressive Jewish theologians, on whose initiatives see Heschel (1998), especially ibid. (106–61).

[18] As Jonathan Klawans has shown, this revised agenda recently has fed back into scholarship on Jesus intimating his rejection of Judaism by way of his protest against the Jewish Temple cult. In the new equation, it is Jesus' symbolic self-sacrifice rather than his execution that signals the birth of a Christian worldview no less estranged from the Jewish tradition than in the classical supersessionist model. See Klawans (2006), especially ibid. (213–45).

[19] Parkes describes this key objective of his project in Parkes (1934: ix–xviii). See also Richmond (2005: 50–105), on the controversial circumstances of the book's publication.

[20] See Wiese (2005: 159–215), on the prevalence of anti-Semitic assumptions in the work of Adolf von Harnack, whose frankly supersessionist account of the so-called late Judaism of Jesus' age looms large over Parkes' study. See also Gerdmar (2009: 143–88), on corresponding themes in the work of Wilhelm Bousset and Johannes Weiss, and ibid. (373–411), on the work of Rudolf Bultmann. I reserve comment here on the overtly anti-Semitic trends in New Testament scholarship sponsored by the Nazi regime, on which see Gerdmar, ibid. (415–575).

in dialogue.[21] Parkes' now seemingly prescient study served that new critical agenda perfectly.

Arguably the most influential scholar of the post-war era to endorse his model of the schism was Marcel Simon. In his 1948 study *Verus Israel*, Simon applied the parting of the ways narrative to a reading of the classical Christian polemic against Judaism predicated on what he construed as an ongoing competition for the hearts and minds of the pagan masses.[22] To Simon, placing Christian and Jew on equal footing in the arena of proselytization was to account for the viciousness of the Christian commentary on Judaism during the centuries following the formal separation of the two religions. To imagine that the Jews actually earned the contempt of their Christian counterparts was to justify the notion that the "parting" of their ancestors was just that, a disjuncture of equals decided by mutual agreement. Simon thereby aimed to provide context for an ancient record of Christian animosity toward the Jew rarely before subjected to the ethical scrutiny now demanded of its interpretation.

Many others followed in Simon's footsteps, applying Parkes' narrative to an ever-expanding assortment of Christian evidences. In time, Simon's augmented rendition of the parting of the ways became the historical model par excellence whereby to describe early Christianity's engagement with Judaism.[23] The ensuing critical discussion reached its pinnacle in the work of James D.G. Dunn, who in the early 1990s published two volumes named for Parkes' narrative, one a monograph and the other a collection of essays assuming the empirical validity of the "parting" model.[24] In his own work, Dunn sought to account for multiple "partings" alternatively predating and postdating the Bar Kokhba rebellion. Drawing upon recent trends in New Testament scholarship, he expanded the sites of conflict proposed by Parkes and Simon to account for the anti-Jewish posturing in the teachings of Jesus and Paul. To Dunn, the originators of the Christian enterprise, while not antagonistic toward Judaism per se, assumed theological positions on the salvation of the gentiles prefiguring the division over Israel's ethnic boundaries later to be asserted in the conflict between Christian and Jew. He thereby opened the conversation on the Christian schism to the stage of the Church's development predating the emergence of its predominantly non-Jewish constitution.

As for its impact on Jewish historiography, the parting of the ways narrative proved no less influential. Following its adoption by Salo Baron in his

---

[21] See the essays in Fredriksen and Reinhartz (2002), and cf. Gerdmar (2009: 609–13). For a more critical view of this new critical venture, see Arnal (2005), who detects in contemporary scholarship on Christianity's Jewish roots a veiled attempt at moral absolution for past Christian abuses of Jews.

[22] See Simon (1986), especially ibid. (xii–xvi), where he explicitly adopts Parkes' terminology and historical scheme.

[23] See M.S. Taylor (1995: 7–21), who focuses on Simon's problematic theory of ongoing competition for converts between Jewish and Christian parties following the supposed schism.

[24] Dunn (2006), especially ibid. (301–38); Dunn (1992a).

landmark *Social and Religious History of the Jews,* Parkes' reading of what
Baron dubbed "the great schism" went on to inform a wealth of scholarship
on the early Jewish response to Christianity.[25] Its influence is perhaps best
exemplified in Lawrence Schiffman's 1985 study *Who Was a Jew?*[26] Surveying
a comprehensive range of textual evidences, Schiffman argues that the early
rabbinic sages articulated a theology of Judaism exclusive of Christian participation well before the decisive parting of the ways. The rabbis, he contends, affixed their responses to Christianity in their earliest expressions of
the *halakhah,* or "the way," the legal-interpretive tradition that defined their
movement. According to the *halakhah,* those Jews who chose to follow the
rabbinic way were to be counted as members of the nation of Israel. Those
who declined, including the prevaricating Christians, were to be shunned as
heretics. Declaring their position by means of the *birkat ha-minim,* Schiffman
concludes, the rabbis thus acknowledged that Christianity's theology represented an irreversible departure from Judaism even before their Christian
contemporaries realized as much.

These are just a few examples of Parkes' influence. The register of others is
extensive and ever growing.[27] I therefore shall conclude by stating simply that
the parting of the ways narrative struck a chord shortly after its debut that
has reverberated ever since. Parkes' measured approach has served the need
of relieving a critical discourse weighed by past abuses, enabling its transformation into one fruitful collaboration across cultural and disciplinary lines.
But despite its ongoing endorsement in some quarters, the parting of the ways
narrative has not been without its detractors. In recent years, a number of
scholars have questioned the validity of Parkes' theory as a universal key to
the Christian schism. The resulting critical reevaluation has posed a serious
challenge to those who would assume the normativity of his model. A review
of the critique is therefore in order before I propose to set the terms of my own
investigation.

CRITICISM OF THE PARTING OF THE WAYS NARRATIVE

Although Parkes created his narrative with good intentions, his argument
rests on a number of questionable interpretive grounds.[28] The criticism leveled
against Parkes' theory can be classified under either or both of two general

[25] Baron (1952–1983: 2.57–88, 2.130–35), and passim.
[26] Schiffman (1985: 1–7, 75–78), and passim.
[27] Even to compile such a list would be a Herculean task. For a valiant attempt to document the
influence of Parkes' theory, see Reed and Becker (2003: 10–15), including further bibliography,
ibid. (10, n. 35). To this list may be added, inter alia, S.T. Katz (1984); Segal (1986: 163–81);
Wilson (1995: 2–11) and passim; Evans (2000); Blanchetière (2001: 245–60) and passim;
Tomson (2003); Crown (2004); Hagner (2012); S.J.D. Cohen (2014: 231–58); Nicklas (2014).
[28] For a corresponding critique noting Parkes' lack of antiquarian expertise, see de Lange (1998:
42–44).

orders. The first addresses the problematic analytical assumptions that motivated his account of the schism as a mutually agreed "parting" of Christian and Jewish parties. The second addresses the reliability of the individual historical data upon which Parkes plotted the schism's major points of disjuncture. In view of those concerns, I should state that my purpose in the summary to follow is neither to question Parkes' interpretive ability nor to challenge his critical objectivity. Rather, I intend merely to show where his account falls short as a comprehensive record of the schism amenable to the Jewish historical record.

I shall begin with Parkes' historiographical method. Despite the honorable intent of its author, the parting of the ways narrative functions on a rather simplistic understanding of historical process. Parkes' approach may be characterized as belonging to the genre commonly described as serial or quantitative history.[29] The logic implicitly ordering historical writing of that type is that change is driven primarily by events of widespread social significance: the careers of influential public figures, major intellectual movements, legal reforms, wars, natural disasters, and so forth. Each such event is construed by the historian as a moment when the people affected by its outcome choose to respond by modifying their attitudes or behaviors. Over time, a sequence of such notable events will lead to a gradual transformation of a society realized by those of its members apt to adjust to the emerging realities of their evolving world or, alternatively, by those who purposefully refuse to adjust. While no single event in the series is necessarily pivotal in effectuating the course of history, the sum of their outcomes amounts to a major turning point.

From an empirical standpoint, the problem with this method of exposition is that it potentially fails to account for the subtle evolutions in popular mentalities demanded of a mass social movement. Serial historiography relieves that prerogative from its subjects and assigns it to the historian. For if an event is to be deemed significant only in view of its potential to affect the next event in a sequence, only one viewing both events in hindsight can assess the historical significance of either. That perforce locates the historian's objective not among his or her subjects of analysis but at a terminal point unknowable to those subjects. Consequently, how those individuals experienced the events in question, that is, their emotional responses and their resulting behaviors, are subordinated to the historian's teleological design. As one critic of the form famously put it, that amounts to writing history without people.[30]

That Parkes' narrative suffers these weaknesses is obvious. According to his theory, the separation of Judaism and Christianity was the net result of a reciprocal process of social disjunction determined by a series of noteworthy events. Yet Parkes' witnesses to those events do not track the movements of the

[29] These terms originate in the work of Pierre Chaunu, notably the essays in Chaunu (1978). For the following critique, in which I assume the validity of Chaunu's social historical method, cf. Ricouer (2004: 188–200).

[30] Ladurie (1979: 285).

undifferentiated mass of human subjects instrumental in making the schism
a reality. Rather, they reflect the rhetorical priorities of the Christian thinkers
and, to a lesser extent, the Jewish thinkers, who wished to impose the distinction between Christian and Jew upon their putative subjects. Consequently,
most of the historical actors implicated in the parting of the ways narrative do
not actually drive that narrative. Rather, it is the narrative that drives them,
impelling them to arrive at the theological schism that Parkes took as a given.
In other words, Parkes knew that the terms Christianity and Judaism ultimately
were to signify some measure of difference and plotted his narrative to speak to
that eventuality. Yet in crafting his history as such, he casually neglected to ask
the majority of those who enduring the parting of the ways what they believed
the terms Christian and Jew to signify at various points in time as or how their
objects of reference related to one another.

   That, in short, is the force of the first major order of criticism pertaining to
Parkes' theory. In the interest of brevity, I shall cite just a few of the scholars
who have questioned the parting of the ways narrative in view of corresponding methodological concerns.[31] In a 1994 article, Judith Lieu argued that the
Parkes' theory, as recently retooled by Dunn, serves a distinctly apologetic
agenda.[32] In asserting that the break between Christianity and Judaism took
place at the close of the apostolic age, Parkes and his followers assume that
the elements of practice and belief later to inform orthodox Christian doctrine
were understood to function independently of Judaism at a fairly early stage
in the Church's evolution. Accordingly, the first Christians would have understood that being a Christian meant not being a Jew, thereby distinguishing
Christianity from Judaism as a natural consequence of believing in Jesus. That
unlikely scenario, though lacking for historical credibility, theoretically justi-
fies the anti-Jewish rhetoric of the New Testament as one reflecting an evenly
matched theological contest between two fully realized religious collectives.[33]

   Lieu developed her critique in her 1996 book *Image and Reality*, in which
she examined the attitudes toward Judaism expressed by Christian authors
of the second century.[34] In her view, the very fact that Christians writing after
the supposed parting of the ways continued to implore their readers to avoid
associating with Jews indicates that its effects were not yet impressed upon the
minds of the Christian masses. Whereas those certain of their theologians preferred to imagine Judaism and Christianity in opposing terms, their target audiences clearly did not. So, Lieu argues, did authors such as Ignatius of Antioch
and Justin Martyr seek to persuade their readers that Christians ought not to

[31] For the following critique, see Reed and Becker (2003: 16–22), as well as the other essays in
that volume. Compare, however, Dunn (2006: xviii–xxiv), for a cogent defense of the general
applicability of Parkes' model in view of the objections of its recent detractors.
[32] Lieu (1994).
[33] The appropriation of Parkes' narrative as an antidote for Christian guilt over past aggression
toward the Jews is sharply noted by Petersen (2005: 45–53).
[34] Lieu (1996). See especially ibid. (277–89), for programmatic conclusions.

live as Jews, worship with Jews, or even think like Jews. Despite, therefore, the affectations of those influential thinkers who wished to believe that a decisive break had severed Christianity from its Jewish roots, their anti-Jewish rhetoric served merely to project their own theological priorities upon a Christian population yet to discern a concrete distinction between Christian and Jew.

Similar arguments have been raised about later Christian evidences. In his 2004 study *Remains of the Jews*, Andrew Jacobs focused on engagements with Judaism among Christian thinkers of the third through fifth centuries active in the heavily Jewish environs of Palestine.[35] Following Constantine's legalization of Christianity in 313 CE, Jacobs contends, the ensuing transformation of the Roman Empire's power dynamic fueled an anti-Jewish rhetoric of domination long gestating among Christian intellectuals. The legal empowerment of the Church forced the Jews now living under Christian rule to play the ugly roles cast for them by theologians of the past. So, he demonstrates, did the exegetes Origen and Jerome exploit Jewish scriptural knowledge in order to characterize Judaism as an anathema to Christian living. So did the historians Eusebius and Epiphanius warn their readers of the Jewish heresy, seizing the Jew's very identity to slander him as a false Christian. The Church's victory over Rome thereby served merely to realize a rupture between Christianity and Judaism conceived long ago.

In her 2008 book *Augustine and the Jews*, Paula Fredriksen traced the evolution of orthodox Christianity's anti-Jewish argument after Constantine's age.[36] Citing the wealth of Christian evidences attesting to the continued cooperation of Christian and Jew during the fourth and fifth centuries, Fredriksen argues that the Christianization of Rome served neither to lure the Jewish masses to the baptismal font nor otherwise to compromise their existence. Wary, therefore, of relinquishing the Church's moral obligation to the Jew, the influential bishop Augustine saw the need for a theological stratagem assigning significance to the Jews' collective refusal of the gospel. Reading Paul's letter to the Romans as an eschatological manifesto attuned to the salvation of the Jews, he thus articulated a rationale of Christian tolerance perhaps no less demeaning of the Jew's beliefs but more protective of one's right to assert them under the authority of the Christian state. Augustine, Fredriksen thereby concludes, indicates the degree to which even the most orthodox of Christians continued to factor Judaism into their theological equations even after the difference between Christian and Jew had been written into law.

To my mind, each of these scholars identifies the same flaw of the parting of the ways narrative, namely its failure to distinguish between theological rhetoric and social reality. Parkes, along with Simon, Dunn, and others, did

---

[35] For the following, see A.S. Jacobs (2004), with reference to the implications of his work toward the conventional scholarly narrative of the schism, ibid. (200–09).

[36] For the following, see Fredriksen (2008), and further, Frederiksen (2003: 35–38), on the parting of the ways narrative.

not adequately account for those ancient Christians who saw no essential conflict between Christianity and Judaism even where others did. The perspectives
of those so-called Jewish Christians should figure in the critical conversation
on the schism no less than those of the more influential Christian thinkers
whose views would go on to inform the dominant narrative of the Church's
early history. While the poorly documented experiences of that history's proverbial losers might not oblige a linear narrative of Christianity's separation
from Judaism, that is no fault of their own. It is the liability of the historian
wishing to impose an artificial interpretive scheme upon what was manifestly
not a straightforward process of social and theological disjunction.

The same might be said of the Jews with whom those Christians found
common ground. In his 2004 study *Border Lines*, Daniel Boyarin extended
the conversation on the Christian side to the Jewish evidences supporting the
parting of the ways narrative.[37] Taking a critical look at the classical Jewish
record, Boyarin questions the role of the *birkat ha-minim* as a catalytic factor in the Christian schism on the grounds that the rabbinic sages of Yavneh
possessed neither the inkling nor the organizational wherewithal to issue a
universal condemnation of Christianity. In fact, he argues, despite expressing
certain apprehensions about the Christians in their midst, the early rabbis were
profoundly impacted by their encounters with Christian thought. Drawing on
Jacobs' work, Boyarin describes a theological discourse indebted equally to
the Jewish and Hellenistic intellectual traditions and sustained by Palestinian
sages, both Jewish and Christian. Not until Rome's legal degradation of the
Jews beginning in the fourth century did the difference between Christian and
Jew prevail upon the rabbinic collective. Only then, Boyarin contends, were
the rabbis compelled to see Christianity as a perversion of their own honored
intellectual discipline rather than merely a variation thereof.

Boyarin's thesis raises a number of interpretive issues to which I shall return
later in my study. For now, I shall say simply that his argument complements
those of the others who have challenged the parting of the ways narrative principally with reference to the Christian literary record. For if one is to acknowledge that the Church Fathers knew of Christians who associated with Jews,
it stands to reason that the rabbinic sages knew of Jews who associated with
Christians. It takes two to tango. If, therefore, we are to assume that the patristic polemic against Judaism distorted the Christian reality to which it ostensibly referred, to imagine that the rabbis preemptively rejected Christianity
would be no less of a distortion of the Jewish reality.

That, in sum, has been the most prominent challenge to Parkes' theory of
the Christian schism posed in recent years. Let us now consider another related
line of criticism. One of the methodological drawbacks of serial historiography
is its dependence on the historian's conferral of significance upon individual

---

[37] For the following, see Boyarin (2004), especially ibid. (1–13), on the methodological pitfalls of
the parting of the ways narrative.

links in the chain of events sustaining his or her narrative. But a chain is only as strong as its weakest link. Were one event in the series proven less significant than the historian first assumed, the entirety of the narrative would suffer as a result.

Parkes' chain, though seemingly strong at the time of its creation, has since been debilitated with respect to nearly every one of its links. Although few have questioned the impact of the Jewish revolts against Rome on the lives of Jews and Christians in Palestine, the specific reactions assumed by Parkes have faced serious challenges.[38] First cited by the Eusebius in the fourth century, the story of the Jewish Christians' flight to Pella during the first revolt has been shown to reflect the theological priorities of a later Christian age.[39] Its implication that the Jewish Christians were prescient enough to leave Judea for a land populated predominantly by gentiles would appear to prefigure the very schism that Parkes submitted had yet to take place. Likewise, the Talmudic narrative tracing the invention of the *birkat ha-minim* to post-war Yavneh has been discredited by scholars wary of its late attestation relative to the event in question. Boyarin has even questioned whether there was a significant rabbinic presence at Yavneh to begin with.[40] As for the second revolt, the sole allegation by Justin Martyr that Bar Kokhba persecuted the Jewish Christians lacks credibility in the absence of evidence for a distinctive Christian estate in second-century Judea. Justin's provocative charge of Jewish lust for Christian blood again implies a schism where one manifestly had yet to take place.[41]

But arguably more challenging than these chips at the foundation of Parkes' narrative is the aforementioned evidence indicating that social relations between Christians and Jews often remained strong well after their supposed parting of ways. For the first few centuries of their coexistence, Jews and Christians were both minority populations in the Roman Empire. In many practical respects, they shared more with one another than they did with the prevailing Greek and Roman cultures of their environs. Despite their occasional signs of hostility, both the Christian and the Jewish traditions speak to the occurrence of peaceable interaction between Christians and Jews in Palestine and elsewhere.[42] Churches and synagogues operated side-by-side, sometimes even catering to

---

[38] See, however, Schwartz's introductory essay in Schwartz and Weiss (2012: 1–19), for a probing discussion of scholarly assumptions and misapprehensions regarding the impact of the failure of the first revolt.

[39] See Koester (1989), who describes the story as that of a local Syro-Palestinian Christian community in search of its apostolic origins, although cf. Verheyden (1990), who ascribes its invention to Eusebius.

[40] See Boyarin (2004: 67–73), on the *birkat ha-minim*, and ibid. (151–201), on the Talmud's tendency to embellish the earliest rabbinic Yavneh traditions.

[41] For similar assessments, see Setzer (1994: 171–72); Lieu (1996: 132–36).

[42] This point is stressed by Fredriksen (2008: 79–102), on the subject of cooperation between Christian and Jews; cf. Fredriksen (2003: 38–61). See also Kinzig (1991); Himmelfarb (1993); Gager (1993).

the same worshippers.[43] Consequently, the efforts of their self-appointed leaders to enforce the separation of Christians and Jews were continually challenged by a reality in which cooperation was the norm.

The foremost signifiers of this climate of mutual support were the Jewish Christians. Amidst the many and diverse allusions to routine interaction between Jews and Christians, none speak more acutely to the failure of the parting of the ways narrative than those attesting to Christians who chose to live as Jews.[44] Beginning with Irenaeus of Lyon in the late second century, select Church Fathers described these alleged Christian heretics as members of a sect called the Ebionites. In time, the Ebionites came to be associated with another alleged sect first identified by Epiphanius as the Nazarenes. Both the Ebionites and Nazarenes are thus described in patristic writings as Christians in mind but Jewish in deed, upholding basic doctrines of the Church rooted in the gospel tradition while following Jewish customs with respect to their habits of worship and ritual observance. Witnesses to the ongoing occurrence of this phenomenon appear in Christian writings into the early fifth century.

The Jewish record speaks to the same situation. The writings of the rabbinic sages attest to the presence of Jewish Christians in their local environs in the Galilee region of northern Palestine. The individuals in question are called *minim* (singular *min*), a Hebrew term roughly equivalent to the Greek *haeretikos* or heretic. The rabbinic construction of *minut* mirrored the contemporary Christian concept of heresy inasmuch as the Hebrew term indicates its subject's dissent from an ideological standard defined by the values of the rabbis.[45] Notices of such heretics espousing Christian beliefs appear in a number of Palestinian and Babylonian rabbinic texts beginning in the third century and continuously through the late ancient period. Like the Church Fathers with respect to their so-called heretics, the rabbis appear to have possessed little clear knowledge regarding the designs of those whom they pegged as *minim*. But just as the Church Fathers begrudgingly counted the Ebionites and Nazarenes as Christians, so did the rabbis presume to count Christian *minim* as Jews.

In view of the foregoing considerations, it would appear that where certain observers saw the relationship between Christian and Jew as a broken bond, others saw an innocent symbiosis. The separation of Christianity and Judaism might therefore best be described not as a singular event but as the net effect of

---

[43] Often cited to this effect are the subjects of John Chrysostom's admonitions toward synagogue-going Christians in late fourth-century Antioch, on which see Wilken (1983: 66–94). Other pertinent evidences are discussed by Fine (1999: 231–36), Liebeschuetz (2001: 249–50), and Stökl Ben Ezra (2003).

[44] For the relevant sources, see Klijn and Reinink (1973), with discussion of the Ebionites and Nazarenes, ibid. (19–52). See also Klijn (1992) for secondary allusions to apocryphal gospel texts assigned to those alleged sects.

[45] On the rhetorical function of this novel rabbinic taxon, see Goodman (1996), followed by Boyarin, (2004: 54–67).

a lengthy process of disjunction involving many subtle movements in thought and social behavior. Those movements transpired in various locations, at various times, and for various reasons, finally to converge in the early fourth century as the Christianization of the Roman Empire commenced. Only following Rome's transformation into a Christian state did the pluralities of Christians and Jews living under her rule find themselves subjected to legislation aiming to regulate their religious identities.[46] Consequently, only in view of centuries of such developments would the ideas of Judaism and Christianity evolve in the minds of both their constituencies to signify distinct theologies and mutually distinguishable categories of religious expression.[47]

To that end, Boyarin proposes to describe the Christian schism not as a separation of two theologies but as the partition of a single theological platform.[48] Prior to the fourth century, he argues, the terms Judaism and Christianity were meaningful only to the relatively few who aimed to create distance between Christian and Jew. In the meantime, the religious system cultivated by Jews and Christians functioned as a hybrid he calls "Judaeo-Christianity," neither categorically Jewish nor categorically Christian in nature. Though rejected by some self-professed Christians and Jews, that hybrid model, he posits, remained viable as long as its proponents possessed the means to support it. Only when the laws of a Christian Roman Empire forced them into orthodox submission did the Christians and Jews once engaged in that common discourse perceive the need to know that a schism had taken place.

Needless to say, Boyarin's attempt to reimagine the Christian schism as the effect of an ideological shift from "Judaeo-Christianity" to "Judaism" and "Christianity" poses a challenge to my project. For the moment, however, I shall speak only to the implications of his thesis toward the viability of the parting of the ways narrative. The prognosis is not good. Nevertheless, I hesitate simply to discount Parkes' model of the schism for its lack of universal functionality. To privilege the positions of those Christians and Jews who knew of no decisive rupture prior to the fourth century is to marginalize the positions of those who believed they did. That so many Christian thinkers of the first through third centuries presumed a theological distinction between Christian and Jew suggests a certain common wisdom.[49] Granted, some saw difference where others did not. But the empirical data attesting to the continual refinement of the

---

[46] S. Schwartz (2001: 179–202). For a complementary assessment probing the Jewish response to Constantine's initial reforms, see Stemberger (2000: 22–47).

[47] For like conclusions, see, e.g., Lieu (1994: 116–17), and further, Lieu (2004: 305–08); Fredriksen (2003: 61–63); Crown (2004: 560–62); Runesson (2008a: 85–87); Lapin (2012: 17–20).

[48] For the following, see Boyarin (2004: 13–33, 202–11), and cf. Petersen (2005: 65–71). Boyarin (2004: 37–44) assigns the invention of this category to Justin Martyr, thereby inferring a point of origin for his "partition" precisely where James Parkes inferred a point of resolution for his "parting."

[49] For similarly circumspect comments, see S. Schwartz (2003: 197–210), speaking primarily to the Jewish record, and Williams (2009), speaking primarily to the Christian record.

terms "Judaism" and "Christianity" beyond the second century does not undermine Parkes' narrative quite to the extent that Boyarin would have us believe.[50]

How, then, should the disciplined historian proceed? I would begin by adjusting the scope of Parkes' theory. In view of the aforementioned criticisms, I cannot accept the premise of describing a decisive break between Judaism and
Christianity prior to the fourth century. That said, I would uphold one's prerogative to consider whether a given population of Jews or Christians perceived such
a break to have occurred prior to the fourth century and, if so, when and by what
means. Since the focus of my project is the Jewish population of Palestine, my purpose moving forward shall be to describe how the experiences of that population
dealing with Christians in their local environs conditioned them to think about
Christianity and its relationship with Judaism. Only in view of those subjective
realities shall I presume to describe their perceptions of the differences between
Christian and Jew in terms of a schism.

But a significant interpretive hurdle remains. Should I base my analysis solely
on the testimonies of the rabbinic sages, I will have to limit myself to a subset
of the Jewish population whose attitudes toward Christianity were not necessarily representative of the whole. Most egregiously, I would have to ignore
the experiences of those Jews whose attitudes toward Christianity earned them
the censure of the rabbis. I refer again to the Jewish Christians. Boyarin, for
his part, dismisses those individuals as mere rhetorical inventions designed to
create illusions of Jewish and Christian orthodoxies where there were none.[51]
While I certainly acknowledge the symbolic value of the Jewish Christian for
both Christian and Jew, I am not ready to discount the wide range of Jewish
and Christian evidences suggesting that such individuals actually existed.[52] To
be clear, I do not assume that Jewish Christians made up a significant part of
Palestine's general Jewish population. But even in their apparently demograph-
ically marginal roles, they demand consideration both as Jews and as conduits
of Christian knowledge to their fellow Jews.

In fairness, Parkes acknowledged the potential of the hardier Jewish
Christians to complicate his narrative. But in casting them as outliers with
respect to what he described as "official" Judaism and Christianity, defined, in
his words, by "the two poles of Catholic and rabbinic orthodoxy," he merely
acquiesced to the spiteful mischaracterizations of their ancient detractors.[53]

---

[50] Compare the balanced assessment of Reinhartz (2006).
[51] For this point, see Boyarin (2004: 202–25), following A.S. Jacobs (2004: 44–51). See also Av.
Cameron (2003: 353–60), who argues that the efforts of the Church Fathers to characterize
Ebionites and Nazarenes as Jews reflected a tendentious rhetorical trope not necessarily determinative of how those individuals saw themselves.
[52] Compare the critique of Carleton Paget (2010b: 373–74), who likewise sets the burden of proof
of their nonexistence on Boyarin's shoulders.
[53] Parkes uses the term "official" to signify both the Judaism of the rabbis (Parkes 1934: 78, 80,
106; cf. ibid., 38) and the Christianity of the Pauline Church (ibid., 95). The latter phrasing
appears in ibid. (94).

Regrettably, this bias has remained a fixture of scholarship on the Christian schism, which typically discounts the Jewish Christians as little more than pesky aberrations from the Christian and Jewish norms.[54] Yet Parkes certainly was correct to identify those historical actors capable of moving between the Jewish and Christian communities as persons of significance to his story. If, therefore, I am to improve upon his theory, I shall have to account for the Jewish Christians more systematically than Parkes did.

THE "JEWISH CHRISTIAN" CHIMERA

Who were the Jewish Christians? To our knowledge, the obscure individuals once cited as Ebionites, Nazarenes, and *minim* never called themselves Jewish Christians. Since our only records of their existence were written with intent to defame them, it is impossible to know precisely who they were or how they understood themselves in reference to their Jewish and Christian contemporaries. All we can presume to know about them depends on those prejudiced testimonials and other such conjectural associations with ancient Christians who supposedly exhibited Jewish tendencies. But what makes one expression of Christianity more or less Jewish than another? The very premise of that distinction assumes an object of Judaism categorically at odds with that of Christianity. That is a problematic assumption. The Christian tradition is rooted in Judaism, sharing its scriptures, its sacred mythology, and the basic elements of its theology. One might therefore wonder whether the very concept of a Jewish Christian assumes a distinction foreign to the mind of its putative subject.

In fact, the ongoing critical reassessment of the parting of the ways narrative has generated some doubt as to the validity of the term "Jewish Christianity." Consequently, it will be helpful to begin our critique by accounting what scholars typically take the terminology to imply in the ancient frame of reference. I quote the following definition from Simon Mimouni, whose work on the subject I consider among the finest: "Early Jewish Christianity is a recent formulation designating Jews who recognized the Messianic in Jesus, who have recognized or not the divinity of Christ, but all who continue to observe the Torah."[55] Notwithstanding the ambiguity of some of his terms, Mimouni thus defines the term "Jewish Christian" in reference to those ancient followers of Jesus whom modern observers have deemed exceptionally given to traditional Jewish ways. His account of their adherence to the Torah accurately reflects a

---

[54] See, e.g., Simon (1986: 237–70); Wilson (1995: 143–59); Blanchetière (2001: 133–51); Dunn (2006: 304–11). The false inference of mainstream Jewish and Christian communities from which early Jewish Christians supposedly deviated plagues the ambitious sociological study of J.T. Sanders (1993), who explains the Christian schism as an effect of the systematic marginalization of Christians within Jewish society.

[55] Mimouni (2012: 51). I have emended the translator's orthography and language of "Judaeo-Christianity" for the sake of coherence with my presentation.

range of Christian witnesses charging the Ebionites, the Nazarenes, and their kind of observing Jewish festivals, circumcising their sons according to the Jewish rite, abiding by Jewish dietary restrictions, and so forth.[56] Those individuals, he suggests, chose to observe those customs because they considered themselves Jews, and, consequently, bound by the same covenantal theology professed by other Jews of their age.[57]

But despite showing an admirable sensitivity to their Jewish identities here and elsewhere in his work, Mimouni casually neglects to recognize his subjects of inquiry as Christians. The fact of their Jewish identities, he implies, excludes their identification as Christians in the normal sense of the word, as though the term "Christianity" demands its subject's refusal of Judaism. His intimation, in other words, of what stands to make one expression of Christianity more or less Jewish than another infers a prior point of dissociation between the concepts of Christian and Jew.[58] To use a convenient point of reference, he assumes a parting of the ways, a prior theological schism in view of which to characterize Christianity as definitively not Jewish. Mimouni thereby assumes the normativity of the categorical distinction between Christian and Jew clearly not assumed by the Jewish Christians themselves.

I do not mean, of course, to question the integrity of Mimouni's work. The ancient phenomenon that he presumes to account was quite real. But Mimouni is among a number of scholars who have questioned the diagnostic value of the discourse he chooses to entertain.[59] Much like the parting of the ways narrative, the language of Jewish Christianity infers a sense of dissonance between the cultural epistemes of Christian and Jew precisely where the evidence suggests there was none. Consequently, the Jewish Christian cannot be defined as such in view of his or her own self-perception. The Jewish Christian is thus not a genuine historical personality but merely a likeness thereof. His existence is reduced to a transitional illusion, a symbol of Christianity's supersession of Judaism inescapably caught between Jewish past and a Christian future that he cannot possibly attain.

Given Parkes' sensitivities, it is a wonder that a figure so dubious entered his mind to begin with. Nevertheless, it would be a mistake to assume that his understanding Jewish Christianity was as plainly problematic as I have made it out to be. It seems, rather, that Parkes innocently thwarted his own theory by forcing his Jewish Christians to make that impossible transition from Jew to Christian, to choose sides in a conflict not of their own making.

---

[56] Note that the Christian record tends to exert greater influence than the comparatively sparse Jewish record in contemporary efforts to locate the phenomenon of Jewish Christianity in its Jewish cultural setting; see, e.g., Visotzky (1989: 50–60); Reed (2006: 332–41).

[57] See Mimouni (2012: 68–69).

[58] To wit, Mimouni (2012: 419–32), offers elements for such a narrative mirroring the parting of the ways model in its timeline and episodic organization.

[59] For the following, see Mimouni (2012: 25–53). For complementary critiques, see J.E. Taylor (1990: 313–34); Reed (2003: 189–96); Boyarin (2009: 27–33).

But what was the catalyst of that conflict if not the difference between Christian and Jew? A judicious reading of Parkes' history points to another cultural duality predicating that difference, namely that of Jew and gentile. In fact, that is the distinction which Dunn and others since have cited as the root cause of the rift between Jew and gentile within the first-century Church later to define the respective "ways" of Judaism and Christianity.[60] It will therefore be instructive to delve deeper into their sources of knowledge in order to discern why and how Parkes and his followers have supposed the ethnic identities of the Jewish Christians conditioned their beliefs.

First in order is an inquiry into the origin of the terminology in question.[61] The term "Jewish Christianity" was born in dialogue with that of "gentile Christianity" in the work of the influential German Protestant theologian Ferdinand Christian Baur.[62] A professor at the University of Tübingen, Baur founded an influential school of historical-critical New Testament scholarship that would dominate that field for much of the nineteenth and early twentieth centuries.[63] His initial formulation of the dichotomy between Jewish and gentile Christian appeared in an 1831 study mining data from the Pauline epistles, the book of Acts, and other Christian texts of the apostolic age.[64] Acknowledging that the separation of Judaism and Christianity was not determined by Jesus, Baur proposed to locate the decisive break between the two religions in a first-century conflict between Christians of Jewish origin and Christians of gentile origin. The former group, he argued, still beholden to their ancestral ways, supported Peter's Torah-oriented version of the gospel. The latter group, unaccustomed to traditional Jewish practice, naturally preferred Paul's antinomian gospel. That tension, Baur posited, finally subsided in the late first century when an ethnically homogenous Christian community now centered in Rome struck a compromise, subordinating Peter's call for obedience to Jewish law to Paul's more spiritual agenda. The result, he

---

[60] Dunn (2006: 185–214); cf. Segal (1986: 160–62); P.S. Alexander (1992: 22–25); Marcus (2006: 99–102).

[61] For a fuller account of the following condensed history of scholarship, see the exemplary study of Carleton Paget (2007: 22–52). Also valuable are the older surveys of Klijn (1973) and Lüdemann (1989: 1–28).

[62] I am not persuaded by the argument recently put forth tying Baur's construction of Jewish Christianity to the English philosopher John Toland, who adduced a similar rhetorical figure in his 1718 treatise *Nazarenus*; see F.S. Jones (2012a). Where Toland looked toward the ancient past for proof of the Jew's potential to embrace Christianity, Baur appealed to the same past only to denigrate the Jew for refusing Paul's gospel; cf. Sutcliffe (2003: 202–03). I find the chain of transmission and rhetorical transformation proposed by Jones tenuous at best.

[63] For general comments on Baur's intellectual and theological foundations, see H. Harris (1975: 159–80), and further, ibid. (181–237), on the contributions of the Tübingen School to modern research on early Christianity.

[64] Baur first articulated this theory in Baur (1831b), later incorporating its major points into two monographs, Baur (1845; 1853). For a summary statement of Baur's position, see Carleton Paget (2007: 30–32).

concluded, was the theological paradigm subsequently to inform orthodox Christian doctrine.

Baur, in short, inferred that the separation of Judaism and Christianity was initiated by Paul as an effect of his mission to the gentiles. But its conclusion was stalled by a subset of self-professed Christians who insisted on maintaining their Jewish identities. Baur referred to those individuals as *Judenchristen*, or Jewish Christians, and to their religious platform as *Judenchristentum*, or Jewish Christianity. Although acknowledging their place in the apostolic Church, Baur stigmatized the so-called Jewish Christians for refusing to heed Paul's advice with respect to the status of the Jewish law in the new Messianic age. Simply recognizing Jesus as the Christ, Baur therefore implied, was not enough to earn one's unqualified Christian credentials. For as long as the Jewish Christians asserted their notion of a covenant particular to their nation, the universal covenant that Paul said had been pronounced by Jesus could not prevail. True Christianity, that is, orthodox, Pauline Christianity, demanded the rejection of Judaism by gentile and Jew alike.

Baur's reading of the ancient Christian record only barely conceals his ulterior agenda. Key to discerning the metanarrative embedded his theory is the social context of its development. Since the late eighteenth century, liberal parties in Germany and throughout Europe had been engaged in a public debate over the emancipation of the Jews from the inferior legal status set upon their estate since the Middle Ages.[65] The humanistic values of the Enlightenment had changed the once commonplace perception that the Jew's Messianic outlook rendered him hostile toward Jesus and thereby fundamentally incapable of assuming the responsibilities of citizenship in a Christian nation-state.[66] Liberal Christian advocates of Jewish emancipation cited the enfranchisement of the Jew as a necessary step toward meaningful social progress. Jewish intellectuals such as Moses Mendelssohn and Abraham Geiger had begun openly to identify with Jesus, proposing the Judaism of the Christian Messiah as a moral foundation upon which to set a new model of cooperation between Christian and Jew.[67] Consequently, European society at large stood at the brink of a transformative admission of the Jewish element it once so vigorously denied.

As Baur crafted his thesis, his student David Friedrich Strauss was unwittingly lending support to the liberal cause.[68] In studies leading up to his

---

[65] On this movement and its momentous social and intellectual implications, see J. Katz (1973), especially ibid. (191–200), on its early nineteenth-century German context. Notably, the Jews of Baur's home state of Württemberg were emancipated in 1828 as he was conducting the research that would support his reading of the schism.

[66] See Roemer (2004), and cf. J. Katz (1973: 92–95).

[67] For detailed discussion of Mendelssohn's sketch of the Jewish Jesus, see Hess (2002: 118–24), as well as ibid. (105–12), on the implications of his work toward the Jewish emancipation effort. On Geiger's presentation, see in general Heschel (1998), especially ibid. (106–26), on his engagement Baur and his followers.

[68] I qualify Strauss' support of Jewish emancipation as unwitting in view of his more overt expressions of hostility against Jews and Judaism, on which see Gerdmar (2009: 121–31).

1835–1836 work *Das Leben Jesu*, Strauss sought to rewrite the traditional biography of Jesus from that of a mysterious saint to one of a relatable Germanic culture hero.[69] He aimed to achieve this effect by demythologizing the gospels, privileging their historical content over what he construed as their more legendary elements. Among his many challenges to conventional wisdom, Strauss denied Jesus' authorship of the Christian religion, boldly asserting that the Jesus of history was born as a Jew and died as a Jew. Baur therefore turned to Paul as the next likely candidate. Insisting that the Jewish elements of the apostolic Church were antagonistic toward those who supported Paul's gospel, Baur characterized the Jewish Christian as a stereotypical Jew: clannish, philosophically repressed, and altogether too stubborn to accept what Paul had correctly realized was the universal significance of Jesus' death and resurrection. In Baur's equation, Jew and gentile simply could not coexist within the proto-orthodox Pauline Church.

The contemporary rhetorical compass of Baur's history is almost too obvious to require comment.[70] His insinuation of an essential conflict between Jewish Christian and gentile Christian rendered his reading of the Christian schism vital to the contemporary debate over Jewish legal emancipation. To Baur, the Jewish Christian's profession of devotion to Jesus was not enough to warrant his full participation in the life of the Church. He was, after all, still a Jew. Only his embrace of Paul's gospel and, conversely, his rejection of Judaism, could justify his membership in the Christian community. Only, Baur thereby insinuated, through baptism into the Christian faith could the contemporary European Jew hope to achieve social equality with his gentile neighbor.

The prejudice of Baur's Jewish Christianity grew more pronounced in the work of his students. Developing his teacher's thesis, Albert Schwegler argued that those apostles who bickered with Paul wished to maintain the Jewish character of the Church as a natural consequence of their Jewish ancestries.[71] Schwegler proposed to demonstrate as much by tracing the genealogy of the Jewish Christians to the Essenes, a radical Jewish sect of an earlier age whose members had cultivated a Hellenistic philosophical discipline similar to that espoused by Jesus and Paul. He further argued that those Essenic Christians maintained their Jewish bloodlines through the late second century, when they would resurface as the Ebionites. Where Baur, in other words, had described the Jewish Christians as such in view of their adherence to Judaism's traditional

[69] Strauss (1835–1836). For an overview of Strauss' work on the historical Jesus highlighting his contemporary political objectives, see Moxnes (2012: 95–120).

[70] For the following, cf. Gerdmar (2009: 97–120). Baur's dichotomy between Jewish Christian and gentile Christian appears to assume a more fundamental, albeit just as prejudiced, categorical ethnic distinction between Jew and Greek, on which see Martin (2001: 32–34).

[71] Schwegler developed his thesis in Schwegler (1846). For a summary treatment of his work on the Jewish Christians, see Carleton Paget (2007: 32–33). Baur had proposed a theory similar to Schwegler's in Baur (1831a).

covenant theology, Schwegler submitted that their seemingly irrational behaviors were an innate effect of their race.

Schwegler's shades of racial bias found fuller expression in the work of another of Baur's students. Building on Schwegler's thesis, Albrecht Ritschl argued that some Jewish Christians chose to live as Jews despite not having been born of Jewish stock.[72] Ritschl proposed to restrict the terminology of Jewish Christianity to those Christians who adhered to Judaism by virtue of their lineage while recognizing Paul's antinomian gospel as authoritative for gentile Christians. Those individuals, he argued, were the Nazarenes. But gentile Christians who elected to observe the Jewish law under the false impression that its covenant theology applied to them were persons of a different sort. These he dubbed *judenchristlichen,* or Judaizing Christians. Ritschl included in this category the Ebionites along with a host of other obscure ancient Christian groups alleged to have exhibited Jewish tendencies. To his mind, that the real Jewish Christians maintained their ancestral ways was abhorrent enough. That their Judaism stood to infect unsuspecting gentiles was far more troubling.[73] To Ritschl, therefore, Jewish cooperation with gentiles was possible, but only to the detriment of the gentile's Christian credentials.

I could say more about the vicious logic at work in Ritschl's thesis. But I do not wish to belabor my point. Suffice it to sat that Baur and his students invented the Jewish Christian to rescue the ancient Church from an emerging rationalist historical discourse prone to acknowledge, if not always to validate, its Jewish matrix. Yet their appeal to the past was merely a pretext. In recasting the seminal conflict between Christian and Jew as one pitting Jew against gentile, they merely reset the terms of Christianity's habituated theological polemic against Judaism. Baur designed his "Jewish Christianity" to function as a cipher for contemporary Judaism and his "gentile Christianity" for contemporary Christianity. Schwegler and Ritschl merely pursued Baur's argument to its logical conclusion, asserting that the Judaism of the Jewish Christian was defined primarily by his disregard for the spiritual welfare of the gentile.[74] Together, they infused the language of Jewish Christianity with a disdain for the Jew based on cultural resentment, xenophobia, and questionable genetic science. The resulting historical construction was anti-Semitic before anti-Semitism had a name.

---

[72] See Ritschl (1857). For a summary treatment of Ritschl's thesis, see Carleton Paget (2007: 33–35).

[73] For a similar critique, see Gerdmar (2009: 133–42), who emphasizes Ritschl's zealous defense of his idealized Protestant state against Jewish influence.

[74] This prejudicial construction is unfortunately maintained by Lüdemann (1989: 28–32), who assumes that all ancient Christian expressions of dissent from Paul's gospel must have originated among Jewish Christians. To my mind, defining anti-Paulinism as a categorical feature of their Judaism relieves none of the bias of Baur's original formulation. It merely redirects his alleged Jewish hostility from actual Pauline (read: gentile) Christians to a disembodied Pauline Christianity.

Before going any further, I should establish some distance between James
Parkes and Baur's so-called Tübingen School. To his credit, Parkes was ahead
of the scholarly curve in depicting the Jewish Christians as noble casualties of
the parting of the ways. Since the Holocaust, the common impetus of Jewish
and Christian scholars to shine positive light on Christianity's Jewish roots
has helped to reinvent the once loathed Jewish Christians as icons of harmony
between Christianity and Judaism. The Jewish scholar Hans-Joachim Schoeps,
for instance, proposed to explain the Jewish Christians' adherence to the Torah
not as a function of their Judaism but of their low Christology.[75] Although
they evidently departed from the Jewish mainstream in recognizing Jesus as the
Messiah, that belief entailed no substantive adjustment of their traditional covenant theology. Taking Schoeps' thesis a step further, the Catholic theologian
Jean Daniélou argued that all expressions of belief in Jesus prior to the second
century not explicitly acknowledging his divine aspect should be qualified as
Jewish because they entailed no substantive reinvention of traditional Jewish
eschatology.[76] To Daniélou, therefore, Jewish Christianity was not a phenomenon limited to a particularly "Jewish" subset of the ancient Christian population. It was, rather, a universal function of formative Christianity's continuity
with the Judaism of its incubation.

The pronounced tonal shift between Baur's and Daniélou's definitions of
Jewish Christianity neatly demonstrates the logical liability of its construction. Should one wish to highlight Judaism's historical relationship with
Christianity, he or she will cast the Jewish Christian as every Christian. Should
one wish to downplay that relationship, he or she will cast the Jewish Christian
as a deviant. Invariably, what is deemed "Jewish" about Jewish Christianity is
determined not by its ancient subject by the contemporary observer. Whether
that assessment is leveled respectfully or disparagingly, its implied objects of
"Judaism" and "Christianity" are fixed in the historian's present reality and
not necessarily in the past that he or she proposes to document. Consequently,
one cannot help but to describe the Jewish Christian without making unverifiable assumptions about his or her subject's own conceptions of Jew and
Christian and the relationship between those ancient cultural epistemes.

Returning, therefore, to the parting of the ways narrative, I find the following conclusions apropos. To set the Jewish Christian in relief against other
Christians and Jews of his day is to denature his self-perception both as a
Christian and as a Jew. More perniciously, the language of Jewish Christianity
categorically denies its subject the personal prerogative to know Christianity as

[75] Schoeps (1949). For a summary treatment, see Lüdemann (1989: 21–23).
[76] Daniélou (1958). For a summary treatment, see Lüdemann (1989, 25–27). Although I laud
the egalitarian principle of Daniélou's approach, I am wary of his presumption to characterize
Jewish Christian theology for its ignorance of Hellenistic philosophy, which assumes a cultural
dichotomy between Judaism and Hellenism unwarranted even in his abstract frame of reference.
For a more thoroughgoing critique to this effect, see Kraft (1972).

a type of Jewish cultural expression.[77] It forces the reader to prioritize its sub-ject's Christian identity, reducing the Jewish Christian's sense of Jewish identity to an instinctive, implicitly recidivist deference to the laws of the Torah.[78] As a result, the Jewish Christian cannot help but to appear antagonistic toward the Christian trained on Paul's gospel. Applied without caution, the terminology of Jewish Christianity thus stands to reinforce the very same hostile notion of Christianity's rejection of Judaism that James Parkes sought to counteract.

THE JEWISH CHRISTIANS IN THE PARTING OF THE WAYS NARRATIVE

In all likelihood, Parkes did not realize that his Jewish Christians were impossi-ble creatures. As noted, he allowed them to function as actual Jews rather than simply as immature Christians, if only within the limits set by his language. Consequently, he portrays the Jewish Christians not as aggressors toward gen-tiles but as victims of gentile and Jewish aggression. That departure from the Tübingen School is to be attributed to his novel impetus to set the ancient Christian record in dialogue with its Jewish counterpart. How Parkes man-aged to defy Baur and his followers is suggested by two notable entries in his bibliography on the parting of the ways.[79] One is Fenton John Anthony Hort's 1894 volume *Judaistic Christianity*.[80] The other is R. Travers Herford's 1903 volume *Christianity in Talmud and Midrash*.[81] Each of these studies offers a unique perspective on the Jewish Christians attuned to their Jewish priorities. Let us therefore consider how Parkes applied their treatments to his theory.

Best known for his text-critical work on the New Testament, Hort was already a scholar of considerable renown when he decided to take on the topic of Jewish Christianity. Since Ritschl, the state of continental scholarship on Christian ori-gins had devolved to the point where the heirs of the Tübingen School were denying the Jewish Christians their places in the early Church. That served to diminish the significance of Baur's proposed ethnic conflict between Jew and gentile, emphasizing instead a supposed philosophical conflict between Jew and

---

[77] This incisive critique is leveled by Strecker (1971) in response to Walter Bauer's evident refusal to validate the apostolic credentials of the Jewish Christians as he had for other alleged Christian heretics of their age (cf. Bauer 1971: 236–38).

[78] For this observation, see Colpe (1987), especially ibid. (64–66). Examplars of this unavoid-able bias include Simon (1986: 237–40); J.E. Taylor (1990: 326–27); Kaestli (1996: 271–72); Carleton Paget (1999: 739–42). Blanchetière (2001: 297–520), tries to overcome this pitfall by contextualizing the ritual practices of Jewish Christians or, in his language, the Nazarenes, within a detailed theological framework reconstructed from classical Jewish and Christian sources. Unfortunately, his method is too conjectural and his logic too tenuous to support the weight of an argument that essentially attempts to historicize Daniélou's model of an abstract theological phenomenon (cf. ibid., 298–305).

[79] Cf. Parkes (1934: 74).

[80] Hort (1894).

[81] Herford (1903).

Greek. The new theory, most famously espoused by Adolf von Harnack, inferred that Paul designed his gospel to relieve Judaism of its archaic national and legal traditions. A Hellenized Jew himself, Paul preserved the monotheistic principle of his ancestral faith for application in a new, universal religion appealing to the enlightened sensibilities of Hellenized gentiles. In accepting Paul's doctrine of the Christ, Harnack argued, the Jew functionally ceased to be a Jew and became a Christian. Consequently, the term "Jewish Christian" should apply only to those Christian heretics who rejected Paul's apostolic authority.[82]

Hort concurred with Harnack's assessment that Jewish Christianity ceased to bear significantly on the Church after Paul's time. But where Harnack attributed the subsequent marginalization of the Jewish Christians to their radical opposition to Paul, Hort saw their estrangement from the Christian mainstream as an unintended consequence of their desires to remain true to their native Judaism.[83] Stressing their pre-apostolic origins, he traced their lineage to the disciples of Jesus and the apostolic Church of Jerusalem. From there he followed their migration to Pella during the first Jewish revolt against Rome, their return to Jerusalem, and their ultimate expulsion after the Bar Kokhba rebellion.[84] After that point, he argued, Jewish Christianity survived only in isolated clusters such as the Ebionites and the Nazarenes, their claims to apostolic authority silenced by a Christian majority who pragmatically opted to distance themselves from the unruly Jews.[85]

Although Hort stopped short of commending the Jewish Christians for their integrity, he effectively countered Harnack's denial of their Jewish roots. To Hort, the Jewish Christians who survived Paul did not reject his gospel outright so much as they disagreed with his premise of erasing the traditional distinction between Jew and gentile. The Jewish Christians thus wished merely to sustain the Church's original Jewish theology, asserting their ancestral prerogatives to live as Jews while deferring to Paul with respect to the gentiles.[86] Consequently, Hort argued, the phenomenon conventionally termed Jewish Christianity "might with at least equal propriety be called Christian Judaism."[87] He thereby envisioned Jewish Christianity as both inalienably Christian and inalienably

---

[82] See, e.g., Harnack (1909–1910: 1.310–34), with summary treatment in Carleton Paget (2007: 36).

[83] For the following, see Hort (1894: 1–8), with summary treatment in Carleton Paget (2007: 36–37). Hort refers to the first edition of Harnack's *Lehrbuch* in Hort (1894: 11).

[84] Hort (1894: 174–80), and cf. ibid. (39–47), on the establishment of the apostolic Church of Jerusalem. Hort, ibid. (178), suggests the Diaspora revolt of 115–117 CE as a factor in Christianity's estrangement from Judaism, although he does not explicitly correlate this episode to the development of Jewish Christianity. For further consideration of this topic, neglected by Parkes, see Goodman (1992: 34–36).

[85] Hort (1894: 194–202).

[86] Hort (1894: 61–83), associates the Jewish Christians' decision to endorse Paul's antinomian gospel for the gentiles with the so-called Council of Jerusalem described in Acts 15 (cf. Gal 2.1–14).

[87] Hort (1894: 5).

Jewish, thereby challenging the distinction conceived by Baur and his followers and still maintained by the likes of Harnack.

Precisely why Hort took exception to the Tübingen School's portrayal of the Jewish Christians is difficult to say. Certainly it was not for any sympathy for their Judaism.[88] One is tempted to attribute his variance with the Germans to his innocence of the continental debate over Jewish emancipation.[89] Yet a more likely explanation is Hort's acculturation to an English intellectual discourse apt to construe Judaism and Hellenism as complementary rather than conflicting philosophical miens.[90] Hort's mentor, Joseph Barber Lightfoot, had already challenged Baur's intimation that the Jewish Christians opposed Paul's gospel out of spite for gentiles, stressing instead what he claimed was the Jew's natural wariness of theological innovation.[91] Hort sustained that critique in reference to Harnack's more malicious assertion that the Jewish Christians, in rejecting Paul's gospel, likewise rejected Christianity. Jew and gentile, he defiantly asserted, could indeed unite under a common Christian banner, even if, in his estimation, the Jew would have done well to follow Paul's advices.

His subtle evangelical angle notwithstanding, Hort presented a historical portrait of Jewish Christianity well-suited to James Parkes' conciliatory agenda. However ambivalently, Hort acknowledged that the Jewish Christians operated principally not as cantankerous Christians but as devout Jews. That novel insight afforded Parkes the opportunity to work the Jewish Christians into a narrative of the Christian schism likewise prioritizing their Jewish identities.

But Parkes' narrative would not be complete without consideration of the ancient evidences situating Jewish Christians in their native Jewish environs. For that perspective, Parkes turned to the more recent work of Herford. An English Unitarian minister, Herford sought to promote Judaism as a viable religion amenable to cooperation with Christianity. His stated aim in writing *Christianity in Talmud and Midrash* was to demystify Judaism's classical sources for the sake of Christian readers apt to discount the Jew's knowledge of Christianity as entirely perfidious.[92] He therefore analyzed what he determined to be all the references to Christians and Christianity preserved in the ancient rabbinic library, interpreting them with the aid of the finest historical-critical Judaic scholarship available in his day.

[88] Hort (1894: 5), shows his personal bias in alluding nonetheless to the Jewish Christians' typically "Jewish point of view" on God's covenant "belonging naturally to the time before Christ came" even after "its national limits were broken down and it had become universal."
[89] I assume here a qualitative difference between the social circumstances that fostered the United Kingdom's legal emancipation of its Jewry in 1858 and those that fostered Germany's in 1871. For an instructive comparison, see Rürup (1999).
[90] On this distinctly English cultural construction, see Martin (2001: 45–48).
[91] See, e.g., Lightfoot (1865: 191–246; 1868: 179–267). For a general comparison of Lightfoot's and Baur's accounts of the conflict between Jew and gentile in the apostolic Church, see Kaye (1984).
[92] Cf. Herford (1903: vii–x).

Although Herford devoted much of his attention to explaining the Talmud's controversial indictments of Jesus, he gave equal time to the rabbinic polemic against the *minim*. Without exception, he identified the targets of that polemic as Jewish Christians and the object of their alleged heresy as Christianity.[93] The earliest references to *minim*, he observed, construe Jewish Christians as opponents of the restorative efforts undertaken by the rabbinic sages following the destruction of Jerusalem in 70 CE. Within the next decade, the rabbis conceived the *birkat ha-minim* as a defensive countermeasure.[94] Just years later, however, the rabbinic affront against Christianity was eclipsed by another. As the Roman authorities persecuted the Church, the rabbis feared being mistakenly associated with the criminal element in their midst. Aiming, therefore, to distance themselves from the Jewish Christians, their deprecations of the *minim* grew more vocal.[95] But by the mid-second century, around the time of the Bar Kokhba rebellion, the rabbinic polemic began to lose steam.[96] Having already driven the Christians from their midst, the sages relaxed their attitudes toward a heresy now seen as more of a curiosity than a threat. Although it would take some time for the Jewish Christians to disappear entirely, their ever-diminishing presence in the hostile climes of Roman Palestine allowed the rabbinic sages and the Jewish people at large finally to see Christianity for what it was, namely a religion distinct from their own.[97]

Despite Herford's questionable methodological presuppositions, his study corrected a critical conversation on the Jewish Christians weighed down by invidious assessments of their designs for the Church's gentile constituency. In situating the Jewish Christians squarely in their Jewish environs, Herford aimed to show that Judaism's most fundamental perceptions of Christians and Christianity were driven not by arbitrary hatred but by the contentious circumstances of the initial encounter of Christian and Jew. More emphatically than Hort, Herford read Jewish Christianity as a Jewish phenomenon, only occasionally referring to the misfit Ebionites and Nazarenes of patristic lore as supporting witnesses for the rabbis.

Herford's lucid presentation of ancient Jewish texts largely unknown to Christian readers opened the door for just the type of the historical synthesis undertaken by James Parkes. But it would be a mistake to infer that Parkes relied solely on Christian informants. In fact, one might surmise that Parkes

---

[93] On Herford's univocal understanding of *minut*, see Herford (1903: 365–81).

[94] Herford (1903: 381–87). Cf. ibid. (125–37), on the Talmudic passages allegedly attesting to that liturgical reform.

[95] Herford (1903: 387–90), referring to supposed rabbinic witnesses to the Roman dragnet at ibid. (137–45).

[96] Herford (1903: 84–85), acknowledges Justin's report of violence toward Christians among Bar Kokhba's supporters. Yet true to his conciliatory agenda, he downplays the likelihood of its historicity and neglects to cite Bar Kokhba's decidedly non-Christian Messianic ambitions as a point of conflict between the Jewish Christians and the Jewish mainstream.

[97] Herford (1903: 390–96).

found credibility in the accounts of Hort and Herford in view of the Jewish historical narrative that provided the structural framework for his study. Before writing *The Conflict of the Church and the Synagogue*, Parkes read the entirety of the eleven-volume *Geschichte der Juden,* a groundbreaking work by the German Jewish scholar Heinrich Graetz that had become standard Jewish fare since its publication in the mid-nineteenth century.[98] Although Parkes referred to Graetz's history only occasionally, its imprimatur is manifest throughout Parkes' work. Graetz's influence on Parkes' account of the Christian schism is especially notable inasmuch as Herford too relied on Graetz.[99] Let us therefore consider Graetz's account of Jewish Christianity before assessing its contribution to the parting of the ways narrative.

Heinrich Graetz was a man of many agendas.[100] A university-trained historian with liberal social leanings, he was a vocal advocate of Jewish legal emancipation in his home country of Prussia and throughout Europe.[101] Nevertheless, as a faculty member at the rabbinical seminary of Breslau, today the Polish city of Wrocław, he assumed a fairly conservative stance regarding how his fellow Jews could achieve social advancement. Attuned to the nascent discourse of anti-Semitism, Graetz was fiercely opposed to the notion that the Jew could achieve true equality with the gentile by converting to Christianity. His mentality shaped by his people's history of subjugation, Graetz unapologetically cast Christianity as a cultural force hostile to Jewish survival. Although, therefore, he acknowledged Christianity's role as a catalyst of Jewish history, Graetz analyzed its human exponents from a decidedly critical perspective often given to outright reproach.[102]

Graetz was just as dismissive of the notion that the Jew could improve his standing by recasting Judaism in a Christian mold.[103] That, to his mind, had been the error of Abraham Geiger and other proponents of the Jewish Reform movement recently undertaken in Germany and rapidly migrating eastward. Compromising one's religious convictions, Graetz believed, not only would fail to impress Christian society but would tear at the fabric of a Jewish society historically bound by the common beliefs and rituals now being subjected to review in the name of social progress. Concomitantly, Graetz disapproved of what he saw as the deliberate anti-intellectualism of the Hasidim, the

[98] Graetz (1853–1875), published in English as Graetz (1891–1898). For ease of reference, I shall cite the German edition followed by the corresponding pages in the English. On Parkes' study of Graetz's work, see Richmond (2005: 84).

[99] See, e.g., Herford's glowing endorsement of Graetz in Herford (1903: 380, n. 1).

[100] For a summary account of Graetz's background and historical objectives, see Brenner (2010: 53–91), and, more extensively, the comprehensive intellectual biography of Pyka (2009).

[101] On Graetz's orientation of his history toward the national debate over the prerequisites for Jewish social improvement, see Schorsch (1994: 286–93); Pyka (2009: 241–57).

[102] For a complementary assessment, see Brenner (2010: 64–68), who notes Graetz's inference of direct correspondence between popular notions of Christian identity and German identity.

[103] For the following, see Schorsch (1994: 282–86); Pyka (2009: 64–86); Brenner (2010: 57–60).

neo-orthodox Jewish mystics then flourishing in the Prussian east who berated the reformers as liars and apostates.[104] Denouncing the Hasidic brand of traditionalism as regressive, Graetz envisioned a Judaism attentive to the past but allowing for moderate innovation for the sake of securing the future of its people in a rapidly evolving world. Further, therefore, to his more overt expressions of resentment toward Christianity, Graetz expressed his uneasiness with those Jews of the past who seemed to have deviated from his ideal path by acculturating to gentile norms.[105]

The Jewish Christians fell squarely into that category. Graetz's portrait of those ancient agitators originated in a notoriously abusive account of Christianity's birth written for the third volume of his *Geschichte*.[106] Taking his cue from Geiger's recent portrait of Jesus as a misunderstood Pharisaic reformer, Graetz contended that the Christian Messiah had operated at the fringes of Jewish society as a member of the mysterious Essene sect.[107] Although his teachings offered a fairly conventional interpretation of traditional Jewish ethics, Jesus' esoteric vision of the end of days attracted the attention of Jewish civil and religious authorities suspicious of his political designs.[108] Following his subsequent trial and crucifixion, some of Jesus' Jewish supporters continued to spread his gospel among their fellow Jews under the cover of Gnostic wisdom. Those erstwhile Essenes, Graetz submitted, would persist as the Ebionites and Nazarenes of subsequent Christian record.[109] It was their knowledge, moreover, that Paul would later exploit in reinventing their failed Messiah as the immortal Son of God and author of a new religion setting Jew against Greek and, ultimately, Christian against Jew.[110]

Distancing the Jewish Christians from what he accounted as the conventional Judaism of the rabbis, Graetz challenged Geiger's intimation that Jesus and his followers were legitimate heirs of the Pharisaic tradition. Yet in order

---

[104] On this aspect of Graetz's rhetoric, see Elukin (1998); Brenner (2010: 68–73).

[105] Note Graetz's decision to begin his publication of the *Geschichte* with the fourth volume (1853), which covers the rabbinic period. He thereby forced his reader's objectification of Judaism into conformity with that of the ancient sages whose ways he aimed to promote over the scriptural traditions typically emphasized by Geiger and the reformers. See Pyka (2009: 175–96).

[106] Cut from the 1856 first edition of the third volume of his *Geschichte*, Graetz's confrontational treatment of Jesus first appeared in a French translation in 1862 before its restoration in the 1863 second edition of the original German work. The following citations of the third volume of the *Geschichte* refer to the second and subsequent editions.

[107] Graetz (1853–1875: 3.272–302; 1891–1898: 2.141–60). On Graetz's debate with Geiger over the early Christian movement's proximity to the Jewish mainstream, see Heschel (1998: 136–37) and passim. For Geiger's views on Jesus and his Pharisaic background, see his summary presentation in A. Geiger (1864–1871: 1.109–38).

[108] Graetz (1853–1875: 3.302–08; 1891–1898: 2.161–66). On Graetz's subversive use of thematic elements culled from the Talmud's polemical portrait of Jesus, see Catchpole (1971: 27–33).

[109] Graetz (1853–1875: 3.308–15; 1891–1898: 2.166–71).

[110] Graetz (1853–1875: 3.408–25; 1891–1898: 2.219–32). On Graetz's implicit accusation of Paul's apostasy, see Langton (2010: 58–60).

to achieve that effect, he had to explain why the rabbis, the successors of the Pharisees, were so alarmed by the so-called heretics supposedly operating on the fringes of their society. Graetz therefore asserted that the rabbis felt compelled to address the Christian element despite their demographic insignificance. As the standard-bearers of the Jewish faith, the Pharisees grew wary of the Jewish Christians when the latter began to absorb pagan beliefs from gentile Christians sharing their Gnostic interests.[111] The fall of Jerusalem in 70 CE. accelerated their estrangement inasmuch as it emboldened the Jewish Christians to amplify their protests against the Pharisees. When, therefore, the surviving Pharisees regrouped at Yavneh to found the rabbinic movement, responding to the Jewish Christians was at the top of their agenda. That, Graetz reasoned, was the genesis of the *birkat ha-minim*.[112] In the years following its implementation, most of the Christians still living as Jews were rousted from the Jewish community. The remainder finally defected from the Jewish camp during the Bar Kokhba rebellion, at which point the last Jewish Christians finally turned on their fellow Jews to become informants to the vengeful Roman authorities. Henceforth, the rabbis would see all Jewish defectors as Christians and all Christians as *minim*.[113]

To Graetz's mind, the rabbinic sages needed to address the Jewish Christians on account of their associations with gentiles, that is, gentile Christians, and Romans. In other words, their enmity toward the *minim* was born of the accused's own hostility toward Pharisaic Judaism. Although he did not acknowledge as much, Graetz's portrait of the Jewish Christians was thus a mirror image of Baur's.[114] Where Baur assented to the Church Fathers in casting those individuals as Christian heretics, Graetz assented to the rabbis in casting them as Jewish heretics. But the effect of Graetz's Jewish Christian was identical to Baur's insofar as both believed that one's Christianity determined his or her path toward the gentile Church. Consequently, despite their opposing rhetorical aims, Graetz's account of the Jewish Christians dovetailed perfectly with Baur's.

But in casting all *minim* as Christians, Graetz did more than simply respond to Baur. Much like his contemporary Jewish reformers, Graetz's *minim* were biblical fundamentalists and falsifiers of the rabbinic *halakhah*. Like the Hasidim, his *minim* were undisciplined mystics corrupted by exotic philosophical influences. To Graetz, all ancient Jews whom the rabbis deemed heretics were no more authentic in their Judaism than the duplicitous Jewish Christians. And just as those *minim* ultimately threw in their lots with the gentiles, so too, he

---

[111] Graetz (1853–1875: 4.77–108; 1891–1898: 2.365–82).
[112] Graetz (1853–1875: 4.104–106; 1891–1898: 2.379–80).
[113] Graetz (1853–1875: 4.154–56, 182–83; 1891–1898: 2.411–13, 430–31).
[114] Although he did not engage Baur directly in the *Geschichte*, Graetz acknowledged the former's work on Jewish Christianity in his earlier study, Graetz (1846: 1–4), in which he first proposed to describe the *minim* as Gnostic Jews exposed to Hellenistic philosophy via pagan and Christian cultural channels.

implied, would the Jewish "heretics" of his own day find themselves alienated from what he envisioned as the genuine Judaism that he claimed to represent.

It is a credit to Herford that little of Graetz's bitterness filtered into his work. But Herford did not have to follow Graetz in choosing to construe all *minim* as Christians. More recently, Moritz Friedländer had argued against Graetz that the category of *minut* applied not strictly to Jewish Christians but, rather, to Gnostic Jews who occasionally traded in Christian knowledge.[115] Herford vociferously rejected that position.[116] He needed to maintain Graetz's wide focus in order to demonstrate the limited compass of the rabbinic polemic against Christianity relative to the whole of the ancient Church. By showing that the rabbis targeted only Jewish Christians, Herford reduced the object of their opposition to one of no consequence toward contemporary Christian-Jewish relations. The rabbis, he thus contended, did not abhor Christianity per se. They abhorred a heterodox form of Christianity equally detested by the Church Fathers. Despite, therefore, affirming their Judaism, Herford depicted the Jewish Christians as the same marginal Jewish actors who figured in Graetz's history.

Let us now return to the parting of the ways narrative. Considering Parkes' influences, it is no wonder that the Jewish Christians function differently in his account of the Christian schism than their pedigree would suggest. His Jewish Christians were not the lying, recidivist Christians of Baur and his followers. Nor were they the debauched Jewish agitators of Graetz. Parkes' Jewish Christians were Hort's misguided but earnest Christian Jews. They were Herford's alarming but ultimately harmless *minim*. And yet, Parkes could not escape the prejudices embedded in the language of Jewish Christianity. Although Parkes allowed his Jewish Christians to operate as Jews, he failed to see that the Judaism he imputed to them was little more than an inferior antitype to their Christianity. Consequently, he failed to see that his Jewish Christians could not function as the legitimate Jewish actors whom he needed them to be.

We are therefore left with a paradox. On the one hand, one cannot describe the Christian schism without accounting for the Jewish Christians. On the other hand, one cannot describe the Jewish Christians without anachronistically inferring the effect of a schism. That interpretive dilemma has complicated a number of recent efforts to locate the phenomenon of Jewish Christianity in historical time and place. Some scholars have sought to resolve the issue by emending the language of Jewish Christianity better to emphasize the Jewish priorities of its subjects, following Hort in renaming the phenomenon "Christian Judaism."[117] Others have offered more inventive tags such as

---

[115] Friedländer (1898). Ironically, Graetz had presented a similar argument in Graetz (1846) prior to his engagement of Geiger's work.

[116] Herford (1903: 368–76) and passim.

[117] Although this reversal of nomenclature is not a new proposal by any means, I refer to recent studies problematizing the terminology of Jewish Christianity and offering Christian Judaism

"Apostolic Judaism" or "Pauline Judaism."[118] Others still have opted for cir-
cumlocution, speaking of "Jewish belief in Jesus" or "Jewish ways of following
Jesus."[119] Frustratingly, some scholars have acknowledged the problem only to
proceed as though there were none.[120]

By recasting the Jewish Christian as a not-quite-Christian Jew, these efforts
seem to suggest that a less prejudicial terminology can rehabilitate the individual in question as an individualist who chose to adhere to an idiosyncratic
Jewish theology rather than accede to the will of the proto-orthodox Christian
majority. In my estimation, this interpretive strategy amounts to little more than
a semantic dodge. Simply to set Judaism and Christianity in a common epistemological framework is to incur some measure of theological prejudice.[121] In
other words, to acknowledge that Christianity evolved from Judaism makes
it impossible for the modern observer not to assume a hereditary relationship
between the categories of Jewish identity and Christian identity. Regardless,
therefore, of what one chooses to call the Jewish Christian, one cannot help but
to see his or her Christianity as atavistic. The ultimate triumph of Paul's gospel stigmatizes the Jewish Christian for his willingness to receive the gospel as
Jewish wisdom, to envision Israel's Messiah as the redeemer of a Jewish nation.
It informs a contemporary objectivity reversing what the Jewish Christian and,
frankly, most ancient observers would have seen as the Church's natural evolutionary trajectory. That is why the Jewish Christian confounds the parting of
the ways narrative. That is why the Jewish Christian inevitably will confound
any historical narrative locating the primary agents of the Christian schism
beyond the Jewish Christian's own frame of reference.[122]

As James Parkes correctly surmised, a narrative of the Christian schism
accurately accounting for the experiences of the Jewish Christians must
acknowledge that those individuals realized their Christian identities in view

---

as an alternative and/or complementary historical category, e.g., Luttikhuizen (1991); Boer
(1998); Jackson-McCabe (2007).

[118] For the former, see Runesson (2008a: 72–73), and the latter, J. Schwartz (2012: 55).

[119] For the former, see Skarsaune (2007a), and the latter, Broadhead (2010: 26–27).

[120] Studies of this order typically acknowledge the fallacy of describing the Jewish Christians as
heretical Christians while minimalizing or simply neglecting the fallacy of describing them as
Christians to begin with. See, e.g., Häkkinen (2005); F.S. Jones (2007: 314–34); Luomanen
(2005; 2012).

[121] For the following, cf. J.Z. Smith (1990: 81–83).

[122] For a recent attempt to redefine the separation of Judaism and Christianity as an intentional
process of cultural disambiguation, see Destro and Pesce (2012: 25–27) and passim. While
I admire the authors' desire to place equal emphasis on the continuities and the discontinuities
between early Christian and Jewish culture, their model entails the same a priori assumption of
epistemological disparity between the categories of Christian and Jew that upends the parting
of the ways narrative. I am less impressed by Broadhead (2010: 371–74), who, despite challenging its suppositions with respect to the motivations of the Jewish Christians, adheres to Parkes'
assumptions quite closely. I find his proposal, ibid. (389), to recast the parting of the ways as a
"forming of the ways" baffling in its redundancy.

of their experiences as Jews. Where Parkes erred was in his assumption that those experiences were defined by a Pharisaic/rabbinic tradition fundamentally opposed to the notion that a Jew could be a Christian. Despite his best intentions, Parkes ceded to the tendentious arguments of Baur and Graetz that the Jewish Christians somehow rejected their Judaism by professing belief in Jesus. That premise is no longer sustainable. That is why I propose to reassess the Jewish Christians as Jews. Only in view of their functions as Jews and sharers in the common Jewish experience can one fairly assess their significance as catalysts of the developments witnessed by the rabbinic sages whose impressions of the Christian schism I aim to describe.

SETTING THE CHRISTIAN SCHISM IN ITS JEWISH CONTEXT

Returning to the agenda set forth in the introduction, I shall now establish some interpretive guidelines for my project informed by the foregoing methodological considerations. I reiterate my intent to describe the Christian schism in reference to just one site of its occurrence, namely Roman Palestine or what the rabbis called *Eretz Yisrael*, the Land of Israel. I shall focus, moreover, on developments spanning the first three centuries of the Common Era, that is, the age before the Roman Empire's Christianization. I choose to analyze this particular historical locus not because it was the only site of the early encounter between Christian and Jew, much less its definitive site.[123] Rather, my interest owes to the presence at that site of the rabbinic sages who formulated the responses to Christianity that would go on to inform the Jewish people's basic knowledge of the Christian other. Per my prior comments, I acknowledge that the initial meeting between Christian and Jew commemorated in the rabbinic record was a meeting between Jews of different ideological persuasions. Yet I also acknowledge that the Jewish Christian was, at the very least, atypical of the general Jewish population with respect to his or her beliefs about Jesus. That, I contend, legitimizes my premise of accounting that meeting as one of the many to influence the more widespread phenomenon to which I refer as the Christian schism.

---

[123] Due to the paucity of the Jewish record, our knowledge of the early Jewish response to Christianity outside of Palestine is largely restricted to tendentious Christian accounts prone to exaggerate the complicity of Jews in the prosecutorial efforts of the Roman authorities; see Setzer (1994); Lieu (1998). Evidence of the early Jewish response to Christianity outside the Roman Empire is entirely lacking. Becker (2003: 382), plausibly suggests that the Jews of early Sasanian Babylonia would have encountered Syriac-speaking Christians on a regular basis. Regrettably, however, the surviving Babylonian rabbinic record exhibits no clear evidence of such encounters prior to the fourth and fifth centuries and, even then, chiefly in figurative terms borrowed from earlier Palestinian texts involving *minim*. It is therefore impossible to deduce from these sources credible information as to the actualities of the initial Jewish encounter with Christianity in Mesopotamia. For comments to this effect, see Kalmin (2006: 5–8).

Second, I take it for granted that the character of Jewish life in Roman Judea/
Palestine was not dictated by the Pharisees or their immediate rabbinic successors. While I recognize a certain degree of continuity between these groups,
I defer to the critical consensus in assuming no power on their parts to enforce
public morals either before or after the destruction of the Jerusalem Temple in
70 CE.[124] Both the Pharisees and the early rabbis participated in movements
of limited popular appeal, professing beliefs and advocating ways of life that
would only begin to influence the Jewish masses following the Christianization
of Rome.[125] Only in conjunction with that process would the rabbinic way
begin to develop the character of a Jewish orthodoxy. Per the assessment of
Steven Fraade, I account the formative *halakhah* as an elaborate legal fiction,
an attempt to construct a discursive world addressing real issues and real social
actors but functional only in the minds of its authors and their consenting
readers.[126] In other words, it represented not normative Jewish custom but the
ideal of a self-styled intellectual elite operating at varying degrees of proximity
to the mainstream of Palestinian Jewish society.[127]

As to the significance of their rhetoric as social commentary, the efforts of
the *Tannaim* to implement the *halakhah* on the broad demographic scale must
be understood as theoretical exercises in popular control. The early rabbis
spoke neither for all Jews nor to all Jews. That fact of itself does not discredit
them as witnesses to the common life of their people. But it does complicate the
premise of reading their academic commentaries as accurate reflections of the
social world in which they operated.[128] Consequently, one must not presume to
read their characterizations of the *minim* as authoritative accounts of how and
where those alleged heretics functioned within that world. At best, the earliest
notices of such individuals, Christian and otherwise, speak to the ambitions of
the rabbis to circumscribe their operation, to exclude them from the pious and
culturally homogeneous Jewish nation of their idyllic imaginations.[129]

Further tempering the popular ambitions of the rabbis was their subjugation by Rome.[130] During the early years of Christianity's development, the
Jews twice tried and failed to uproot the foreign regime that had occupied
their land since the first century BCE. The harsh repercussions of the ensuing

---

[124] For the following, I rely primarily on S.J.D. Cohen (1984), especially ibid. (36–42). For representative statements bolstering what I describe as the emerging critical consensus, see Hezser
(1997: 69–77); S. Schwartz (2001: 91–98, 105–123); Lapin (2012: 45–55).

[125] S. Schwartz (2001: 259–74); Lapin (2012: 155–67).

[126] Fraade (2011: 12–15).

[127] So, e.g., S.J.D. Cohen (1999b: 959–61); S. Schwartz (2001: 119–23); Lapin (2012: 65–76). For
comments on how the elitism of the rabbis impacted their ethical objectivity in reference to
Jewish actors outside of their immediate social circles, see Schofer (2005: 30–40).

[128] For comparable comments, see Miller (2006: 21–26).

[129] So, e.g., Goodman (1983: 104–07); S.J.D. Cohen (1984: 41–42); Miller (2006: 2–3).

[130] For the following, see S. Schwartz (2001), especially ibid. (127–61). The awareness of the
Tannaim of their provincial domestication and its impact on the formative *halakhah* is discussed by Goodman (1983: 135–54), and, more recently, Lapin (2012: 105–09) and passim.

wars eventually conditioned most of Palestine's Jews to accede to their roles as minor players in a local social hierarchy dominated by Rome's provincial administrators.[131] The establishment of the office of the Jewish Patriarch or, in Hebrew, the *nasi*, around the turn of the third century afforded the rabbinic sages access to a political apparatus whereby to seek the state's intercession in Jewish civil affairs.[132] But the Patriarchate was not a rabbinic office. It was a Jewish office commissioned to serve the needs of the many over the desires of the few. Consequently, while the rabbis often boasted of their close ties with the Patriarchs and other local Roman officials, their actual power of persuasion over their fellow Jews was quite limited. The rabbis, like all provincials, acted only insofar as Rome allowed them to act. These factors inhibited their ability to exercise their legislative authority among those of their fellow Jews who preferred Roman judicial procedure to the *halakhah*.

That the rabbinic sages functioned almost indistinguishably within Palestine's general Jewish population speaks to the terms of their encounter with Christianity. As Joan Taylor demonstrated in her 1993 study *Christians and the Holy Places*, the Christian estate appears to have left no unique mark on the landscape of Palestine prior to the fourth century.[133] Although travelers of the late ancient period spoke of lively Christian cult sites dotting the terrain where Jesus once lived, those traditions were likely fabricated centuries after the fact by local believers wishing to establish their claims to a land still occupied chiefly by Jews and pagans. To our knowledge, the relatively few Christians who sustained the churches of Palestine prior to Rome's Christianization did not erect shrines to Jesus or other New Testament luminaries. They did not build architecturally distinctive houses of worship. As far as the material record indicates, the Christians most likely deemed *minim* by their rabbinic neighbors cultivated their sense of difference from the general Jewish population just as the rabbis did, namely in their own minds.[134]

To the extent that one can securely locate Christians amidst that population, our objectivity is conditioned by a rabbinic literary record not especially forthcoming about its ideological and social prejudices. By their very nature, therefore, our primary Jewish witnesses to the Christian schism cast the Christian both as an insider and as an outsider, one standing within the actual Jewish society of Roman Palestine but outside of the idealized Jewish

---

[131] This key observation informs the recent studies of S. Schwartz (2010), especially ibid. (110–65), and Lapin (2012).

[132] For the following, see S. Schwartz (2001: 119–23); Lapin (2012: 52–55). I shall discuss this institution in greater detail in Chapter 5.

[133] For the following, see J.E. Taylor (1993), especially ibid. (318–32), on the supposed identification of traditional Jewish Christian cult sites in Byzantine Palestine. For a more recent critical assessment probing the possibility that Palestinian Christians of the Roman era maintained a subdued private estate while concomitantly operating as Jews, see Meyers and Chancey (2012: 185–94).

[134] J.E. Taylor (1993: 25–31).

society envisioned by the rabbis. Contemporary scholars seeking to describe the schism in reference to the rabbinic record generally have followed Heinrich Graetz in emphasizing the latter, externalizing aspect of the *min*'s characterization. Following the institution of the *birkat ha-minim*, the argument goes, the rabbinic construction of *minut* referred no longer to Jews but to gentiles.[135] The Jewish Christians are thereby allowed only a brief window of time in which to have operated as Jews. That mistake is in need of correction. The critical reader of Jewish history must forgo Graetz's outdated assumption that the rabbinic sages represented authoritative voices of Judaism during Christianity's formative age. Accordingly, one must not assume that the *halakhah* represented a normative system of practice and belief precluding members of Palestine's Christian demographic from identifying as Jews. What the rabbinic sages chose to remember about the schism is not the same as what was. The responsible historian must therefore distinguish between the Christian schism as it occurred within that demographic and for its idiosyncratic representation among the rabbinic collective. So shall I attempt to differentiate between the facts of the past and their selective representation in the rabbinic record.

Although I am reasonably confident of the originality of my project, I am not the first to try to read the Jewish experiences of the Christian schism through the lens of the rabbis. The most substantial recent effort to that effect is the aforementioned study of Daniel Boyarin.[136] In accounting the rabbinic concept of *minut* as a functional analogue to the Christian construction of heresy, Boyarin submits that Jewish and Christian theologians participated in a mutual discourse sustained until the catalytic political developments of the fourth century forced its resolution. Up to that point, he argues, Jews and Christians of all varieties operated on a common Judaeo-Christian theological plane neither typically Jewish nor typically Christian but, rather, an organic amalgam of the two.

Boyarin's tactful language clearly improves a conventional discourse on Jewish Christianity hopelessly at odds with itself over the cultural priorities of its subjects. It naturalizes those ancient actors whom their critics sought to alienate as heretical *minim*, Ebionites, and Nazarenes, allowing the historian to read their kind as genuine Jews and Christians rather than defective variations thereof. Yet while I find Boyarin's "Judaeo-Christianity" superior to Baur's *Judenchristentum*, I am not sure of its advantage to the historian. In order to recast the Christian schism as a partition of a hybrid cultural platform, Boyarin intimates that neither the rabbis nor the Church Fathers knew of Judaism and Christianity as distinct theological systems prior to the fourth century.[137]

[135] See, inter alia, Avi-Yonah (1976: 137–45); Alon (1980–1984: 288–307); Flusser (1988); P.S. Alexander (1992: 22–25); Krauss and Horbury (1995: 7–10); Basser (2000: 61–71); S.T. Katz (2006: 287–93); Teppler (2007: 135–64).
[136] Boyarin (2004); see also Boyarin (1999: 1–21).
[137] Boyarin (2004: 1–13) and passim.

Those categories, he argues, were meaningful only insofar as proto-orthodox Christian theologians used them to establish boundaries of thought and practice within the Christian collective. I find that thesis wanting for credibility with respect to the rabbinic record. To be clear, Boyarin is correct to note the internecine quality of the initial polemic against *minut*. Yet while he appropriately dispels the worn-out notion that the rabbis realized their exclusionary agenda by means of the *birkat ha-minim*, I find his insistence that they conceived no such agenda difficult to accept. The only Christianity of which the rabbis knew was the type practiced by Jews. They therefore had no reason to construe it as anything but an indigenous Jewish phenomenon.

The fact that the originators of the concept of *minut* presumed to characterize Christians as Jewish heretics was not due to their innocence of the difference between the concepts of Christian and Jew.[138] For all of their talents, the ancient rabbis were not visionaries. They could not have foreseen the need to objectify Judaism and Christianity as discrete theological categories. But neither were they as naïve as Boyarin intimates. That they presumed to steer their disciples away from Christian Jews indicates their sense that those individuals were somehow different from most other Jews of their day. As I shall argue in Chapter 4, the *Tannaim* had reason to be cautious of Christianity even if they did not yet possess the language to articulate their concerns as such.

But one must not mistake their lack of terminological precision for philosophical indecision. The historian must seek to determine what the rabbis meant to communicate to their readers by construing what we know as Christianity as a symptom of *minut*. To that end, I believe that the pivotal question to be posed to the rabbis is not why they failed to call Christians Christians but how the persons in question functioned in the world onto which they sought to map the *halakhah*.

As noted, past efforts to account for their stance on Christianity *qua minut* typically have plotted the rabbis' response in reference to the parting of the ways narrative. The advantage of that model as a key to the rabbinic record is its intimation that the difference between Christian and Jew was more-or-less resolved by the middle of the second century. The earliest rabbinic commentaries on Christianity, preserved in the Mishnah and the Tosefta, date to the early third century. Consequently, the parting of the ways narrative permits the reader of those works to think about Christianity's relationship with Judaism in the past tense. Their depictions of Christian *minim* are thereby read as historical memories of Jews who rejected the rabbinic *halakhah* and, by extension, their own Jewish identities, rather than as witnesses to an ongoing process of cultural disambiguation still taking place.

To my mind, the most effective study of that nature is Lawrence Schiffman's aforementioned *Who Was a Jew?* Forgoing the assumption that the rabbis dictated the norms of Jewish society during the early days of their movement,

---

[138] Boyarin (2004: 220–26); cf. Boyarin (1999: 22–41).

Schiffman seeks to describe the Christian's function within the discursive world of the *halakhah*. Outlining what the *Tannaim* deemed acceptable and unacceptable behaviors for Jews, Schiffman argues that the typical Christian would have faced great difficulty adhering to the rabbinic way. Whether Jewish or gentile, the Christian's endorsement of a theology placing the two on equal covenantal footing would have offended the sensibilities of a guarded rabbinic collective apt to see God's relationship with Israel in terms exclusive to the Jewish nation.[139] That, in his estimation, is why the rabbis chose to cast even Torah-observant Jewish Christians as heretical *minim*. They feared the Jewish Christian's potential to lapse in his Judaism on the pretext of cooperating with the gentile Christian per the terms of Paul's gospel. That fear is what compelled the very first rabbis to institute the *birkat ha-minim*. That fear, moreover, was to be vindicated during the Bar Kokhba rebellion when the last of the Jewish Christians defected to the gentile camp.[140]

That Schiffman's cautious assessment of the rabbinic record improves upon Graetz's tendentious reading of the same goes without saying. But in assuming the validity of the parting of the ways narrative, Schiffman incurs several of its fallacies, namely its episodic trajectory, its a priori distinction between the epistemes of Christian and Jew, and, most problematically, its forced characterization of the *minim* as Jewish Christians of the vintage variety. Like Graetz, moreover, Schiffman assumes that those Christians who lived as Jews were acquainted with Paul's gospel and its subscribers. He thereby infers that the rabbis had just cause to suspect the Christian *minim* of sympathizing with gentiles.[141] That inference is impossible to verify on the basis of a Tannaitic record evincing knowledge neither of Paul nor of gentile Christians.

Schiffman furthermore assumes that the *minim* categorically denied the authority of the Torah in the manner of a Jewish apostate.[142] To the contrary, the rabbis consistently depict *minim* as avid readers of the Torah prone to observe its laws, albeit not according to the *halakhah*.[143] Consequently, while Schiffman does not follow Graetz in denying the *minim* their Jewish identities, neither does he allow them much space in which to function as Jews. Rather, he forces them to meet the rabbis not as dialogical equals but as would-be agents of apostasy. His resulting effort to describe the Christian schism as a Jewish event is therefore no less tendentious than Graetz's and, to my mind, no more historically feasible.

More recent studies assessing the Christian *minim* from similar perspectives have yielded equally problematic results. In his 2005 book *Le judaïsme et l'avènement du christianisme*, Dan Jaffé reviewed many of the same textual evidences surveyed by Schiffman in a game attempt to set the rhetoric of

---

[139] Schiffman (1985: 4–7).
[140] Schiffman (1985: 51–61, 75–78).
[141] Schiffman (1985: 53).
[142] Schiffman (1985: 41–49).
[143] For this observation, see Hayes (2007: 258–59).

the *Tannaim* in a social world populated by Jews of many varieties including, but not limited to, Christians.[144] In Jaffé's estimation, the Christians whom the rabbis cast as *minim* were Palestinian Jews of the heterodox variety elsewhere accounted as the *am ha-aretz*, the "people of the land."[145] These were Jews who observed the laws of Torah and attended the same synagogues as the rabbis but who did not align themselves with the rabbis or their *halakhah*. The rabbinic construction of *minut*, Jaffé therefore argues, was meant to denounce those Jews among the *am ha-aretz* whom the sages believed stood to thwart their orthodox vision by rejecting their particular methods of scriptural exegesis. The Jewish Christians fit that bill, thereby justifying their censure by the rabbis by way of the *birkat ha-minim*. That, in turn, prompted their estrangement from Judaism.

I find Jaffé's study problematic in several respects. Indiscriminately drawing upon texts of varied temporal and geographical provenance, he fails to account for the wide cultural gaps separating rabbinic literary compositions of Roman Palestine, Byzantine Palestine, and Sasanian Babylonia. Consequently, he does not account for the dynamic quality of the rabbinic polemic against Christianity over the centuries-long course of its development. His refusal, moreover, to question the documentary qualities of his sources complicates his thesis to no end.[146] Furthermore, while Jaffé is correct to locate the Christian *minim* within the boundaries of Palestinian Jewish society during the age of the *Tannaim*, his conflation of those alleged heretics with the reviled *am ha-aretz* of subsequent rabbinic record unfairly slants his assessment of their abilities to function as Jews.[147] Finally, although Jaffé alludes to recent research questioning whether the categories of orthodoxy and heterodoxy are rightly applied in his frame of reference, he rejects that critique as irrelevant to his defiantly rabbinocentric agenda.[148] That he ends up retreating to the parting of the ways narrative in spite of its acknowledged flaws is not surprising.[149]

A more formidable attempt to contextualize the early rabbinic response to Christianity is Adiel Schremer's 2010 study *Brothers Estranged*.[150] Contrary to Schiffman and Jaffé, Schremer opts to set the rabbinic construction of *minut* in a diachronic evolutionary scheme. The rabbinic rhetoric of heresy, he argues, originated as a common Jewish rhetoric of exclusion implying its subject's rejection of Judaism's traditional covenantal theology. Developed during the late Second Temple period, he contends, the *Tannaim* took up this existing

---

[144] Jaffé (2005).

[145] Jaffé (2005: 38–41).

[146] Jaffé (2005: 70–75).

[147] Jaffé (2005: 337–77). Sustained primarily in the Babylonian Talmud, the image of the unlearned masses of Palestinian Jewish society as the truculent *am ha-aretz* has been thoroughly dispelled by Rubenstein (2003: 123–42); see also Hayes (2007: 260–62).

[148] Jaffé (2005: 58–70). For the term "rabbinocentrism" and its critical implications, see S. Schwartz (2001: 5–6).

[149] Cf. Jaffé (2005: 409–18).

[150] Schremer (2010).

polemical discourse in response to the crisis of faith that fell upon Palestinian Jewry following the disastrous revolts against Rome. Facing the popular perception that God had abandoned his people, the founders of the rabbinic movement aimed to head off further deterioration of their nation by marking as heretics those of their fellow Jews who expressed support for the Romans.[151] That those caught in their polemical dragnet included Christians was due to the adherence of the latter to a gospel casting the fall of Jerusalem as a sign of God's rejection of the Jewish people. To the rabbis, Schremer argues, that belief amounted to a denial of Judaism itself.[152]

Yet although the rabbis devised the language of *minut* in reference to persons within the Jewish community, Christianity's subsequent evolution compelled them to expand their heresiological repertoire. By the age of Constantine, the figurative *min* no longer stood primarily for a Jewish Christian harboring Roman sympathies but, rather, for a gentile Christian of Roman cultural orientation. What their forebears devised as an anti-Roman polemic thus gradually transformed into a typically anti-Christian polemic.[153] Unlike the original Jewish *min*, the new gentile *min* was of no accountability to the *halakhah*. Nevertheless, the gentile *min* was to continue to command the attention of rabbinic sages now forced to combat dissent both from within the Jewish community and from without.[154] Thus, Schremer concludes, did the later rabbinic sages, the *Amoraim*, gradually come to apply the exclusionary rhetoric of *minut* to persons of all ethnic, religious, and political persuasions who stood to challenge their collective enterprise.

Schremer's study offers a provocative new perspective on the early Jewish response to Christianity. Deferring to Boyarin's observation that one cannot speak of a decisive break between Judaism and Christianity until the fourth century, Schremer nevertheless proposes to describe a preliminary parting of ways between Christian Jews and non-Christian Jews as early as the first century. Their object of contention, he posits, was not Jesus but God. Although still living as Jews, the first Christian *minim* rejected a Jewish intellectual tradition conditioned by the belief that God protects with his chosen people through thick and thin. By denying Judaism's traditional covenant theology, those Jews aligned with a Roman regime thought to scoff at the notion of God's covenant with Israel.[155] That the rabbis presumed to exclude them from that collective was not on account of their Christianity. It was due to their belief offensive to all right-thinking Jews that God had abandoned his people.[156]

Schremer's departure from the parting of the ways narrative allows him to pursue an innovative and nuanced argument regarding the history of the

[151] Schremer (2010: 25–42).
[152] Schremer (2010: 49–57).
[153] Schremer (2010: 121–38).
[154] Schremer (2010: 138–41).
[155] Schremer (2010: 65–68).
[156] Schremer (2010: 87–99).

minim. He is also to be commended for reminding us that the early rabbis were far more guarded about their theology than Boyarin's intimation of their "Judaeo-Christian" hybridity demands of them. Nevertheless, I am highly skeptical of Schremer's thesis. His suggestion that the exclusionary rhetoric of the *Tannaim* originated prior to the rabbinic movement relies on tendentious readings and conjectural reconstructions of texts of questionable relevance to their milieu. The weakness of his argument with respect to these evidences undermines Schremer's case for reading the rabbinic construction of *minut* as a reflection of the attitudes of the general Jewish population. Nor am I persuaded by Schremer's intimation of its pervasive anti-Roman sentiment. While the sages never forgot the past offenses of their imperial subjugators, the working relationship between Romans and Jews was quite healthy by the early third century. One wonders why rabbinic scribes of that era would have sustained a polemic out of step with their times.

But perhaps most puzzling about Schremer's thesis is his insinuation the authors of the category of *minut* foresaw the Church's alignment with Rome. The Roman government was not favorably disposed toward Christians during the age of the *Tannaim*. While some Christians undoubtedly exulted in what they saw as God's punishment of the Jews, that theological conceit by no means amounted to a pledge of allegiance to the Roman state. The rabbinic sages who first supposed to cast Christians as heretics could not possibly have seen a day when those Christians would willingly collaborate with the Roman authorities. Nor, for that matter, could they have foreseen a day when those authorities would be Christians. The distinct anti-Roman animus that Schremer detects amidst the variegated rabbinic polemic against the *minim* makes sense only in view of developments yet to take place at the time of its commencement.

I appreciate Schremer's desire to redirect the bitterness of the *Tannaim* from Christians to Romans. It helps him to imagine that Christians and Jews of their era managed to remain "brothers" even as a third party, hostile to both, worked to mitigate their filial bond. But Schremer makes a tremendous logical leap in order to discern echoes of political protest in a rabbinic discourse on heresy concerned primarily with matters of practical *halakhah*. At best, his reading of the invention of *minut* as a response to Roman imperialism is merely anachronistic. At worst, it is an elaborate rehashing of Graetz's xenophobic account of the *minim*, and, by extension, all early Christians as traitors to the Jewish nation. Consequently, while I find Schremer's treatment stimulating, I do not see his as an advantageous interpretive framework in which to set my own analytical objective.

A WAY FORWARD

The nature of the evidence at our disposal makes it difficult for the modern reader to avoid judging the early Jewish response to Christianity from the vantage point of the rabbis. Nevertheless, efforts to tie the rabbinic perspective to that of all their fellow Jews have yielded unsatisfactory results. There is a certain danger in attempting to widen the scope of the rabbinic polemic against *minut* beyond its natural discursive capacity. Viewing its subjects through the rabbinic lens makes it difficult to see the *minim* as legitimate Jewish actors. It forces the reader's perspective into compliance with the rabbis, invariably casting their Christian opponents as defective Jews. While I do not mean to dismiss the opinions of the rabbis, to consent to their prejudices is to surrender one's objectivity as an observer of the common Jewish experience. I therefore reassert the need of the critical historian to set all of the Jewish actors involved in the Christian schism on a common dialogical plane.

In the chapters to follow, I shall attempt to supply a revised historical framework in which to analyze the Christian schism in its Jewish context. Rather than proceeding on the basis of the rabbinic record, I shall begin by describing the idea of Judaism at regnant in their society as a variable object of cultural identification. That variable episteme, I shall argue, informed the range of typically Jewish ideologies and behaviors that defined Christianity's evolution in the environs of Roman Palestine later to witness the scene of the encounter between Christian and Jew attested in the rabbinic polemic against *minut*. I thereby aim to demonstrate that the rabbinic sages, though not speaking for all of their fellow Jews, spoke to a common process of negotiation whereby other Jews of their age came to distinguish between Christian and Jew.

The results of my investigation will not amount to a cohesive "Jewish" narrative of the Christian schism. I am not sure that such a narrative can exist. Nevertheless, I believe it feasible to describe the Christian schism as a concrete historical event rather than merely as a synthetic memory discernible only in hindsight. The singular aspect of that event that I aim to document was perhaps of minor significance relative to other points of disjuncture between Christian and Jew. But as I hope to show, the impression that it left upon the memories of the Jewish people would prove exceedingly meaningful in the centuries to follow.

2

Jewish Identity in Classical Antiquity: Critical Issues and Approaches to Definition

In order to comprehend how Christianity took root in ancient Jewish society, we must begin by considering what it meant to be Jewish in the context of classical Judea and Palestine. But defining Jewish identity in antiquity is no simple task. The key questions of who was a Jew and on what grounds have proven difficult to disentangle from corresponding conversations on what constitutes Jewish identity in the contemporary frame of reference. The sensitivities, moreover, of scholars wishing to avoid casting ancient Jews as mere Christian antitypes have yielded a dizzying variety of approaches whereby to describe their collective sense of self. These efforts are too many and too complex to survey here.[1] Nevertheless, an overview of the key arguments and evidences at issue will help me articulate my own analytical assumptions as to what made a Jew a Jew at the time of Judaism's initial encounter with Christianity. Those assumptions, in turn, will furnish the standards by which I shall proceed in Chapter 3 to assess the Christian's ability to function as a Jew at the site of that encounter.

JEWS, JUDAISM, AND JEWISH IDENTITY: METHODOLOGICAL SOUNDINGS

Until fairly recently, sincere efforts to define ancient Judaism typically were predicated on the particular type of Jewish cultural expression inscribed in the works of the rabbinic sages.[2] The idea that the Judaism of the rabbis represented the normative Judaism of its day was both convincing and convenient

---

[1] For recent studies of this order, see Frey et al. (2007); Levine and Schwartz (2009); Eckhardt (2012).

[2] By "sincere" I mean to exclude those disingenuous portraits of ancient Judaism drawn by modern Christian theologians as negative counterpoints to formative Christianity as well as to those drawn by modern Jewish theologians as idealistic designs for contemporary Jewish practice and belief. For critical comments on the fallacies of both these approaches, see S.J.D. Cohen (1986).

to scholars mindful of the influence that the rabbis would later exert upon Jewish life and thought in the Middle Ages and continuously to this day. That their Judaism stood in direct continuity with that of their immediate forebears, the Pharisees, and of their predecessors, the prophets of Israel, was taken for granted. Judaism was thus assessed as a constant and immutable trait of the Jewish people, the religion that defined their national ethic and, for better or for worse, set them apart from other nations.[3] Consequently, to be a Jew in antiquity meant to practice the Judaism of the rabbis. It meant following the laws of the Torah as encoded in the *halakhah*. It meant professing the covenant theology of a nation obliged to serve the God of Israel. It meant living a life of conscience and community, of continually striving to maintain purity of mind and body in a world full of profane influences.

Yet the modern correlation of Jew and Judaism does not translate easily into the ancient frame of reference. As noted in Chapter 1, the premise of defining ancient Judaism as the religion of the Pharisees and rabbis is no longer viable. Those groups, we must now assume, were atypical in their exacting standards of practice and thought. Consequently, we must not assume that the classical *halakhah* was received in its day as a universal design for Jewish life. That observation naturally raises the question as to how the typical Jew of Roman Judea/ Palestine would have understood the idea of Jewish identity to function in reference to those operating within and without his or her social sphere. But before attempting to identify that common cultural benchmark, I shall briefly discuss two theoretical treatments that stand to problematize the premise of my inquiry.

I shall begin with perhaps the most influential contemporary scholar to tackle the question of Jewish normativity in antiquity. In a series of studies published during the 1970s and 1980s, Jacob Neusner challenged the prospect of reading the works of the rabbinic sages as a coherent record of their Judaism. Calling attention to the manifold inconsistencies and contradictions exhibited in the classical rabbinic literary corpus, Neusner demonstrated a previously unappreciated diversity of thought among its authors. Acknowledging that the individual components of the rabbinic library were compiled over the course of several centuries and in diverse socio-cultural settings, he subjected each one to rigorous literary analysis with the intent to demonstrate its singular theological agenda.

The aggregate results of Neusner's form-critical project yielded a theory accounting for both the continuities and the discontinuities in religious thought manifest in rabbinic Judaism's intellectual canon.[4] Although the sages whose

[3] S. Schwartz (2001: 5–7), reasonably traces this still prevalent scholarly model to the efforts of early Zionist scholars of classical Jewish history to support the positivistic historical claims of a contemporary nationalist movement raised on the strictly orthodox and fairly parochial historicism of the classical rabbinic tradition. On the origins of this historiographical trend, see Myers (1995: 89–93) and passim.

[4] For an autobiographical account of what Neusner calls his "documentary approach" to rabbinic research, see Neusner (1995a: 1–20), with relevant bibliography (ibid., xvi–xxv).

interpretive traditions are preserved in the rabbinic library consistently appealed to the authority of the Torah, Neusner observed that those rabbis pursued a variety of hermeneutical agendas as unique as their circumstances demanded. Rather, therefore, than reading theirs as a monolithic ancient Judaism, he concluded that one should more accurately recognize multiple ancient Judaisms, that is, a family of Judaic religions bound by a shared history but entailing diverse principles of belief and religious outlooks.[5] Extending his argument to the Second Temple period, Neusner further argued that the diversity of the rabbinic record was born of corresponding diversity in Jewish thought preceding the formation of the rabbinic movement. The multiple Judaisms of that age, he thus posited, includes those of the Pharisees and their sectarian peers including, notably, the first Christians.[6]

This is not the occasion to critique Neusner's rigid structuralist approach to defining Judaism.[7] Suffice it to say that his limitless inventory of unique Judaisms has little bearing on the lived Jewish experience. According to Neusner, Jewish identity qua Judaism is a self-affirming theological construction entailing a variable measure of identification with the ancient nation of Israel.[8] His premise of validating every given expression of that principle on record as a unique Judaism entails that no one Jew's sense of self should be judged more or less Jewish than another's regardless of the ideological differences between them. If, in other words, the basic defining element of a Judaism is its theology of Torah, to compare the interpretive strategy of one Jew's Judaism with another's would be to violate the prerogatives of both.[9]

In so reducing the idea of Jewish identity to an egalitarian theological principle, Neusner removed the idea of Judaism from the avenue of historical research.[10] For if one is to forfeit the right to compare one mode of Jewish cultural identification to another, one cannot presume to document the dynamic evolution of any given expression of Judaism across a given range of time or space. So, for instance, one cannot fairly assess the relationship of the Judaism of the Pharisees with the Judaism of the Babylonian Talmud without inferring negative value judgments about the theological integrity of one or the other. Likewise, one cannot assess the Judaism of the Jewish Christians in reference to the implicitly more normal Judaism(s) of other, non-Christian Jews. Indeed, following Neusner's logic, one might argue that Christianity has never ceased to be a Judaism inasmuch as its adherents continue to identify as children of Israel with respect to their own diverse interpretations of that concept.[11]

---

[5] See, e.g., Neusner (1988: 9–15).

[6] Neusner (1988: 89–92).

[7] For a recent critique obliging to my critical aims, see S. Schwartz (2011: 210–16).

[8] So, e.g., Neusner (1989), especially ibid. (8–18).

[9] So noted by Neusner (1978).

[10] For the following, cf. Satlow (2006: 843–45).

[11] For this forensically dubious argument, see Boccaccini (1991: 15–18), and more cautiously, Peterson (2005: 65–71). Neusner, for his part, rejects this notion, asserting that Christianity evolved into a closed religious system after 70 CE accruing its own terms of cultural reference at odds with that of its Judaic past; see Neusner (1988: 97–100).

I do not mean, of course, to suggest that Neusner's ideas about ancient Judaism are wrong. I find much to commend in his effort to avoid imposing anachronistic standards of rabbinic orthodoxy upon an ancient Jewish population unapprised of that notion.[12] But in choosing to privilege the ideological variance within classical Jewish thought as its defining characteristic, he inevitably obscures the shared social and cultural experiences that made the Jewish people a people. In other words, in suggesting that everything Jewish was a Judaism, Neusner implies that there was no Judaism, that is, no standard or practice or belief by which one Jew could recognize another Jew of a different ideological persuasion as a member of his or her own group.[13] In declining to acknowledge that the Jew's identification with the nation of Israel is more than simply a theological metaphor, Neusner marginalizes the aspect of ethnicity or national identity that made and continues to make Judaism more than just a religion.[14]

The criterion of ethnicity is the focus of Steve Mason's more recent study analyzing the range of meanings signified by the terms Jew and Judaism in antiquity.[15] Surveying a range of literary and epigraphic evidences, Mason demonstrates that the term Jew was used in antiquity primarily to indicate one's national origins with respect to the geopolitical territory of Judea. That "Judean" ethnic distinction, he argues, took on a different range of meanings among the early Christians. In their hands, both the Greek term for Judean (*ioudaios*) and its verbal abstractions Judaizing (*ioudaizein*) and Judaism (*ioudaismos*) were refashioned as theological distinctions referring not to Judeans per se but to Christians alleged to be excessively given to the ways of those ancient enemies of Jesus.[16] The theological construction of the Judean as a Christian antitype ultimately came to inform the self-perceptions of actual Judeans when they fell under the authority of Christian Rome in the fourth century. Judaism became a religion, albeit, of course, a false religion, according to the new Christian convention. Only then, Mason concludes, were the Judean people compelled by force of law to reconceive what they traditionally knew as their ethnic identities in theological terms. Only then,

---

[12] In this respect, Neusner's theory supports the emerging consensus on the fourth-century time frame of the decisive break between Jew and Christian accounted in Chapter 1. See, e.g., Neusner (1987), especially ibid. (13–28).

[13] This consequence of Neusner's Jewish anthropology is emphasized by J.Z. Smith (1982), who argues against the fairness of associating one ancient Jew's Judaism with another's more accurately than one might associate it with a "pagan" or a "Christian" cultural system exhibiting similar symbolic and/or ritualistic traits. Compare, however, S. Schwartz (2011: 216–21), on the historiographical liabilities of Smith's phenomenological approach.

[14] See, e.g., Neusner's somewhat forced argument in Neusner (1995b), responding to Dunn's rightful attention to the ethnic dimension of the Christian schism (cf. Dunn 2006: 29–32, 185–214, 324–29).

[15] Mason (2007).

[16] Ibid. 460–80.

therefore, did the terms Jew and Judaism begin to take on their present religious aspects.[17]

Although points of Mason's philological commentary are open to debate, I shall comment here only on his central argument.[18] To my mind, Mason's insistence on the primary ethnic significations of the terms Jew and Judaism is on the mark. Before the Christianization of Rome, the term religion (Latin: *religio*) referred only to those Roman cults deemed instrumental to the welfare of the state. Previously, the national cult of the Jews had been deemed a superstition (Latin: *superstitio*) in the eyes of the Roman law, albeit one lawful for members of the Jewish ethnic polity to practice.[19] Only when the official religion of Rome ceded to Christianity were her Jewish subjects forced to recognize as "religious" the ethnic culture that their imperial masters now presumed to characterize as such.[20] The efforts of Christian legislators of the fourth century to define the orthodoxy of the new imperial religion in contradistinction to the alleged heresy of the Jews thus served to define Judaism as a system of belief exceeding the functions of a national cult.

Mason's analysis supports Boyarin's argument with respect to the difficulty of distinguishing Judaism and Christianity as discrete categories of religious expression prior to the fourth century. In view of Mason's work, Boyarin has augmented his conception of "Judaeo-Christianity" to entail that no effect of rabbinic thought or practice ought to be characterized as Jewish until after the "Judeans" became Jews under the influence of Roman law.[21] If the concept of Judaism was, as Mason contends, a by-product of Christian orthodoxy, that the rabbinic sages lacked the "religious" awareness to distinguish between Jew and Christian would logically follow. The *Tannaim*, Boyarin therefore asserts, knew the Jew as a categorically ethnic entity. That they thought to distinguish other Jews as *minim* suggests that, despite their misgivings, they had no choice but to recognize those alleged heretics as members of their ethnic group.

---

[17] Mason (2007: 488).
[18] For the following, compare the more thoroughgoing critiques of D.R. Schwartz (2007) and S. Schwartz (2011: 223–27). See also J. Schwartz (2012: 64–67), who questions the functionality of Mason's theory vis-à-vis interethnic relations between Jews and gentiles in the early Church.
[19] This shift in Judaism's legal definition was already observed by S. Schwartz (2001: 194). See also Martin (2004: 135–39), on the Christian assumption of the Roman language of "religion" and its deprecating effect upon the legal construction of the Jewish cult.
[20] See Nongbri (2013: 26–32, 35–37), on the semantic transformations of the Latin term *religio* and its Greek equivalent *thrēskeia* in early Christian culture. As Nongbri (ibid., 26), correctly points out, the Hebrew and Aramaic languages sustained by many Jews in the ancient Near East have no known words corresponding with those Indo-European terminologies. Compare, however, D.R. Schwartz (2014: 93–99), who submits that Josephus routinely used the term *thrēskeia* to indicate a dimension of Jewish thought and practice reasonably defined as "religious" by contemporary epistemological standards.
[21] Boyarin (2009: 8–12).

Consequently, he concludes, the Christian *minim* were not quite the Jewish outsiders whom the sages wished their disciples to believe they were.[22]

Despite Boyarin's endorsement, I find Mason's distinction between "Judean" ethnicity and religion fundamentally flawed.[23] As his critics have noted, at no point in our storied history have the Jewish people presumed to objectify our practices and beliefs as anything but functions of our shared national history. Conversely, the theological and ritual traditions typically construed as functions of the Jewish religion have been with the Jewish people from the very beginning of our corporate existence. Mason's insistence that the "Jew" was and is nothing more than a contrived Christian antitype neglects the copious evidence indicating that his "Judeans" sustained ideologies and behaviors conforming to the religious phenomenon today known as Judaism long before they knew to call their culture by that name. That ancient Jews, therefore, did not uniformly use the terms "Jew" and "Judaism" is not a useful indicator of how those individuals functioned as a group. It merely indicates that they did not speak English. While ancient Jews, moreover, might not have defined their collective enterprise as a religion until Roman law compelled them to do so, neither did they define it strictly in as an ethnicity.[24] That categorical indecision has always been a property of Judaism and remains so to this day.[25]

What I take from Neusner is his observation that the literary and material remains of ancient Jews exhibit a notable diversity in thought and practice. That observation upends the once commonplace notion that Judaism in antiquity was defined exclusively by the designs of the Pharisees and rabbis. What I take from Mason is the need to tread carefully when attempting to describe classical Jewish culture in religious terms. While that category, I would contend, is not intrinsically problematic, its intimation of doctrinal normativity stands to obscure the primary ethnic connotations of the terms Jew and Judaism. Acknowledging, however, that the category of ethnicity is equally problematic, I shall take care not to rely too heavily on either categorization in my comments to follow. Rather, I shall attempt to account for the ancient idea of Jewish identity on the basis of the common experiences of the Jews as best as I can describe them utilizing the technically inadequate language at my disposal.

---

[22] Boyarin (2009: 33–36).

[23] My conclusions here follow S. Schwartz (2011: 236–38), and D.R. Schwartz (2007: 5–7) (cf. D.R. Schwartz (2014: 3–7).

[24] My own understanding of ethnicity and its attendant terminology in the premodern frame of reference is informed by the balanced methodological discussion of S. Jones (1997: 56–83). See also S. Jones (1998) for an instructive exercise in ethnographic definition pertaining to ancient Jewish culture.

[25] As noted by Satlow (2006: 839–42). For a more thoroughgoing discussion of this persistently agitating ambiguity in Jewish cultural politics, see Gitelman (2009: 303–19).

THE GENEALOGY OF JEWISH IDENTITY: A HISTORICAL SKETCH

If not a religious or an ethnic ideology, what was Judaism in antiquity? In view of the foregoing considerations, I propose to define ancient Judaism as a dynamic objective connoting different characteristics in different contexts. Nevertheless, I maintain that the idea of Jewish identity guiding that objective was predicated on certain fixed assumptions as to its subject's cultic, ethical, and intellectual orientation. In other words, while ancient Jews were not subject to a monolithic standard of cultural identification, they generally perceived their collective as one bound by a set of practices and beliefs unique to their nation, if not always to the exclusion of practices and beliefs learned from other nations.[26] I shall proceed by explaining how the idea of Jewish identity came to acquire its characteristic versatility of meaning, highlighting developments in the common life of the Jews that conditioned their collective sense of self.

Let us begin at the beginning. The term Jew can be traced to the classical Hebrew term *yehudi* (plural *yehudim*), a demonym first attested in the biblical book of Jeremiah in reference to the Kingdom of Judah (Hebrew: *yehudah*).[27] The Kingdom of Judah existed from its obscure date of foundation sometime before the seventh century BCE until its conquest by the Neo-Babylonian Empire of King Nebuchadnezzar II in 597 BCE. The prophecies of Jeremiah were composed and edited in several stages before, during, and after the Babylonian conquest. It is therefore difficult to say whether the book's language reflects the conventions of the former kingdom or of its immediate political successor, the Babylonian province of Yehud.[28] In any case, the ethnic designation *yehudi* appears to have remained with the survivors of Judah driven from the province during what would be known as the Babylonian Exile, thereby functioning outside of Yehud as a Diasporan ethnic identification.[29]

---

[26] I do, however, demur from Schwartz's characterization of ancient Judaism, (S. Schwartz 2001: 105), as "a nonexclusive religious option in a religious system that was basically pagan." The association of Jewish popular culture with paganism implies an ethical breach that was hardly the intent of those Jews who willingly partook of Persian, Greek, and Roman customs. While infer no such assignment of intent in Schwartz's use of the language of paganism, I am wary of its potential to offend the sensibilities of contemporary readers conditioned to misconstrue the pagan as a negative Christian antitype. For comparable considerations, see Al. Cameron (2011: 14–32).

[27] See Jer 32.1 et al., and cf. 2 Chr 32.18. For the following etymological observations, cf. Blenkinsopp (2009: 19–28). Also useful is the lexical register of Harvey (1996: 11–20), who highlights the consistency of the term *yehudi* in the later books of the Hebrew Bible with earlier references members of the tribe of Judah (e.g., 2 Kgs 16.16, 25.25).

[28] In other words, I acknowledge that those Judahites who remained in Yehud during the expulsion of their kingdom's former ruling class were genuine *yehudim* rather than merely the poor, supposedly unworthy "remnant of Judah" (Hebrew: *she'arith yehudah*) mentioned in Jer 40.7–41.18 and 2 Kgs 25.22–26. On these individuals, see Lipschits (2005: 102–07).

[29] In addition to the ample scriptural evidence to this effect, see Pearce and Wunsch (2014: 7–8) on recently discovered epigraphic witnesses to the establishment by the Judahite exiles of a unique territorial estate in Babylon known in Aramaic as *āl-yāḫūdu*.

Following the defeat of the Babylonians by the Achaemenid Empire of Persia in 519 BCE, the restoration of Yehud to the exiled *yehudim* served to return their self-appointed ethnic marker to the site of its origin. Moving forward, the name *yehudi* would be applied both to those former exiles who resettled the land of their ancestors as well as to those who remained in Babylonia and in other Diaspora locales.[30] Upon the establishment of the Second Temple of Jerusalem, the name took on further significance with reference to the revived cult of Yahweh. So did the name *yehudi* come to refer to all who patronized the Jerusalem Temple, whether in Yehud or from abroad.[31] In time, corresponding nomenclatures in Aramaic (*yehudai*), Greek (*ioudaios*), and Latin (*iudaeus*) would arise as *yehudim* encountered peoples of other nationalities in their Near Eastern and Mediterranean environs. Like the Hebrew *yehudi*, each of these terms connoted both its subject's ethnic and cultic orientation. Each, in other words, connoted a mode of identification commensurate with that today known by the term Jew.

The Jews of Yehud enjoyed relative calm under Persian rule, developing a thriving Temple economy in Jerusalem and healthy relations with an imperial hierarchy supportive of its subjects' cultic rights. That order endured little change when Alexander of Macedon passed through the Near East in 333 BCE during his victorious campaign against the Persians. Yet although the resulting transformation of Persian Yehud into the Hellenistic province of Judea had no immediate effect on the Jews or their cult, the subtle cultural changes that followed in its wake would prove significant.[32] The onset of Greek rule brought with it a new political philosophy. To identify as a member of the Hellenic nation did not necessarily mean that one was born of Greek parentage. To be a Greek, rather, was a

---

[30] Instances of this usage include Zech 8.23; Ezra 4.12 et al.; Neh 1.2 et al.; Esth 2.5 et al.; Dan 3.8, 12. Bar-Asher (2002) points to the book of Esther's characterization of Mordecai as a *yehudi* as an unmistakable sign of the early migration of the ethnic demonym to the Jewish Diaspora, as Mordecai is said both to live and to have been born outside of Yehud. The same might be said of the self-described "Judahite" garrison (Aramaic: *ḥayla yehudaya*) stationed at the southern Egyptian border town of Elephantine during the late fifth century BCE, on which see Cowley (1923: 60–76) (nos. 21–22).

[31] On the general coherence of Yahwistic ritual culture between Yehud and the Persian-era Jewish Diaspora, see Knowles (2006, 121–28). A helpful register of data on this rather poorly documented era of Jewish history appears in Grabbe (1999).

[32] Josephus reports that Alexander's seizure of the Near East occasioned the construction and consecration of the Samaritan Temple on Mount Gerizim near Shechem, or modern-day Nablus; see Josephus, *Ant.* 11.321–25, 340–47. By his account, this development bore significantly on the idea of Jewish identity inasmuch as it realized the Samaritans' rejection of the cult of Yahweh in Jerusalem and, in effect, their difference from Jews. That Josephus does not hide his distrust of the Samaritans renders his account of this event problematic. Furthermore, recent archeological finds at Mount Gerizim indicate that its Temple dates to the turn of the fifth century BCE, if not earlier. It is therefore doubtful that the Macedonian conquest significantly impacted a schism between Jew and Samaritan already centuries in the making. For critical commentary on Josephus' account, see Kartveit (2009: 90–96), and ibid. (209–16), on the epigraphic evidence for prior Samaritan cultic activity at Mount Gerizim.

matter of choice, a distinction attained by acceding to the political constitutions of ancient Athens. Following Alexander's example, politicians, scholars, and aesthetes from Egypt to India thus sought to align themselves with the new ruling class by adopting classical Greek culture as their own.[33]

Over time, the Hellenization of the Near East transformed the environments where the Jews had planted their roots. The idea of Jewish identity took on new shades of meaning as the children of Israel began to reimagine their ancestral traditions in terms consonant with the dominant cultures of their surroundings.[34] Jews in Judea and in the Diaspora read their sacred scriptures not merely as archival records of their people's past but as philosophical treatises and political manifestos, testaments to a rich national heritage comparable in age and in excellence to that of the Greeks themselves. To identify as a Jew meant more than to worship Yahweh. It meant to represent one's self as an heir to Moses, the inspired lawgiver who authored the Torah, to David and Solomon, the great kings who oversaw their nation's rise from tribal chieftaincy to imperial power, and to all of the luminaries of Israel's past. To be a Jew meant to exemplify the culture of a Hellenized Israel, to uphold her time-honored values, and to profess her ancient wisdom.[35]

Around the turn of the second century BCE, Judea changed hands from the Ptolemaic kingdom of Egypt to the Seleucid kingdom of Syria.[36] Though insignificant at first, the change in Greek administrations took a turn for the worse in 175 BCE upon the accession of the Seleucid king Antiochus IV. A puppet of Rome, the emerging superpower of the Mediterranean world, Antiochus quickly proved himself a poor study of his Jewish subjects. When residents of Jerusalem eager to improve their city's standing in the Seleucid administrative hierarchy sought the king's permission to educate their youngsters at a Greek gymnasium near the Temple Mount, Antiochus agreed. He did not consider the qualms of those Jews who stood to be offended by the establishment of a shrine to the body and mind opposite their sacred precinct.[37] When dubious claimants sought

---

[33] On the transferable conception of Greek ethnicity in the classical age, see Hall (2002), especially ibid. (172–228), on its facilitation of Greek cultural profusion in the wider Hellenistic world.

[34] On early Hellenistic-era Jewish texts reflecting this accommodating cultural trend, see Gruen (1998: 246–91; 2002: 213–31).

[35] On the influence of Greek culture upon popular modes of Jewish identification, see L.I. Levine (1998), in reference to Hellenization in Judea/Palestine, and Collins (2000), in reference to the Mediterranean Diaspora. See also Collins' more recent survey of scholarship in Collins (2005).

[36] The following account of the Maccabean revolt generally follows that of Bickerman (1979), with additional insight into the subtlety of the cultural exchange that took place during the initial Jewish overtures to the Seleucids from Collins (2001: 38–55). Although I defer to Collins (ibid., 47–52), in associating the rebellion of the Hasmoneans to the relatively late Seleucid interference with the Jewish cult, I acknowledge that the precise sequence of events precipitating this breach of administrative etiquette is notoriously difficult to reconstruct on the basis of the highly stylized accounts of the incident at our disposal (cf. Weitzman 2004).

[37] With respect to Bickerman (1979: 83–88), the arrival of the gymnasium did not perforce compel its supporters or its students to forsake their ancestral customs for Greek ways. It seems, rather,

the king's appointment to the office of the High Priest, Antiochus indulged their requests. He did not consider the sensibilities of those Jews who wished their chief representative before God chosen for his virtue rather than his political clout. When rival priestly appointees liquidated the Temple's treasury to pay the king for his favors, Antiochus happily accepted the bribes. He did not consider the needs of those Jews who had supplied the Temple treasury with charitable donations to be disbursed on behalf of the public good.

When in 167 BCE those rival priests came to blows over who would control the Temple and its finances, Antiochus' record of mismanagement reached a terrible crescendo. Marching back to Syria after a strategic fumble in Egypt, Antiochus invaded Jerusalem, wreaking havoc for several days as his troops pillaged the city. With the help of his most recent priestly pawn, the king liquidated the Temple's coffers before leaving Jerusalem in a huff. In his stead, Antiochus left a small military garrison at the Temple Mount to protect his local supporters. The presence of gentile soldiers in their holy city agitated a Jewish population now fearful that their self-appointed civic leaders had gone too far in the ways of the Greeks. As the Syrian soldiers built altars to their gods beside the Jewish Temple, many Jews fled Jerusalem for the unsullied Judean countryside. And as their civil disobedience coalesced into a movement of resistance, their Greek overseers took note. In short time, Antiochus dispatched more soldiers to Judea with an order of suppression of the Jewish cult. He commissioned his generals to enact a compulsory program of public sacrifice whereby the Jews were to offer unclean animals to Greek deities. He decreed noncompliance punishable by death.

The reforms of Antiochus posed an acute challenge to the Jews. To those trained on their ancestral traditions, the king seemed to wish to destroy the very notion of Jewish identity, replacing it with an order of cultural affiliation alien even to their Hellenized sensibilities.[38] It was from among those Jews that the champions of tradition emerged. The Hasmoneans were a priestly family whose patriarch, Mattathias, had left Jerusalem upon the initial arrival of the Greeks. Spurred by their father's zealous defense of the old ways, Judah the Maccabee and his brothers launched a rebellion against Antiochus' forces that would over the course of several years see the rebels seize control of the Temple Mount along with other strategic positions in and around Judea. Their rededication of the Temple in 164 BCE and reinstatement of its suspended sacrificial liturgies signaled not only a victory for the Hasmoneans but the rebirth of a Jewish political ideology dormant since the Babylonian conquest.[39]

that the foreignness of its intellectual and physical curricula alarmed the more conservative elements of Jewish society to the danger of apostasy. See Doran (2001: 94–111).

[38] For the following assessment of the Jewish resistance to Antiochus' decree as a matter of cultural survival, cf. Weitzman (2005: 34–54). Cf. S. Schwartz (2001: 33–36), for an alternative explanation emphasizing the political dimension of the rebellion even during its earliest stages.

[39] For a complementary assessment of Judah's nationalistic ambitions and support base during his initial campaign, see Sievers (1990: 41–67). See also Nongbri (2005), who stresses the political

The death of Antiochus around the time of the Temple's rededication proved a lucky break for the rebels. Following a few years of instability, the accession of a new royal dynasty in 161 BCE led to improved relation between Jerusalem and Antioch. Though the following year would see Judah killed in battle, the continuing decline of the Seleucid state prompted a dramatic policy reversal by the new king Demetrius I. Facing upheaval elsewhere in his realm, Demetrius withdrew his troops from Judea, leaving the province under the control of Judah's surviving brother Jonathan. When in 153 BCE Demetrius was challenged by the royal pretender Alexander Balas, Jonathan exploited the rivalry to secure his appointment to the vacant office of the High Priest. In time, and with the aid of further administrative changes in Antioch, Jonathan expelled the last remaining royalists from Jerusalem along with their military escorts.

Upon Jonathan's death in 143 BCE, the leadership of the now semi-autonomous Judea fell to his brother Simon. Already acknowledged as the leader of his people's national cult, Simon took advantage of the Seleucids' continuing absence from the region and declared himself king of Judea around the year 141 BCE.[40] The creation of the Hellenistic kingdom of Judea was secured by its recognition by the Roman Republic in 139 BCE, a move which deterred the fractured Seleucid clan from attempting to retake their former territory. Though closely allied with Rome and Antioch, the Hasmonean state was the first independent Jewish commonwealth since the fall of the Kingdom of Judah. The novelty of a state ruled by Jews fueled the imaginations of their countrymen at home and abroad. No longer mere provincials, the children of Israel now had achieved the political independence needed to know theirs as a nation in every sense of the word.[41]

The establishment of a Jewish nation-state profoundly impacted the idea of Jewish identity. Chief among its effects was the need for the Hasmoneans to enfranchise those peoples within the political borders of their state who were not Jews.[42] Judah and his successors had gradually expanded Judea's territory in order to secure their hold of Jerusalem. By the order of Simon's son John Hyrcanus (r. 134–104 BCE), the borders of Judea were extended northward into the region of Samaria and southward into the kingdom of Idumea, both areas with significant Jewish settlement but populated primarily by non-Jews.

---

ambitions of the early Hasmoneans over the religious zeal traditionally ascribed to them in contemporary accounts of their campaign for Jerusalem.

[40] On the Hasmoneans' appropriation of the traditional Israelite rhetoric of divine kingship, see Rajak (1996).

[41] On the Hasmoneans' assumption of typically Hellenistic political strategies, see Rajak (1990, 261–80); Gruen (1998: 12–39); J. Geiger (2002a).

[42] On this development, see Goodblatt (2006: 144–59), who keenly observes that the Hasmonean rhetoric of territorial sovereignty extended beyond the borders of the ancient Kingdom of Israel. Cf. Mendels (1987: 47–53), who associates the Hasmonean propaganda with expressions of sacred geography in earlier Hellenistic Jewish texts.

As a result, the Jews found themselves imposing their national agenda upon people who did necessarily share their values.

The Samaritans posed little problem by way of integration as they too identified as Israelites and worshiped Yahweh. Hyrcanus needed only to demolish their cultic installation at Mount Gerizim and order them to worship in Jerusalem.[43] The Idumeans, however, were more problematic. Although their culture was similar in certain respects to that of their Jewish neighbors, they did not worship Yahweh or abide by his Torah. Hyrcanus therefore tried to make them Jews by means of proselytization, compelling them under the threat of violence to adopt the ways of the Jews as their own.[44] Similar measures were taken by his successors Aristobulus (r. 104–103 BCE) and Alexander Jannaeus (r. 103–76 BCE) as they expanded Judea further northward into the Galilee and Golan regions, eastward across the Jordan River into Perea and the Hauran, and westward in hostile takeovers of the Greek cities lining the Mediterranean coast. Although the Jews living in these areas welcomed the Hasmoneans, their neighboring gentile populations had either to become Jews or to accept their inferior social statuses in order to remain in the good graces of their new sovereigns.[45]

How successful the Hasmoneans were in their efforts to integrate these foreign peoples is not entirely clear.[46] In any event, impetus of the Hasmonean kings to make gentiles into Jews by governmental fiat added a new element to the traditional formula for Jewish identity. From time immemorial, the will of the Jews to serve Yahweh had been informed by the notion that their God was bound by an everlasting covenant with their ancestors to reciprocate their devotion. That divine logic functioned in part on an assumption of genealogical continuity between their nation and the storied nation of Israel. The efforts of the Hasmoneans to impose the laws of the Torah upon their gentile subjects debased that assumption by opening the Jewish covenant not only to self-professed heirs of Judah but to everyone who happened to live within the borders of their ethnically heterogeneous Judean state.

To be sure, the Jews long welcomed the interests of foreigners who wished to serve their God. They called such individuals proselytes or, in Hebrew, *gerim*, reflecting the scriptural ordinances for their affiliation with the nation of Israel.[47] The premise, therefore, of turning gentiles into Jews was not an

---

[43] So S. Schwartz (2001: 37).

[44] On Hyrcanus' expansionist designs, see Kasher (1988: 44–78).

[45] On the Hasmoneans' campaigns in the Syrian and Transjordanian regions, see Kasher (1988: 70–105), and on their incursions into Greek cities, see Kasher (1990: 132–69).

[46] Josephus dubiously reports that Hyrcanus ordered all the men of Idumea circumcised according to the Jewish custom (*Ant.* 13.257). On the questionable veracity of this claim, see S.J.D. Cohen (1999a: 115–16), who observes that the Idumeans practiced ritual circumcision before their alliance with Judea, although cf. Kasher (1988: 57–58).

[47] See, e.g., Exod 12.48–49; Lev 19.33–34; Num 9.14, 15.14–16. On the relationship of the law of the *ger* and the classical Jewish construction of the proselyte, see S.J.D. Cohen (1999a: 140–74).

innovation of the Hellenistic age. What was new about the Hasmoneans' approach to proselytism was their subordination of conviction to political pragmatism. The kings of Judea could not reasonably have expected their newly realized Jewish subjects to undergo a process of collective reinvention akin to a mass religious conversion. Their aim, rather, was to offer those subjects a convenient means whereby to declare their loyalties to their new rulers. Much as the Seleucids had once wielded the idea of Greek identity to dominate their Jewish subjects, the Hasmoneans used the idea of Jewish identity to exercise power over the ostensibly nonnative peoples now under their rule.[48]

For Jews both old and new, life in Hellenistic Judea brought new political opportunities that would further shape the idea of Jewish identity. Access to a local power base representing both their nation's priestly and civic leadership generated competition between Jewish parties eager to ply their influences among the masses.[49] The reign of John Hyrcanus saw the emergence of the Pharisees and Sadducees, the former advocating a populist approach to cultic governance and the latter a more conservative approach generally more to the taste of the Hasmonean court. A third sect, the Essenes, soon took shape in opposition to the Hasmoneans, its members often withdrawing from civil society to live in the wilderness in protest of what they saw as the corruption of the Temple cult. Although none of these groups spoke for more than a fraction the Jewish people at any given time, their efforts to influence the policies of the Hasmoneans further democratized a popular discourse on Jewish identity no longer given to instinctive deference to Judea's national leadership.

In the year 63 BCE, the Hasmonean state fell under the direct governance of Rome. Once allied with Judea from afar, the Republic had since expanded its presence in the eastern Mediterranean.[50] The Romans at first allowed the Hasmoneans to serve as client kings, maintaining a semblance of the civic economy built by their ancestors. But Rome's tolerance for the Jewish royal family extended only as far as the Roman senate desired. In 37 BCE, the Romans installed a new king of Judea, Herod, a man of no relation

---

That the preservation of genealogical continuity remained a priority despite this custom is evident in the efforts of certain Jewish sectarians of the late Second Temple period to deny the proselyte's Jewish legitimacy in spite of the scriptural legislation to the contrary; see Hayes (2002: 68–91).

[48] On the function of ethnic rhetoric in the imperialistic stratagems of the Hasmoneans, see S. Schwartz (2007: 232–35), who posits that they sought to justify their colonization of gentile areas by implying their nation's recovery of territorial and demographic losses sustained since the dissolution of the Kingdom of Israel centuries ago.

[49] For an overview of the major Jewish sectarian movements of the late Second Temple period, see Stemberger (1995). On their origins as would-be mediators of popular influence among the Hasmonean kings, see Baumgarten (1997), especially ibid. (42–58).

[50] For the following history of the initial Roman colonization of Judea and the surrounding region, see Goodman (2007: 47–62).

to the Hasmoneans but whose family had proven loyal to the Republic in their recent affairs in the region. Although of Idumean descent, Herod was accepted by his Jewish subjects as a patron of their nation and a loyal servant of Yahweh. And while he often governed his client state with the fervor of a despot, his outgoing support for the Temple cult and its priesthood secured the stability of Judea's once contentious social order.[51] Herod and his successors thereby proved that the transnational program of Jewish identity fashioned by the Hasmoneans remained palatable to the masses even in the absence of an autonomous Jewish state.

But just as Rome once wore down the Seleucids, so did their gradual takeover of Judea wear down the Herodians.[52] The rebirth of the Republic as the Empire of Augustus in 27 BCE brought great changes to her eastern provinces. New administrative hierarchies were installed. Old alliances with local client kings were weakened by the arrival of governors and other diplomats from the west. Military occupation increased throughout the imperial state's vast frontier regions. The Jews endured these changes along with the rest of Rome's provincial subjects. But the marginalization of their monarchy by new superiors not attuned to their unique cultural needs sowed an ideology of resistance in the minds of many. Rome became a symbol of spite to those Jews who yearned for the bygone days of the Hasmoneans and the legendary kings of Israel and Judah. Hope for divine intervention was in the air.

In time, that hope gave way to action. The revolt of 66–73 CE brought great destruction to the Jews and their land.[53] By the end of the debacle, Jerusalem was in ruins. The Temple of Yahweh was torn down and its cult suspended indefinitely. Judea was stripped of her vestigial kingship and placed under heavy military surveillance. Her economy and infrastructure crumbled. Thousands of her people were dead, thousands more taken into captivity. Jews throughout the Roman Empire were made to pay indemnities for the insolence of their countrymen. The net effect of these disasters on the mentalities of the Jews is impossible to capture in its devastating totality. Both their nation and their cult had been thoroughly humbled. Not since the Babylonian Exile had the Jewish nation faced an existential crisis of the magnitude brought on by their ill-advised rebellion against Rome.

---

[51] On subsequent Jewish notices of Herod's mixed ethnic heritage, see S.J.D. Cohen (1999a: 13–24), who notes how the prejudices of later authors rueful of his abuses of power serve to obscure Herod's popular acceptance as a Jew during his reign over Judea.

[52] The following account of the causes of the first Jewish revolt reflects that of Martin Goodman, who assesses the situation as one of gradual breakdown of Rome's sensitivities toward the unique rights and needs of their Jewish subjects; see Goodman (2007: 379–99). For a more typical, if less theoretically informed, treatment assigning the revolt to the apocalyptic ambitions of Jewish religious fanatics offended by the mere presence of Romans in their land, see Hadas-Lebel (2006: 439–54).

[53] For the following history, cf. Goodman (2007: 7–25).

The Jews did not give up in the face of their crises.[54] Doubtless many were moved by their people's defeat to relinquish their Jewish identities. Others, however, continued to express hope for imminent salvation, construing their latest crisis as a prelude to another great national renewal.[55] Some of the Pharisees who survived the war pursued that objective by resolving to remain firm in their service of Yahweh in spite of the loss of their Temple.[56] Jews the world over turned their attentions from the Temple to the synagogue, reinventing their ancestral customs in view of the new circumstances of their cult's operation.

Yet others refused to accept the new reality. So powerful was their desire for freedom that it prompted another armed uprising against Rome.[57] The Bar Kokhba rebellion of 132–135 CE was fueled in part by Messianic fervor, its leadership hoping to repeat the success of the Hasmoneans in retaking Jerusalem from the heathen horde. But the superior might of Rome again proved too much for the rebels. This time, the Jews were made to pay a symbolic price for their mutiny. The emperor Hadrian stripped Judea of its name and rebranded the province with the archaic Greek toponym Palestine, subordinating its governance to the neighboring province of Syria. A military force of unprecedented scale was deployed to police the region and its unruly people. The city of Jerusalem was refounded as the Roman colony of Aelia Capitolina and populated with foreign soldiers and veterans.[58] As far as the Roman government was concerned, the nationalistic ambitions of the Jewish people were thoroughly put to rest.

The wars with Rome exhausted the energies of the Jews in Judea/Palestine and throughout the Empire, ensuring that their people would be denied their

---

[54] On the range of surviving Jewish responses to Rome's victory, see Weitzman (2005: 138–57), who discusses strategies of cultural survival even among those Jews who admitted the folly of their people's recent strategic misstep.

[55] On this short-lived but significant apocalyptic trend, see Stone (1981); Collins (1998): 194–232; Hadas-Lebel (2006: 455–87).

[56] On this development, see S.J.D. Cohen (1984: 27–31) and passim. See also Goldenberg (2006: 199–202), who likewise reads the initiation of the rabbinic movement as a reaction to the loss of the Temple.

[57] For the following history, see Goodman (2007: 424–69), who argues that Bar Kokhba's Messianic vision was compounded by the cause of securing the Jewish people's release from the debilitating financial penalties levied upon them in retaliation for the first revolt.

[58] Following Cassius Dio, *Historia Romana* 69.12.1, it seems that the Roman emperor Hadrian planned to found a military colony in or near Jerusalem during a diplomatic tour of Judea in 129 or 130 CE. Though not necessarily by design, that decision appears to have incited the Jewish rebels to take up arms in defense of their still ruined holy city for fear of its defilement by gentiles; cf. Goodman (2007: 461). Yet it is unclear whether any significant action to the effect of implementing Hadrian's order was taken until after the war, which lends credence to the commonplace assumption that the establishment of Aelia Capitolina and the installation of Roman shrines on the Temple Mount were punitive measures exacted after the war. In all likelihood, intentions both pragmatic and punitive played roles in these developments. See Isaac (1998).

political independence for the foreseeable future. Nevertheless, Rome's victories over the Jews did not spell the end of Judaism. Save for a brief and apparently ineffectual ban on circumcision issued in the wake of the second revolt, participation in the Jewish cult remained lawful.[59] In time, the Jews learned how to be obedient subjects of Rome, ultimately achieving an acceptable modus vivendi alternatively given to preserving their ancestral values and collaborating with the gentiles in whose midsts they operated. Both in their ancestral homeland and abroad in the ever-expanding Mediterranean Diaspora, the Jews learned how to be compliant subjects of Rome. Not until the unexpected developments of the fourth century would their people again be compelled to reevaluate their cultural priorities on the mass scale in the face of the new and daunting challenge to their survival posed by the rise of Christianity.

Lest the reader fault me for flouting my own warnings about the ills of serial history, I should stress that my purpose in the foregoing account was not to suggest that the developments in question impacted the self-perceptions of all Jews in precisely the same ways. Nor do I mean in concluding my narrative with the Bar Kokhba rebellion suggest that the aftermath of that event represented a terminal point in the evolution of Jewish identity. To the contrary, the writings of the rabbinic sages speak to the efforts of their people to express their Jewish identities in all sorts of new ways for centuries to follow.[60] That observation is fundamental to my premise of reading the rabbinic response to Christianity as part of an ongoing Jewish conversation.

Nevertheless, I follow the scholarly consensus in maintaining that the abolishment of the Jewish state and the Jewish Temple cult served as major catalysts in the transformation of a popular discourse on Jewish identity once tied to those institutions. Following the wars with Rome, the Jews no longer had civic or cultic leaders capable of making policy decisions on behalf of their entire nation. They therefore knew no one with the capacity to dictate who was a Jew and who was not. Consequently, what made a Jew a Jew henceforth was to be a matter of tradition and, more importantly, a matter of perception.

---

[59] Here I depart from Goodman (2007: 462), who cites a universal ban on genital mutilation reportedly enacted by Hadrian as evidence for an imperial ban on Jewish circumcision; cf. *Scriptores Historiae Augustae*, Hadrian 14.1–2. Later rabbinic traditions also intimate that the failure of the rebellion incurred certain unspecified difficulties involving that rite (see, e.g., *m.Shabbat* 19.1; *y.Shabbat* 19.2 [17a]; *y.Yevamot* 8.1 [9a]; *Genesis Rabbah* 46.13; *b.Yevamot* 72a). By most recent critical accounts, however, the reputed ban was, at worst, a temporary punitive measure briefly enforced in Palestine immediately following the war; so, e.g., Oppenheimer (2003). Compare, moreover, Boustan (2003), who questions whether the circumcision of Jewish newborns was formally restricted at any point before or after the war in view of the absence of reliable evidence to that effect.

[60] On this wide-ranging topic, see S. Stern (1994), especially ibid. (1–50), on the rabbinic understandings of the scriptural distinction between Israel and the nations. That the rabbis themselves routinely indulged in casual acculturation to gentile norms is rightly emphasized by Eliav (2009).

CONTINUITY AND CHANGE

Let us now return the question of what defined the idea of Jewish identity dur-ing Judaism's formative age. Despite the transformative changes in the common life of their people surveyed above, the Jews in general remained committed to their God and their nation. And while those commitments certainly were tested at times, the bonds of tradition never were quite broken, at least not on the mass scale. Why not? What about their conceptions of God and nationhood made the Jewish enterprise resilient to failure even in the face of devastating injuries to their cult and country? Here is where I would contend that the cate-gories of religion and ethnicity are advantageous to the historian. Each of those phenomena incurs mimetic modes of thought and behavior supportive of the discourse of identity.[61] It is not without reason, therefore, that contemporary scholars have proposed to describe the idea of Jewish identity in religious and ethnic terms. Let us therefore consider some of those proposals in order to assess their heuristic merits with respect to my project.[62]

I shall begin with the category of religion. As noted, the term religion tech-nically did not apply to the culture of the Jews prior to the fourth century. But did Jews assume a characteristically religious agenda before their culture was formally defined as a religion by Christian Rome?

As it is normally understood today, the term religion implies something in the order of spirituality, an elective system of belief relating to the divine and operating independently of human authority.[63] It is, ideally, the right of the individual to profess the religion of his or her choosing. But this was not the case in antiquity, when the primary objective of seeking communion with the divine was to serve the common good of one's nation or state. Religious thought and its attendant behavioral prescripts were understood to govern the activities of its subscribers as a statutory moral code. Religion, therefore, did not exist independently of the social and political structures licensed by human authorities to implement its rules, if not always to enforce strict compliance with those rules among its adherents.

In order to discern whether ancient Jews presumed to operate in such a religious economy, one must consider their perceived relationships with God

---

[61] Cf. Assmann (2011: 137–39), who sees the course of Jewish history from the Babylonian Exile to the fall of Jerusalem in 70 CE as a cultural evolution from one emphasizing religion to one more characteristically ethnic but no less predicated on religious myth. While my discus-sion below will problematize the application of these categorical distinctions, I find value in Assmann's description of ancient Judaism as a culture insofar as his analytical model accom-modates the shifting modalities of Jewish identification for which I attempt to account.

[62] The following analysis will focus primarily on the evolution of Jewish identity in Judea on account of the geographical emphasis of the foregoing discussion. For complementary com-ments regarding the general consistency of Jewish modes of identification between Judea and the Diaspora, see Bohak (2002).

[63] My comments here follow Nongbri (2009); see especially ibid. (154–59), on the questionable applicability of the category of religion in the ancient frame of reference.

and his laws. The theology of the Torah dictates obedience to those laws for the sake of maintaining God's storied covenant with the nation of Israel. The implication of a divine economy upheld by the ideological and ritual compliance of its human subjects certainly suggests something like a religion inasmuch as it projects the values of a state onto the polity of Israel. That that polity operated as a nation even when denied its political independence might therefore be construed as proof of her people's religious resolve long before they or anyone else thought to describe their culture as a religion per se.

To that end, a number of scholars have sought to define the religious aspect of ancient Judaism on the basis of its covenantal theology. Most prominent among them is E.P. Sanders, who characterizes what he calls the "common Judaism" of the late Second Temple period as "a standard by which loyalty to Israel and to the God of Israel was measured."[64] Supporting this definition was an immutable theological principle that Sanders calls covenantal nomism, that is, the idea that perpetual adherence to the laws of the Torah would serve to secure the Jews' covenantal relationship with God. That notion, nurtured by the promises of Yahweh's eternal patronage inscribed upon their sacred memories, ensured a common devotion to God, his Torah, and his Temple in Jerusalem manifest throughout the diverse record of surviving Jewish textual and material evidences of the age. In a similar vein, Dunn borrows from the language of Islam in proposing to define the religion of ancient Judaism in view of its "four pillars," comprising the three objects of cultivation cited by Sanders along with the elaborate theological construction that is the nation of Israel itself.[65] Martin Hengel and Roland Deines describe a "complex" rather than a common ancient Judaism allowing for the occurrence of greater variety in thought and practice than Sanders acknowledges.[66] Extending that logic to the rabbinic period, Stuart Miller proposes a "complex common Judaism" likewise defined by its consistency on some matters and its diversity on others.[67]

To my mind, each of these scholars offers a reasonable account of a coherent and widely practiced ancient theological system functionally analogous to that of today's Judaism. The concepts of God, Torah, Temple, and Israel were subjects of tremendous interest, if not of unanimous agreement, among ancient Jews of all ideological varieties.[68] But whether those interests constituted a discrete religious system is another matter. Per Neusner, the diversity of thought typical of ancient Jews precludes the possibility of describing any one strain of

---

[64] See E.P. Sanders (1992), especially ibid. (47–49), on "common Judaism" as a normative standard of Jewish identification. Sanders' terminology of covenantal nomism originates in his earlier study, E.P. Sanders (1977), especially ibid. (419–28), where he describes that principle of traditional Jewish theology as a functional counterpoint to Paul's formative Christian theology.

[65] See Dunn (2006: 24–48).

[66] Hengel and Deines (1995), especially ibid. (53–54).

[67] Miller (2006: 25–26).

[68] For detailed elaboration on this point, see S. Schwartz (2001: 49–74), on the Torah and the Temple, and ibid. (74–87), on the related mythology of Israelite nationhood.

their cultural expression as "Judaism" regardless of how generically that term is to be understood.[69] The prominence, moreover, of certain elements of practice and belief across the range of Jewish textual and material evidences must not be taken to indicate a universally accepted program of collective identification. Popularity, in other words, does not imply commonality.[70] Finally, to reduce ancient Judaism to its supposed theological essentials is to force the phenomenon in question into an interpretive framework that does not account for its diverse cultural ramifications beyond the religious realm.[71]

To be a Jew in antiquity meant more than simply to support a sacrificial cult. It meant more than to profess a given theology. It meant partaking of a national culture predicated on those conditions but regulated by the habits of the Jewish collective. In order, therefore, fairly to assess the religious aspect of the idea of Jewish identity, one must consider its regulatory function. How did the cult of Yahweh function as an agency of Jewish group definition? To what extent did compliance or noncompliance with its ritual and ethical statutes dictate one's ability to function as a Jew amidst others claiming that distinction? When and by what means did the laws of the Torah come to define the construction of Jewish nationhood?

In his recent study *Judaism, the First Phase*, Joseph Blenkinsopp argues that the Jewish connection of law and nationality runs deep. By his account, the leaders of the restored Jewish community of Yehud were authorized by the Persian crown to use the Torah as a kind of ethnic constitution, implementing its laws as binding statutes among their province's native polity. While the endorsement of the Torah did not supplant Persia's own civil statutes, it empowered the priestly and scribal administrators of Yehud to regulate the revived cult of Yahweh in Jerusalem on behalf of all self-professed Jews throughout in the Achaemenid realm.[72] In effect, Blenkinsopp argues, the Persian kings and their Jewish administrative agents instituted a regulatory law for the Jewish cult from the very moment of its revival. The exacting standards of ritual purity and practice thus instituted by the governate of Yehud constituted the first expression of the religious system later to be known as Judaism.[73]

Although Blenkinsopp might be too eager to label the Temple cult as Judaism tout court, I find his effort to show that the term Jew has always

---

[69] See Neusner (1993), especially ibid. (275–95), for an effective, if overstated, critique of Sanders' construction of "common Judaism" in reference to the supposed *halakhah* of the Pharisees and early rabbinic sages.

[70] See the critical assessment of Stemberger (2001), and cf. S. Schwartz (2001: 66–68).

[71] For this incisive critique, see Eisenbaum (2005), who notes the tendency of contemporary New Testament scholars to describe ancient Judaism in terms apposite to Christianity without due attention to those of its socio-cultural aspects of the former not readily classified as functions of theology or religion.

[72] This impression is most clear in Blenkinsopp's interpretation of the biblical portrait of Ezra as an archetypical symbol of Jewish priestly-scribal authority; see Blenkinsopp (2009: 46–85).

[73] See especially Blenkinsopp (2009: 32–37).

implied a certain inalienable standard of religious observance persuasive. His intimation, moreover, of the Torah's endorsement by the Achaemenids would seem to account for the currency its legislation would attain among the Jewish masses during the centuries to follow.[74] But there is little to suggest that the Persian authorities sanctioned the priests and scribes of Yehud to exercise their leadership privileges beyond the immediate purview of the Temple cult.[75] Consequently, the likelihood that Jerusalem's civil leadership actively promoted the ritual legislation of the Torah as a binding bill of reform does not explain why their regulatory efforts evidently worked so well.

To my mind, one must look beyond its religious function in order to discern the other major draw of the Torah as a benchmark of Jewish identification in antiquity. In addition to its laws, the books of Moses represent the foundational documents of a national myth attuned to the sensitivities of a nation distressed by the Babylonian Exile. That is no coincidence. The Torah as we know it likely was compiled in Babylon and given its final priestly overlay in Persian-era Yehud.[76] To abide by its legislation thus meant more than simply to serve the God of Israel. It was to be Israel, to locate one's self in the story of a nation buoyed by the belief that God would never abandon his chosen people even when hope of salvation seemed lost.

These are some of the more salient points raised by David Goodblatt in his book *Elements of Jewish Nationalism*.[77] The Torah, Goodblatt argues, instilled a collective sense of purpose, providing not only a code of cultic regulations but an ideology of nationhood. Its central narrative relating Israel's exodus from Egypt spoke to the aspirations of a Jewish people yearning to free themselves from the Persians, the Greeks, and the Romans.[78] The Torah thereby sustained the Jews through the trials of the classical age, informing a remarkably consistent discourse on national identity expressed in reference to Israel, Judah, and Zion. Coupled with the Torah's intricate priestly legislation, its legends of cultural perseverance sustained a national culture grounded in religion but far exceeding its domain. Jewish identity in antiquity was not simply about cultic reverence. It was about kinship and tradition, about loyalty to a proud and

---

[74] Blenkinsopp here presents a moderate view on a subject of debated historical import, to which cf. Blenkinsopp (2001). For a comprehensive survey of research on the theory of a Persian authorization of the Torah, see Lee (2011).

[75] This perhaps would explain the passive-aggressive nature of Ezra's effort to regulate the marriage practices of the Jews by making them stand in the rain outside the Temple until they agreed to desist from taking foreign wives (Ezra 9–10). On this incident, see Blenkinsopp (2009: 63–71).

[76] For critical overviews of these late-stage textual developments, see Carr (2011: 252–303), on the Babylonian-era compilation of the sources of the Pentateuch and ibid. (214–21), on the Persian-era revisions.

[77] Goodblatt (2006).

[78] Ibid. 28–48, highlights the efforts of various Jewish administrative agencies of antiquity to cultivate popular awareness of the Torah and other Hebrew scriptural texts by means of educational and liturgical reforms.

historic people destined to withstand their political subjugation in order to reclaim the past glories documented in their sacred scriptures.[79]

Despite some misgivings with respect to his stance on the political dimensions of ancient Jewish nationalism, I find Goodblatt's case quite compelling.[80] If one is to assume that the Torah was the founding document of Judaism's religious constitution, it stands to reason that its ethnic constitution derived from the same source. Consequently, what the modern observer might distinguish as the respective religious and ethnic elements of ancient Jewish culture are functionally inseparable. That observation offsets Blenkinsopp's argument that Judaism was a typically religious venture from its outset. Even if the idea of Jewish identity was tied to the cult of Yahweh from the moment of its inception, it was the Jews' perception of their shared national history that demanded their reestablishment of that cult after the Babylonian Exile. Simply put, there would have been no Jewish religion had there not been a cohesive Jewish ethnic polity to support it. One therefore cannot account for one without accounting for the other.

Both Blenkinsopp and Goodblatt emphasize continuity over change as a defining trait of the ancient idea of Jewish identity. Consequently, neither draws equal attention to the subtle changes in the popular and official discourses supporting that construction over the course of the classical age. That makes it difficult to apply either of their theories to the central problematic of my investigation. For even if I am to frame the initial encounter between Christian and Jew as a meeting of Jewish parties, I must acknowledge some measure of disagreement between those parties with respect to the relative values of the religious and ethnic components of the cultural paradigm that the presumed to share. In other words, to assess the nature of the conflict between Christian Jew and non-Christian Jew, I must allow some space for negotiation between their respective viewpoints on what made one a Jew.

The tendency among those attempting to describe that space has been to propose an evolutionary trajectory whereby the idea of Jewish identity changed from a typically ethnic distinction into one more closely resembling a religious distinction. One prominent advocate of this approach has been Shaye J.D. Cohen, who proposes to locate the pivotal point of that transition during the reign of the Hasmonean king John Hyrcanus.[81] The decision of Hyrcanus

[79] See especially Goodblatt's methodological statement in Goodblatt (2006: 14–27). Compare, however, Assmann (2011: 175–205), who characterizes the same sense of cultural rootedness in the narrative of the Torah as the defining element of the Jewish religion in the classical age, thereby prioritizing the religious aspect of Jewish identity over its ethnic aspect where Goodblatt attempts just the opposite.
[80] Compare Weitzman (2008), who stresses that Goodblatt's understanding of nationalism qua political independence seems to overstate the aims of the ancient Jews who typically yearned only for social improvement within the various imperial infrastructures in which they operated.
[81] For the following, see S.J.D. Cohen (1999a: 109–39), especially ibid. (137), on his proposed definition of Hasmonean-era Judaism's "ethno-religious" character. For endorsements of Cohen's model, see, e.g., J. Geiger (2002b); Wilson (2004a).

to open the doors of Jewish nationhood to the Idumeans served to transform a traditional Jewish discourse on group identity by downgrading its primary ethnic aspect. In effect, Cohen argues, Hyrcanus and his successors asserted that being a Jew was just like being a Greek, that is, a matter of cultural conformity rather than hereditary happenstance. Henceforth, Judaism was to function as an "ethno-religion" still predicated on the ethical and ritual values of the Torah albeit now on a platform of universal accessibility. In other words, what was traditionally understood as a law for Israel was reconceived as a law for all the peoples of greater Judea, a rubric of thought and practice serving the regulatory function of an institutionalized religion.

Cohen certainly is correct to note that the encounter with Greek culture prompted many Jews to reimagine their ancestral traditions as ones no longer specific to their ethnic group. The impetus of the later Hasmonean kings to impress those traditions upon the non-Jewish peoples in their political dominions was well in line with that trend. But Cohen's argument rests on a questionable assumption. As he acknowledges, receiving proselytes was an established Jewish custom long predating the Hellenistic age. Hyrcanus, he asserts, circumvented that custom by compelling the Idumeans to join the Jewish nation without voluntarily committing to the legislation of the Torah, if not necessarily against their wills.[82] Yet winning converts for Yahweh was not the purpose of the Hasmonean reform. As Seth Schwartz has argued, Hyrcanus and his successors extended the rhetoric of Jewish nationhood only to indigenous peoples reasonably to be construed as fellow descendants of Abraham.[83] The Torah, they reasoned, counted the Idumeans and their other gentile neighbors as members of the same ancestral line as the Jews. One might therefore posit that the expansionist policies of the Hasmoneans amplified the ethnic element of Jewish identity rather than diluting it.

Furthermore, as Martha Himmelfarb has shown, many Jews of the age evidently influenced by classical Greek philosophical ethics had taken to questioning the value of kinship long before the rise of the Hasmoneans.[84] As early as the third century BCE, Jewish thinkers chose to emphasize personal piety over ancestral merit as the defining element of one's Jewish identity, heeding the Torah's call to live as "a kingdom of priests" (Exod 19.6).[85] Citing virtuous

[82] S.J.D. Cohen (1999a: 130–32).
[83] See S. Schwartz (2007), who regards the Hasmonean policy as an emulation of the Hellenistic custom of striking friendships with one's political allies by adopting their ethnic constitutions, and cf. S. Schwartz (2011: 233–34), responding to Cohen more directly. See also Osterloh (2008), who detects a corresponding rationale in the efforts of the Hasmoneans to establish fictive kinship ties with the peoples of Rome and Sparta (1 Macc 12.1–23).
[84] For the following, see Himmelfarb (2006). Compare Collins (2000: 157–60), on what he describes in complementary terms as the "common ethic" of Jewish life and thought in the Hellenistic Diaspora.
[85] See Himmelfarb (2006: 1–8). Himmelfarb (ibid., 160–85), sees a reversal of this trend after 70 CE, when the neutralization of the Jewish priesthood and the concomitant rise of Christianity appear to have prompted a retreat to the hierocratic and distinctly ethnic modes of cultural identification espoused by the rabbinic sages.

conduct as the calling card of their nation, these reighteous ideologues asserted that their fellow Jews had to earn their covenantal birthrights. To their minds, Jews born into God's chosen nation were no less responsible than proselytes to prove their credentials through faithful adherence to God's law. One might therefore make the case that the will of the Hasmoneans to impress obedience to the Torah upon their foreign subjects was an effect of an established moral discourse prioritizing the religious element of Jewish identity to its ethnic element.[86]

Another evolutionary model of ancient Jewish identity has been proposed by Doron Mendels, who sees the rise of the Jewish religion as a response to the decline of Jewish nationalism. Mendels sees the rise and fall of the Hasmonean state as a bellwether of mass psychological upheaval among the Jewish people.[87] The gradual liquidation of Judea's political autonomy at the hands of the Romans beginning in the first century BCE served to temper the political ideology inscribed upon the idea of Jewish identity since its inception. The fall of Jerusalem during the first Jewish revolt forced Jews around the world to abandon hope for an imminent restoration of the Kingdom of Israel. The erasure of Judea from Rome's political map in the wake of the second revolt deprived the Jews of their very basis of their national identity. The Judaism that survived these disasters, Mendels thus argues, was no longer substantively ethnic in character insofar as the Jews had been drained of their nationalistic resolve. What was left, therefore, was a religion.[88]

But while the disappearance of the Jewish nation-state surely curtailed the political ambitions of the Jews, to characterize that as a failure of their national enterprise would be a mistake. As Goodblatt has shown, the fact of their past subjugation under the Persians and the Greeks had not killed the sense of ethnic unity of the Jews who lived through those times. It only stands to reason that their descendants were equipped to maintain that element of their culture upon their return to subjugation under the Romans. Moreover, their dreams of a return to political independence are well attested in the eschatological aspirations of generations of Jews who survived the wars.[89] The losses of their

---

[86] Compare, however, Himmelfarb (2006: 74–78), who discerns traces of a negative response to the mass entry of Idumeans into Jewish society in Jubilees, a sectarian work of the Hasmonean age exhibiting hostility toward proselytes and other nonnative Jews.

[87] Mendels (1992). For arguments likewise associating the emergence of the Jewish religion with cessation of the Jewish sacrificial cult in 70 CE, see Goodman (1989), who sees grounds for a semantic shift in Rome's decision to levy punitive taxes against Jews irrespective of their countries of origin, and D.R. Schwartz (2005), who detects a similar trend in Josephus' postwar depiction of the Herodian monarchy as patrons of a nongeographically delimited ethnic cult. See also Modrzejewski (2003), who notes an increase in Roman legislation addressing participation in the Jewish cult during the late first and second centuries CE, a development arguably anticipating the Christian laws on Judaism to be issued in the fourth century and thereafter.

[88] See, e.g., Mendels (1992: 391).

[89] So noted by Weitzman (2005: 108–14), who highlights the figurative return to the scene of the Babylonian Exile in Jewish apocalyptic texts of the late first century CE. Similar coping mechanisms would evolve among the rabbinic sages, on which development see Milikowsky (1997). On the roots of this phenomenon, which Goodblatt describes as "Zion nationalism," (2006: 167–203).

kingdom and Temple undoubtedly disoriented the nationalistic outlooks of many Jews. But the consequent need to recondition their habits of worship and communal organization was not an insurmountable obstacle to those who wished to see their nation endure in perpetuity.

To my mind, one need not infer a wholesale reinvention of a discourse in order to discern the effects of change over time. The alternating emphases on the ethnic and religious aspects of Jewish identity observed over the course of antiquity merely attest to the elasticity of the idea in question.[90] A Jew in one context reasonably could have perceived his or her Jewish identity differently than a Jew in another context. Moreover, the observation of difference between their respective perceptions need not imply a qualitative comparison of their cultural assumptions. In view of these considerations, I reaffirm my prior characterization of ancient Judaism as neither a religion nor an ethnicity, much less a nationality, a political ideology, or a genealogy. Even my preferred term "culture" is not quite up to the task of describing the phenomenon at issue. Ancient Judaism was none of these and all of these. Like the many other ancient peoples amongst whom the Jews of antiquity operated, theirs was a sui generis collective enterprise resistant to such neatly sorted modern classifications.

And yet, the absence of a fixed religious rule analogous to today's Reform Judaism, Orthodox Judaism, or Conservative Judaism did not preclude the recognition among ancient Jews of such common organizing principles as God, the Torah, the Temple, and the nation of Israel. What remains to be considered is the extent to which Jews of different ideological persuasions diverged from one another in translating those objects of cultural orientation into the observable behaviors and social modalities that defined their respective expressions of their Jewish identities. Identifying the preconditions and limitations of variety within the Jewish collective will serve to establish key interpretive principles for the negotiations with Christianity to be accounted in the chapters to follow.

VARIETY AND ITS IMPLICATIONS

The condition to which I refer as variety is often construed as a function of sectarianism. That description is not unfitting inasmuch as the ancient Jewish population did play host to a few notable sects (Greek: *haereseis*), including the aforementioned Pharisees, Sadducees, and Essenes.[91] One might even infer

---

[90] For like considerations, see Janowitz (2000), and cf. Weitzman (2005: 158–59); Goodblatt (2006: 204–10). S. Schwartz (2011: 238), prefers to avoid all categorical descriptions of ancient Judaism, although I believe that his concomitant assertion of both its enduring ethnic and religious qualities supports my conclusions.

[91] The sectarian designation belongs to Josephus, who uses the typically philosophical term *haeresis* or "choice" in his accounts of the Pharisees, Sadducees, and Essenes in Josephus, *J.W.* 2.117–66; ibid., *Ant.* 13.171–75, 18.11–22 et al. See Baumgarten (1997: 3–4), for these and other usages of the Greek and possibly related Hebrew terms in classical Jewish and Christian texts.

that the earliest Christians saw themselves as a Jewish sect.[92] But the language of sectarianism implies its subject to be an offshoot of a religious group driven by ideological disagreement significant enough to drive some of its members toward separation from that group.[93] That definition is not entirely appropriate for an ancient Jewish collective bound not strictly by religious principles but also by a sense of shared national history. So, for example, while the Pharisees might have cultivated their own self-regulating discourse on Jewish identity, they were recognized as Jews even by persons outside their group. Nor, to our knowledge, did the Pharisees deny the Jewish identities of those who declined to join their group. The same seems to have been the case for the Sadducees, the Essenes, and, at least initially, those Christians who chose to live as Jews.[94]

So what made a Jewish sect in antiquity? And what difference did their differences make to the general Jewish collective? A return to our historical sketch will be instructive. Scholars seeking to describe ancient Jewish sectarianism often trace its roots to the very beginning of the Jewish enterprise. The books of Ezra and Nehemiah indicate that the Jews who returned to Yehud from their exile in the east differentiated themselves from those of their countrymen who had remained in their ancestral homeland after the Babylonian conquest.[95] Representing the self-styled priestly and scribal elites, the former exiles looked down upon those who they dubbed the *am ha-aretz*, the "people of the land," for their perceived failures to maintain their ritual obligations to Yahweh during the suspension of the Temple cult.[96] That moral distinction, the argument goes, would go on to influence those Jewish prophets of the era who envisioned a socially stratified Israel excluding those whom they deemed undeserving of God's favorable judgment at the end of days. The implication that some Jews were more worthy of the title than others thus sowed the seed of dissent later to flower into the phenomenon of sectarianism.[97]

---

[92] In other words, I take it for granted that the three groups whom Josephus construed as sects were but three of the most prominent among a wider range of Jewish sectarian movements attested sporadically in his work and in other ancient Jewish texts. For a similar assessment, see Goodman (2000a). On the earliest Christians as a Jewish sect, see S.J.D. Cohen (2014: 165–67).

[93] So according to Bainbridge (1997: 22–23).

[94] For a comparable attempt at definition specific to the ancient Jewish context, see Baumgarten (1997: 5–9), who describes the sectarian modus operandi as one of subordinate group definition within the wider Jewish collective.

[95] For the following, see Blenkinsopp (2009: 189–227), and cf. M. Smith (1971: 99–147); Hanson (1979: 209–79).

[96] On the social dynamics of Yehud's population, see Weinberg (1992: 62–74), who argues for the development of the terminology of *am ha-aretz* from one of internal to external group demarcation between the sixth and fourth centuries BCE. See also Weinfeld (2005a) on the origins of the opposite language of "exilic" self-definition and its persistence in later sectarian modes of Jewish identification.

[97] I refer to the authors of the prophecies recorded in such texts as Isaiah 24–27 and 56–66, Haggai, Zechariah 9–14, and Malachi. On these developments, see in general Hanson (1979), and cf. Weinfeld (2005b).

Alternatively, however, one might submit that the social differentiation witnessed in Persian-era Yehud actually confirms the unity of the Jewish nation during its formative age. The prophets envisioned an Israel united in practice and in purpose. But the Achaemenid endorsement of the Torah as the de facto civil law of Yehud meant that all who agreed to abide by the Torah's legislation were to be considered Jews.[98] That, in turn, relieved the prophets of the prerogative to distinguish good Jews from bad. They therefore reset the terms of their traditional theological critique to imagine an eschatological scenario wherein only those Jews who had proven themselves exceptionally devoted to Yahweh would be counted among the true nation of Israel. But the conceits of the prophets did not necessarily reflect genuine sectarian divisions within the Jewish body politic. They merely denoted the occurrence of varying degrees of religious observance within the Jewish collective.[99]

The rhetoric of social differentiation devised by the prophets of Yehud was sustained in the Hellenistic era by the obscure authors behind such noncanonical Jewish texts as 1 Enoch and Jubilees. These works might be characterized as sectarian on account of their concomitant adherence to the laws of the Torah and opposition to the Temple administration. Where Jerusalem operated on a 354-day lunar calendar, the authors of these texts advocated a 364-day solar calendar as though speaking to readers operating at variance with their nation's official cult. In practice, this meant that those Jews observed certain Jewish festivals on different dates than the majority of their fellow Jews. Notably, the same alternative calendar would be adopted by the Essenes.[100] But their expressions of defiance against the Temple cult and its leadership did not amount to their rejection of Judaism. The Torah remained central to their lives and, presumably, they continued to identify as Jews even if not quite to the same effect as those Jews who opted to defer their people's cultic establishment.[101] Nor, to our knowledge, did they deny the Jewish identities of those of their countrymen who operated beyond their social circles.[102]

---

[98] Following Blenkinsopp (2009: 46–47), I put little stock in the dubious report in Neh 10 indicating that Nehemiah enjoined all the people of Yehud to adhere to the laws of the Torah by means of a binding social contract.

[99] Compare the sober sociological account of Albertz (1994: 443–50). See also S.J.D. Cohen (2014: 135–42), who declines to identify formal sectarian divisions in Persian-era Yehud despite the manifest occurrence of ideological variety amidst its population.

[100] On calendrical disagreements between the Essenes and their sectarian rivals, see S. Stern (2010), with attention to 1 Enoch and Jubilees at ibid. (234–35).

[101] So, e.g., Nickelsburg (2003: 44–48); Stone (2011: 138–39).

[102] So Himmelfarb (2006: 80–84), on the sectarian language of Jubilees, and ibid. (118–24), on the Rule of the Community and War Scroll documents from Qumran, each of which acknowledges Jews outside their projected readership communities as members of Israel, even if sometimes ambivalently. 1 Enoch makes no such explicit compromise, although that might be attributed to the composition's pre-Israelite narrative setting. See, however, Mendels (1987: 23–24), on the geographically expansive vision of Hasmonean-era Israel articulated in 1 Enoch 85–90.

As noted, the ancient Jewish groups acknowledged as sects in their own times appear to have emerged during the early years of the Hasmonean state. Prior to Judea's movement toward political autonomy, Jews hoping to achieve popular influence had few options. The Temple priesthood, the de facto civic bosses of Judea, operated as a closed hieratic caste. Their offices guaranteed by their Zadokite lineage, the High Priests and their families dictated the norms of the Jewish cult from positions of unimpeachable authority.[103] Would-be dissenters had little recourse but to express their dissent in the manner of the solar calendar enthusiasts. That situation changed under the Hasmoneans.[104] The corruption of Antiochus IV had served to extinguish the Zadokite line, effectively vacating the office of the High Priesthood until its assumption by Jonathan the Hasmonean in 153 BCE. When in 141 BCE his successor Simon assumed the title of king, the reins of the Temple cult, the civic authority once exercised by the kings of Persia, Egypt, and Syria now rested in Jerusalem.[105] Consequently, Jews from without the priestly caste who wished to participate in the administration of their state had only to position themselves as supporters of the Hasmoneans in order to achieve their ambitions.[106]

Judging by the account of Flavius Josephus, it seems that the Pharisees, Sadducees, and Essenes first found their callings as advisors and critics of the Hasmoneans.[107] The differences between their sectarian platforms were principally what each group aimed to accomplish by way of influencing the regulation of the Temple cult. The Pharisees maintained that they possessed a tradition (Greek: *paradosis*) of interpretation pertaining to the laws of the Torah that obliged them and, theoretically, all Jews all Jews to maintain rather stringent standards of ritual purity and practice traditionally observed only by priests.[108] The

---

[103] The Zadokites, who claimed descent from the last High Priests of the Kingdom of Judah, were apparently recognized by the Achaemenids as the rightful heirs of Yehud's cultic administration. On the history of Zadokite dynasty from the Persian restoration until the Maccabean revolt, see VanderKam (2004: 43–239).

[104] I refer to the change in the aristocratic conduct of the priesthood, which apparently ceded to a more populist regime with the rise of the Hasmoneans. As to the disputed Zadokite lineage of the Hasmoneans, see Schofield and VanderKam (2005), who tentatively weigh in favor of that possibility.

[105] Note, however, the operation of an alternative Jewish cult site at Leontopolis in Egypt evidently established by Zadokite priests chased from Jerusalem during the reign of Antiochus IV. On this poorly documented but no less fascinating satellite operation, see Modrzejewski (1995: 121–33).

[106] So Baumgarten (1997: 188–95). See also the concluding remarks of Sievers (1990: 157–58).

[107] On the political activities of the earliest Pharisees and Sadducees, see Sievers (1990: 146–52), and, on later developments, McLaren (1991: 54–79), along with the overview of Stemberger (1995: 104–14). Both Sievers (ibid., 38–40), and Stemberger (ibid., 96–104), are justified to discount the fairly weak but frequently cited argument that the Essenes predated the Hasmonean era as the so-called *hasidim* (Greek: *asidaioi*) or "tremblers" said in 1 Maccabees already to have been active during the outbreak of hostilities in 167 BCE; cf. 1 Macc 7.12–18, 2.42.

[108] Josephus, *Ant.* 13.297 et al. For attestations of this concept in early Jewish and Christian texts, see Baumgarten (1987), who associates the Pharisaic *paradosis* with the tradition of

Sadducees, representing the old Zadokite guard, asserted that the letter of the law was sufficient. They therefore advocated a code of ritual conduct more relaxed than that of the Pharisees but no less beholden to the Torah. The Essenes appear to have preferred it both ways. Styling themselves as the true Zadokite priests in contradistinction to the Sadducees, many chose to withdraw from a Jewish society that they believed had been sullied by the Hasmoneans and their illegitimate Temple administration. Waiting in the wilderness for the restoration of their ideal Israel, they pursued lives of perpetual holiness exceeding even the demands of the Pharisees.[109]

Yet although the Jewish sects differed from one another with respect to their positions on how best to serve God, they agreed upon the principle that proper service of God was of paramount importance to their nation. Each, in other words, recognized the imperative of maintaining their ancestral culture per the instructions of the Torah.[110] Where they differed from one another was in their approaches to interpreting the Torah's legislation. In the cases of the Pharisees and Essenes, their interpretive strategies yielded modalities of ritualized behavior that lent their sectarian enterprises distinctive social profiles. But that did not make them any more or less Jewish than other Jews who declined those behaviors. The same can be said of what Josephus accounts as the philosophical constitutions of the sects. The Pharisees, Sadducees, and Essenes maintained different positions on the doctrines of fate, free will, and the afterlife. These were subjects of great interest among ancient Jews. But they are not expressly addressed in the Torah. Consequently, whether a given sectarian chose to affirm or to deny the validity of any one of those doctrines did not determine his Jewish credentials.

Rome's removal of the Hasmoneans in 37 BCE undermined the administrative hierarchy that had fostered the growth of the sects. In contrast, the Herodians appear to have had little interest in sectarian politics.[111] The

"oral Torah" later asserted by the rabbinic sages as the authoritative basis of the *halakhah* (cf. Baumgarten 1997: 21). Compare, however, Stemberger (1995: 88–95), for a more circumspect assessment of that association.

[109] My account of the Essenes assumes a certain kinship between that sect and the Qumran community, the authors of the Dead Sea Scrolls. For methodological considerations supporting this commonplace identification, see VanderKam (2010: 97–125), and, more briefly, Stemberger (1995: 124–30). Compare, however, Collins (2009: 122–56), for a compelling argument to identify the Qumran sectarians as a splinter group indebted to the Essenes yet sufficiently distinct from its parent sect not to qualify as Essenes themselves. Without evaluating either of these positions here, I should state that the interpretive issues at stake in the debate over the Essenic affinities of the Qumran group are immaterial to my argument.

[110] For the following, see Baumgarten (1997: 55–58), and, more extensively, Klawans (2012: 137–79). Klawans (ibid., 14–17) notes the tendency of scholars to overemphasize the differences between the Pharisees and Sadducees over matters of legal exegesis, a negative stereotype reinforced by later Jewish and Christian portraits of those sects and regrettably extended to the Essenes since the publication of legal texts from Qumran.

[111] Note, however, the exceptions during the reign of Herod's grandson Agrippa I (r. 41–44 CE), a man of partial Hasmonean descent recalled in later Jewish and Christian traditions as having

Pharisees and Sadducees thus assumed new roles as mediators of influence between the Temple priests and the Jewish masses, now aiming to affect local politics from below.[112] In time, however, the failures of the old sects to change in Judea's rapidly constricting social order yielded the more volatile ideology that Josephus would derisively call the fourth philosophy.[113] Convinced that the Romans and their Herodian clients had tarnished their land and their cult, various rebel factions converged by the middle of the first century CE to instigate the first Jewish revolt. The ultimate failure of their offensive makes it impossible to say precisely what its leadership aimed to achieve beyond expelling the Romans. Consequently, precisely how the sectarian ideologies of the Pharisees, Sadducees, and Essenes contributed to the outburst of nationalistic fervor is unclear. Nevertheless, that members of those groups threw in their lots with the rebels suggests that they were not as alienated from the rest of their countrymen as their sectarian affiliations might suggest.[114]

Although some individual Jewish sectarians survived the war, their sectarian platforms did not fare as well.[115] With no Temple cult to support or to protest, their calls for its regulation and reform were silenced. Moreover, the added pressure exerted by Rome's military occupation presumably made it difficult for would-be sectarians to operate in public.[116] Evidently, only the Pharisees seem to have been prepared to endure the loss of the Temple with some semblance of their sectarian ideology intact. Unlike the Sadducees, the Pharisees had trained themselves to serve God both at and away from his Temple. And unlike the Essenes, the Pharisees had trained themselves to live their lives interspersed among their fellow Jews. Those qualities of their discipline allowed the surviving Pharisees who regrouped at Yavneh to embark upon the new sectarian venture that would evolve into the rabbinic movement.

---

entertained the political designs of persons variously aligned with the High Priest and against the Jerusalem Church. On these texts and their possible indications of Agrippa's sectarian allegiances, see D.R. Schwartz (1990: 116–30).

[112] For the following, see Saldarini (1988), especially ibid. (277–308), for a historical synthesis emphasizing the diminished intermediary roles of the Pharisees and Sadducees under the Herodian kings.

[113] See Josephus, *Ant.* 18.23. As noted by Klawans (2012: 163–65), Josephus' description of the rebel factions as adherents to a distinct "fourth" philosophy did not preclude his inclusion in that column of affiliates of the other sects.

[114] On sectarian politicking as a factor in the breakdown of Jewish social relations during the early first century, see Goodman (1987: 76–108). On corresponding bellicose rhetoric among the Qumran sectarians, see Eshel (2008).

[115] For the following, compare Goodman (2009) (cf. Goodman 2007: 424–28), who focuses on rabbinic literary evidences for the persistence of sectarian behaviors after the war, and, further, Magness (2012) on archeological finds ostensibly speaking to the same phenomenon.

[116] On the exacerbation of Rome's military presence after the fall of Jerusalem, see Magness (2002), especially ibid. (189–91), on the police activities in the Judean desert that culminated in the siege of Masada in 73 CE. On the significance of the desert as a site of popular resistance in the years preceding the war, see D.R. Schwartz (1992b).

Although most of our information on the Yavnean sages comes from relatively late rabbinic texts, it seems as though one of their key priorities was to distance themselves from their sectarian pasts.[117] The earliest *Tannaim* maintained a good deal of the practices and beliefs once credited to the Pharisees while envisioning a somewhat more open means of access to their intellectual discipline. Acknowledging the variety of thought and practice among their fellow Jews, these self-styled rabbis opted to forgo the sectarian pretenses of their predecessors in favor of a more permissive stance toward Torah observance, if only within what they deemed reasonable limits of their received interpretive tradition.[118] Henceforth, what they called the *halakhah* would be typified by an ever-shifting balance of tradition and innovation that they believed could accommodate all Jews who wished to live by their ancestral laws.[119]

Nevertheless, the revised agenda of the rabbinic sages was still fairly sectarian in character.[120] What the rabbis knew as the Jewish people was not the same as what they preferred to know as Israel. So, for instance, did they mar as *minim* those Jews who professed to live by the values of the Hebrew Scriptures but chose to interpret them in ways potentially threatening to the rabbinic enterprise.[121] Likewise, later *Tannaim* would revive

[117] For the following, see S.J.D. Cohen (1984), although cf. Stemberger (1995: 140–47), for a more cautious assessment of the sectarian ideology of the Pharisees and its translation into the organizational platform of the nascent rabbinic movement.

[118] S.J.D. Cohen (1984: 36–42).

[119] S.J.D. Cohen (1984: 47–50). Daniel Boyarin has taken issue with Cohen's account of the Yavnean sages. In his estimation, Cohen's image of the Yavnean sages as an egalitarian coalition is a fairly late Babylonian fiction meant to obscure the efforts of the early Palestinian sages who, in his estimation, devised the Mishnah as a proto-orthodox *halakhah* allowing for minimal difference of opinion within the Jewish collective; see Boyarin (2004: 44–45, 155–57). Boyarin is certainly mistaken here. Although the Babylonian sages doubtless embellished their distant memories of the Yavneh tradition, they did not fabricate that tradition whole cloth. Some (if not all) of the sources supporting the historicity of Cohen's account of the Yavneh assembly are Tannaitic and long predate the Babylonian Talmud. Furthermore, the multiplicity of halakhic opinions preserved in the Mishnah, the Tosefta, the Tannaitic *midrashim*, to say nothing of earlier Amoraic texts, counters Boyarin's assertion that the Babylonian sages in their own commitment to exegetical indeterminacy rejected a prior rabbinic intellectual tradition defined by uniformity. That the same type of polysemy exhibited in the Babylonian Talmud was a constant feature of classical rabbinic textual production is shown by Fraade (2007), especially ibid. (37–40), commenting on Boyarin's tendentious methodological assumptions. Although Fraade's insights do not speak directly to the reliability of Cohen's portrait of the Yavnean sages, they do problematize Boyarin's objection to Cohen to persuasive effect.

[120] For the following critique, see Goodman (2009).

[121] S.J.D. Cohen (1984: 41–42). I leave aside for the moment the related Tannaitic constructions of the Sadducee (*tzadoqi*), a caricature of the historical Sadducee, and the Epicurean (*apiqoros*), a Jew implicitly given to Greek philosophy. Although Tannaitic texts reveal little about whom the early rabbis thought these people were (or, in the case of the Sadducee, if they actually were), they function in those texts as analogues to the *minim*, i.e., as Torah-reading Jews at odds with the sages over their approaches to scriptural interpretation. For like observations, see Hayes (2007: 259).

the Persian-era construction of the *am ha-aretz* to demean those Jews who declined to observe the purity laws of the *halakhah* or to pay tithes to their now unemployed priests.[122] These novel rabbinic taxonomies speak to continued divergences in thought and practice amidst the Palestinian Jewish society in which the rabbis operated. Hence, where sectarianism subsided, variety persisted.[123] Even as the sages of subsequent generations cultivated their *halakhah*, the Jews on the whole possessed no formal regulatory agency whereby to measure one's sense of Jewish identity against another's. Such comparisons doubtless were attempted. The ongoing efforts of the rabbis to assert their unique views amidst their fellow Jews attest to that.[124] Yet it is no less clear that the bonds of tradition precluded them from denying others their rights to be Jews.

That conceptions of Jewish identity varied in antiquity is beyond question. But the resulting diversity of opinions must not be mistaken for a lack of control.[125] Those Jews who chose to express their Jewish identities generally presumed to do so with reference to a common set of practical and theoretical objectives rooted in the Torah.[126] Divergences in their pursuits of those objectives prompted some Jews to imagine that they belonged to an idealized nation of Israel more exclusive than that which they knew in real life. The emergence of formally organized sects offered opportunities for those Jews disposed to profess such conceits to realize their perceived differences by adopting unique modes of behavior. Yet even as those sectarians disagreed with other Jews on certain points of practice and belief, they generally agreed with one another on the imperative to maintain the religious and ethnic commitments of their ancestors. Even, therefore, when those commitments were put to the test by strife from within and from without the Jewish collective, they remained integral to the formula for cultural identification traditionally understood to define that collective.

---

[122] S.J.D. Cohen (1999b: 959–61). On the perceived ritual failings of the Tannaitic *am ha-aretz*, see Hayes (2007: 260–61).

[123] So Goodman (2009: 212–13). Cf. S.J.D. Cohen (1984: 50–51), who sees the dearth of evidence for Jewish sectarianism after 70 CE as an indication of a popular movement toward social homogenization akin to that devised by the rabbis.

[124] On this long-standing rabbinic discourse, see S. Stern (1994: 87–138), especially ibid. (127–35), on the conceptual distances and commonalities between the real variegated Israel and the utopian rabbinic Israel, and cf. Harvey (1996: 257–66). Related but less germane to my investigation is the effort of Peter Tomson to differentiate the terms "Jew" and "Israel" as alternating external and internal modes of group identification; see Tomson (1986). For a recent critique of Tomson's approach, see Thiel (2014: 85–91).

[125] For the following, compare S. Schwartz (2001: 91–98).

[126] Note that the Temple remained an object of identification even in its ruined state among those Jews who dreamt of its restoration. On the rebuilding of the Temple as a casus belli of Bar Kokhba, see Goodman (2007: 467–68). On the lingering memories of the Temple, its physical space, and its bygone cult in rabbinic thought, see, e.g., Eliav (2005: 189–236); Mandel (2006a); Fraade (2009: 246–56); Cohn (2013: 119–22) and passim.

AN INDEX CASE: THE CONSTRUCTION OF JUDAISM IN 2
MACCABEES

To this point, I have probed the ancient concept of Jewish identity from the detached standpoint of a modern observer. Before concluding my treatment of this subject, I would like to offer a test case representing a more authentic perspective. The book of 2 Maccabees is part of the Apocrypha, a collection of ancient Jewish texts not considered sacred in the Jewish tradition but included in the early Christian biblical canons.[127] 2 Maccabees deals primarily with the disturbances in Jerusalem in the year 167 BCE, its romantic narrative plotted around the actions of the villainous King Antiochus and the valiant Judah the Maccabee. In relating the details of the Seleucid persecution, the author offers a snapshot of what he accounts as the Judaism (Greek: *ioudaismos*) of Judah and his supporters, that is, the ideology that impelled their revolt against the imperious policies of the Greek king. Consideration of his construction of Judaism will offer instructive data as to what the author of 2 Maccabees meant to convey to his readers by means of that novel cultural abstraction.

Written in Greek, 2 Maccabees assumes the form of a narrative attached to a letter dated to 143/142 BCE (2 Macc 1.7). That letter is attached to another letter dated to 125/124 BCE (2 Macc 1.10). Said to have originated in the Hasmonean court of Jerusalem, the letters are addressed to the Jewish community of Ptolemaic Alexandria. They enjoin the Alexandrian Jews to observe the festival of Hanukkah, recently established by the Hasmoneans to commemorate their reestablishment of the Temple cult in 164 BCE (cf. 2 Macc 10.1–8). The attached history of the persecution and the ensuing Jewish revolt is described by its anonymous author as an epitome of a five-volume work by one Jason of Cyrene (2 Macc 2.23). It is impossible to ascertain where the words of Jason ends and those of the epitomizer begins. Nor is it clear whether the epitome was produced in conjunction with either of the two surviving letters or, conversely, the letters were attached to the epitome by its author or by a later editor. Consequently, we do not know precisely when, where, or by whom 2 Maccabees was written.[128]

What is clear enough, however, is that the book was meant to function as a voice of support for the Jewish cult during the early years of the Hasmonean administration.[129] Beyond its overt appeal for the celebration of Hanukkah

---

[127] For a critical overview of 2 Maccabees supporting the following assessment of its history and design, see van Henten (2011). Of great value are the recent critical commentaries of D.R. Schwartz (2008) and Doran (2012).

[128] Van Henten (2011: 16–17), acknowledging its favorable impression of Rome, dates 2 Maccabees to between 125/124 and 63 BCE and locates its author's perspective in Jerusalem. Compare, however, D.R. Schwartz (2008: 11–15), who dates the book to between 161 and 143/142 BCE and locates its author's perspective in the Egyptian Diaspora, the putative home of Jason of Cyrene (ibid., 43–56). For an evenhanded discussion of the interpretative dilemmas at issue in determining the precise provenance of the book, see Doran (2012: 14–17).

[129] For the following, compare D.R. Schwartz (2008: 6–10); van Henten (2011: 11); Doran (2012: 13–14).

in the Egyptian Diaspora, the author of 2 Maccabees is fairly transparent in his effort to bolster the cultic governance of Judah's successors. The author seems to know that the Hasmoneans were not rightful heirs of the priestly offices vacated by the Zadokites.[130] He therefore attempts to besmirch Jason the Oniad, the last Zadokite High Priest, by suggested that he surrendered his right to the office by colluding with Jewish parties in Jerusalem allegedly given to "the Greek way of life" (*ton hellēnikon*; 2 Macc 4.10) to the detriment of "the divine laws" of Jason's sacerdotal order (*toi theioi nomoi*; 2 Macc 4.17). Discrediting Jason as "impious and no true High Priest" (*asebous kai ouk archiereōs*; 2 Macc 4.13), the author proceeds to juxtapose his scandalous downfall with the ascent of Judah and his righteous brothers to the fore of Judea's popular front. Their subsequent efforts to restore the Temple cult and other of their ancestral customs outlawed by the Seleucids thereby make the Hasmoneans seem justified in assuming Jason's former office.

Though writing in a Hellenized idiom, the author of 2 Maccabees knew where the customs of the Greeks overstepped the boundaries of what he calls "the ancestral laws" of the Jews (*toi patrioi nomoi*; 2 Macc 6.1 et al.). And while those boundaries never were quite as clear as he seems to suggest, he aptly describes what lay on one side as Judaism (*ioudaismos*; 2 Macc 2.21, 8.1, 14.38) and on the other as Hellenism (*hellēnismos*; 2 Macc 4.13).[131] Neither of these abstruse neologisms clearly explains its intended object of reference. To infer, therefore, an adversarial relationship between the two would be misleading.[132] But the author of 2 Maccabees surely means to imply some measure of difference in setting each of his novel "-isms" in relief against the other. Simply on the basis of his verbiage, one may reasonably conclude that his "Judaism" was meant to indicate typically Jewish ways and his "Hellenism" typically Greek ways. Only, in the author's estimation, when the Jewish people's

---

[130] D.R. Schwartz (2008: 12–13), and Doran (2012: 36–37), are correct to dismiss the likelihood that the author patronized the Zadokite-staffed temple at Leontopolis, at least not to the extent of rejecting the cultic services performed at the Hasmonean-staffed Jerusalem Temple.

[131] The resonance of the author's *ioudaismos* with the contemporary term "Judaism" has yielded much critical debate about his intended object of reference. For philological comments supporting the following interpretation, see Himmelfarb (1998); D.R. Schwartz (2008: 170, 224; 2014: 105–12); Doran (2012: 67–68, 105–06). Compare, however, Mason (2007: 468), who, asserting its exclusively ethnic object of reference, rather tenuously describes 2 Maccabees' *ioudaismos* as an "ironic counter-measure" to the term of *hellēnismos*, generally understood in the classical world to connote only the adoption of the Greek language by non-Greek persons. I am not persuaded by Honigman (2014: 120–21), who follows Mason in proposing to read the author's contrast between Judaism and Hellenism as a statement of his ethnic priorities as opposed to his religious priorities.

[132] So, e.g., Gruen (1998: 3–4); S.J.D. Cohen (1999a: 105–06); Collins (2001: 39–40); D.R. Schwartz (2008: 66). This position counters previous scholarship asserting a fundamental conflict of interests between Judaism and Hellenism owing to the insular religious sensibilities of the Jews. For variations of this argument, see, e.g., Tcherikover (1959: 193–201); Hengel (1974: 1.303–309); Bickerman (1979: 76–92).

adoption of Greek ways threatened to disrupt their traditional Jewish ways did the two become incompatible.[133]

Let us now consider what the author of 2 Maccabees chose to characterize as the more distinctive and sacrosanct elements of Judaism. The author marks two stages in the Seleucid affront, one preceding Antiochus' edict and one following it. The first stage begins with Jason's forceful seizure of the office of the High Priest from his brother Onias III around 175 BCE. Following that transfer of power, Jason is sanctioned by Antiochus to build a gymnasium in Jerusalem, a facility for training would-be Seleucid civil servants in the Greek ways that they would need to function as such (2 Macc 4.9).[134] Ignoring the civic freedoms granted by previous Seleucid kings, Jason lures young priests away from their cultic duties at the Temple, inviting them to dress like Greeks and to test their mettle in athletic competitions (2 Macc 4.12–15). All the while, Jason continually extorts funds from the Temple treasury to pay his bribes to Antiochus as well as for other expenditures unbecoming of his sacred office (2 Macc 4.18–22). These offenses continue unabated when Jason is ousted by the equally odious priestly pretender Menelaus around 172 BCE (2 Macc 4.23–50).

These, then, are the violations of the "ancestral values" that precipitated the edict of Antiochus (*patrōous timas*; 2 Macc 4.15). The next stage arrives in 167 BCE. The rivalry between Jason and Menelaus has provoked an armed standoff between their supporters, a conflict setting priest against priest and Jew against Jew (2 Macc 5.5–6). The civil row erupts at an inopportune time. Having recently aborted an invasion of Egypt under the threat of Roman reprisal, Antiochus is heading north when he learns of the disturbance in Jerusalem. Incensed and in need of funds to pay his restless troops, the king takes a detour to Judea. There, he routs Jason's supporters and allows his soldiers to ransack Jerusalem (2 Macc 5.11–14). With the aid of his loyal client Menelaus, Antiochus enters the Temple and strips it of its valuables (2 Macc 5.15–16, 21).[135] Finally, after leaving the battered city, he dispatches a unit of bloodthirsty soldiers who promptly violate the sanctity of the Jewish Sabbath (2 Macc 5.22–26).[136]

---

[133] For this crucial qualification, see Collins (2001: 41–42), and cf. Himmelfarb (1998: 38); Doran (2011: 432–33).

[134] I here follow the critical consensus characterizing Jason's appeal to the king as an effort to win for Jerusalem the formal status of a colony of the Seleucid mother city of Antioch, an effort for which the establishment of a Greek gymnasium would have been essential; see, e.g., D.R. Schwartz (2008: 530–32); Doran (2012: 101–02).

[135] The Temple is a recurring subject of apprehension throughout the book, its sanctity continually under threat before, during, and after the reign of Antiochus (cf. 2 Macc 3.1–40, 14.28–33, et al.). On the cultic rhetoric of these and other notices of the Temple throughout the book, see Doran (1981), especially ibid. (47–76), and, more recently, Zsengellér (2007: 183–87). Compare, however, D.R. Schwartz (2008: 46–48), who downplays the centrality of the book's Temple rhetoric in view of what he characterizes as its Diasporan perspective.

[136] The violation of the Sabbath by uncaring Seleucid parties is another of the book's recurring themes (2 Macc 6.11, 15.1–5), as is its observance by the Jewish rebels (2 Macc 8.26–28, 12.38). On the contrasting rhetorical functions of these tropes, see Doering (1999: 561–62).

As the situation in Jerusalem continues to deteriorate, Antiochus unexpectedly issues a proclamation compelling the Jews to change "the ancestral laws" (*tōn patriōn nomōn*) and no longer to live by "the divine laws" (*tois tou theou nomois*; 2 Macc 6.1). In short time, Jerusalem's Temple precinct is seized by the Seleucid soldiers and contaminated by their strange and depraved rituals (2 Macc 6.2–5).[137] As a result, devout Jews can no longer offer their regular sacrifices to Yahweh nor even "confess themselves to be Jews" (*haplōs ioudaion homologein einai*; 2 Macc 6.6). The Jews are forced to enroll in the cult of Antiochus' beloved deity Dionysius (2 Macc 6.7).[138] Circumcision is outlawed (2 Macc 6.10). Sabbath observance is forbidden (2 Macc 6.11). Jews are forced to eat pork cut from unlawful heathen sacrifices (2 Macc 6.18–20, 7.1). Those who refuse "to change to the Greek ways" are threatened with execution (*metabainein epi ta hellēnika*; 2 Macc 6.8–9). These violent reforms are to remain in effect until Antiochus' sudden death in 164 BCE.[139] In the interim, they elicit noble acts of passive resistance among those principled Jews who dare to refuse the king's orders (2 Macc 6.18–7.42) and, in time, the proactive insurrectionary efforts of Judah the Maccabee and his supporters (2 Macc 5.27, 8.1ff.).

Among the many "ancestral" and "divine" laws said to have been breached over the course of the events in question we may discern what the author perceived as two orders of inviolability. The first order of laws, violated prior to Antiochus' edict, includes the preservation of the Temple's sacrificial liturgies, support for the Temple's civic treasury, and training of priests for cultic service.[140] Committed by Jews, these offenses are not egregious enough to incite significant popular remonstration. As long as some dedicated priests remained at their posts in the Temple, the questionable pursuits of Jason and his company do not pose a dire threat to the welfare of the Jewish nation as a whole.[141] But the outbreak of hostilities between Jason and Menelaus, the author asserts,

---

[137] Here the author seems to confuse the cultic rites of the Syrian soldiers stationed in Jerusalem for the Greek rites of their Seleucid employers. See Bickerman (1979: 73–75); D.R. Schwartz (2008: 276–77).

[138] Note the recurrence of this motif in 2 Macc 14.33, where Nicanor threatens to raze the Jerusalem Temple and replace it with a shrine to Dionysius.

[139] Although the author of 2 Maccabees is likely correct to associate the repeal of the persecution with the death of Antiochus IV, his sardonic account of the king's deathbed policy reversal (2 Macc 9.13–27) seems contrived on the basis of the rescript of his successor Antiochus V recorded out of proper sequence later in the book (2 Macc 11.22–26). On the questionable historicity of the former episode, see D.R. Schwartz (2008: 351–52).

[140] According to the parallel account of 1 Maccabees, the latter offense might have been a matter of modesty. Students at the Greek gymnasium routinely exercised naked and in public, a habit that allegedly prompted some of its Jewish patrons to grow ashamed of their circumcisions in the company of uncircumcised gentiles (cf. 1 Macc 1.14–15). See Doran (1990: 106–08).

[141] The author tries to obscure this fact by ending his account of Jason's civic reforms with an ominous warning of the "heavy disaster" to befall him in times to come (2 Macc 4.16–17); on this technique see D.R. Schwartz (2008: 64–65); Doran (2012: 107).

provoked God to retaliate against all of his people at once (2 Macc 5.17–20, 6.12–17). Hence, the laws targeted by Antiochus are of a higher order of sanctity than those flouted by the crooked priests, their neglect liable to threaten the entire Jewish nation. The king bids his Jewish subjects, that is, all of his Jewish subjects, to forsake their divine ordinances against idolatry, tolerating the practice of idolatry in their land, eating food sacrificed to idols, and eating pork.[142] He challenges them to forsake their cultic regulations concerning circumcision, Sabbath observance, and the public sacrifices ordained by God to be offered by their Temple priests daily, weekly, monthly, and during seasonal festivals.[143] Consequently, the author suggests, where the policies of Jason and Menelaus challenged the sensibilities of some Jews, the policies of Antiochus challenged the sensibilities of all Jews by disrupting the cultic economy traditionally thought to maintain God's covenant with Israel.

Although we must not assume that the author of 2 Maccabees spoke for all ancient Jews, his account of those who withstood the Seleucid persecution is telling of a more widely recognized set of cultural assumptions. His appeal to conventional wisdom is underscored by his assumption that the "Judaism" defended by the heroes of his story would be intelligible to readers both in Judea and in the Diaspora.[144] That he alternatively describes the laws underlying the values of those heroes as "ancestral" and "divine" neatly encapsulates his sense of the inseparable ethnic and religious qualities of the cultural model to which he refers.[145] To the author's mind, the exceptional courage of those individuals who adhered to their laws helped sustain their people for the duration of the Seleucid persecution.[146] That explains the author's valorous portraits of the Jewish martyrs who tragically surrender their lives in defense of their ancestral laws. It explains his portrayal of Judah the Maccabee as a champion not only of God and his holy Temple but, moreover, of the entire Jewish nation.[147]

---

[142] Foreign deities: Exod 20.3–6, 23.13, 32–33, Deut 5.8–10, 12.29–31; idolatry in the Land of Israel: Exod 34.11–16, Deut 7.16, 12.2–4; food sacrificed to idols: Exod 34.15–16; pork: Lev 11.7, Deut 14.8.

[143] Circumcision: Gen 17.9–14, Lev 12.3; Sabbath: Exod 20.8–11, 23.12, 31.12–17, 34.21, 35.2–3, Lev 23.3, Deut 5.12–15; daily sacrifices: Exod 29.38–42, Num 28.2–8; weekly sacrifices: Num 28.9–10; monthly sacrifices: Num 28.11–15; festival sacrifices: Exod 23.14–17, 29.38–42, Lev 16.1–34, 23.3–43, Num 28.16–29.39, Deut 16.1–7.

[144] For the following, see Collins (2000: 78–83). D.R. Schwartz (2008: 46–47), is especially assertive on this point in view of his estimation of the Diasporan provenance of the book's main narrative.

[145] For a similar assessment, see Osterloh (2008: 27–31), on the apparent lack of distinction between the various types of Jewish law cited throughout the book, and cf. D.R. Schwartz (2014: 111–12).

[146] So van Henten (2011: 21–22); D.R. Schwartz (2008: 50).

[147] Note that the author prefers the demonym Jew/Jews (i.e., ioudaios/ioudaioi), which appears sixty-one times in the main narrative (2 Macc 3.1–15.37), to Israel and Hebrews, which appear three times apiece. This usage is consistent with what Goodblatt calls an uptick in "Judah

According to Cohen, 2 Maccabees is the first known Jewish text to use the term Jew in its conventional religious sense inasmuch as the author depicts the Jews as a nation bound by a fixed order of ritual legislation.[148] It seems to me, however, that the author's account of that order merely gave a new name to an old idea no less religious than ethnic in its constitution.[149] Of course, the assortment of Pentateuchal statutes reportedly targeted by Antiochus' agents did not categorically define the Jewish identities of those who suffered under the king's decree. But they did constitute a firm dividing line between the "Judaism" that the author sought to communicate to his readers and the sense of Greek "otherness" occasioned by the persecution (*allophylismos*; 2 Macc 4.13). Here, I contend, is where the Judaism of 2 Maccabees might reasonably be cited as an index of the ancient idea of Jewish identity. If one is to imagine the other as a mirror of the self, one need only reverse the author's gaze in order to reveal the sense of Jewish otherness embedded in his work. From the standpoint of the Seleucid administration, the Jews were the ones who were different. They were the ones who chose to worship a singular, invisible God rather than the gods of the Olympian pantheon. They were the ones who chose to mark themselves as different through their peculiar rites of circumcision, Sabbath observance, and dietary restraint. These practices were routinely ridiculed by the gentiles as hallmarks of the Jews' peculiar superstition.[150] And no wonder. These were the outward expressions of an ancestral culture that distinguished the Jews from the countless other Hellenized peoples who populated the classical world. These, therefore, were the aspects of their culture that functioned most prominently as measures of their Jewish identities.[151]

nationalism" during the Hasmonean age; see Goodblatt (2006: 144–48). See also Goodblatt (2012: 22–23), where he accounts the prevalence of "Jew" over "Israel" in 2 Maccabees as a reflection of Judea's newly realized political momentum as a semi-autonomous nation-state.

[148] S.J.D. Cohen (1999a: 89–93).

[149] On this point, see Honigman (2014: 141–45), who demonstrates the general consistency of the author's construction of *ioudaismos* with the socio-cultural order prevalent in Judea since the Persian era.

[150] So said many of the ancient Greek and Roman authors who commented on the Jews and their cult. For alternating perspectives on the context of this critique, see Feldman (1993: 149–70), who sees Greek and Roman expressions of negativity toward Jews as a symptom of intellectual prejudice, and cf. Schäfer (1997: 34–105), who sees such expressions as xenophobic.

[151] I leave aside here the presumably frequent, though poorly documented, occurrence of apostasy or voluntary neglect of the Torah among native Jews, a subject to which I shall return in Chapter 4. For now, note that the first-century Alexandrian Jewish philosopher Philo famously criticized those of his countrymen who, in his estimation, wrongly neglected some of the Torah's practical teachings in favor of strictly allegorical readings of the type later to be professed by Christian exegetes; see Philo, *Migr.* 89–93. The offended laws enumerated by Philo are participation in the Temple cult, Sabbath and festival observance, and circumcision. While Philo does not characterize those forgoing these laws as apostates, his comments are well in line with his generally deprecating view of those who seemed to have relinquished their ties to the Jewish community in order to pass as Greeks. See Wilson (2004b: 36–43), with attention to this passage, ibid. (39).

As noted, the destruction of the Jerusalem Temple in 70 CE and the suspension of its sacrificial rites would force a dramatic conceptual reevaluation of that institution's role in the Jewish cultic economy. But those Jews who elected to continue expressing their Jewish identities in the wake of that disaster remained fixed on the Torah. That the rabbinic sages and their followers continued to live by its laws hardly requires demonstration. By their own accounts, many Jews outside their discipleship circles did as well, even if not always in accord with the *halakhah*. As for those laws cited in 2 Maccabees as uniquely emblematic of Judaism, the rabbis naturally counted circumcision, Sabbath observance, and dietary restriction (Hebrew: *kashrut*) among those rites that distinguished Israel from the nations.[152] Indeed, those practices continue to play important roles in defining the idea of Jewish identity both within and without the Jewish collective to this very day.

Again, the Judaism of 2 Maccabees must not be mistaken as an archetype of the Judaism of the rabbis or any subsequent Jewish person or party. But the cultural model represented by that term is no less recognizably Jewish today than in its author's age.[153] Apropos is the invocation of the classical Hebrew prayer *Al ha-Nisim* ("On the Miracles"), traditionally recited during Hanukkah: "When the wicked Greek kingdom arose against them, against your nation Israel, to make them forget your Torah and to make them violate the laws of your will."[154] Long after the precise causes and effects of the Seleucid persecution faded from popular memory, the perception that it had targeted both their nation and their law has continued to resonate with the Jewish faithful. Though not without variation in expression, the bond between ethnicity and religion assumed in the very first documented expression of Judaism has remained characteristic of its discourse on identity ever since.

CONCLUSIONS

At the beginning of this chapter, I set out to define the idea of Jewish identity in antiquity. I have argued that while there was no fixed standard of practice or belief comparable, for example, to the modern phenomena of Reform,

---

[152] For examples, see S. Stern [1994: 63–65 (circumcision), 76–77 (Sabbath), 56–59 (forbidden foods), and 151–52 (foods prepared by gentiles)]. See also S.J.D. Cohen (1999a: 204–07), on the rabbinic conversion ceremony described in *b.Yevamot* 47a–b, which involved warning the potential proselyte about the difficulties of observing laws of Sabbath and *kashrut* and of the painful procedure of circumcision (presuming that the subject is male).
[153] Although evidence for the Jewish reception of 2 Maccabees is scarce, the enthusiastic first-century CE adaption today known as 4 Maccabees tellingly reiterates its prototype's *ioudaismos* at 4 Macc 4.25. For comments, see D.R. Schwartz (2008: 85–86).
[154] Although referenced in the Byzantine-era Talmudic tractate *Soferim* (20.4), the earliest surviving text of *Al ha-Nisim* appears in the liturgical order ascribed to the ninth-century Babylonian sage Amram bar Sheshna; see Goldschmidt (1971: 97–98). On the commemorative function of the prayer, see Firestone (2012: 38–40).

Orthodox, or Conservative Judaism, those ancient Jews who chose to maintain their ancestral customs generally presumed to maintain the cultic laws and national mythology inscribed upon the Torah. From that authoritative body of knowledge derived a dynamic and polyvalent cultural model conditioned by developments in the common life of the Jewish people that served to prioritize their religious and ethnic values in alternating, though never exclusive, turns. The consequent discourse of Jewish identity initiated during the Babylonian Exile grew more complex as its practitioners sustained generations of change brought about from within their collective and in response to the Persian, Greek, and Roman cultural stimuli of their surroundings.

But the resulting variances in Jewish practice and thought were effects not of deviance from an established doctrine. The only religious rule deemed authoritative across the wide expanses of time and space was that of the Torah. Customs and beliefs exceeding the Torah's express cultic regulations were not universally considered binding. To be a Jew in antiquity thus meant to reserve for one's self a certain freedom in applying the ritual ordinances of the Torah to one's everyday life. In practice, this meant general agreement over the basics of Jewish observance, including laws such as circumcision, Sabbath observance, *kashrut*, and, until 70 CE, patronage of the Temple cult, even if allowing for disagreement over precisely how to observe those laws in view of one's own abilities and intellectual proclivities.

That, in short, is the metanarrative to inform my account of the Christian schism in the chapters to follow. The popular discourse on Jewish identity that faced those early followers of Jesus alternatively given and opposed to its cultural assumptions was negotiable, although only within certain limitations fixed by tradition. Some, I shall show, presumed to respect those limits where others opted to defy them. Their resulting divergences of opinion with respect to the formative idea of Christian identity will be the keys to understanding why those Christians whom the early rabbinic sages preferred to know as *minim* opted to maintain their Jewish identities even as the greater part of the Church grew detached from its Jewish roots.

3

Early Christian Negotiations with Jewish Identity

Having now established my field of inquiry, my next task is to assess how early followers of Jesus responded to the idea of Jewish identity. In this chapter, I will outline two major strategies of cultural negotiation whereby the first generations of Christians sought to account for the relationship between their new collective enterprise and the Jewish traditions to which they traced its origin. The first, initiated by the apostle Paul, inhibited the practice of Jewish identity among all followers of Jesus. The second, initiated by Christian parties not beholden to Paul's interpretation of the gospel, supported the practice of Jewish identity, if only among those followers of Jesus predisposed to identify as Jews. Setting each of these approaches in its proper social context will illuminate the uniquely Jewish type of Christian expression to which the early rabbinic sages applied the language of *minut*.

Inevitably, my account of these two trends in early Christian self-definition will occasion reference to the categories of "Pauline Christianity" and "Jewish Christianity" that I previously disavowed as invidious fabrications. My intent is not to rehabilitate those problematic terms. As I shall explain, I believe that all thinking Christians of the period under consideration had to entertain the alternative strategies of identification posed by Paul and by the Jewish tradition against which he defined his vision for the Church. That some chose to reject Judaism where others accepted it does not necessarily indicate that the two camps were categorically opposed to one another. I hope to show that the distance between Pauline Christians and Jewish Christians should be measured not by the disparate outcomes of their negotiations with the idea of Jewish identity but, rather, by the disparate contexts from which they proceeded.

One further terminological note is in order. In this chapter and for the remainder of the study, I shall use the term "church" with a lower-case "c" in reference to local Christian communities or congregations. I shall use the term "the Church" with the definite article and a capital "C" in reference to the broader Christian enterprise and its constituents. Although I do not wish to characterize the formative Church as unilaterally given to post-Nicene orthodoxy, I shall qualify its theology as proto-orthodox where my argument calls for a distinction between Pauline Christians and Jewish Christians within its ranks.

PAUL AND JUDAISM

Renowned as the apostle to the gentiles, Paul has been a central figure in scholarly discussion of the Christian schism since the mid-nineteenth century prime of the Tübingen School.[1] As noted in Chapter 1, F.C. Baur was the first to posit a model of the emergent conflict between Christian and Jew pivoting not on the identity of the Messiah or, in Greek, the Christ, but on the Torah and the question of its applicability in the Messianic age. Filtered through the lens of traditional Protestant theology, that observation was interpreted to denote what Martin Luther upheld as Paul's doctrine of justification by faith. In Luther's reading, Paul taught that Jesus' self-sacrifice had served as an eternal atonement for the sins of the world. In order, therefore, to achieve salvation, one need not adhere to the impossible ritual restrictions of the Torah that Paul dismissively termed the works of the law. One need only profess belief that Jesus is the Messiah and to avail one's self of his sacrifice in order to receive God's grace. To Baur and his followers, that idea was what drove Paul to depart from those of his fellow apostles who preached a gospel demanding adherence to traditional Jewish ways. Where his competitors thus maintained that Christian initiates submit to Judaism's onerous "legalistic" protocols, Paul urged only introspective conviction.[2] From this divergence in theological priorities arose the transitory conflict between Jew and gentile within the ancient Church, which was in turn to yield the enduring conflict between Christian and Jew.

Yet while Baur's basic analytical model is widely upheld today, recent critical reevaluations of Paul's letters have cast doubt on the premise of casting the apostle to the gentiles as the author of the Christian schism. During the late 1970s and early 1980s, scholars departing from the notion that Paul rejected the Jewish law as a matter of ethical protest developed a more sympathetic approach to understanding his relationship with what he describes as the "Judaism" of his life before his apostolic calling (*ioudaismos*; Gal 1.13–14).[3] Advanced most substantially by E.P. Sanders and James D.G. Dunn,

---

[1] For the following, see Zetterholm (2009: 33–40), on Baur and the Tübingen School, and ibid. (58–63), on the Lutheran grounding of its proponents' negative views of Judaism.

[2] The infamous caricature of Judaism as a religion of "legalism" originated in Weber (1880), a highly tendentious study of classical rabbinic theology casting the Jew's perceived relationship with God as an impersonal system of merits and demerits based solely on the individual's compliance with the laws of the Torah; see especially ibid. (47–48). On Weber's impact on Pauline scholarship, see E.P. Sanders (1977: 33–59); Zetterholm (2009: 63–67).

[3] What Paul calls his "earlier life in Judaism" (*tēn anastrophēn pote en tōi ioudaismōi*; Gal 1.13) need not imply that he no longer considered himself a Jew at the time he wrote to the Galatians.

the so-called "new perspective" on Paul built upon the earlier observations of Johannes Munck and Krister Stendahl that the apostle's letters, though occasionally touching on the philosophical distinction between works and faith, are more immediately concerned with the traditional Jewish distinction between Israel and the nations.[4] For even when writing to gentiles, Paul remained aware of the need to counter the expectations of those who believed that they could partake of God's covenant with Israel only by adhering to the laws of the Torah in the conventional Jewish fashion.

According to Sanders, Paul's central theological concern was the Jewish concept of covenant.[5] Having encountered other apostles preaching a thoroughly Jewish gospel, Paul's audiences were uncertain of how the gentile might achieve the same privileged covenantal status as the Jew. Where the others urged proselytism, Paul rebutted the need of gentiles to become Jews in order to be counted among the faithful when Jesus was to return to earth to deliver God's final judgment of the nations. The Torah, Paul asserted, had been given to the Jews to keep them in line until the arrival of the Messiah. Now that he had arrived, its laws had been abrogated, their regulatory bonds broken by the expiatory sacrifice of God's anointed agent of salvation. Henceforth, Paul argued, Jew and gentile alike were to uphold the supposedly more accessible moral covenant of Jesus, a mature covenant unencumbered by the liabilities of Israel's sinful past. Accordingly, Paul's objective was not to reject Judaism but to reinvent it for the benefit of those unable to commit to Jewish ways of life and thereby to impede the imminent second coming of the Messiah.

Seen through this interpretive lens, Paul's cutting remarks on Jews and Judaism reveal a surprisingly sensitive side. Where conventional wisdom knows Paul as a catalyst of the Church's departure from its Jewish past, the new perspective casts him as a theological innovator within his native Jewish milieu. His aim, accordingly, was not to convince Jews to desist from Judaism but to convince gentiles of their potential to achieve soteriological parity with Jews. In Sanders' view, Paul devised a new religion distinct from Judaism with respect to its apparatus of participation.[6] Where Jews of his day typically believed that obedience to the Torah was the only way to maintain God's favor, Paul argued

He seems, rather, to suggest that his former pursuits, including his persecution of the Church, were no longer suited to his current agenda. For like comments, see Wilson (2004a: 162). Mason (2007: 469–70), contends that Paul refers to his own past "Judaizing," i.e., forcing followers of Jesus to behave like Judeans, now trying to dissuade the Galatians from doing the same.

[4] The term "new perspective" was coined by Dunn (1983) in reference E.P. Sanders (1977); see especially Dunn, ibid. (97–103). Both scholars were indebted to the groundbreaking critical essay of Stendahl (1963) (reprinted in Stendahl 1976: 78–96), who in turn was influenced by Munck (1959).

[5] I refer to Sanders' aforementioned account of Judaism's logic of "covenantal nomism," articulated in E.P. Sanders (1977: 419–28). For the following, see ibid. (431–523), with reference to Paul's critique of the conventional Jewish thinking of his day at ibid. (511–18).

[6] For the following, see E.P. Sanders (1977: 543–52). Sanders developed his theory of Paul's relegation of the Torah to a status of secondary instrumentality in E.P. Sanders (1983).

that its laws were meant only for the Jewish people and only until the revolutionary death and rebirth of the Messiah had served to renew their covenantal relationship with God. In his revised theological system, neither Jew nor gentile could rely on the Torah alone as an instrument of salvation. To Paul, faith in the saving grace of Jesus Christ was the prerequisite of all who wished to win God's mercy at the end of days.

Sanders' account of Paul's challenge to conventional Jewish thinking has influenced a number of scholars to plot Christianity's emergence along similar lines. Among the first to engage his theory was Dunn, who submitted that Paul's issue with Judaism was not its method for maintaining God's covenant but its means of accessing that covenant in the first place.[7] Stressing the importance of Israel as a Jewish religious concept, Dunn argues that Paul was bothered by the attendant conceit of divine election and its intimations toward the definition of Jewish nationhood. While gentiles were welcome to become Jews, they had first to forfeit their native ethnic identities at the risk of alienating themselves from their friends and families. Paul therefore challenged the ethnocentric outlook of his Judaism by devising a less restrictive model of covenantal participation entailing no functional distinction between gentile and Jew.

I will have occasion to refer to other studies offering variations of these ideas in the pages to follow.[8] But I do not wish to delve too deeply into Paul's own beliefs here. My purpose, rather, is to gauge the effect of his words on the practice of Jewish identity among early readers of his letters. The observations of Dunn and Sanders legitimize that premise by undermining the arguments of Baur and the Tübingen School regarding Paul's determinative role in severing the Church from its Jewish roots. They also upend Heinrich Graetz's polemical counterportrait of the apostle to the gentiles as a deliberate falsifier of Judaism. The "new" Paul wished nothing more than to see his fellow Jews accept gentiles as equals even if at the cost of reevaluating some dearly held convictions about their supposed differences.

In view of these considerations, I do not assume that those early Christians who chose to live as Jews deliberately rejected Paul's apostolic authority or otherwise operated at odds with the Church's gentile demographic. I find it more plausible to infer that those so-called Jewish Christians simply did not see themselves as Paul's target audience. To that end, it will be helpful to examine those of Paul's letters that speak most directly to his critique of Judaism. In his letter to the Galatians, Paul addresses the question of whether gentile followers of Jesus need to practice the Jewish law in order to partake of God's covenant

---

[7] See Dunn (1983: 103–22), and cf. Dunn (2006: 185–97). See also the essays collected in Dunn (2008).

[8] For an overview of scholarly contributions to the "new perspective" since Sanders, see Dunn (2008: 1–97). Of special interest here are the studies of Segal (1990) and Boyarin (1994), which are among the rare scholarly offerings assaying to locate Paul's outlook amidst the prevailing Jewish intellectual trends of his age.

with Israel. In his letter to the Romans, he reframes that question to address whether any followers of Jesus are permitted to practice the Jewish law and, if so, whether it offers any soteriological advantage to the practitioner. In both letters, Paul utilizes his well-honed knowledge of traditional Jewish covenant theology to instruct his gentile addressees how not to go about winning God's mercy in what he perceived was the new eschatological age.[9]

The volume of scholarship on Paul's letters is far too abundant to review here.[10] I will therefore offer only brief analyses of those points of Paul's arguments most pertinent to my study. Throughout, I will assume the validity of the "new perspective" as outlined by Sanders and Dunn, if only as one of many legitimate interpretive strategies less serviceable to my project. Finally, I should reiterate that my interest in Paul is not to probe his mind but, rather, his words and the responses they elicited among early Christian readers. Only then shall I attempt to explain why some readers, even if they supported Paul's mission to the gentiles, evidently responded differently to his gospel than most.

THE DEMOGRAPHIC PARAMETERS OF PAUL'S MISSION

In order to determine how Paul meant his words to impact his readers, it is essential first to establish who those audiences were. Paul clearly indicates that he preached his gospel to gentiles.[11] He refers in his letters to the Galatians and the Romans to his role as the apostolic representative to the gentile churches (Rom 1.5, 13–14, 11.13, 15.16, 16.4; Gal 1.16, 2.7–9). He frequently takes issue with the tendencies of his readers toward what he calls idolatrous worship (1 Cor 6.9–11, 8.7, 10.1–14, 12.2; Gal 4.8; 1 Thess 1.9). He insists that they refrain from the rite of circumcision (Gal 5.2–12; Phil 3.2–3). In every respect, therefore, Paul indicates that his addressees were neither born Jewish nor previously integrated into their local Jewish communities as proselytes. Undoubtedly, some Jews of Paul's day learned of his gospel through contact with his gentile audiences. Among those were some fellow apostles who insisted that gentiles hoping to achieve salvation had to serve the God of Israel in the traditional Jewish fashion (cf. 2 Cor 11.4–5; Gal 1.6–9, 3.1).[12] But Paul did not need to invite his fellow Jews to join the nation of Israel. As far as his surviving writings indicate, the apostle to the gentiles pitched his gospel toward

---

[9] In focusing on Paul's comments on Judaism in Galatians and Romans, I should acknowledge his tendency elsewhere to apply typically Jewish laws and modes of legal exegesis in assessing the ethical responsibilities of his gentile audiences (e.g., Rom 13.8–10; 1 Cor 6.9–11; Gal 5.14, 19–23). On this topic, see Tomson (1990), especially ibid. (187–220), for an enlightening counterpoint to Paul's critique of the Jewish law in view of his affirmative exposition of the Pentateuchal proscriptions against idolatry in 1 Cor 8–10.

[10] For recent summaries, see Riches (2011) and Elliott (2011).

[11] For the following, see, inter alia, Munck (1959: 200–06); Stendahl (1976: 2–3); E.P. Sanders (1983: 179–90).

[12] E.P. Sanders (1983: 190–92), and, more extensively, Setzer (1994: 58–65).

those liable to take advantage of what he understood as the new covenantal order brought about by Jesus (cf. 2 Cor 3.4–6).

Reading Paul's letters in view of the "new perspective," one might get the impression that his novel ideas about God, Israel, and the Torah were not meant to undermine those traditional Jewish concepts but to provide functional alternatives more palatable to gentiles. The apostle therefore would seem to have envisioned two parallel paths to salvation, one for gentiles and the other for Jews, to be upheld on disparate covenantal grounds.[13] Were that the case, one might further suppose that those early followers of Jesus who subscribed to Paul's gospel likewise presumed his advices on the Jewish law to apply only to gentiles. Naturally, that would eliminate the need to consider Paul's role in shaping the Christian negotiation with Jewish identity. For those who understood his gospel as intended, there was no essential conflict between being a Jew and recognizing Jesus as the Messiah. Only when Christian readers lost sight of Paul's rhetorical objective did they come to see Judaism as an anathema.

But Paul's letters tell only part of the story. The seven New Testament epistles reliably ascribed to Paul, that is, Romans, 1 and 2 Corinthians, Galatians, Philippians, 1 Thessalonians, and Philemon, date to a relatively late stage in his missionary career. The book of Acts credibly depicts Paul as originally having preached his gospel to Jews. Paul himself acknowledges this phase of his ministry. Writing to his supporters in Corinth, he states, "To the Jews I became as a Jew, in order to win Jews (1 Cor 9.20; cf. 2 Cor 11.22)."[14] That is an odd choice of words for a man who elsewhere affirms his Jewish lineage and Pharisaic education (Rom 11.1; Gal 2.15; Phil 3.4–6). One therefore assumes that Paul had come to view his own Jewish identity in the past tense by the time he wrote his letters. That naturally raises questions as to the motives behind Paul's subsequent advices toward gentile followers of Jesus deliberating whether to adopt the lifestyle that he had chosen to forgo (cf. Phil 3.7–11).[15]

Unfortunately, information on Paul's earliest missionary efforts is not easy to come by. Most of his surviving letters are addressed to individuals and

[13] This has been the interpretive tack of those who prefer to read Paul's covenantal theology as one meant strictly for gentiles and of no consequence to God's prior covenant with the Jews; see, e.g., Gaston (1987); Gager (2000). Although I have learned much from these studies, I find it difficult to accept that Paul would have been so cavalier in disparaging his fellow Jews had he not meant to compare their concepts of covenant unfavorably to his own.

[14] For the following, cf. E.P. Sanders (1983: 99–100).

[15] Here I follow Segal (1990: 17–25), although I decline his account of Paul's personal stance vis-à-vis traditional Judaism as that of an apostate and convert to a new mystical Judaic religion later to be called Christianity (cf. ibid., 1–20). With Stendahl (1976: 7–9), I see Paul's departure from traditional Jewish ways as a vocation on the apostle's part to reimagine those ways for the sake of persons whom he believed needed to enter the Church as gentiles rather than as Jews. Compare, however, Rom 9.1–5, where Paul explicitly counts himself with the Jewish people amidst his all-inclusive definition of Israel. I thank Nathan Thiel for bringing this passage to my attention.

communities visited by Paul during his later missionary ventures. His final letter to the Romans addresses a community established by other apostles that Paul hoped to visit in the near future. It is therefore difficult to determine whether the values that Paul aimed to impress upon the gentile recipients of his letters speak to those that he had formerly preached to his fellow Jews.

The book of Acts is of little help here. Traditionally ascribed to the evangelist Luke, possibly an acquaintance of Paul during his later days, Acts depicts the apostle's interactions with Jews in a highly stylized manner. In city after city, Paul is shown plying his gospel in the synagogue before being shown the door by the local Jewish establishment. He then turns his attention to the Greeks, gentile associates of the Jews who repeatedly show themselves more receptive to Paul's gospel.[16] That Paul regularly initiated contact with Diaspora Jews during his journeys abroad is quite credible. But the formulaic narrative of Acts casts those Jews as vicious stereotypes, unrelenting in their antagonism toward Paul and his fellow apostles. The book's clear anti-Jewish bias suggests the perspective of an author who, unlike Paul himself, had given up on the Jewish mission. Acts therefore does not provide an especially convincing account of Paul's meetings with Jews beyond merely attesting to their occurrence.[17]

In the account of Paul's missionary career to follow, I will limit my comments to those that seem to me most useful in diagnosing Paul's positions on matters of Jewish concern in his letters to the Galatians and the Romans. As a rule, I shall privilege the autobiographical comments occasionally provided in Paul's letters over what are, at best, the secondhand witnesses in the book of Acts. Acknowledging, however, that none of these sources is entirely forthcoming about the facts at issue, I will rely on my own critical instincts to compile a synthetic account of Paul's early missionary career tailored to the needs of my investigation.[18] By necessity, my sketch will be incomplete.[19] I recognize that I will present a Paul whose relationship with his ancestral culture might seem inordinately driven by his adversarial experiences with his apostolic competitors. Nevertheless, I maintain that those experiences were of fundamental

[16] Paul is shown using this technique in Damascus (Acts 9.19–20), Salamis (Acts 13.5), Antioch-in-Pisidia (Acts 13.14–15), Iconium (Acts 14.1), Thessalonica (Acts 17.1–2), Beroea (Acts 17.10), Athens (Acts 17.16–17), and Corinth (Acts 18.4), and twice in Ephesus (Acts 18.19, 19.8). Moreover, he is shown expressly denying having used this technique in the synagogues of Jerusalem (Acts 24.12).
[17] For similar observations, see Kee (1992: 188–89, 194–95). On the failure of the Jewish mission as a presupposition in Luke-Acts, see Wilson (1995: 64–66).
[18] Much has been written about the difficulty of reconciling the portrait of Paul presented in Acts with that offered in piecemeal in his letters. See now Marguerat (2013: 23–27), with further bibliographical references in notes ad loc. My own methodology is informed by the balanced approach offered by Marguerat, ibid. (27–32).
[19] That is to say that I will not attempt to provide an account of Paul's missionary dealings with Jews. For a study of that comprehensive scope, see Hengel and Schwemer (1997), although note that the authors proceed on the assumption of general agreement between Paul's self-portrait and that provided in Acts; see ibid. (6–11).

significance in shaping the attitudes toward Jews and Judaism voiced in his letters and thereby communicated to his early Christian readers.

I shall begin by locating Paul in the time line of Jewish history presented in Chapter 2. Paul's involvement with the apostolic Church began at a time when its mission was still a decidedly Jewish initiative. Assuming that Jesus was crucified around 30 CE, it would have been shortly afterwards when some of his remaining followers regrouped in Jerusalem to carry on with his ministry under the leadership of Jesus' brother James and his disciple Peter, to whom Paul refers by his Aramaic name Cephas. At the time, Jerusalem was under the control of an unusually cohesive ruling class.[20] Representing the city's cultic establishment were the priests, led by the High Priest Joseph Caiaphas. Caiaphas, however, was subservient to the Roman governor Pontius Pilate, whose predecessor Valerius Gratus had appointed Caiaphas during a temporary vacancy of the throne ordinarily occupied by a descendant of Herod.[21] As a result, the priests in control of the Jewish cult at that time were strictly beholden to the Romans. If we are to trust the Gospel of John, the priests were also aligned with the Pharisees, a sect whose members were instrumental in bringing Jesus to the attention of Caiaphas and, ultimately, to the attention of his executor Pilate.[22] Consequently, the Church established in the wake of Jesus' crucifixion had to contend with the same hostile parties who had persecuted their revered teacher, their version of his gospel now evolved to account for the resurrection and imminent return of the Messiah rather than merely for his arrival.

It was evidently in the service of one or more of these parties that Paul was introduced to the Church. As noted, Paul was an enthusiastic young Pharisee at the time of the Church's establishment (Phil 3.5; cf. Acts 23.6, 26.5).[23] One therefore can only surmise that it was at the behest of Jewish cultic officers working in cooperation with the Pharisees that the man then known by his Hebrew name Saul was charged to apprehend fugitive followers of Jesus in Syria and return them to Jerusalem for trial (1 Cor 15.9; Gal 1.13; Phil 3.6; cf. Acts 8.1–3). According to Acts, it was on the road to Damascus that Saul the Pharisee became Paul the apostle, experiencing a vision of the risen Jesus that profoundly changed his mind

[20] For the following, cf. McLaren, (1991: 89–101), on Judea's administrative hierarchy during the recent trial of Jesus.

[21] Josephus, *Ant.* 18.35. Allusions in the New Testament to another High Priest by the name of Annas refer to Caiaphas' father-in-law Ananus, who had formerly held the position and is implied to have wielded some measure of control over his young successor (Luke 3.2; John 18.19, 22; Acts 4.6; cf. Josephus, *Ant.* 18.34).

[22] On cooperation between priests and Pharisees in the first century, Josephus, *J. W.* (2.409–17), *Life* (20–23), and cf. John (7.32, 43, 11.47, 57, 18.3), with discussion in Saldarini (1988: 101–05).

[23] On Paul's Pharisaic background, see Saldarini (1988: 134–43). Segal (1990: xi–xiii), is correct to emphasize this aspect of his persona as an important factor in his theological presuppositions. Unfortunately, Segal's anachronistic tendency to assign Paul knowledge of later rabbinic traditions detracts from his argument for the apostle's radical departure from the Jewish tradition of his upbringing.

about the Church (Acts 9.1–9).[24] It was at that juncture, Paul later asserts, that he received his divine commission to deliver to the gentiles the good news about the Messiah (1 Cor 15.8; Gal 1.15–16).

Paul states in his letter to the Galatians that he spent the next three years in Arabia before returning to his original destination of Damascus (Gal 1.17).[25] He seems to refer here to the Kingdom of the Nabateans, a Roman client state encompassing a region today comprising western Jordan, the Negev desert in southern Israel, and the northernmost reaches of Saudi Arabia. Elsewhere, Paul dates his time in this region with reference to an incident in Damascus when he claims to have been aided by a local governor in the employ of one King Aretas (2 Cor 11.32). Paul most likely refers here to the Nabatean king Aretas IV Philopatris, who reigned from approximately 9 BCE to 40 CE. The Roman occupation of Damascus early in 37 CE following a row between Aretas and the Jewish king Herod Antipas makes it unlikely that Paul would have found a Nabatean administrator residing in the city later than that date.[26] That, in turn, would date Paul's conversion to no later than 34 CE, that is, within just a few years of the establishment of the Jerusalem Church.

What Paul did in Arabia is something of a mystery. Given the developments that followed, one surmises that he spent some of his time formulating his doctrine of a new covenant for all nations. Nevertheless, Paul implies that he devoted some of his earliest missionary efforts to preaching to Jews. Adjacent to Judea and the Herodian territories of Galilee and Perea, the Nabatean kingdom was home to an Aramaic-speaking Jewish population culturally indistinguishable from that which Paul had known in Jerusalem.[27] It is therefore conceivable that Paul simply followed in the footsteps of others who had crossed the Jordan River to spread the gospel to their countrymen abroad.

In any case, it would seem that Paul spent some time away from Damascus before having to make his hairy escape. Only after his departure from that city did Paul formally introduce himself to the founders of the apostolic Church. Upon returning to Jerusalem, Paul recounts having met with Peter and James for fifteen

[24] My idiom "changed his mind" reflects the Greek term *metanoia*, typically translated as "repentance" and the only term which Paul uses to indicate a Jew's decision to call on Jesus as the Messiah; see Rom 2.4, and cf. 2 Cor 7.9–10, 12.21. With respect to Segal (1990: 20), I see no significance in the fact that Paul uses no such language to describe his own apostolic calling.

[25] In contrast, Acts refers compresses all of Paul's apostolic activities in Damascus into one continuous narrative (Acts 9.19–25). Hengel and Schwemer (1997: 106–07), plausibly infer that the author simply did not know of Paul's venture to Arabia.

[26] On the date of Paul's encounter in Damascus, see Millar (1993: 56–57). On the dispute between Herod Antipas and Aretas, see Josephus, *Ant.* 18.109–15, with discussion in Kasher (1988: 176–83).

[27] On Jewish life in first-century Arabia, see Newby (1988: 30–32), and cf. Hengel and Schwemer (1997: 112–13).

days (Gal 1.18–19).[28] His purpose at that summit would have been to persuade those men to affirm his apostolic credentials. After all, they had never met this man before, much less entertained his story of a personal encounter with Jesus. By his account, Paul wanted their blessing in advance of his upcoming venture into the predominantly Greek-speaking regions of western Syria and Cilicia in Asia Minor, today south-central Turkey (Gal 1.21).[29] Once having obtained their consent, Paul avers, he proceeded to travel northward along the Mediterranean coast, taking care to avoid contact with local churches founded by other apostles preaching a decidedly Jewish gospel (Gal 1.22).

Paul's primary site of activity during the next phase of his missionary career was the Syrian metropolis of Antioch-on-the-Orontes, home to a historic and sizable Jewish community well integrated into the city's urban landscape.[30] Paul might have chosen to initiate his gentile mission in Antioch on account of his familiarity with the city. The book of Acts reports that he had been born in the nearby Cilician city of Tarsus (Acts 9.11, 21.39, 22.23). It also relates that a church already had been established in Antioch under the aegis of the original apostolic mission, suggesting that Paul might have chosen the city to take advantage of its favorable climate for itinerant Jewish preachers (Acts 11.19–26).[31] Paul himself says little about this phase of his mission, revealing only that he spent fourteen years away from Jerusalem following his initial visit with Peter and James (Gal 2.21). It was likely during those years that Paul founded the churches addressed in his letter to the Galatians, as the province

[28] The parallel account of Paul's first encounter with the Jerusalem Church in Acts 9.26–30 depicts him as an already renowned apostle, an image at odds with Paul's own humble recollection of the event. For an attempt to reconcile the two versions, see Hengel and Schwemer (1997: 134–42).

[29] Acts 9.27 indicates that Paul first undertook his mission to the gentiles as an assistant to another apostle called Barnabas (cf. Acts 4.36 et al.). In Paul's recollection, it was Barnabas who followed his lead (Gal 2.1). In this case, the account of Acts seems more plausible than Paul's own, as it is unlikely that the leaders of the Church would have entrusted Paul, a newcomer, with the organizational prerogative he would later assume. As for Barnabas, the author of Acts recalls him as a colleague who left Paul's company at an intermediate stage of the latter's mission (cf. Acts 15.36–41). I shall therefore refer to the gentile mission as Paul's initiative for the sake of continuity with the discussion to follow. For consideration of Barnabas' influence on Paul, see Hengel and Schwemer (1997: 205–20).

[30] On the history of the well-documented Jewish community of Antioch, see Zetterholm (2003: 18–42).

[31] More accurately, Acts indicates that Barnabas summoned Paul to Antioch following the latter's expulsion to Tarsus (Acts 11.22–25). Again, it is difficult to reconcile this account with Paul's own. The author's claim, moreover, that followers of Jesus were first called Christians, i.e., Messianists, upon Paul's arrival in the city seems contrived (Acts 11.26). Not until the end of the first century, well after Paul's day, would Christian writers begin to call their group by that name. For comments to this effect, see Lieu (2004: 250–59), although cf. Hengel and Schwemer (1997: 225–30), who suggest its original use by opponents of the Church in Antioch.

of Galatia bordered Cilicia to the northwest. Acts reports that Paul journeyed from Antioch to a number of cities in Asia Minor and Cyprus, unfailingly offering his gospel first to reluctant Jews and then to more receptive Greeks (Acts 13–14, 16).[32]

Paul's decision to take his mission beyond the Church's original Jewish demographic was likely motivated by two factors. On one count, he perceived a need to integrate gentiles into the community of Israel in order to bring to fruition the ancient Hebrew prophecies foretelling an eschatological age when all nations would turn to Yahweh.[33] That is the crux of his presentations to the churches in Galatia and Rome. But Paul would have had practical concerns as well. By the time he first conferred with Peter and James, it had been several years since the crucifixion. It therefore had been several years since the risen Jesus was said to have appeared to his disciples promising his epochal second coming.[34] The message that those men went on to preach was beginning to wear thin among Jewish audiences accustomed to an eschatological myth involving no death or resurrection of the Messiah. In their imaginations, the very premise of a second coming demanded a leap of faith. To the few Jews willing to make that leap, the failure of Jesus to reappear, much less to establish himself as the king of Israel, made that element of his message difficult to sustain.

As the agents of the apostolic mission began to branch out into the Jewish Diaspora, Paul saw an opportunity to revitalize their flagging initiative. Having failed to accomplish much in Arabia and Damascus, Paul realized the difficulty he would face should he have continued his missionary work among his fellow Jews. He knew that he needed to reach new audiences more open to his evolving understanding of the gospel and its new ideas about the nature of Jesus' Messianic reign. He needed, in other words, to preach to individuals willing to adjust their expectations as to what the Messiah was supposed to do to match the reality of Jesus' prolonged absence. The most likely candidates were not his

---

[32] The chronology of Acts is confused here, suggesting that Paul passed through central Asia Minor twice, first with Barnabas (Acts 13–14) and then again after their separation en route to the Mysian city of Troas (Acts 16.1–5, with reference to Galatia at 16.6). Problematically, none of the cities associated with these journeys actually was in Galatia. Antioch-in-Pisidia was in Pisidia (Acts 13.16, 14.19, 21; cf. 16.6), Iconium (Acts 13.51, 14.1, 19, 21, 16.2) was in Phrygia, Lystra (Acts 14.5, 8, 21, 16.1–2) and Derbe (Acts 14.6, 20, 16.1) were in Lycaonia, and Perga (Acts 14.25; cf. 13.12) was in Pamphylia. It is therefore difficult to say whether Paul also founded other unidentified churches in Galatia, or, alternatively, whether he mistakenly addressed as Galatian those founded in the aforementioned cities. See Meeks (1983: 42–43).

[33] I refer to the scriptural prophecies foretelling of gentiles who would give themselves to the worship of Yahweh at the end of days: Isa 2.2–4, 25.6, 56.3–7; Mic 4.1–5, 11–13; Zech 8.25; cf. the more ominous prophetic notices of the eschatological lot of the gentiles at Isa 49.23, 54.3; Mic 5.9–15, 7.16–17; Zeph 2.1–3, 8 et al. On the influence of these oracles on Paul's soteriology, see Fredriksen (1991: 544–47).

[34] On the inception of the Church's gentile mission as a response to the persistent absence of Jesus, see Gager (1975: 37–49), and cf. Gager (2000: 61–64).

increasingly skeptical Jewish brethren but the gentiles who stood to join the community of Israel in what he still believed to be the imminent end of days.[35] If the Jews could not be relied upon to embrace the gospel, it would have to be the gentiles whose faith in Yahweh would bring about the Messiah's return. This realization evidently drove Paul to his conclusion that the gentiles needed their own means of access to the gospel.[36] He therefore tailored his message to speak specifically to their cultural sensibilities rather than to the traditional Jewish mores preached by the other apostles. But Paul's success hinged on his ability to relate to gentile audiences what were still basically Jewish ideas. He needed to target gentiles already somewhat familiar with the concepts vital to his theological argument. He needed gentiles inured to the idea of a universal God bound by a covenant to his chosen nation of Israel. And he knew that he would not find them in the shallow backwaters of Arabia. Paul migrated to the cities of the Roman east to seek out the cosmopolitan environments where gentiles easily comingled with their Jewish neighbors, attending their synagogues and learning about their exotic ways.[37] These were the people, he likely reasoned, most susceptible to receive Paul as he presented himself, as a Jewish preacher bearing promises of great things for all who were to recognize Jesus as Israel's Messiah.

Despite, therefore, its anachronistic anti-Jewish subtext, the modus operandi assigned to Paul in Acts is entirely convincing.[38] Upon arriving in a given city, Paul would present himself as a visiting Jewish sage in order to gain entry into the local synagogue. Once he established his credentials, he would preach his message of Messianic renewal to audiences of Jews and their gentile associates. Eventually, the Jews would grow wary of Paul's talk of new covenants and new ritual dispensations. They would ask him to leave. But some of those gentiles (and reportedly some of the Jews) moved by Paul's message would

---

[35] Paul most clearly expresses his anticipation of the second coming of Jesus in 1 Thess 4.13–18 (cf. 1 Thess 1.9–10). On the context and implications of this aspect of Paul's Messianism, see Gager (1975: 43–44); Segal (1990: 163–64).

[36] Compare the following to Fredriksen (1991: 555–56). My comments here are heavily indebted to her engaging and insightful reconstruction of Paul's thought process.

[37] That gentiles attended synagogue meetings in the classical world is taken for granted by the author of Acts, who variously characterizes such individuals as fearers (*phoboumenoi*; Acts 10.2, 10.22, 35, 13.16, 26) or worshippers (*sebomenoi*; Acts 13.43, 50, 16.14, 17.4, 17, 18.7) of God. While it is unclear whether the persons in question formally identified as devotees of Yahweh, the involvement of gentile sympathizers in Jewish communal life throughout the ancient Mediterranean Diaspora is confirmed by a range of archaeological and literary evidences independent of the New Testament. See, e.g., Gager (1986); Fredriksen (1991: 533–43); Trebilco (1991: 145–66); Liebeschuetz (2001: 240–41). Also of interest here is the possibility that some Jewish communities worshipped alongside non-Jewish devotees of the "the highest god" (*theos hypsistos*), the subject of a monolatrous Greek cult prevalent in Asia Minor, on which see Mitchell (1999, 110–21), and cf. Trebilco (127–44).

[38] For the following, cf. Acts 13.13–52, relating Paul's activities in Antioch-in-Pisidia. For general comments on Paul's use of Jewish contacts to establish local footholds for his ministry, see Meeks (1983: 25–29).

invite him to take up residency elsewhere in the city and preach his gospel to all comers. The company of gentile believers would serve as the basis of that city's church, their knowledge of the gospel mediated primarily by Paul and only subsequently, if ever, by other apostles preaching more conventionally Jewish interpretations of Jesus' teachings.

Writing to the Galatians, Paul recalled his triumphant return to Jerusalem after fourteen years in Antioch and Asia Minor (Gal 2.1–2).³⁹ Conferring again with Peter and James, he explained the gospel he had been preaching, demonstrating its gentile orientation and its variances with that preached by the other apostles. Buoyed by the reports of his success in the field, the leaders of the Jerusalem Church recognized Paul as the foremost apostle to the gentiles and pledged their ongoing support for his mission (Gal 1.7–10). The significance of this agreement toward the future demographic makeup of the Church cannot be understated. While others preached the Jewish-oriented gospel to ever diminishing returns, Paul was founding functioning outposts of gentile believers at a healthy clip. He thereby set in motion what would become a dramatic change of course for an initiative originally devised by Jews and for Jews.

It is to Paul's credit that he saw the need to redirect the Church's missionary agenda in order to avert its impending collapse within just years of its initiation. But a distressing incident in Antioch ultimately would compel the apostle to the gentiles to question the compatibility of his personal vision for the Church with that of its founders. Sometime after his second visit to Jerusalem, Paul returned to Antioch from an unspecified missionary journey to find a troubling scene. Peter had since appeared in the city to minister to the local Jewish church. Under the influence, however, of certain unnamed emissaries from Jerusalem, Peter had refused to dine with members of Paul's gentile church for fear of some unspecified breach of etiquette (Gal 2.11–13).⁴⁰ Paul was incensed. He publicly denounced Peter, accusing him of betraying his own ethical principles (Gal 2.14–21). Paul had left his second meeting with the

---

³⁹ Acts 11.29–30 plainly contradicts Paul here, reporting that he and Barnabas delivered funds to the Jerusalem Church during their residency in Antioch. Hengel and Schwemer (1997: 242–43), tenuously suggest that Paul himself declined to enter Jerusalem during these visits, leaving to Barnabas the task of actually handing the monies to James.

⁴⁰ Precisely what Peter was supposed to have done wrong is unclear. Traditional interpreters typically assume that it was the substance of Peter's meal that offended the Jerusalem delegation inasmuch as he had eaten food not deemed ritually clean or *kosher* according to the Torah (cf. Acts 11.1–9). But it seems unlikely that Paul would have expected Peter to transgress his Jewish mores so blatantly. In all likelihood, Peter violated no law but merely appeared to have acted inappropriately to visitors unaccustomed to seeing Jews dining with gentiles. Accordingly, Paul's reaction would have implicated Peter for betraying Paul's principle of accepting gentiles as equal covenantal partners. For this interpretation, see Zetterholm (2009: 24–28) (cf. Zetterholm 2003: 136–42); Bauckham (2005: 121–30). Alternatively, Dunn (2006: 172–79), reads Peter's concession as a sign of his failure to grasp Paul's concept of justification by faith, while Tomson (1990: 227–36), sees it as a sign of his vulnerability to critics within the Antiochene church advocating standards of *kashrut* more stringent than those of the Torah.

founders of the Church under the impression that his gentile supporters were to be treated as equals within the organization, their understanding of the gospel no less valid than that of the Jews. In order for the Jews to achieve the salvation promised by Jesus, Paul believed that they had to cooperate with those gentiles willing to forsake their past lives to serve the God of Israel. Refusing to commune with their fellow believers was no way for Peter and his Jewish supporters to welcome the gentile newcomers into their fold.[41]

Omitting the incident's more acrimonious details, the book of Acts reports that the dispute was resolved amicably.[42] Paul himself gives no such word, indicating only that the affair strained his relationship with his fellow apostles. In any case, Paul went on from Antioch to pursue his mission further west into the Aegean region, establishing churches in the cities of western Asia Minor and Greece. Although this last phase of his career would see him undertake a collection of charitable funds for the Jerusalem assembly, whether he maintained contact with Peter and James is uncertain (Rom 15.25–33; 1 Cor 16.1–4; 2 Cor 8–9; cf. Gal 2.10). Those were the journeys during which Paul began to write to those of his supporters now reportedly entertaining the overtures of other apostles of the aggressive variety he had encountered in Antioch. Evidently, those emissaries of the Church remained convinced that gentiles had to become Jews in order to achieve the salvation that Paul had promised. It is little wonder, therefore, that Paul presumed to defend the integrity of his gospel by challenging the beliefs of his apostolic competitors.

It is in view of these circumstances that we must consider Paul's comments on Jews and Judaism. Put simply, he did not try convince Jews to relinquish their Jewish identities. He tried to convince gentiles that they did not have to

---

[41] Zetterholm (2003: 164–66), is correct to infer that the Jerusalem delegation would have appeared to prevail on the occasion of their arrival in Antioch insofar as they persuaded Peter to question the authority of Paul's gentile-oriented gospel in the latter's absence. Paul, in other words, was right to have felt insulted on behalf of the gentiles from whose company Peter had been persuaded to withdraw.

[42] The corresponding account of the incident in Acts 15 implies that the matter at issue related to the question of whether gentile followers of Jesus had to undergo circumcision in order to join the Church, a rite that in effect would have made them Jewish proselytes (Acts 15.1, 5; cf. Gal 2.7–9). The reported resolution dictated that gentiles were exempt from circumcision but obliged to uphold a code of ethics known in the Jewish tradition as the Noahide laws (cf. Acts 15.19–20, 28–29). See Bockmuehl (2000: 164–72). Assuming the priority of that alleged apostolic decree to the Antioch incident, J. Taylor (2001) argues that Paul, having previously agreed to those laws, took issue with Peter for trying to press further ritual obligations on his gentile supporters in Antioch. I find this theory difficult to accept. Paul was something of a fanatic in respect to gentile observance of Jewish laws. It seems implausible that he would have consented to the logic of Mosaic authority that James reportedly offered in support of the limited gentile contract (cf. Acts 15.21). In all likelihood, the author of Acts contrived his account in an attempt to rationalize James' otherwise unexplained endorsement of Paul's antinomian gospel at a time when he believed the Jewish mission was still viable. If so, the entire sequence would appear to be a literary pretense immaterial to the facts of the dispute in Antioch. For a more thoroughgoing assessment to this effect, see Zetterholm (2003: 143–49).

become Jews. That he chose to pursue this argument by attacking the Jewish convictions of his apostolic competitors was, in retrospect, an unfortunate decision. But it is an understandable decision in view of Paul's strained relationships with his fellow apostles, a relationship that reached its nadir not long before he began writing his letters. Let us now turn to those texts to see how he accounted for the traditional discourse on Jewish identity in his novel reading of Israel's salvation history. Ultimately, his words rather than his intent would be what would color the self-perceptions of those Christian readers who would later presume to see themselves reflected in Paul's rhetorical mirror.

THE LETTER TO THE GALATIANS

Chronologically, the first of Paul's surviving writings touching on the question of Jewish identity is his letter to the Galatian churches. Writing sometime after the Antioch incident, Paul responds here to the inquiry of an unidentified church community or communities regarding the need for gentile followers of Jesus to undergo circumcision. As noted in Chapter 2, the rite of circumcision was one of the most prominent indicators of Jewish identity in the ancient world.[43] To Jews, it was a symbol of covenantal participation, a nonnegotiable prerequisite for enrollment in the Jewish nation. To gentiles, it was a mark of ethnic distinction shared by Jews and other peoples of the Near East. Since Paul's departure from their company, his supporters in Galatia had been visited by other apostles (Gal 1.6–9, 3.1). Those men had insisted that the Galatians, though gentiles, nevertheless had to be circumcised (Gal 3.19–29, 5.2–12). In other words, they were told that they had to become Jews or, more accurately, Jewish proselytes, in order to partake of God's covenant with Israel.[44]

For the Galatians, as for other gentile followers of Jesus, to undergo circumcision would have been a daunting prospect. As adults, they would have found the surgical procedure itself quite painful. Moreover, the condition of being circumcised would have marked them as different from their friends and neighbors in a Roman society that prized cultural conformity.[45] Though they seem to have understood that these liabilities came with the territory of being Jewish, they apparently balked at the advices of their latest apostolic contacts for the simple fact that Paul already had told them that circumcision was not required for their entry into the eschatological community of Israel. The Galatians had a dilemma on their hands: to circumcise or not to circumcise. It was in view

---

[43] On the significance of circumcision in Jewish covenantal theology, see Collins (1985); E.P. Sanders (1992: 213–14). Note the androcentric implications of this particular marker of Jewish identity, which, though not available to women, was not thought to exclude them from the community of Israel; see S.J.D. Cohen (2005: 133–35).

[44] For this inference, see Fredriksen (1991: 561), and cf. Gager (2000: 98).

[45] On circumcision as a social stigma in Roman culture, see A.S. Jacobs (2012: 15–19), and on Paul's sensitivity to concerns of his readers regarding the procedure, ibid. (22–25).

of this question that some unknown agent or agents of their church decided to write to Paul for an explanation as to why he was right and the other apostles were wrong in their opposing viewpoints on the formality at issue.

Judging by his response, Paul did not take kindly to this latest challenge to his apostolic authority. He begins his letter by avowing his apostolic credentials, which, as noted, he claims to have received from Jesus and from the leaders of the Jerusalem Church (Gal 1–2). He then offers a detailed exposition of his views on the Jewish law and its relevance to gentiles. Alluding to a theological argument attested elsewhere in his writings, Paul asserts that the Jewish law sets a standard of righteousness impossible for normal human beings to achieve (Gal 3.10–12).[46] The Torah, in his estimation, was no reward for Israel's faith. It was a sentence for their infidelity, a yoke laid upon the necks of God's chosen nation in view of their predilection for sinful behavior. God, in other words, imposed his law upon the Jews as a preventative measure in order to keep them in line with his will (Gal 3.19, 21, 23).[47]

But that precautionary measure, says Paul, was no longer necessary. The crucifixion of Jesus, he avers, had alleviated God's concern for Israel's sins. The Messiah had given his life on behalf of his people as a vicarious and everlasting sacrifice of atonement (Gal 3.12–14, 22, 24–26, 29; cf. 2.15–21).[48] The covenantal partnership between God and his chosen people was thereby restored to its original state of mutual commitment (Gal 3.6–9, 15–18). Consequently, Paul asserts, the divine privileges once reserved for those bound by the Jewish law were now available to all who elected to be baptized or, in his language, "immersed into the Messiah" (*eis christon ebaptisthēte*; Gal 3.27). No longer relevant were the differences between Jew and Greek, slave and free, or even male and female. Jesus, he asserts, had united all people by eliminating the boundaries thought to give meaning to those limiting ethnic, social, and gender distinctions (Gal 3.28).[49]

---

[46] Compare, however, Paul's advice that his readers adhere to an ethical code suggestive of the Torah's (Gal 5.16–21). On this seeming inconsistency in Paul's logic, see Räisänen (1987: 115–16). Tomson (1990: 87–89), attempts to explain Paul's demurral from circumcision as a function of his belief that gentiles need not observe the *halakhah*, or post-biblical Jewish law, in contradistinction to the laws of the Torah. Despite Paul's confusing advice to the Corinthians regarding a distinction between "circumcision" and "the law," I am unconvinced that Paul would have seen circumcision as anything but a Pentateuchal statute (1 Cor 7.19; cf. Gen 17.10–14; Lev 12.3).

[47] I do not infer here a blanket indictment of the Jewish people as living in a chronically sinful state. To wit, Paul himself asserts that he used to follow the Jewish law to perfection (Phil 3.6). He seems, rather, to observe that everyone sins sometimes. God, Paul therefore reasons, imposed the law upon Israel to instruct them how to act according to his will, thereby ostensibly diminishing their opportunities for sin. For similar readings, see Stendahl (1976: 12–13); E.P. Sanders (1983: 65–70); Dunn (1990: 249–50).

[48] On this central theme in Paul's soteriology, see E.P. Sanders (1977: 463–68).

[49] On the ethnic dimension of Paul's social critique, see Johnson Hodge (2007: 126–31), and cf. Lieu (2004: 126–32).

This is not the occasion to delve into Paul's soteriological reasoning. For now, it will suffice to say that his account of the Torah as a preemptive disciplinary measure represented a counterintuitive spin on the traditional Jewish notion of Israel's election. Jews of Paul's day typically imagined their covenant with God to pivot on their status as the chosen people, the only nation on earth worthy of his patronage. And their merit was not unwarranted. As told in the book of Exodus, the Israelite ancestors of the Jews had enthusiastically welcomed God's commandments upon their arrival at Mount Sinai. They had witnessed the miracles that their divine protector had wrought on their behalf to secure their liberation from enslavement. They therefore readily submitted to his ritual and ethical ordinances, reciprocating the devotion that God had shown them during their escape from Egypt (Exod 19.1–9).[50]

One assumes that Paul knew this. But Paul also knew that the commandments comprising the Jewish law were meant specifically for the Jews. In the book of Deuteronomy, Moses is said to have instructed those Israelites about to enter the land promised to their ancestor Abraham that their descendants were to observe the commandments in perpetuity should they hope to maintain God's commitment to their national enterprise (Deut 26.16–19, 29.10–29).[51] As a result, Jews of Paul's day typically believed that they and they alone were obligated to observe God's law. Gentiles simply had no role to play in the rapport between Israel and Yahweh.[52] The Galatians were therefore justified to question Paul's antinomian gospel when presented with the conventional Jewish wisdom of his apostolic competitors. Evidently, they had been told that the God of Israel works only for those who agreed to the terms set forth at Sinai. Paul needed to discredit that notion, to show that the God of Israel welcomed the faith of all peoples regardless of whether they kept to the laws of the Torah. He therefore had not merely to circumvent the argument of his apostolic competitors but to upend the ethnocentric principle on which their concept of covenant was founded.[53]

[50] For an account of the Sinai covenant as a function of Israel's particular national experience, see Kaminsky (2007: 85–91).

[51] On the construction of the Deuteronomic legislation as an ersatz national charter, see Goodblatt (2006: 29–30); Himmelfarb (2006: 11–15).

[52] On the anomalous place of gentiles in classical Jewish covenantal theology, see Goldenberg (1998: 9–27), who compares the Jewish position to those of other ancient peoples who regarded their gods as uniquely bound to their own national collectives. I should reiterate here that while ancient Jews typically did not account for gentiles in their constructions of God's relationship with Israel, they did perceive a place for those who wished to join their nation as proselytes. The conceptual distance, however, between the desire of the proselyte to identify with Israel and the desires of the Jews to protect Israel's ethnic boundaries prompted many native Jews to recognize proselytes as proselytes even as gentiles recognized them as Jews. See S.J.D. Cohen (1999a: 156–62).

[53] Here I follow Dunn (1990: 247–48); see also Sanders (1983: 17–22), who places less emphasis on the ethnic dimension of Paul's soteriological rationale. On Paul's challenge to what we can reasonably surmise was the more conventional Jewish thinking of his fellow apostles, see Segal (1990: 210–18); Boyarin (1994: 130–35).

In order to accomplish this delicate interpretive task, Paul delved deeper into Israel's history than the events at Sinai. In the book of Genesis, God is said to have assured Abraham great things for his descendants and, in turn, to all the nations of the earth (Gen 12.2–3, 15.5, 17.8, 22.17–18; cf. Gal 3.8). That promise, Paul observes, preceded the covenantal agreement struck at Sinai by hundreds of years (Gal 3.17). God, he reasons, must have deemed Abraham righteous not because he observed the Jewish law but simply because he put his faith in God (Gal 3.6; cf. Gen 15.6). Consequently, Paul tells his readers, "Those who believe are the descendants of Abraham ... those who believe are blessed with Abraham" (Gal 3.7, 9). In other words, the Jewish people are not the only beneficiaries of God's promise. Whether Jews or gentiles, all who abide by Abraham's covenant of faith share in his righteousness. That was the fundamental order of faith that Jesus professed. Thus, Paul assures his readers, "If you are with the Messiah, then you are the offspring of Abraham, heirs according to the promise" (Gal 3.29).[54]

Not content to rely on that covenantal loophole, Paul buttresses his argument with an even more inventive appeal to the Genesis narrative. He explains that Abraham's two sons each represent two aspects of God's relationship with Israel. According to the scriptural text, Abraham spurned his elder son Ishmael, born to his Egyptian servant Hagar, in favor of his younger son Isaac, born to his wife Sarah (Gen 21.8–14). As a result, Jews of Paul's day typically believed that Isaac was the one who inherited God's devotion to Abraham as it pertained to their nation, the nation of Israel. Ishmael, on the other hand, inherited his father's divine reward as it pertained to the other nations of the world, that is, the gentiles (cf. Gen 25.12–18). Paul, however, reverses these positions in a clever allegorical twist.[55] Ishmael, he asserts, born into servitude, represents the Jewish people, on whom God had placed the yoke of the Torah. Isaac, born into freedom, represents the gentiles, who never had to shoulder the burden of its punitive legislation. Contrary to the intimations of his apostolic competitors, Paul claims that God's vow to Abraham applied not to those bound by the Jewish law but to those who yearned to be like Isaac, the favored son and the one born to Abraham as a function of God's word (cf. Gen 18.10, 21.1–2). All people, therefore, were now free to avail themselves of the covenant of faith that God had struck with their common ancestor Abraham (Gal 4.21–31).

---

[54] On Paul's construction of God's promise to Abraham as a dialogical complement to the Sinai covenant, see Johnson Hodge (2007: 96–100).

[55] My reading here is indebted to Gager (2000: 92–97), who likewise sees Paul's allegory as a play on the expectations of his readers with respect to the disparate covenantal statuses of Jews and gentiles. In other words, Paul means not to suggest that Ishmael's gentile descendants have usurped the ethnic privileges of Isaac's Jews, but, rather, that the spiritual heirs of both sons are to be regarded as such on the basis of their faith. See also Gaston (1987: 83–91), who offers a considerate reading of Paul's allegorical exegesis in view of ancient Jewish understandings of Ishmael's relationships with Abraham and Isaac.

Rather than challenge the established notion that God's covenant was only open to Jews, Paul argued that its terms had been dramatically altered by the Messiah. The upshot of his exegetical demonstration is that Israel's renewed relationship with God does not require observance of the Jewish law, much less the particularly unnerving rite of circumcision (Gal 5.6, 6.15). The Galatians, Paul therefore assures them, need not worry about the issue that had prompted their inquiry. In fact, he asserts, they would do best not to undergo the procedure lest they set the law above their faith and forget the lesson of the crucifixion (Gal 5.2–5). Thanks to Jesus, the Jewish people were now freed of the parochial bonds of the Torah. They were free to revert to the terms of God's original, intended covenant with all of humanity. That was the covenant, Paul now tells his readers, of which he had spoken while in their company.

Paul's elision of the ethnic distinction between Jew and gentile was not necessarily as radical as it might appear at first glance. I have already mentioned Himmelfarb's observation that many Jewish thinkers of the Second Temple period sought to deemphasize the significance of kinship toward establishing one's credentials with God. Paul's impetus to place faith before obedience to the law might well reflect that intellectual trend, albeit to the unprecedented end of denying altogether the soteriological value of ancestral merit. According to Himmelfarb, Paul sought to provide gentiles a means of accessing the community of Israel entirely on the basis of their own virtues, thereby obviating the premise of joining an ethnically delimited nation of Israel that had troubled his friends in Galatia.[56]

Others have suggested even less revolutionary ideas. According to Martin Hengel, Paul took a page directly from the playbook of the Hasmonean king John Hyrcanus.[57] Paul's symbolic allusion in Gal 4.25 to "Mount Sinai in Arabia" might offer a glimpse into a thought process dating as early as his stay in that region. If so, it is possible that Paul devised his allegorical reading of Ishmael's legacy in reference to the Arab nations whom Jews of his day typically construed as descendants of Abraham's elder son.[58] Much as Hyrcanus had declared the Idumeans Jews in view of their common ancestry, Paul might have plotted his initial missionary appeal to the gentiles on the premise of genealogical affinity between Jews and Arabs. Only later would he extend that logic to non-Arab peoples in the manner exhibited in his letters to the Galatians and other gentile churches.

In a similar vein, Caroline Johnson Hodge has suggested that Paul's thoughts about Ishmael might speak to the legal sensibilities of the Galatians.[59] According

---

[56] Himmelfarb (2006: 175–77).
[57] For the following, see Hengel (2002), and cf. Hengel and Schwemer (1997: 113–20).
[58] Hengel (2002: 50); Hengel and Schwemer (1997: 118). On ancient Jewish perceptions of Arabs as descendants of Ishmael, see Josephus, *Ant.* 1.220–21, with discussion in Millar (1993: 8–9), and, for later rabbinic evidence, Bakhos (2006: 67–74).
[59] For the following, see Johnson Hodge (2007: 68–72).

to the matrilineal principles of classical Greek and Roman law, Ishmael, born to an Egyptian mother, ordinarily would have possessed no right of inheritance in his father's household. But if, as Paul suggests, Abraham recognized Ishmael as an heir of God's promise, their relationship would resemble that which existed between a father and his adopted son. According to the Roman civil law to which the Galatians were beholden, the male head of a household reserved the right to transfer his property and social status to a male heir born outside of his family line. Analogously, Ishmael, though born a slave, was deemed a son of Abraham and a party to God's promise, his kinship having been fully established by legal right if not necessarily by ancestral right. Were that Paul's implication, he would have evaded the ethnic logic of the Torah's covenantal language by appealing to that of another code of law meaningful to the experiences of his readers.

Yet although it is likely that Paul based his advice to the Galatians on what he deemed a sound contextual reading of Genesis, there can be little doubt of his unconventional design. In order to convince his gentile readers of their covenantal right, Paul needed to circumvent the primary ethnic and religious elements of what he and they knew as the conventional formula for Jewish identity. Consequently, while Paul's counterintuitive exposition of the purpose of the Jewish law stood to ease the apprehensions of gentiles, it stood equally to raise the hackles of Jews committed to the traditional equation of Torah and covenant. That much is clear in the reactions of his apostolic competitors.

Of course, I do not mean to suggest that Paul meant to offend his fellow Jews. Given the occasion of his writing to the Galatians, it would be unfair to conclude that Paul's disparaging comments about those who would uphold the Jewish law referred to anyone but those apostles whom he believed stood to thwart his mission.[60] Speaking to gentiles, Paul likely felt justified to assert his apostolic authority in contradistinction to those of his peers who questioned the validity of his approach. Nevertheless, that Paul chose to justify his gospel by deprecating the Jewish law lent his words a distinct polemical edge. In insinuating that God no longer expected Jews to abide by their law, Paul naturally implied that the Jewish mission was operating on an obsolete model of God's relationship with Israel. If, as he argued, the Torah was instituted as a temporary measure, its expiration meant that neither gentile nor Jew were now to abide by its regulations. Those apostles, therefore, who insisted that gentiles observe the same law as Jews implicitly failed to grasp the significance of Jesus' life, his teachings, and his death on the cross. For Paul, in other words, to assert

[60] Note that Paul appears in his recollection of the Antioch incident to recall having issued a broad indictment of "those gentiles who presumed to act as Jews" (*ta ethnē anagkazeis ioudaizein*; Gal 2.14). Given, however, the reassuring tone of his letter, it seems unlikely that Paul meant to accuse the Galatians for "Judaizing" in the same pejorative sense in which the late first-century bishop Ignatius of Antioch would introduce that term to the Christian lexicon; see Ignatius, *Magn.* 10, with discussion in Townsend (2008: 225–30). On the contrasting rhetorical objectives of Paul and Ignatius, see Zetterholm (2003: 203–11).

the right of his antinomian gospel meant to deny the right of that originally conceived for the Jews.

While it is not difficult to see how Paul's approach would have relieved his gentile readers in Galatia, neither is it difficult to see the potential of his words to alarm Jewish readers. Insisting that Jews were no longer bound by the laws of the Torah, Paul undermined the very foundation of their collective sense of self. For followers of Jesus predisposed to identify as Jews, to forsake their law would have been to forsake God himself, to refuse the terms of their ancestral covenant and to sever their descendants from what they knew as the nation of Israel.[61] In effect, they would have had to forgo their very identities as Jews in order to comply with Paul's novel covenantal theology. Irrespective of Paul's abiding interest in drawing gentiles into communion with his fellow Jews, his interpretation of the gospel as an antidote to the Torah would have been a pill difficult for many of those Jews to swallow.[62]

THE LETTER TO THE ROMANS

Paul's letter to the Romans is the latest and arguably most mature exposition of his gospel drafted by the apostle himself. Addressed to gentile followers of Jesus residing in the imperial capital (Rom 1.5–6, 11.13 et al.), the letter offers a series of position statements pertaining to his concept of justification by faith and its implications toward issues of covenant, community, salvation, and so forth. Amid those advices, Paul regularly touches upon the question of whether his readers are to practice the Jewish law and, by extension, to identify as Jews in the conventional fashion.[63] As in his letter to the Galatians, Paul's opinion here is in the negative, his views on the temporary nature of the Torah's legislation unchanged since his earlier missive. But where he once allayed the apprehensions of his readers by refracting the ideology of Jewish identity through the lens of allegory, Paul now engages the sensitivities of those of his readers

---

[61] In other words, were Jewish followers of Jesus to forsake the laws of the Torah, they would have become apostates, removing themselves and their children from the nation of Israel per the dictates of the Torah. That should not have been a problem to Paul, who urged his followers to join a community of Israel not bound by the terms of the Torah. Yet he warns his gentile readers in Corinth to avoid marrying idol worshippers lest their unions yield ritually "unclean" offspring (*akatharta*; 1 Cor 7.14; cf. 2 Cor 6.14–71). Ironically, therefore, Paul there seems to uphold the principle of ethnic continuity that he implicitly rejects in his letter to the Galatians. See Hayes (2002: 92–98), and cf. S.J.D. Cohen (1999a: 272).

[62] That Paul regularly encountered resistance during his missions suggests that some of the Jews he encountered in his travels saw his gospel as an invitation to apostasy. According to Acts, that was among the allegations leveled against Paul prior to his arrest in Jerusalem (Acts 21.28, 25.8). For like considerations, see Barclay (1995: 111–19).

[63] My understanding of Paul's dismissive stance toward Judaism in this letter as an effect of his fading confidence in the Jewish mission is typical of the aforementioned "new perspective." For representative statements, see, e.g., E.P. Sanders (1983: 29–43); Segal (1990: 255–67, 276–84); Dunn (2006: 194–97).

prone to construe Israel's covenant with God as one available exclusively to Jews. As a result, one of the letter's recurring motifs sees Paul defending his stance on the relationship between the historical nation of Israel and the new spiritual Israel embodied in the Church. This element of his argument famously culminates in chapters 9–11, where Paul, acknowledging his disappointment over the failure of his fellow Jews to take to the apostolic mission, nevertheless expresses his confidence that they soon would.

The elaborate nature of Paul's final extant letter likely owes to its function as a letter of introduction. Paul had not founded the church in Rome. Presumably, it was established by an apostle espousing a Torah-oriented gospel.[64] Having heard about their initiative from unknown informants, Paul aimed to assert his right as the Jerusalem Church's officially sanctioned apostle to the gentiles (Rom 15.14–16). He therefore wrote to Rome in advance of a planned visit to the city during which he hoped to preach his gospel to the appropriate gentile audiences (Rom 1.8–13). But Paul's reputation preceded him, if only, perhaps, in his own mind. Anticipating resistance to his message, Paul wrote his letter in the hope of forestalling conflict between the Roman church's existing Jewish and gentile constituencies (cf. Rom 1.7, 15.1–13).[65] He therefore designed his letter not merely to demonstrate the validity of his gospel but also to expose the faulty soteriological assumptions of those apostles who had preceded him.

Paul realizes his dual purposes with the aid of a classical Greek rhetorical style formally known as the diatribe.[66] This technique sees the speaker present two alternating sides of a single argument, allowing one to speak both as a protagonist for his or her own case and a theoretical antagonist against that case. The effect is that of a speaker conducting a debate with his or her self. Clearly, the strategic advantage in the diatribe is with the protagonist, who sets up the counterargument of his or her rhetorical opponent for effortless deflection. In his letter to the Romans, Paul naturally positions himself as the protagonist. His implied antagonists are Jews, specifically Jewish followers of Jesus, in

[64] The precise origins of the Roman church are difficult to trace. Paul, for his part, acknowledges only that it was founded by someone other than himself (Rom 15.20; cf. Acts 28.14–15). For an attempt to recover its lost history on the basis of Paul's letter and other Christian texts of the apostolic age, see P. Lampe (2003: 69–79). Also useful here is Spence (2004: 15–65), whose synthetic profile of first-century Rome's synagogue community offers a plausible, albeit unverifiable, Jewish context for the local church's first formal contacts with the apostolic mission.

[65] So P. Lampe (2003: 69–75). Spence (2004: 290–308), assumes that Paul's intent was primarily pastoral, to raise the spirits of a gentile constituency marginalized by the Jewish-oriented gospel on which their church was founded. I find this position wanting for credibility in view of Paul's derogatory statements about the church's "sickly" Torah-observant members (Rom 14.1, 15.1), a tendentious characterization, which Spence declines to question. While the gentiles might have felt unsure of their roles as parties to what was still a Jewish enterprise, it seems reasonably clear that Paul aimed to intercede primarily to assert that his apostolic competitors had no territorial right in Rome.

[66] For the following, see Stowers (1994: 11–12). My reading of Paul's comments on Jews in his letter to Rome as advice meant for gentiles is much indebted to Stowers' treatment.

whose mouths Paul sets a version of the argument against his gospel similar to that implied in his letter to the Galatians.[67] Speaking in his own apostolic voice, Paul methodically deflects the qualms of his fictive Jewish adversaries, in the process expositing his own missionary ideology.

The apostle's utilization of this unique rhetorical form offers fascinating insight into Paul's self-awareness as a Jew and an agitator of Jews. He seems to know that he must reconcile those adversarial identities should he hope to persuade his readers of his noble intentions. It is therefore vital to recognize that Paul here pursues an argumentative strategy more apologetic than that of his letter to the Galatians. Whereas Jews appear in his earlier letter as opponents of Paul's mission, they appear in his letter to the Romans as potential allies merely in need of correction regarding their misconceptions of his gospel. Of course, the Jews who figure in Paul's dialogic exposition say only what Paul allows them to say. One must not assume that the arguments they voice reflect the attitudes of the actual Jews involved in the Roman church along with Paul's gentile addressees.[68] Nevertheless, it will be helpful to consider his perceptions of those whom he expected to hold fast to the old covenant of the law in order to gauge the effect of Paul's latest appeal for the renewed covenant of faith.

True to his earlier comments to the Galatians, Paul appeals to his readers in Rome on the premise that the Jewish law had been abrogated by Jesus. Sensitive, however, to the needs of those who might object to this notion, he now explains his position in a more subdued tone. So, for instance, where Paul previously stated that the Israelites had brought the yoke of the Torah upon themselves, he now tells his gentile readers that their own ancestors were no less prone to violate God's will (Rom 1.18–32, 3.9–20). God, he says, might seem to have judged the Jews, but that was only because they were the first people to partake of his covenant. They received the punishment of the law because God expected them to know the difference between wrong and right (Rom 2.1–16, 3.1–8). In fact, Paul asserts, God is partial neither to the Jew nor to the Greek (Rom 2.11). Lest his readers judge their Jewish friends negatively on account of their predilection for the law, he warns that the law itself is no hindrance to righteous living for those inured to its regulations. Only if one not previously disposed toward those regulations chooses to become a Jew does

---

[67] On Paul's invention of his opponents, see Stowers (1994: 16–21) and passim. I should note that while I agree with Stowers' assessment of Paul's rhetorical stratagem, I do not mean to dismiss his figurative Jew as a complete fabrication. Paul, after all, was a Jew and presumably understood the misgivings of his Jewish detractors. I therefore feel it appropriate to read his contrived Jewish antagonist in light of the unfortunate dealings with the actual Jewish antagonists recounted in his letter to the Galatians.

[68] This position typifies the traditional Christian interpretation of the letter as having been written for the benefit of all the constituents of the Roman church, both Jewish and gentile, thereby serving to censure those of its members who had previously voiced opposition to Paul's gospel. On the questionable historical inferences necessitated by this still ubiquitous interpretive approach, see Stowers (1994: 22–33).

the law become a liability, unnecessarily multiplying his or her opportunities for sin (Rom 2.17–29, 3.21–31).[69] "For one is a Jew," Paul avers, "not merely in appearance, nor is circumcision that which can be seen in the flesh. Rather, one is a Jew on the inside and circumcision is of the heart. It is spiritual, not literal. That individual is commended not by men but by God" (Rom 2.28–29).

Paul does express sympathy for those followers of Jesus prone to invest meaning in the Jewish law. "Do we mean to overturn the law?," he asks. "By no means! On the contrary, we uphold the law!" (Rom 3.31). And yet, he remains firmly convinced that the covenantal principle embodied in the Torah's legislation is no longer in effect. Revisiting the exegetical argument that he presented to the Galatians, Paul adduces God's promise to Abraham as proof that his promise to Israel was predicated not on the law but on faith (Rom 4.1–5). Now, however, he avoids his previous intimation that the Jews had lost their stake in God's arrangement with Israel's patriarch. Abraham too, says Paul, observed the law, confirming his treaty with God with the blood of his circumcision (Rom 4.9–12; cf. Gen 17.9–14, 23–27). Nevertheless, he points out, according to the sequence of events narrated in the book of Genesis, God reckoned Abraham righteous before bidding him to undergo that procedure. Paul thereby nuances his previous explanation to the Galatians, now affirming the function of the law as the ancestral prerogative of the Jews. And although that right was not usurped by the covenant of faith renewed by Jesus, he nevertheless asserts that it had outlived its precautionary purpose (Rom 4.13–25).[70] Obedience to the Torah, while still permissible for faithful Jews, was no longer essential for their salvation.

The lesson here is fairly simple. The Jews had chips on their shoulders just like the gentiles. Where the gentiles had to overcome the abject depravity that had ruled their lives before their embrace of Jesus, Jews had to overcome their reliance on the ritual obligations that dominated them to equally stultifying effect (cf. Rom 6.15–23).[71] The problem, as Paul saw it, was that not enough Jews appreciated that that was case. He thus proceeds to apologize to his readers on behalf of those of his countrymen who, by his account, had removed themselves from Abraham's lineage and from the nation of Israel by failing to heed the word of God (Rom 9.1–29).[72] The Jewish mission, Paul concedes,

---

[69] In other words, Paul leaves open the possibility that those born under the law might still practice it without offense, just unnecessarily so. Here I depart from the readings of Gaston (1987: 122–23, 138–39), and Gager (2000: 114–17, 120–23), who cite Paul's stance as evidence of his conception of alternative covenantal models for gentiles and Jews. Paul seems to me merely to tolerate Jews habituated to Torah observance, not to equate their standard of faith with that which he wishes to impress upon his gentile readers.

[70] On Paul's exegetical logic as a complement to his argument to the Galatians, see E.P. Sanders (1983: 33–34); Johnson Hodge (2007: 86–89).

[71] For this reading of Paul's exhortation, see Stowers (1994: 255–58).

[72] Paul achieves this effect by qualifying his prior distinction between "children of the flesh," i.e., circumcised Jews, and "children of the spirit," i.e., uncircumcised followers of Jesus (Gal 4.23

had failed to win significant numbers of supporters. Even those Jews who did acknowledge Jesus as the Messiah continued to operate under the misperception that they were still bound by the law (Rom 9.30–10.4). In other words, Paul believed that the gentile members of the Church had achieved righteousness while their Jewish counterparts continued to err in their soteriological assumptions. That, he seems to have realized, stood to thwart his appeal to a gentile readership in Rome still cooperating with Jews who saw no such error in their ways.

Bearing in mind this concern, Paul reiterates his belief that the Jewish people are bound for salvation along with all the nations (Rom 10.5–21). Even those Jews who had yet to attach themselves to the Church, he avers, would embrace the gospel in due time (Rom 11.1–10, 25–36). But this eventuality would be realized only when the Jewish people were to see all the nations of the world align themselves with the community of Israel (Rom 11.11–24). Until then, Paul urges his readers, it will be their responsibility to cultivate their belief in the God of Israel not by doing as the Jews do but by paving their own paths of faith. Until then, the gentiles would have to serve the traditional function of the nation of Israel, to bear witness to the God of the Jews, and Israel the function of the gentiles, to disregard that witness in advance of God's judgment (Rom 11.30–32). The purpose of this eschatological role reversal, says Paul, is a mystery (Rom 11.25). But given the circumstances, that is how it had to be.[73]

Paul concludes his teaching on the gospel with a reminder of its availability to Jew and gentile alike (Rom 15.7–13). Yet he enjoins his readers not to begrudge their brothers and sisters whom he deems "sickly in faith" (*asthenounta tē pistei*; Rom 14.1, 15.1) in view of their preoccupations with such matters as dietary restrictions and Sabbath observance (Rom 14.1–12). As long as Jewish followers of Jesus remain true in their covenantal intentions, says Paul, their gentile confrères should not give them grief (Rom 14.13–15.6).[74] Nor should they abstain from acting like Jews themselves while interacting with their steadfastly Jewish friends. Better, he argues, that his readers should show consideration to their weaker partners than to upset the peace of the church. Only those gentiles, he asserts, who act like Jews for fear of God's

---

et al.). Where Paul once declared these types mutually exclusive, he now implies that Jews who adhere to his gospel can move from the former category to the latter (Rom 9.6–13). See Johnson Hodge (2007: 100–03). Instructive here is Boyarin's treatment of Paul's hermeneutical distinction between physical and spiritual existence in Boyarin (1994: 69–76).

[73] The precise object of Paul's hope regarding the eschatological fate of the Jewish people is famously enigmatic. That he presumed, however, to address the subject suggests a desire to assure his gentile readers that their salvation ultimately would depend on the salvation of the Jews and vice versa. Paul, in other words, though regretful of the declining state of the Jewish mission, remained convinced of its instrumentality in bringing about the second coming of the Messiah. See Stowers (1994: 298–312); Gager (2000: 138–42).

[74] On Paul's concession to law-abiding members of the Roman church as a plea for harmony between its Jewish and gentile constituents, see Stowers (1994: 320–23), and, further, ibid. (66–74), on the apostle's recurring call for his readers to conduct themselves with ethical forbearance.

judgment are in the wrong, as their adherence to the law comes not from faith but from willful neglect of his gospel (Rom 14.23). For it was his gospel, he finally asserts, and his gospel alone that God had authorized as the charter of the gentile mission (Rom 15.14–21).

As a statement of Paul's stance on Judaism, his letter to the Romans is noticeably less confrontational than his letter to the Galatians. He appears entirely genuine in his desire to unite Jew and gentile in common purpose. But just as in his earlier work, the apostle to the gentiles ultimately prioritized the needs of his own constituents over those of his apostolic competitors.[75] Speaking primarily his intended gentile readers, Paul obliged them to see the Jew as a spiritual inferior. His rhetorical Jew was weak in spirit, beholden to a covenantal conceit no longer meaningful to God. He was weak in mind, too, dull to understand or too obstinate to accept what Paul knew as the true salvific significance of Jesus' life and death on the cross. And that was the Jew who actually did recognize Jesus as the Messiah. As for those Jews who declined even that basic sign of faith, Paul deemed them the most deluded of all.

"There is no distinction," Paul wrote to the Romans, "between Jew and Greek. The same Lord is the Lord of all and is generous to all who call on him, for everyone who calls upon the name of the Lord shall be saved" (Rom 10.12–13; cf. Joel 2.32). And yet, perhaps unwittingly, his effort to dispel the notion that the Jew would possess an advantage over the Greek when they were to stand before the heavenly tribunal saw Paul place the Greek at a tremendous advantage on the terrestrial plane. While the apostle to the gentiles remained ever eager to welcome Jews into the Church, his ideal Church was one in which they were no longer to function as Jews. Built on time-honored principles of ethnic privilege and regulatory ritual, the idea of Jewish identity as Paul knew it had no place in a community of Israel henceforth to be defined primarily by faith and open to all peoples on equal terms.

But persuading gentiles not to become Jews was easier than selling Jews on the mandate to cease being who they already were. As the veteran apostle well knew, old habits die hard. Jews were bound to think like Jews. Even, therefore, those Jews who supported Paul's mission to the gentiles would have had difficulty adjusting their religious and ethnic mentalities to his expectations. In that respect, the apologetic responses to his would-be detractors voiced in his letter to the Romans were, in effect, no less aggressive than the indictments of his apostolic competitors in his letter to the Galatians. Although not entirely without cause, Paul had come to believe that all of his fellow Jews were as hostile toward his mission as those who had humiliated him in Antioch years ago. His unremitting resentment of those who had presumed to question his

---

[75] For the following assessment of the likely effect of Paul's remarks on his readers' perceptions of their Jewish associates, compare Barclay (1996: 303–08).

apostolic authority would leave a lasting impression on Paul's legacy as the Church's principal spokesperson for the Jewish people.

NEITHER JEW NOR GREEK

Paul's letters do not indicate whether he ever made it to Rome to preach his gospel. The book of Acts reports that the apostle was arrested by the Roman authorities upon his return to Jerusalem, transferred to the care of Judea's provincial government in Caesarea, and, ultimately, deported to Rome to languish in prison (Acts 21–28). The author implies that Paul's offense had been bringing a gentile into the sacred precinct of the Jewish Temple, although that allegation alone probably would not have warranted a hearing before the imperial tribunal (Acts 21.28–29, 24.6, 25.6–12).[76] In all likelihood, his arrest was the result of bad blood between his advocates in the Jerusalem Church and those local Jewish authority figures still suspicious of that fading institution.[77] The canonical account dates the apostle's last stand in Judea to the governorship of Antonius Felix (ca. 52–59 CE; Acts 23.24 et al.) and logs his subsequent incarceration at two years (Acts 28.30). It therefore would have been no later than 61 CE when Paul was unceremoniously executed.[78]

Paul accomplished a great deal in his roughly thirty years as an apostle. His devotion to the gentile mission had seen Paul breathe new life into what was already a failing apostolic initiative by the time of his introduction to the Jerusalem Church. Yet Paul could not have accomplished this turnaround without dramatically recasting the gospel of Jesus as a call to all nations speaking to their needs as strangers to the God of Israel. He thereby opened door for gentile involvement in the Church even as the door for Jewish participation was closing. Paul's mission also seems to have proved more successful than the efforts of those apostles who affirmed the traditional belief that the laws of the Torah were essential for all worshippers of Yahweh. Although precise numbers are difficult to ascertain, it appears as though the Church, founded in Judea as a Jewish enterprise, was already populated predominantly by gentiles toward the end of Paul's lifetime. That was almost certainly the case within the first generation of his death.[79]

---

[76] On the restriction of gentiles from entering the Temple court, see Philo, *Embassy* 212; Josephus, *J.W.* (5.193–94, 6.124–26, *Ant.* 14.417). On the circumstances of Paul's arrest and trial, see McLaren (1991: 139–45).

[77] In other words, the Jewish authorities likely turned to the Romans for prosecutorial assistance just as Jesus' critics had done several years earlier. For like comments, see McLaren (1991: 142–44); Setzer (1994: 73–74).

[78] On early Christian literary traditions detailing Paul's execution, see Eastman (2011: 16–24).

[79] I base my assessment on that of Sim (2005: 433–36), contra Hopkins (1998: 212–16). Given the speculative nature of the enterprise, I find Sim's text-based analytical method more persuasive than Hopkins' sociological approach. While hardly a reliable statistical indicator, no less telling is the assertion of Justin Martyr that Christians of gentile origin outnumbered those of Jewish and Samaritan ancestry by the mid-second century (Justin, *1 Apol.* 53).

But Paul's instruction that his supporters be "neither Jew nor Greek" was not easily accomplished. The society in which they lived valued these ethnic affiliations as a matter of the public welfare. Greeks were supposed to patronize the syncretistic Hellenic cults of the Roman deities thought to ensure the vitality of the state.[80] Followers of Jesus who declined to identify as Greeks or Romans thus left themselves open to charges of atheism for refusing their civic duties to the gods and goddesses of the Roman pantheon.[81] They also left themselves open to accusations of sedition by Diaspora Jews. Jews were by special decree exempted from Rome's sacrificial liturgies in deference to their own venerable ethnic cult.[82] The Jews, moreover, evidently wanted no part of the controversial new sect that claimed to venerate their ancestral deity in ways not sanctioned by their treasured edicts of protection.[83] Paul's will to dissolve the ethnic categories that stood to divide his readers thus became a liability for their successors, rendering them outliers in the Roman Empire's highly regimented social structure. That was the concern that prompted the heirs of the apostolic mission to devise the new mode of cultic identification called Christian.[84]

Yet almost as early as Christians began to identify as such, they found themselves retreating to the ethnic reasoning once repudiated by Paul.[85] By the turn of the second century, Christian thinkers were rationalizing their new collective enterprise as one structured quite like those that the apostle had sought to dissolve. An early second-century treatise known as the Preachings of Peter is perhaps the first known text to speak of Christians as a "third race of worshippers" (*tritō genei sebomenoi*) distinct from Greeks and Jews yet comparable in its constitution.[86] Around the same time, the

---

[80] On the cultic logic of the Roman *religio*, see Ando (2008: 95–100), and on the presumption of interchangeability between Greek and Roman deities, Beard et al. (1998: 171–74).

[81] For comments on early Roman skepticism toward Christians and their cultic habits, see Beard et al. (1998: 225–27). Also useful here are the case studies of Wilken (1984).

[82] On the acquisition of special cultic freedoms by Roman Jews, see Pucci Ben Zeev (1998: 1–11). Rome's official recognition the Jewish cult as an inoffensive conceit or *superstitio* was consistent with the state's usual policy of tolerance toward the ethnic habits its foreign subjects; cf. Ando (2008: 100–05); Beard et al. (1998: 214–25).

[83] Deriving entirely from the Christian tradition, the evidence for Jewish involvement in the persecution of the Church during the first and second centuries is catalogued by Setzer (1994: 110–46), although one must question whether Jews would have wished to draw negative attention to persons associated with their communities given their own subjection to official scrutiny on account of the recent civil wars in Judea.

[84] On this development, see Lieu (2004: 250–59), who infers that the name Christian was originally a disparaging term devised by critics of the Church and later adopted by its members. Compare, however, Townsend (2008: 215–25), who argues for its origination as a self-designation for gentiles members of the early Roman church.

[85] I borrow the term "ethnic reasoning" from Buell (2005), who surveys a wealth of evidence on the use of the interchangeable categories of race and ethnicity in early Christian writings. See also Simon (1986: 107–11); Lieu (2004: 259–66).

[86] This lost treatise is quoted in Clement of Alexandria, *Strom.* 6.5.41. See Buell (2005: 29–33).

anonymous author of an apologetic tract called the Epistle to Diognetus set about to explain the origins of "this new race" (*kainon touto genos*) defined by the Christian habit of "divine worship" (*theosebeia*).[87] The slightly later Apology of Aristides speaks of Christians as a fourth race among the Greeks, the Jews, and the barbarians, tracing their genealogy to their originator Jesus Christ not through kinship in the manner of those nations but, rather, through adherence to the gospel.[88]

Through rhetorical strategies such as these, the expression of faith that Paul had sought to purge of Judaism's ethnic bias ended up forging new ones in its place.[89] Where Paul had spoken only of "the Church of God" (*tē ekklēsia tou theou*; 1 Cor 10.32; Gal 1.13), the survival of the Christian enterprise depended on the ability of its members to relate to those outside of their collective who were prone to question their motivations. Christians needed to stake their claim to legitimacy, to find their places in a Roman society generally intolerant of cultic difference. Consequently, those who aimed to cast the nascent idea of Christian identity in positive terms went to great lengths to justify their differences by drawing negative comparisons with their antagonists. That process of negotiation invariably resulted in the rhetorical vilification of those non-Christian others, of Romans, Greeks, and especially Jews.

The perceived relationship between Christian and Jew was of pivotal significance here. To casual Greek and Roman observers, the premise of venerating the God of Israel put the Christians in league with the Jews.[90] For Christians, this meant having not only to distinguish themselves from Jews in the public sphere but also in their self-perceptions. The premise of seeing Christianity as a distinct race meant erasing the memory of its Jewish roots. Leading Christian thinkers thus conditioned their associates to forget the Jewish identities of Jesus, Paul, and other pillars of the apostolic Church. Relating their movement's past according to their new Christian perspectives, they interpreted the internecine arguments between those men and their fellow Jews as extramural debates between Christian and Jew and, eventually, existential conflicts between Christianity and Judaism. Moreover, those Christians who followed

---

[87] *Diogn.* 1. The apologetic nature of the treatise is hinted at by Tertullian, who would later intimate that their critics derided Christians as a third race (*Nat.* 1.8.1, 9, 11, 20.4, *Scorp.* 10.10). See Buell (2005: 154–56).

[88] *Arist.* 2, according to the edition of J.R. Harris (1891: 36–37). The Syriac text reads *gensā* for the original Greek *genos*. See Buell (2005: 35–36).

[89] E.P. Sanders (1983: 171–79), infers that Paul meant to inscribe a "third race" ideology in his denial of difference between Jew and Greek, although it seems unlikely that he or his apostolic contemporaries would have foreseen the emergence of Christian as a distinct social estate in need of its own racial or ethnic identity; cf. Lieu (2004: 264–65).

[90] The most exemplary Greco-Roman indictment of Christians as apostate Jews is that of the second-century philosopher Celsus, preserved in fragmentary quotations by Origen; see, e.g., Origen, *Cels.* 2.4, with discussion of this and related passages in Wilken (1984: 112–17). For a more benign assessment of the relationship of Christian and Jew, see Galen, *De pulsibus* 2.4, 3.3, with discussion in Wilken, ibid. (72–73).

Paul's advice resented Jews not merely for seemingly having rejected his gospel but for maintaining the cultic rights and exemptions that they lacked.

The twin defeats of the Jews at the hands of the Romans in 70 and 135 CE vindicated the conviction held by many Christians of those times that God was dissatisfied with the old nation of Israel. God, they reasoned, had used the Romans to destroy their central cultic institution in order to show the Jews that Jesus had made the ultimate sacrifice, his crucifixion having signaled the end of the Jewish cult and the initiation of his renewed covenant of faith.[91] The Romans, like the Greeks of Paul's letters, now seemed to work in the service of God's eschatological plan. And yet, Judaism endured while Christians continued to suffer the indignities of disenfranchisement and persecution. In time, the dissonance between Paul's promise of salvation and the reality of their existence compounded the frustration of those Christian thinkers prone to blame the Jews for inhibiting the timely return of their Messiah.

A new fold was thus added to the emerging notion of the Christians as a new kind of people. Writing in the wake of the Bar Kokhba rebellion, the apologist Justin Martyr is the first on record to assert that the Christians were the only deserving claimants to the title Israel and the only true heirs to God's promise to Abraham.[92] To Justin's mind, the national history of the Christians supplanted that of the Jews. Judaism itself was nothing more than a Christian heresy, an illegitimate corruption of the Messianic prophecies of the Hebrew Scriptures.[93] The new Christian race thus was refashioned as a nation neither Jewish nor Greek but, from a functional standpoint, an amalgamation of the two. Subsequent Christian theologians would trace the roots of their Church to the culture heroes of the Jews, to Noah, Abraham, Jacob, Moses, and David, to the prophets of Israel, establishing a pedigree for their race as ancient as those of the Greeks and Romans. In the Christian scheme of salvation history, those men and all their virtuous Israelite ancestors were cast as Hebrews, custodians of a sacred spiritual legacy later to be claimed by imposters operating under the name Jews. Only, accordingly, since the arrival of Jesus had that long lost inheritance been restored to its rightful owners.[94]

These were among the factors that contributed to the development of what I described in Chapter 1 as the classical Christian theological polemic against Judaism. The model of Christianity that flowered in the wake of Paul's missionary career was resolutely inhospitable toward those Jews in whose salvation

[91] On this subject, see, e.g., G.W.H. Lampe (1984); Wilson (1995: 8–10, 44–45, 53–54, 62–64, 76–78, 131–36).
[92] See, e.g., Justin, *Dial.* 119, 123, with discussion in Lieu (2004: 265–66). On Justin's sophisticated argument for Christianity's priority to Judaism in his *Dialogue*, see Buell (2005: 94–115).
[93] Hence, in Boyarin's estimation, Justin invented the Christian concepts of heresy and Judaism in one deft literary motion; see Boyarin (2004: 37–40). For a more reserved assessment of Justin's invidious construction of Judaism, see Lieu (2004: 136–40).
[94] On "Hebrew" ethnicity as an anti-Jewish trope in classical Christian historiography, see A.S. Jacobs (2004: 21–51); Buell (2005: 63–93); Johnson (2006: 94–125).

its apostle had expressed genuine hope. In Christian eyes, the Jews became enemies of Jesus, falsifiers of the gospel, and bearers of a false doctrine in its own right. Those would be the chief allegations against Judaism to inform proto-orthodox Church doctrine during its arduous early centuries and, eventually, through its evolution into the imperial apparatus of religious law under Constantine and his Byzantine successors.[95] In view of this reversal of power, the disbelieving Jew became an object of universal contempt in the eyes of those who submitted to the authority of Rome. Attenuated by centuries of denial and deliberate misconstruction, the memory of the Church's Jewish roots was thereby banished from the Christian imagination.[96]

All of which leads me to the following interim conclusions. By the end of the second century, the Church was largely populated by persons whom Jews likely would not have mistaken for members of their own group. The establishments founded by Paul and grown by his successors attracted participants predisposed to identify not as Jews but, according to conventional Jewish reasoning, as gentiles. They were trained on a gospel that specifically instructed them not to identify as Jews irrespective of their ethnic origins. They were not to observe the laws of the Torah in the typical Jewish fashion. Moreover, they were not to condone the grave theological errors of other Christians who presumed to do the same.

To the heirs of Paul's gospel, to be a Christian meant, among other things, not to be a Jew. The typical Pauline Christian was neither born a Jew nor prone to behave like a Jew in accordance with the laws of the Torah. To the best of our knowledge, the typical Pauline Christian had no reason to go through the motions of Jewish ritual observance while secretly disavowing those rites as self-destructive. That observation makes it difficult to imagine that those followers of Jesus whom the rabbinic sages initially characterized as Jewish heretics or *minim* subscribed to Paul's gospel.

So what kind of Christians were they? Here is where one might consider the early Church's other, less celebrated demographic. I refer, of course, to the Jewish Christians. Per my comments in Chapter 1, I do not assume that the individuals and groups typically assigned to that problematic category opposed Paul's mission. Nor do I assume that they uniformly took exception with Paul's stance on the relevance of the Jewish law for gentiles. I mean merely to suggest that not all early Christians aware of Paul's gospel took to his novel exposition of Judaism's covenant theology quite as eagerly as he would have preferred. Let us therefore consider just who those individuals were.

---

[95] For a thoroughgoing overview of the relevant history and literature, see Fredriksen and Irshai (2006).
[96] For a similar assessment, see A.S. Jacobs (2004: 51–55), who likens this process of historical revisionism to one of naturalizing the Jewish other into the conceptual boundaries of the new Christian Empire.

TRACES OF THE JEWISH MISSION

When Paul embarked on his mission to the gentiles, he left the Jerusalem Church at a crossroads. With the Jews rapidly losing interest in their initiative, the leaders of the original apostolic mission were unsure of whether or how to present their case to the gentiles. Judging by his own testimony, Paul's way was one of several approaches tested simultaneously and without coordination. Presumably, the showdown between Peter and Paul in Antioch was one of many such impasses elicited by the diffusion of conflicting interpretations of the word of God concerning Jesus and his Messianic reign.[97] Despite Paul's reasonable protests, other apostles of his age continued to urge all who would hear their call to seek salvation in the laws of the Torah as their ancestors had for generations.

What became of those apostles is not clear. If history is written by the victors, it would be fair to say that Paul's competitors were the losers. Aside from Paul's letters, we possess no unambiguous contemporary witnesses to what was happening in Jerusalem or at other outposts of the apostolic mission to the Jews during the course of its operation.[98] Though written after its dissipation, the book of Acts provides some general information on the parameters of the Jewish mission. Yet its author identifies primarily with the gentile mission, which naturally casts doubt over its sources for events ancillary to Paul's storyline. Finally, we have the recollections of later Christian writers whose secondhand testimonials are also subject to question. Only should one choose to take all of these sundry evidences at face value is it possible to compile a coherent record of the Jerusalem Church and its missionary initiatives beyond Paul's realm of influence.[99] I therefore should warn the reader that the following sketch of the Jewish mission is but an impression of an impression offered in lieu of a more empirically demonstrable account.

The apostolic mission to the Jews evidently began shortly after the crucifixion of Jesus. The impetus of his surviving disciples to sustain the ministry of

[97] This observation is salvageable from the treatment Lüdemann (1989: 35–111), despite the author's unfortunate decision to objectify such alternate readings of the gospel as a cohesive "anti-Paulinist" (read: pro-Jewish) faction within the Jerusalem Church (ibid., 112–15).
[98] By unambiguous, I mean to disqualify the Epistle of James, a New Testament text traditionally ascribed to the eponymous principal of the Jerusalem Church (cf. Jas 1.1). Espousing an ethical code balancing faith and unspecified works or ritual activities, the letter is generally regarded as a "Jewish Christian" wisdom text framed in an epistolary form in homage to Paul's preferred literary medium. Although its provenance cannot be determined with certainty, the fairly late date of its initial attestation (ca. early fourth century) suggests that its allusive ascription to the brother of Jesus is a literary affection. For like comments, see Llewelyn (1997), although cf. Lockett (2011). In any case, the text offers no clear criteria by which to assess its value as a witness to the Jewish mission.
[99] See, e.g., the careful but inevitably speculative accounts of Bauckham (1995) and Horbury (2006).

their departed teacher was driven by the same apocalyptic impulses that later compelled Paul to extend its reach. Although theoretically open to gentiles, the eschatological vision preached by James, Peter, and their associates pertained primarily to their fellow Jews (Acts 1–3). The first apostles expected those who recognized Jesus as the Messiah to fulfill the terms of their ancestral covenant with Yahweh in the manner to which they were accustomed. In other words, their reading of Jesus' gospel amounted to a call for national reform based on the traditional Jewish belief that their observance of the laws of the Torah would ensure the salvation of Israel in the coming end of days.[100]

That the founders of the apostolic mission first presented their message as a matter of common Jewish interest is apparent in the reported resistance to their group by the High Priest Caiaphas and his supporters (Acts 4.1–22) and, later, their suppression by the priests (Acts 5.17–42, 6.8–8.3) and the Herodian king Agrippa I (Acts 12.1–5). While the scale of these reported events might be exaggerated, there is no reason to doubt that the Jewish civil authorities would have seen Jesus' followers as troublemakers.[101] After all, they were espousing the teachings of a man who had been executed for prophesying the divine overthrow of the Roman regime. The heat in Jerusalem is probably what drove the apostles to seek audiences elsewhere in provincial Judea, taking the gospel to Samaria (Acts 8.4–25), then to the local Greek cities of Gaza (8.26), Azotus (8.40), Lydda (Acts 9.32–34), Joppa (Acts 9.36–43), and Caesarea (Acts 8.40, 10.24), and finally to more remote sites of Jewish settlement in the neighboring regions of Phoenicia, Cyprus, and Syria (Acts 11.19–30). Although those emissaries reportedly met Samaritans, Greeks, Romans, and other gentiles receptive to their message, their target audiences and objectives remained almost invariably Jewish (cf. Acts 11.19).[102] That, apparently, is why the Jewish authorities deemed it expedient to send men like Paul to rein in the apostles as they ventured beyond the borders of Judea.

Unfortunately, however, Paul's appearance in the book of Acts marks the end of its author's interest in the Jewish mission. Henceforth, the Jerusalem Church is mentioned only in conjunction with Paul's visits (Acts 15.1–35, 21.17–26).

[100] Although the book of Acts does not expressly account for the covenantal theology upon which the apostolic mission was founded, its typically Jewish character is implied throughout. For like inferences, see Bauckham (1995: 422–28); Horbury (2006: 36–38).
[101] On the realities behind these highly dramatized reports, see McLaren (1991: 102–14), commenting on the priestly interferences, and D.R. Schwartz (1990: 119–24), on the king's.
[102] The notable exception to this pattern is the story of the Roman soldier Cornelius, who is said to have received a divine vision compelling him to meet with Peter in Caesarea (10.1–33). The lesson for Peter in learning of the man's piety is that God shows no partiality to the Jew over the gentile (Acts 10.34; cf. Rom 2.11). This prompts the immediate conferral of the Holy Spirit upon other gentiles present at the meeting (Acts 10.44–48). Acknowledging the Pauline tendency of this miraculous story, it seems significant that Peter does not tell his new gentile associates to think or to act contrary to the Jewish law. The incident thus seems to serve as a divine license for the formal mission to the gentiles soon to be undertaken by Paul (cf. Acts 11.1–16). For comments, see Horbury (2006: 63–64).

As for the fruits of its earliest missionary efforts, the author offers only a salutary reference to the abiding peace of the churches in Judea, the Galilee, and Samaria (Acts 9.31). Aside from its muddled account of the Antioch incident (Acts 15.1–5), we read nothing more in Acts of those members of the Church who presumed to know Jesus as Jews. As noted, that is probably a function of the author's subjective bias. Writing in the late first century, his was a Church positively defined by Paul's gospel and, consequently, disabused of the Jewish missionary platform against which he had defined his own.

Evidence for the fate of the Jerusalem Church beyond the book of Acts is both scarce and highly problematic. According to Josephus, its founder James was executed several years prior to the outbreak of the Jewish revolt of 66–70 CE.[103] Peter, its leading missionary proponent, was probably dead before the war was through.[104] What became of their survivors is less certain. The fourth-century Church Father Eusebius famously reports their mass removal upon the outbreak of hostilities to the Greek city of Pella east of the Jordan River.[105] Yet per my comments in Chapter 1, that story is not especially credible. In fact, the same author preserves a number of conflicting testimonies to the fate of the Jerusalem Church after the war. Quoting the late second-century Christian author Hegesippus, Eusebius recounts the death of James and the subsequent transfer of the congregation's leadership to his cousin Simeon son of Clopas.[106] He also quotes Hegesippus on the involvement of other relatives of Jesus in the Jerusalem Church up to the reign of the emperor Domitian (r. 81–96 CE) and, ultimately, its dissolution into heresy.[107] Elsewhere, Eusebius cites another second-century author, Ariston of Pella, who states that the church was continually overseen by Jewish bishops through the Bar Kokhba rebellion of 132–135 CE. Following that war, Ariston avers, the city of Jerusalem was closed to Jewish settlement and its episcopal seat given to a gentile bishop called Marcus.[108]

All told, the testimonies compiled by Eusebius do not make for a cogent record of the fate of the Jerusalem Church after the death of James.[109] His

[103] Josephus, *Ant.* 20.199–203, dates the execution of James to a brief window of time between the governorships of Porcius Festus (ca. 59–62 CE) and Lucceius Albinus (62–64 CE).
[104] Though not the first Christian author to note Peter's death, Tertullian, *Scorp.* 15.13, credibly associates it with the emperor Nero's infamous persecution of Christians in Rome sometime late in his reign (54–68 CE). On the timing and impact of this episode, see P. Lampe (2003: 82–84).
[105] Eusebius, *Hist. eccl.* 3.5.3. See also Epiphanius, *Pan.* 27.7.7–18, 30.2.7, whose knowledge of the legend seems to depend on the account of his slightly older contemporary.
[106] Eusebius, *Hist. eccl.* 2.23.3–18 (James), 3.11.1–2, 4.22.4 (Simeon).
[107] Eusebius, *Hist. eccl.* 3.20.1–8 (Jesus' relatives), 4.22.5 (the heresy of the Jerusalem Church).
[108] Eusebius, *Hist. eccl.* 4.6.3–4. Lüdemann (1989: 205–06), plausibly infers that Ariston provided Eusebius the legend tracing the migration of the original Jerusalem Church to his own hometown. In any case, one must question Eusebius' placement of another Jewish church in its stead. Epiphanius, *De mensuris et ponderibus* 15, appears to correct Eusebius' editorial oversight, asserting that the Pella refugees returned to Jerusalem after the first war.
[109] I therefore demur from the cautious acceptance of Eusebius' confused testimonials by Horbury (2006: 67–72), and considerably more freely by Bauckham (1990: 79–106).

sources seem to agree only on the fact of the Church's decline and eventual disappearance. We can only surmise that the Jewish mission met the same unobtrusive end. Ostensibly the last living witness to the original apostolic endeavor is Justin Martyr, who, channeling Paul, derided certain unnamed Christians whom he alleged were still urging their gentile fellows to submit to the Jewish law even in the wake of the second revolt.[110] If we are to take Justin at his word, it would appear that the more dynamic apostolic initiative founded by Paul relinquished its last remaining links to its Jewish past just as the Church began to take on the corporate character of a new ethno-racial polity predicated on a constitution of faith rather than a charter of kinship.

That is, of course, if we are to define the Church strictly according to Paul's terms. Presumably, the demise of the Jewish mission did not retroactively erase its theological platform from the minds of its former supporters. Considering that there were Christians who preferred to know the Messiah as the savior of the Jewish people, one easily conceives why they chose to continue living as Jews irrespective of their waning influence in the Church. These followers of Jesus who lived in places where Paul did not preach his gospel, in Judea and Samaria, and in the robust Jewish communities of Syria and Arabia that Paul had failed to penetrate. These were Christians who taught their children the Torah, sustaining the practices and beliefs of their ancestors as a matter of sacred obligation to their God and to their fellow Jews. These were the Jewish Christians or, if you prefer, the Christian Jews, who believed that they stood to realize Paul's unfulfilled hope for the salvation of the whole of Israel.

Or so one might surmise. In fact, we know nothing about what motivated the Jewish Christians to think or act as they did. Paradoxically, the very sources that constitute our principal witnesses to the existence of Jewish Christians are nearly impossible to quarry for useful information about their theological designs. The ancient references to the Ebionites and Nazarenes do not give those alleged heretics much credit for their beliefs. In general, the Church Fathers acknowledged those folks only to denounce them as false Christians. Nor do the Jewish witnesses to Christian *minim* reveal much about what made those pilloried individuals tick. We are therefore left only to guess where the subjects of these polemics placed themselves in the apostolic tradition to which they presumably traced their understandings of the gospel according to the conventional Christian wisdom of their day.

---

[110] Justin, *Dial.* 47–48. One might recall here Justin's comments on the supposed persecution of Christians during the Bar Kokhba rebellion (*1 Apol.* 31.6) and the expulsion of Jews from Jerusalem in its aftermath (*1 Apol.* 47.5–6). One therefore wonders whether his resilient Jewish missionaries were real or simply rhetorical figures foolishly asserting God's desire that Israel observe the law despite the recent imperial ban on circumcision. For this argument, see Lieu (2004: 119–23).

Fortunately, we have some clues. Recent studies on some of the earliest surviving Christian literary traditions have shed light on a long lost chapter in the history of the Church. Resisting the overt anti-Jewish biases exhibited in those texts, scholars have detected what appear to be signs of Jewish life within their very pages. Considered in context, these scattered evidences offer precious snapshots of an age before Judaism became a Christian heresy, when Jewish followers of Jesus struggled to reconcile their old and new identities. The internal conflicts projected in their writings resemble Paul's diatribe to the Romans, although with a notably different inflection. Evidently, the authors of these texts knew of the categorical distinction between Christian and Jew gaining traction in the Church. But they were not quite ready to accept it. They therefore appear at times to respond to Paul as though the impressions of Jews and Judaism that the apostle had left on the emerging discourse on Christian identity were still subject to negotiation.

In what follows, I shall briefly survey three of these documents, namely the Gospel of Matthew, the Didache, and an obscure literary source preserved in the Pseudo-Clementine Recognitions. I choose to focus on these texts because they appear to speak to roughly the same Christian demographic operating in the Roman Near East during the late first and early second centuries.[111] My purpose here is neither to argue that these documents preserve evidence of a united anti-Pauline front in the eastern churches nor to suggest that those churches were breeding grounds for heresies of the Jewish variety. In other words, I do not wish to suggest that the readership communities implied in these texts were the progenitors of the Jewish Christians of subsequent record.[112] I mean only to show that the authors of these texts spoke to readers whom they themselves implicitly or explicitly identified as Jews. I thereby aim to establish a proximate socio-cultural context for the occurrence of the Christian *minim* attested in Palestinian rabbinic texts of roughly the same vintage.

[111] Conversely, I shall not deal with other second-century Christian texts of less certain provenance often associated with Jewish Christians in view of their engagements of Jewish cultural concerns, e.g., the Apocalypse of Peter, the Epistle of Barnabas, and the Infancy Gospel of James. Per my comments in Chapter 1, the impetus of the authors of these texts to repudiate those concerns marks them as Jews only if one assumes that they composed their works with the decisive split between Judaism and Christianity already in hindsight. Naturally, I find that inference untenable. One need not assume that Christians of Jewish origin were the only ones obliged to critique Judaism as a means of confirming their own beliefs. I therefore prefer to read the misgivings about Judaism expressed in these and other arguably "Jewish" Christian texts as apologetic arguments in the Pauline vein meant for Christian readers of no particular ethnic or cultural persuasions.

[112] While I would not rule out the possibility of continuity between the communities reflected in these texts and the Jewish Christians of later patristic and rabbinic legend, I do not believe that the evidence on either side of the proposed equation is strong enough to sustain the necessary historical inferences. For efforts of this speculative nature, cf. Blanchetière (2001: 97–103, 109–12); Skarsaune (2007c: 756–60); Broadhead (2010: 384–88), and for less historically positivistic arguments to similar effect, Luttikhuizen (1991); Segal (1992); Horrell (2000).

THE GOSPEL OF MATTHEW

One of the four canonical gospels, Matthew is arguably the latest book of the New Testament to entertain the idea of Jewish identity as a possibility for followers of Jesus. Likely written toward the end of the first century CE, the book is traditionally attributed to its namesake disciple, Matthew the tax collector (cf. Matt 9.9, 10.3). Although that ascription is doubtful, the association is not trivial. Among the features unique to his rendition of Jesus' teachings are the author's concerns for wealth and social standing among its implied readership community. Most notable, however, for our purpose is the author's implication of a Jewish readership or, alternatively, one whose prior situation within Jewish society was still a recent memory. Scholars assessing that aspect of the gospel's social outlook have highlighted a number of rhetorical strategies and thematic motifs locating its target audience in or near the cultural orbit in which the rabbinic movement took root.[113] It therefore behooves us to consider whether Matthew's portrait of Jesus provides salient information on the practices or beliefs of the local Christian demographic whom the rabbinic sages were later to acknowledge as *minim*.

A full account of Matthew's history of composition is beyond the scope of this study.[114] I offer here only a few of the details relevant to the foregoing discussion. Along with the Gospel of Luke, Matthew is based on the Gospel of Mark, the earliest of the four canonical narratives of Jesus' life. Matthew also appears to draw upon a number of undocumented oral or written sources including, but probably not limited to, the author's own literary embellishments. The author's use of materials situating Jesus' ministry squarely within his native Jewish environment of the Galilee naturally suggests a Jewish readership. But that aspect of its rhetoric must not be mistaken as a sign of the book's provenance. In fact, the composite tract later to be attributed to Matthew is first attested around the turn of the second century in the writings of Ignatius of Antioch.[115] Tellingly, where the other gospels locate Jesus' earliest ministry strictly in the Galilee, Matthew shows him visiting Syria as well (Matt 4.23–25; cf. Mark 1.28, 39; Luke 4.14, 16, 31). Finally, Matthew uniquely promotes Peter as Jesus' favorite disciple, a theme likely reflecting that apostle's influence in Antioch's earliest church community (Matt 4.18–22, 10.2, 16.16–18, 17.1–8 et al.; cf. Gal 2.11–12).

---

[113] For major studies of this variety, see Overman (1990); Saldarini (1994); Sim (1998); Repschinski (2000); Gale (2005). Key articles include Segal (1991); Carter (2007); Runesson (2008b).
[114] See now Runesson (2011), with relevant bibliography (ibid., 75–78). My account of the book's likely Antiochene provenance reflects the common opinion as articulated, for instance, by John Meier in Brown and Meier (1983: 15–27). Sim (1998: 40–62), offers a thorough review of the arguments for and against Antioch, arguing in favor of that location at ibid. (58–62).
[115] Indications of Ignatius' familiarity with an early form of Matthew's gospel appear in Ignatius, *Eph.* 14.2 (cf. Matt 12.33), 17.1 (cf. Matt 26.7), *Smyrn.* 1.1 (cf. Matt 3.15), 6.1 (cf. Matt 19.2), *Pol.* 2.2 (cf. Matt 10.6), and possibly elsewhere. See Meier in Brown and Meier (1983: 24–25); Sim (1998: 56–57).

For these reasons, it seems most likely that Matthew was written in Antioch or a nearby locale in the Greek-speaking region of coastal Syria.[116] Its intended audience was probably a church community not unlike that which Paul locates in Antioch in his letter to the Galatians. In other words, Matthew's readers probably were made up of persons of Jewish and gentile ancestry who invariably chose to identify as Jews by virtue of their adherence to the laws of the Torah.[117] But the events of the years since Paul's activity in their region seem to taken a toll on their number. By the time of Matthew's composition, the apostolic mission to the Jews was dead or dying. The demographic of the wider Church was already leaning toward Paul's decisively non-Jewish model. Furthermore, the destruction of the Jerusalem Temple and suspension of its sacrificial cult had undermined the covenantal logic of the gospel through which Matthew's readers had been drawn to the Church. Consequently, his agenda is to address the concerns of disillusioned readers habituated to Jewish lifestyles but conditioned by circumstance to question whether their adherence to the Jewish law would be enough to ensure their salvation.[118]

Matthew's multigenerational and multisituational discourse on Jewish identity is difficult to reduce to a simple position statement. In contradistinction to Paul, the question for Matthew is not whether followers of Jesus must observe the laws of the Torah. It is whether those predisposed to observe those laws must do more than that. His answer is in the affirmative. In several instances,

---

[116] My comments here follow L.M. White (1991), who stresses the possibility of Matthew's origin in any number of Jewish communities in the Greek cities of Syria liable to have been in contact with apostles from the Galilee (see especially ibid., 228–36). Some stressing Matthew's Jewish rhetoric have argued for the location of his community in the Galilee itself; see, e.g., Overman (1990: 158–59); Saldarini (1992: 26–27) (although cf. Saldarini (1994: 26); Gale (2005: 46–63)); Runesson (2008b: 106–08). I find the inference of a predominantly Jewish social setting for Matthew's community forced. The gospel includes nothing to suggest that its critique of Judaism was specific to the temporal or geographical setting of its narrative. Nor is there reason to suppose that Matthew's community would have known a Jewish population in Syria substantially different from that of the Galilee. The general rapport between Palestinian and Syrian Jews is indicated by a range of evidences in locating those two geographically proximate populations in close cultural contact. For evidence and discussion to this effect, see Roth-Gerson (2001: 46–50), and cf. Segal (1991: 25–29), for similar considerations with respect to Matthew's community.

[117] On Matthew's church as a Torah-observant community of mixed Jewish and gentile ancestry similar to the type addressed by Paul in his letter to the Galatians, see Sim (1998: 103–06); Zetterholm (2003: 211–16).

[118] I do not mean to suggest that Matthew's view of the Jewish law as a legitimate option for his readers amounted to a general endorsement thereof. In other words, that his community continued to sustain its practice does not necessarily imply Matthew's expectation that all followers of Jesus (read: gentiles) had to adhere to the legislation of the Torah per the convention of the Jews. For recent studies predicated on this crucial distinction, see Deines (2004), summarized in Deines (2008), Foster (2004), and Cuvillier (2009), with further bibliography in Cuvillier (145–47, n. 7). Although the question of Matthew's views regarding gentile observance of the Jewish law is beyond the scope of this study, I shall comment on his view of the gentile mission later.

Matthew's Jesus is shown asserting the permanence of the Jewish law as a binding obligation for his fellow Jews. But in each case, he adds conditions of his own.[119] So, for instance, Jesus hails the law as the key to righteousness before offering a series of antitheses contrasting its ethical directions with alternative positions attuned to his ethical outlook (Matt 5.17–20, 21–48).[120] Asked whether a man can divorce his wife for any reason he should choose, Jesus cites the Pentateuchal statute confirming that right only to repudiate it as unfair to the woman (Matt 19.1–9; cf. Deut 24.1–4). Asked by a wealthy young man how to achieve the eternal life of the righteous, Jesus instructs him to follow the commandments of the Torah as well as to donate all his assets to the poor (Matt 19.16–22). To Matthew, therefore, followers of Jesus predisposed to observe the laws of the Torah had also to abide by Jesus' moral teachings as though his revealed wisdom had qualified and improved the legislation of Moses.[121]

Yet offsetting his implicit support for readers wishing to maintain their Jewish identities, Matthew expresses a great deal of hostility toward Jews outside of his church community. Much of the gospel's vituperative content appears to have originated in older narrative traditions documenting conflicts between Jesus and his fellow Jews. But Matthew's personal animus surfaces throughout. Matthew's Jesus is shown constantly arguing with the Pharisees and scribes, who seem to follow his every move from the outset of his ministry to his arrest in Jerusalem.[122] He thus upbraids those local Jewish authority figures as blind men, hypocrites, and vipers, reproving their sanctimonious pretensions and condemning them to hell (Matt 15.3–9, 13–14, 23.1–36). Elsewhere Jesus appears to vent his frustration at the Jewish people in general in anticipation of their eventual rejection of his gospel (Matt 7.15–20, 8.11–12, 22, 12.33, 21.42–44, 23.37–39). In one notorious passage, the author seems to implicate the Jews en masse in his persecution and death (Matt 27.24–25). Finally, Jesus foretells the fall of Jerusalem and the destruction of the Temple as signs that God will have rejected the sacrificial cult of the Jews in favor of

---

[119] Hence Deines' argument that Matthew's Jesus "transformed" the Torah by subordinating its legislation to his moral authority (2004: 645–51; 2008: 84), Foster's that he "reprioritized" the status of the Jewish law (2004: 260), and Cuvillier's that he "radicalized" it (2009: 146–47 and passim). For corresponding comments on the following examples, see Deines (2004: 95–434), summarized in Deines (2008: 73–82); Foster (2004: 94–143); Cuvillier (2009: 148–57).

[120] Note that the innovative readings of the Pentateuchal laws assigned to Jesus in this sequence appears to owe to modes of Jewish exegesis later to be practiced by the rabbinic sages. See Ruzer (2007: 11–34), and cf. Vahrenhorst (2002: 24–26), for general comments on Matthew's use of Jewish exegetical techniques.

[121] Here I follow the central argument of Byrskog (1994); see especially ibid. (199–218), on Matthew's unique depiction of Jesus as a teacher of Torah.

[122] The Pharisees and scribes appear as opponents of Jesus in Matt 9.9–17, 12.1–14, 22–32, 38–42, 15.1–20, 16.1–4, 19.1–9, 21.23–27, 22.15–22, 23–33, 41–45. Discussion of these stories, their sources, and their Matthean redaction are the principal concerns of Repschinski (2000); see ibid. (294–342), for programmatic comments.

the new covenantal dispensation that he was to inaugurate (Matt 23.37–39, 24.1–2, 15–28).[123] Each of these tropes sees Matthew embellish his source materials to toxic effect.

The tension between Jesus' Jewish tendencies and his misgivings about Jews likely mirrors Matthew's own conflicted persona.[124] Though likely a product of the apostolic mission to the Jews, Matthew clearly was frustrated by its recent failure. He also regretted the failure of the Jewish revolt and the resulting destruction of the Jerusalem Temple, tragedies no less upsetting to his community than to all Jews of his day. As for his derogatory views on the Pharisees and scribes, one might infer that Matthew saw those men as competitors in a field of popular influence that, to his mind, belonged solely to Jesus. The survival of some of those learned interpreters of the Torah is manifest in a rabbinic literary tradition counting such men among its earliest proponents.[125] It is possible that Matthew uniquely saw those historical adversaries of Jesus as potential rivals of his own apostolic initiative liable to hound his readers despite their distance from Judea (cf. Matt 23.15).[126] Hence Jesus' telling advice to his disciples regarding involvement with Pharisees and scribes: "Do what they teach you and follow it, but do not do as they do, for they do not practice what they teach … You are not to be called rabbi, for you have one teacher and you are all students" (Matt 23.3, 8).[127]

In light of these considerations, scholars acknowledging Matthew's Jewish frame of reference have described his community as a sectarian movement within the wider Jewish collective similar in organization to the Pharisees, Sadducees, and Essenes.[128] Although I hesitate to overstate the structural design

---

[123] The predictions of the destruction placed in Jesus' mouth are not unique to Matthew's gospel; cf. Mark 13.1–8, 14–23. But Matthew's juxtaposition of Jesus' patronage of the Temple with his warnings of its downfall lend his account the rueful tone of a lament in contrast to Mark's vindictive stance. See Gurtner (2008).

[124] For the following, compare Freyne (1985: 119–23, 129–31, 132–35, 137–39); Dunn (1992b, 203–10); Saldarini (1994: 44–67); Sim (1998: 118–23). For a corresponding assessment locating Matthew's rhetorical objective outside of the Jewish tradition, see Luz (2005a).

[125] On the social profiles of the surviving Pharisees as reflected in the works of Josephus and the rabbis, see S. Schwartz (1990: 170–208), although cf. S. Schwartz (2001: 112–13), on the fallacy of overstating the degree of popular influence that those reputed founders of the rabbinic movement would have exercised during their own days.

[126] For a similarly reserved assessment, see Repschinski (2000: 343–49). Other commentators have been too confident in the organizational wherewithal of the earliest proponents of the rabbinic movement to present an authoritative Jewish stand against Christianity; see, e.g., Overman (1990: 38–62); Saldarini (1994: 13–18); Sim (1998: 150–51); Gale (2005: 17–23); Runesson (2008b: 108–11).

[127] Matthew's application of the title "rabbi" to the Pharisees and scribes thus serves to distance Jesus from other Jewish teachers prone to such pretension; see Byrskog (1994: 284–87). But his use of that common Hebrew honorific does not necessarily indicate Matthew's familiarity with the nascent rabbinic movement.

[128] See, e.g., Overman (1990: 154–57); Saldarini (1994: 84–123); Sim (1998: 115–50); Repschinski (2000: 50–56); Runesson (2008b: 120–30). Less tenable are the proposals of Luomanen (2002), who sees Matthew's community as a deviant cult given to Roman concepts of divinity, and Gale

of a group known only through Matthew's allusive testimony, I certainly will grant their sectarian function. Matthew addresses his readers as Jews shunned by their countrymen for their belief that Jesus is the one and only authoritative interpreter of the Torah, the defining benchmark of Jewish identity in their locale and throughout the ancient world.

Whether that renders Matthew's rhetorical objective pro-Jewish or anti-Jewish is a matter of perspective. According to the former reading, his affirmation of the Torah as the basis of the gospel implies his affirmation of Judaism as a reasonable choice for followers of Jesus. According to the latter, Matthew's relegation of the Torah to a status of inferior didactic authority implies his rejection of all interpretations of Judaism apart from that which Jesus ostensibly preached. While some scholars, therefore, prefer to locate Matthew's readership community within the limits of a culturally diverse Near Eastern Jewish society, others choose to locate his community just beyond those limits.[129]

To my mind, the very inference of such boundaries is illusory. Given the time and place of his writing, Matthew had no reason to know his readers as anything but Jews.[130] If he did know of the idea of Christian identity, he evidently did not feel obligated to apply that new rubric to his own group. Matthew's commendation of the Jewish law as a key element of their communal discipline is enough to qualify those readers as Jews, if, by definition, Jews of a specific and idiosyncratic variety. That he sometimes condemns Jews of other varieties puts Matthew in league with Paul as a voice of dissent leveled against the Jewish status quo from within the Jewish collective. And as in Paul's case, that Matthew's social commentary contributed to the process whereby later readers chose to realize their identities as Christians does not retroactively render his objective anti-Jewish. Others may disagree. But that is the angle that I choose to assume in reading Matthew's gospel as a product of Jewish design.

A few examples will help to illustrate my point. Matthew is not unique among the gospels in depicting Jesus as a Torah-observant Jew.[131] But it is the

---

(2005, 30–32), who sees a community of wealthy and educated Jewish scribes at odds with other scribes advocating the more traditional Jewish values of the Pharisees.

[129] Compare the studies cited earlier to those arguing for the decisive removal of Matthew's community from their prior Jewish social setting, e.g., Stanton (1992: 113–45); Senior (1999), Hare (2000); Hagner (2003); Luz (2005b).

[130] In other words, the inference that Matthew meant to define his community as something other than Jewish depends on the assumption of a decisive "parting of the ways" between Judaism and Christianity prior to the composition of his gospel; cf. Stanton (1992): 124–31; Luz (2005b: 9–13). Several studies predicated on this questionable sequence of events appear in Senior (2011).

[131] That is to not to say that the gospels depict Jesus as a strict observer of the Torah's precepts. The Jesus of the gospels is a man knowledgeable of the Torah's contents but prone to question its wisdom when it offended his ethical sensibilities. If this characterization is at all accurate, it would appear that the Jesus of history carried himself as a Jew with a defiant streak. For more nuanced comments supporting this impression, see, e.g., Vermes (1973: 28–29); E.P. Sanders (1985: 245–69); Freyne (2004: 20–23); Meier (2009: 26–47).

only one to indicate that he wished his disciples to follow his example. The most notable statement to this effect appears in Matthew's account of Jesus' Sermon on the Mount (Matt 5–7). In that pivotal sequence, Jesus is shown preaching in public for the very first time to an assembly of curious onlookers in the Galilee.[132] Among the lessons included in his speech are the aforementioned legal antitheses whereby Jesus sets forth his ethical objective in reference to selected directives drawn from the legislation of Moses. He prefaces his exposition with a noteworthy proviso. "Do not think," Jesus tells his audience, "that I have come to abolish the law or the prophets. I have come not to abolish but to fulfill" (Matt 5.17). Promising not to change one letter of the Torah, Jesus urges his audience to follow its commandments to perfection should they wish to be known as righteous and enter into the eschatological kingdom of heaven (Matt 5.18–20).

As a prelude to the gospel, this statement is striking. Matthew's Jesus unmistakably affirms the need of his followers to observe the Jewish law. From the standpoint of his narrative, it makes perfect sense that Jesus would have spoken these words to an audience consisting entirely of Jews. But Matthew further draws his own audience into Jesus' discursive range by implication of their common social context. Assuming, in other words, that Matthew meant to speak primarily to Jewish readers, we may reasonably deduce that he meant to impart Jesus' words on the relevance of the Jewish law to those very readers.[133] Of course, one must bear in mind that Jesus immediately proceeds to qualify the law with his own ethical stipulations. It therefore would be a mistake to construe Matthew's affirmation of the Jewish law as a general order for Christian living.[134] Nevertheless, his equation of gospel and Torah imbues Matthew's tract with a tacit defense of Judaism as an acceptable, if not necessarily obligatory, mode of cultural identification for some within the ethnically

---

[132] Presenting a summary statement of his moral teachings, Jesus' debut speech appears to have originated as an abstract pedagogical tradition. On its narrative function in the gospel, see Betz (1995: 80–88), who posits its general independence of Matthew's own covenantal theology. For a rebuttal aligning the Sermon on the Mount with Matthew's worldview, see Stanton (1992: 307–25).

[133] This point is emphasized by those arguing for Matthew's Jewish discursive objective; see, e.g., Overman (1990: 86–89); Saldarini (1994: 5–6); Sim (1998: 124–27).

[134] In other words, the "law" cited in Matt 5.17 might represent a conceit synonymous with Jesus' creative rereading of the Torah in the verses immediately following. According to this reading, Jesus' expression of support for the law would function not as a general endorsement of Jewish practice but, rather, as a hermeneutical principle conferring his pedagogical authority upon the legal antitheses that he proceeds to articulate. For this reading, see Stanton (1992: 300–03); Betz (1995: 173–79); Foster (2004: 182–86); Meier (2009: 40–47). Deines (2004: 257–87) (cf. Deines 2008: 74–75), reads the verse as a confirmation of Jesus' fulfillment of the law rather than an explanation of his own agenda. Although I take much from these readings, I do not consider Matthew's equation of gospel and Torah to imply his valuation of one over the other. Both are necessary ingredients in his formula for righteousness. Only if one assumes that Matthew meant to address Christians of gentile ancestry does his position seem problematic.

variegated Church. For those in his community concerned about the prospect of maintaining their Jewish identities as members of that Church, Matthew's positive reinforcement presumably would have been quite welcome.

Hints of Matthew's Jewish rhetorical objective also appear in more subtle variations from Mark's gospel. In Mark, for example, Jesus is shown attracting the suspicion of the Pharisees for eating without washing his hands (Mark 7.1–23). In a narrative aside, the author explains that the Pharisees and all Jews are preoccupied with the concept of ritual cleanliness, causing them to wash their hands, their food, and their cookware to obsessive lengths (Mark 7.3–4). After deflecting his critics, Jesus explains to his disciples that one is not defiled by what goes into his mouth but by what comes out. He thus at once debases the concerns of his critics while teaching his followers a valuable lesson about proper speech. The evangelist then infers that Jesus' words amounted to a declaration that all foods are to be considered ritually clean or *kosher* (Mark 7.19). In Matthew's retelling of this incident, he omits Mark's disparaging remarks on the Jews' odd predilection for washing and his inference regarding Jesus' views on their dietary restrictions (Matt 15.1–20). It therefore would appear that Matthew expected that his readers would understand the objection of the Pharisees without further explanation. Perhaps more notably, he expected Jesus to have upheld the essential Pentateuchal requirements of *kashrut* despite rejecting the ancillary concerns of his Pharisaic critics.[135]

Another notable example of Matthew's abiding Jewish temperament appears in his account of Jesus' vision of the fall of Jerusalem (Matt 24.13–28). In Mark's account of that prophecy, Jesus tells of the city's residents fleeing for the hills following the violent desecration of their Temple (Mark 13.14–23). Warning his disciples that the refugees will not have time even to gather their coats, he chillingly cautions them, "Pray that it shall not be in winter" (Mark 13.18). In Matthew's version of the same premonition, the author emends Jesus' warning to "Pray that your flight shall not be in winter or on a Sabbath" (Matt 24.20). Despite the efforts of some to explain Matthew's editorial addition as disingenuous, the most obvious explanation is his intimation of danger for followers of Jesus forced to violate the sanctity of the Jewish day of rest.[136] It seems that Matthew likewise expected his own readers, the putative subjects of Jesus' prediction, to have been just as troubled by that possibility.

The author of Matthew's gospel casually implicates his readers as Jews by virtue of what he says and what he chooses not to say. Arguably the most notable silence in his exposition of the gospel pertains to his views on the gentile

[135] For complementary readings of these passages, see Overman (1990: 82–84); Saldarini (1994: 134–41); Sim (1998: 132–35); Vahrenhorst (2002: 393–403).
[136] So Saldarini (1994: 126–27); Vahrenhorst (2002: 381); Doering (2010: 248–50) (cf. Doering 1999: 402–03). Compare Stanton (1992: 192–206), who offers the rather forced view that Matthew meant to warn his readers of having to expose themselves to attacks by Jews prone to persecute them for violating the Sabbath.

mission still flourishing in his day. Although Matthew's Jesus seems to endorse the Jewish law as a necessary code of conduct for Jews, he states nothing directly regarding its relevance for gentiles. Set almost entirely in Jewish social environments, Matthew's narrative features only occasional value-neutral references to non-Jews whom Jesus happens to encounter during his ministry (Matt 8.5–13, 15.21–28).[137] Nevertheless, Matthew does appear to acknowledge the apostolic mission to the gentiles in one pivotal passage. In the very last verses of the book, the risen Jesus appears to his disciples in the Galilee with express instructions to "go and make disciples of all nations," teaching them to "obey everything that I have commanded you" (Matt 28.18–20; cf. 24.14). Looking forward to the present situation of the Church, the evangelist thus recognizes and accepts the eventual need of the apostolic mission to expand beyond its original Jewish ambit.[138]

But whether Matthew supposed that Jesus' message to the gentiles was to include their obedience to the Jewish law he does not say. This leaves ambiguous the matter of how he expected his followers to function as Jews within a Church already predominated by Pauline Christians. One commentator has argued that Matthew's endorsement of the Jewish law speaks to his deliberate rejection of Paul's gospel and his assertively Jewish social outlook to his community's isolation from the wider Christian collective.[139] I find that implausible. Although Matthew's Jesus is shown expressly telling his disciples not to evangelize beyond the nation of Israel during his lifetime (Matt 10.5–6), his unqualified endorsement of the gentile mission confounds the premise of setting him in opposition to the Church's Pauline demographic. Matthew undoubtedly agreed with Paul in construing the teachings of Jesus as the filter through which his followers had to process the legislation of the Torah in the present eschatological age.[140] He invokes Paul's own language in speaking of

[137] On these stories as premonitions of the gentile mission, see Saldarini (1994: 70–74); Foster (2004: 227–30). Amy-Jill Levine argues for a more measured approach, citing Jesus' reported indifference to his gentile contacts as evidence of Matthew's sense that the covenantal status of the nations underwent a profound transformation following the crucifixion; see A.-J. Levine (1988: 107–52).

[138] On this crucial turning point in Matthew's ethnic rhetoric, see A.-J. Levine (1988: 165–92), and cf. Overman (1990: 127–28); Saldarini (1994: 78–81). I depart from A.-J. Levine (1988: 193–239), with respect to her argument for Matthew's rejection of the Jews tout court in light of the negative opinions he expresses toward the Pharisees, the scribes, and others who declined to receive the gospel.

[139] For this argument, see Sim (1998: 236–47), who reads Matt 5.17–20 as an expression of the author's intransigent desire to see all members of the Church abide by the Jewish law irrespective of their ethnic origins. Less forceful arguments in favor of Matthew's expectation that gentile initiates into his community adopt Jewish customs appear in Saldarini (1994: 68–83); Repschinski (2000: 345–48).

[140] My assessment here follows that of Foster (2004: 219–52), with reference to Matthew's version of the apostolic commission at ibid. (239–47). See also Deines (2004: 447–51) (cf. Deines 2008: 55); (Cuvillier 2009: 158–59).

Jesus' fulfillment of the law (Matt 5.17; cf. Rom 3.31, 8.4, 10.8–10). He echoes Paul's assertion of the preeminence of God's commandments (Matt 5.19, 8.4, 15.3, 19.17, 22.34–40; cf. Rom 25–27, 1 Cor 7.19, Gal 5.14). He emulates Paul's scheme of salvation history in citing Jesus' primary role as the savior of the Jewish people (Matt 1.21; cf. Rom 9–11).

Clearly, Matthew admired the apostle to the gentiles. It therefore seems reasonable to surmise that he accepted Paul's gospel, if only as it applied to gentiles. The evangelist, in other words, correctly understood that Paul had pitched his gospel to people wary of becoming Jews, offering his gentile readers a protocol for joining the community of Israel on terms conducive to their lifestyles. But Matthew presumed to speak to people who were already Jews. He therefore articulated a gospel for Jews that he believed complemented Paul's, inverting his predecessor's ethnic reasoning to his own rhetorical advantage. Paul had urged his readers in Rome to tolerate their "sickly" brethren given to Jewish habits (Rom 14.1–15.6). Matthew, on the other hand, affirmed the Jewish identities of his readers, advocating tolerance of those of their associates not beholden to their own privileged rights of covenantal participation. From his point of view, the gentiles were the ones in need of compassion.

One wonders whether Matthew was really so aloof from his people's dwindling share in the wider Church. But the eclipse of the Jewish Christians by adherents of Paul's gospel does not diminish the remarkable quality of Matthew's testimony. In time, his readers would circulate their book widely enough to ensure its consecration as one of Christianity's few authoritative witnesses to the life of Jesus. And even as Matthew's native Jewish perspective faded from the agendas of most, some Christians continued to read his gospel as it was meant to be read. Within living memory of the evangelist's lifetime, the early second-century bishop Papias of Hierapolis reported that certain unnamed Christian parties were circulating a version of Matthew's gospel in the Hebrew language.[141] Several years later, Irenaeus of Lyons would connect that tract to a rumored population of Torah-observant Christians operating under the name Ebionites. Later patristic authors would go on to tell of Matthew's popularity among those and other "Jewish" heretics allegedly infesting the Near Eastern churches.[142] Evidently, the evangelist's brand

---

[141] Cited in Eusebius, *Hist. eccl.* 3.39.16. Papias seems to have inferred that the Hebrew text was Matthew's original composition and, therefore, the source of the canonical Greek text. But as Eusebius acknowledges, Papias was not very smart (*Hist. eccl.* 3.39.13). Bizarrely, Eusebius also cites the second-century Alexandrian scholar Pantaenus as having found a Hebrew edition of Matthew in India (*Hist. eccl.* 5.10.3). One wonders whether the Greek-speaking traveler innocently mistook one exotic script for another.

[142] Irenaeus, *Haer.* 1.26.2, 3.1.1, 3.11.7; cf. Epiphanius, *Pan.* 29.9.4, 30.3.7, 30.6.9, 30.13.1–5, 30.14.1–4; Jerome, *Pelag.* 3.2, *Vir. ill.* 3, *Comm. Matt.* 12.13. For a valiant attempt to locate these testimonies in relation to other apocryphal gospel tracts associated with Jews, see Klijn (1992: 27–30).

of radical conservatism remained a feasible option for quite some time, if only to those few of his readers attuned to his subtle Jewish métier.

THE DIDACHE

The ancient Christian text known as the Didache is quite enigmatic. Attested in several patristic writings as an early entry in the formative Christian scriptural canon, its contents were lost to that tradition at a relatively early date. The discovery in 1873 of a medieval manuscript including the Didache among a number of other documents of the apostolic age quickly commanded the attention of those hoping to mine its ancient record for new information about the foundations of the Church. The results of more than a century of scholarship now point to the Didache's function as a collection of materials explaining a number of early Christian rites and ethical directives through synthetic exegesis of the Hebrew Scriptures and the teachings of Jesus.[143] From the outset of its modern study, scholars have noted apparent instances of correspondence between its text and classical Jewish concepts, liturgical texts, and ritual practices otherwise lost to the Church. That quality of its composition is today widely taken to indicate the Didache's origin amidst a Christian community of Jewish descent still inclined to express their faith in a Jewish idiom.[144]

More precise details regarding its provenance have proven difficult to ascertain. The Didache's conventional title, Greek for "the teaching," is short for "the teaching of the Lord through the twelve apostles to the nations." Although the title is likely secondary to the text itself, its literary pretense is that of a treatise composed by the leaders of the apostolic Church of Jerusalem for use by Jewish apostles preaching the gospel among the gentiles. The Didache utilizes an edition of the gospel identical to Matthew's or closely related, echoing, for instance, in its first section the latter's unique account of the Sermon on the Mount. Although the genealogical relationship between the two texts is impossible to establish, it seems reasonable to infer that they originated in the same general time and place, if not necessarily within the same readership community.[145] This would place the

---

[143] On the ancient reception of the Didache and the circumstances of its modern rediscovery, see Niederwimmer (1998: 4–29). Also instructive is the critical overview of Draper (1996b). A number of important twentieth-century studies are reprinted in Draper's volume.

[144] The Jewish elements of the Didache are treated in detail in van de Sandt and Flusser (2002) and Del Verme (2004). For a succinct overview of theories relating to its Jewish sources, see Draper (2007). The document's proposed Jewish provenance is a guiding hermeneutical principle in the voluminous, though often erratic, study of Milavec (2003); see especially ibid. (xxix–xxx), for relevant methodological comments.

[145] In other words, while it is clear that the Didache's author was aware of textual traditions also attested in Matthew, it is not clear whether one text draws directly upon the other. For like comments, see Niederwimmer (1998: 46–51), and cf. Draper (1996b: 16–19). Recent studies probing the relationship between the two documents appear in van de Sandt (2005) and van de Sandt and Zangenberg (2008). Milavec (2003: 695–739), argues for the Didache's complete independence of Matthew in view of their divergent religious systems, a hermeneutic which I do not see as applicable to the question at issue.

composition of the Didache in western Syria around the turn of the second century. That said, as in Matthew's case, some of its source materials are likely older than the text's final recension.[146]

For lack of verifiable data on its textual evolution, I shall attempt to diagnose the Didache's Jewish profile not on the basis of its proposed source materials but on the function of those materials in the document's received form.[147] The first five sections of the text feature an ethical discourse plotted in reference to what its author describes as "two ways, one of life and one of death" (*Did.* 1.1). The proceeding instructions on righteous and unrighteous living evoke a dualistic model of moral objectification attested in a document recovered among the Dead Sea Scrolls known as the Rule of the Community. In that text, the "two ways" motif is used to educate potential initiates into the Qumran community about that group's sectarian anthropology (1QS 3.13–4.26). The motif serves a similar function in the Didache, which relates the contours of Jesus' ethical program to potential Christian initiates.[148] Whether the author of the Didache was aware of its currency among Jewish sectarians of a slightly earlier era is unclear. But it seems reasonably certain

---

[146] So Niederwimmer (1998: 42–52); Draper (1996b: 22–24). Milavec (2003) assumes an oral-traditional context for the text's development allowing for the flexible dating of its contents; see especially ibid. (xxxii–xxxiii, 715–25), and cf. Draper (ibid., 19–22), for comments on earlier theories positing the text's organic evolution as a rule of order in its author's Christian community. While I concede the likelihood that the Didache's final text conceals successive stages of prior editorial activity, I do not take that observation as a sound methodological pretext for paring away the text's undifferentiated editorial accretions in the interest of recovering its putative sources.

[147] I depart here from the methods of those who propose to isolate strands of traditional Jewish material on the basis of their affinities with Jewish texts of later provenance. This unfortunate tendency affects the treatments of van de Sandt and Flusser, Milavec, and Draper, who interpret the Didache in light of rabbinic sources chosen indiscriminately and analyzed without regard to their contexts and histories of composition. Their resulting efforts to demonstrate the text's Jewish features thus incur numerous false assumptions as to the respective states of Jewish ethical discourse, halakhic observance, and apocalyptic thought in the Didache's rhetorical world. More cautious is Del Verme, who seeks to contextualize the text's features in view of its contacts with Jewish cultural phenomena of the Second Temple period; see especially Del Verme (2004: 74–88), and cf. Jefford (2001). Yet I am unmoved by his situation of the Didache (and the entirety of the Christian tradition) within a distinctive milieu of "Enochic-Essene Judaism," on which see ibid. (21–24). While I find it plausible that the author of the Didache drew upon a foundation of knowledge shared with Essenes and other Jewish sectarians, I find Del Verme's submission of the Didache as an Essene or Essene-inspired communal manifesto lacking for evidence and credibility.

[148] On the Didache's introduction of this discernably Jewish tradition into Christian ethical discourse, see the seminal treatments of Audet (1996) and Rordorf (1996) and, more recently, Draper (1996b: 13–16); Niederwimmer (1998: 30–41). On its relevance toward the proposed Jewish background of the book, see van de Sandt and Flusser (2002: 55–80); Del Verme (2004: 126–33).

that he emulated a Jewish model in applying the "two ways" to the purpose of his didactic exercise.[149]

Later in its text, the Didache rehearses a series of benedictions meant to be recited by Christians after sharing a Eucharistic or thanksgiving meal (*Did.* 10). The content and structure of those blessings seem to anticipate a liturgical cycle later to circulate among Jews as the *birkat ha-mazon* or the "blessing of the meal."[150] Although versions of this liturgy were known to the early rabbinic sages, our earliest surviving witnesses to its text date to the Middle Ages. That makes it difficult to say how closely the Christian adaptation in the Didache resembles its putative Jewish source text.[151] But the likelihood that the Didache's formula traces to the same liturgical tradition claimed by the rabbis is remarkable enough. In adopting the Jewish rite, the author reveals a connection to contemporary Jewish practice indicative of his or his informant's recent acquaintance with actual Jews.

What these furtive Jewish connections say about the cultural persuasions of the Didache's addressees is not certain. Unlike the author of Matthew's gospel, the author of the Didache nowhere alludes to followers of Jesus as Jews. In fact, he is sufficiently confident in the idea of Christian identity to apply that new mark to his readers (*Did.* 12.4). But beyond that distinction, his social commentary is frustratingly ambiguous. At one point, he refers to certain unnamed hypocrites who allegedly fast on Mondays and Fridays and pray differently than the author would prefer (*Did.* 8.1–2). That Matthew applies the same derogatory term to the Pharisees, the scribes, and other Jews of Jesus' day raises the possibility that the author of the Didache likewise means to refer to Jews here.[152] Elsewhere, he warns his readers of itinerant apostles and prophets

---

[149] I am less confident in the premise of situating the Didache's use of the "two ways" motif in a continuous discursive tradition extending from the Dead Sea Scrolls through the late ancient Christian pseudepigrapha known as the Testaments of the Twelve Patriarchs and the post-classical Talmudic treatise *Derekh Eretz Zuta*. For this argument, see van de Sandt and Flusser (2002: 140–90), and cf. Milavec (2003: 62–65); Draper (2007: 263–67).

[150] So, e.g., Niederwimmer (1998: 155–61); Draper (1996b: 26–29); van de Sandt and Flusser (2002: 310–29); Milavec (2003: 416–21).

[151] The earliest surviving allusions to the text of the *birkat ha-mazon* providing data comparable to the Didache appear in *t.Berakhot* 4.6, 6.11. On the development of the rabbinic rite, see Shmidman (2007: 121–25).

[152] Compare the reserved commentaries of Niederwimmer (1998: 131–35); Draper (1996a); van de Sandt and Flusser (2002: 291–96); Del Verme (2004: 143–88), although cf. Milavec (2003: 301–03), who argues against the correlation of the Didache's hypocrites with Matthew's while nevertheless maintaining their Jewish identities. Scholars assessing the text's likely allusion to contemporary Jewish practice have had trouble explaining its unprecedented intimation that Jews tend to fast on Mondays and Thursdays; see, e.g., Draper (233–35); van de Sandt and Flusser (291–93); Milavec (293–95); Tomson (2005). I find the effort of Del Verme (ibid., 168–86), to expose a dispute between Essenic Christians and Pharisees over competing liturgical calendars frankly farfetched.

preaching lessons contrary to his own (*Did.* 11–12). It is tempting to discern in these notices hints of competition with Christian preachers of persuasions other than the author's own. But unlike those apostles whom Paul once derided as his competitors, the Didache's are allocated no specifically Jewish biases or missionary designs.[153]

More indicative of the Didache's social outlook are its comments on the Jewish law.[154] Amidst his various virtues constituting the more admirable of the "two ways," the author enjoins his readers not to neglect the commandments of the Lord, neither adding nor subtracting from what they have received (*Did.* 4.13). This phrasing evokes that ascribed to Jesus in Matthew 5.17–20, perhaps indicating the author's assimilation of that gospel's stance on the Jewish law. More telling is the author's advice following his initial moral demonstration. Referring to his previous advice, he tells his readers, "If you can bear the entire yoke of the Lord, you will be complete. But if you cannot, do what you can. And concerning food, bear what you can. But certainly stay away from what is sacrificed to idols, for it is worship of dead gods" (*Did.* 6.2–3).

The author's reference to the Torah as a yoke corresponds with the euphemism utilized by Matthew, Paul, and the author of Acts (Matt 11.29–30; Gal 5.1; Acts 15.10). He thereby acknowledges a readership consisting of persons whom he judged generally but not uniformly obliged to the Jewish law. In other words, the Didache speaks on behalf of a predominantly Jewish church community open to the inclusion of gentile members. The book's literary pretense is thus not entirely misleading. Despite its unusual medium, the tract communicates a typically Jewish rendition of the gospel yet distinctly sensitive to the needs of its non-Jewish readers. The author is aware that undertaking to observe the Jewish law would pose certain challenges to those not previously given to Jewish lifestyles. That is why he exhorts all of his readers, without casting aspersions, to bear as much of the burden as they can manage.[155] His one exception clearly resonates with Paul's plea that his readers in Corinth avoid ritually polluted meat (1 Cor 8–10), a need also stressed in the book of Acts

---

[153] So, e.g., Niederwimmer (1998: 169–70); van de Sandt and Flusser (2002: 340–50), although cf. ibid. (353–60), on analogous evidence for the occurrence of such behaviors among contemporary Near Eastern Jewry. For a fairly tendentious argument identifying the Didache's itinerant preachers as Jewish Christians urging strict adherence to the legislation of the Torah, see Draper (1996c: 346–52).

[154] For the following, see Niederwimmer (1998: 121–24); van de Sandt and Flusser (2002: 238–70); Draper (1996c: 352–59).

[155] Milavec (2003: 771–82), takes issue with the intimation of Draper (1996c: 357–59), that the author expects all of his readers to resolve to observe the whole of the Jewish law in advance of the end of days, a position which Draper defends in Draper (2003). Yet while Milavec is correct to counter Draper's original inference of tension between the Didache's author and Pauline Christianity, he seems to want to erase the Didache's variegated ethnic outlook by forcing the text through a Pauline sieve. That interpretive maneuver does not ring true to me. Although the author expresses no specific bias against gentiles, he clearly does assume a functional distinction between gentile and Jew in his scheme of salvation history (cf. *Did.* 1.3, 14.1–3).

(Acts 15.20, 29, 21.25). The author of the Didache seems to be aware of the issue faced by his apostolic predecessors. He therefore expresses in no uncertain terms what he believes is the one procedural condition potentially ruling out communion between his congregation's Jewish and gentile constituents. The Didache's stance on the Jewish law is well in line with Matthew's position.[156] Yet where Matthew merely implies that all followers of Jesus ideally should follow the commandments, the author of the Didache states it outright. His willingness to hold some members of his community to different standards of practice than others realizes Matthew's will for collaboration between the Jewish and gentile missions. One can only speculate as to whether the Didache speaks to the existence of an ethnically variegated Christian population modeled on Matthew's gospel or a similar apostolic charter. That intriguing possibility is supported by its reception as a handbook of high repute in the early Church. Clearly, some readers identified with its author's rare vision of a Christian community still connected with their Jewish past yet ready to compromise with potential supporters of their apostolic initiative who assumed cultural priorities different from their own.

THE PSEUDO-CLEMENTINE RECOGNITIONS

The Pseudo-Clementine literature comprises a set of Christian texts originating in fourth-century Syria and sharing a common pretense of having been written by the first-century bishop Clement of Rome.[157] The most substantial of these, the Homilies and the Recognitions, are based on a common literary source presenting a novelistic account of Clement's travels in the east with the apostle Peter during the years leading up to the latter's celebrated mission to Rome.[158] Likely dating to the early third century, the apparent function of this now lost book was to invent an alternative history of the apostolic Church catering to readers who traced their genealogies not to Paul's missionary enterprise but to the original Jewish mission spearheaded by Peter. Where the book of Acts loses interest in the Jewish mission upon picking up Paul's narrative thread, the Clementine novel apparently followed Peter and Clement through the cities of the Near East preaching a gospel predicated on continuity between the teachings of Jesus and the teachings of Moses.

That the authors of the Homilies and Recognitions chose to make use of the Clementine novel suggests their positive identification with the earlier

---

[156] For the following, see Draper (2007: 280–82), although cf. Draper (2005: 239–41), for a more sober assessment of the viability of the communal model envisioned in these texts.

[157] For an overview of the Pseudo-Clementine corpus, see F.S. Jones (2012b), with further bibliography, ibid. (41–49).

[158] On this lost document, see F.S. Jones (2012b: 16–17). Typically called the basic writing or *grundschrift,* Jones associates the lost Clementine novel with a document known as the Circuits of Peter, which Epiphanius alleges was written by Clement but subsequently corrupted by the Ebionites (*Pan.* 30.15.1–3).

document's portrait of a Church founded on resolutely Jewish principles. But their connection to Judaism evidently was not just a fond memory. The authors of both texts regularly urge their readers to observe certain vaguely Jewish dietary restrictions and standards of ritual purity otherwise eschewed by Christians of their age. That observation has led many scholars to posit that the books were written for the benefit of an obscure population of Syrian Christians who also identified as Jews.[159] Considering, moreover, their circulation in the Near East, their alleged predilections for Jewish ritual behavior have drawn comparisons between the readership communities who apparently sustained the Pseudo-Clementine literary tradition and the Ebionites, as well as other reputed Christian heretics of their ilk documented in patristic writings of the fourth century.[160]

My interest here is not to test these intriguing hypotheses.[161] I wish to focus, rather, on a section of the Recognitions generally thought to derive from a source even older than the Clementine romance, encompassing an independent narrative of unmistakable Jewish provenance (*Recog.* 1.27–71). According to the detailed and disciplined analysis of F. Stanley Jones, this section of the text appears to derive from an independent history of the apostolic Church of Jerusalem up to roughly 40 CE synchronous with the narrative of Acts.[162] For reasons I shall explain subsequently, that document appears to have been composed by a Jewish author and for Jewish readers in Palestine during the late second century.[163] It therefore bears asking whether the text, even in its present

[159] On the Jewish aspects of the fourth-century texts, see F.S. Jones (2005; 2007). Influential in this respect has been Strecker (1981) (cf. Strecker 1971: 257–71).

[160] Arguably the most notable early advocate of this identification was Schoeps (1949: 45–61) and passim, who built upon the earlier, though unsubstantiated, efforts of F.C. Baur and the Tübingen School to demonstrate this connection on the basis of Epiphanius' account of the Ebionites in *Pan.* 30. Although typically avoided in contemporary scholarship of the Pseudo-Clementines, the connection to the Ebionites remains popular among commentators on that alleged Jewish sect; see, e.g., Wilson (1995: 148–52); Bauckham (2003: 164–71); Häkkinen (2005: 258–65); Luomanen (2007: 92–95; 2012: 38–41) and passim. Lüdemann (1989: 182–83, 191–92), assigns the Recognitions to an unidentified community of formerly Jewish Christians disillusioned by the failure of the first Jewish revolt and the Homilies to the Elchasites, another alleged Jewish sect reputedly of Persian origin.

[161] Recent efforts to this effect include several articles by Annette Yoshiko Reed, who questions the diagnostic value of characterizing the Pseudo-Clementines as distinctly Jewish in view of the recent critical reevaluation of the parting of the ways narrative; see, e.g., Reed (2003, 2008b, 2008c, and 2012). See also Stanton (2007), who argues against describing the books as Jewish in view of their complicated and impenetrable histories of tradition and redaction among Christian readers not categorically identifiable as Jews.

[162] F.S. Jones (1995), summarized in F.S. Jones (2012b: 24–25). The Jewish character of this section has been upheld even by those hesitant to apply that generic label to the entire Pseudo-Clementine corpus; see, e.g., Reed (2003: 204–13); Stanton (2007: 317–33). Buell (2005: 71–73), although not denying the possibility of the text's Jewish provenance, reads its appeal to Jewish sensibilities as an early example of the historiographical construction of the Hebrew as a primordial Christian ethnic category.

[163] Earlier studies following Strecker (1981: 221–54), isolated the source as *Recog.* 1.33–71 on the pretext of correlating it with the aforementioned Preachings of Peter and/or another obscure

redacted form, might preserve pertinent information about the circumstances of its composition.

Due to the text's literary style and the state of its preservation, it is difficult to differentiate between the original text and its subsequent emendations.[164] I therefore shall forgo consideration of the redacted version's dialogical exposition between Peter and Clement and focus my analsyis on its proposed source. The section in question begins with a whirlwind account of the history of Israel up to the advent of Jesus before transitioning to a more focused narrative involving the first apostles. The narrative setting of the latter is roughly coterminous with that of Acts 5–10, namely Jerusalem several years after Jesus' resurrection. Facing resistance to their mission among the local Jewish establishment, the apostles assemble at the Temple to engage their critics in debate. In the process, they offer a systematic defense of their beliefs as legitimate interpretations of the ancient Hebrew prophecies concerning the Messiah. That strategy goes well for a while as certain members of the opposition including the Pharisaic sage Gamaliel and the High Priest Caiaphas soften to their message. Directed by James, the apostles are just about to baptize a large number of Jews including Caiaphas and his fellow priests when an unnamed enemy charges into the Temple and incites a riot. The ensuing melee sees James nearly killed and the rest of his company put to flight, eventually to regroup in Jericho. The narrative breaks off following a notice that the violent interloper, implied to be Paul, was next to pursue Peter to Damascus under the impression that the apostle had sought refuge in that city.

From a literary standpoint, the story reads like an alternative history of the early years of the apostolic mission dovetailing with the account of Acts yet told from a decidedly different perspective.[165] Its principal departure from the earlier treatise is its wholesale substitution of the martyrdom of the deacon Stephen for the near-martyrdom of James (*Recog.* 1.70.1–8; cf. Acts 7). Less conspicuous, though no less striking, is its divergent ethnic outlook. Speaking chiefly through Peter and other of Jesus' disciples, the author assumes an emphatically Jewish agenda. Narrating the origin of Israel, he characterizes

---

pseudo-apostolic treatise known as the Ascents of James, the latter of which Epiphanius associates with the Ebionites (Epiphanius, *Pan.* 30.16.6–9); see, e.g., Lüdemann (1989: 171–85); Wilson (1995: 152–55). Compare F.S. Jones (1995: 4–38), for a comprehensive survey of prior scholarship critical of the premise of identifying the source with any known text or textual corpus.

[164] Originally written in Greek, the text of the Recognitions survives primary in Syriac and Latin translations of the fifth century. Parallel English versions of these and other relevant witnesses appear in F.S. Jones (1995: 51–109). Per Jones (ibid., 39–49), neither ancient translation seems superior to the other with respect to its fidelity to the Greek text. I therefore shall not differentiate between the two in my citations except in cases of significant divergence.

[165] On the text's contrapuntal relationship with Acts, see F.S. Jones (1997), and cf. F.S. Jones (1995: 141–42). Compare Stanton (2007: 318–19), who downplays the affinities between the accounts in characterizing the Pseudo-Clementine source as a functionally independent apologia for Jewish followers of Jesus.

Abraham as a man of "our race, the Hebrews, who are also called the Jews" (*Recog.* 1.32.1).[166] He praises the land of Judea and its holy city of Jerusalem (*Recog.* 1.30.3, 1.57.4). He speaks of Hebrew as a holy language (*Recog.* 1.30.5). Later, he states that Jesus himself was a Jew, an exceedingly rare affirmation for Christians of his age (*Recog.* 1.60.7). Naturally, he appeals to all of his fellow Jews to recognize Jesus as the Messiah. But as for those who choose not to, the author nonetheless implores them to respect Jesus as they would any other decent person (*Recog.* 1.60.5–6).

Amidst his Jewish apologetics, the author articulates a missionary platform neatly aligned with those of his apostolic forerunners. He adduces Paul's ethnic reasoning in construing the mission to the gentiles as a necessary means for the fulfillment of God's promise to Abraham (*Recog.* 1.42.1; cf. 1.33.1–3). He alludes to Paul's soteriology in speaking of Jesus' self-sacrifice as a means of atoning for his people's sins in advance of their admission to the kingdom of heaven (*Recog.* 1.51.1–2). Like Paul and Matthew, the author prioritizes the Jewish mission to the gentile mission (*Recog.* 1.50.1–4). He likewise speaks of Jesus as a teacher of the law who came to fulfill its potential (*Recog.* 1.62.3, 1.69.1–3). Though hailing Moses a prophet of great repute in his own right, he asserts that Jesus was greater than Moses inasmuch as he was both a prophet and the Messiah (*Recog.* 1.59.1–3). Yet, like Matthew, he offers no indication that his readers should abandon the Jewish law, confidently stating that the only issue dividing their nation is the contested identity of the Messiah (*Recog.* 1.43.2, 1.50.7).

Yet his opinions on the Jews and their law are not entirely positive. He appropriates the rhetoric of Paul, Matthew, and other apostolic authors in faulting some of his people for refusing to believe in Jesus despite their having been primed to do so (*Recog.* 1.40.2, 1.50.5–6). He implicates those same stubborn Jews in Jesus' persecution (*Recog.* 1.53.1–2, 1.59.7). He accuses the Pharisees and scribes of concealing the key to the kingdom in their inscrutable teachings on the law (*Recog.* 1.54.6–8; cf. 1.59.1). And despite his support for the practice of that law, the author unleashes a familiar tirade against its regulations regarding sacrificial worship. Moses, he asserts, had allowed Israel to perform those rites as a concession to the idolatrous habits they had picked up in Egypt (*Recog.* 1.36.1; cf. Acts 7.42). God, he claims, preferred piety to sacrifice and punished his people each time they put that archaic form of worship at the fore of their national agenda (*Recog.* 1.37.3–4, 1.64.1–2). In any event, the period of sacrificial worship was meant to be temporary from the outset (*Recog.* 1.37.1–2). The arrival of Jesus had put an end to that period (*Recog.* 1.39.1, 1.48.5–6, 1.54.1, 1.63.4). Those Jews, he therefore warns, who were to continue patronizing the Temple cult would soon

---

[166] I quote here from the Syriac text (*gensā d'iylan ebraye d'metqreyn ap yihudaye*). The Latin text reads "our race of the Hebrews" (*nostrum hebraeorum [...] genus*); cf. F.S. Jones (1995: 58).

be uprooted from Judea, leaving only the followers of Jesus in their stead (*Recog.* 1.39.3, 1.64.1–4).[167] Yet even amidst his criticism, the author exhibits an unusual degree of sympathy for the subjects of his reproof. Though warning of the fall of Jerusalem and the destruction of her Temple, he faults the Samaritans for neglecting the Jewish holy city in favor of Mount Gerizim (*Recog.* 1.54.4). Though he introduces Caiaphas as a villain, he shows the High Priest willingly acceding to James' gospel before Paul's untimely intervention (*Recog.* 1.69.8). Conversely, he depicts Paul as a dutiful supporter of the old cult and a hindrance to the apostolic Church (*Recog.* 1.70.6–7, 1.71.3). Despite expressing hostility for the Pharisees and scribes, the author asserts against the Gospel of Matthew that those men had secretly been baptized by John, the herald of the Messiah, before the arrival of Jesus (*Recog.* 1.54.6–8; cf. Matt 3.7–10). He thus embellishes the sympathetic depiction of Gamaliel in Acts to indicate that that noted Pharisee was both the head of the entire Jewish nation and a secret supporter of the apostolic mission (*Recog.* 1.65.2, 1.66.4–67.7; cf. Acts 5.33–39, 22.3).

All told, the Pseudo-Clementine source presents a suggestive portrait of its author. As noted, he asserts his Jewish identity with no apparent reservation. And while he has choice words for some of his fellow Jews, his critique infuses established polemical tropes with a sense of awareness of their destructive potential for Jewish readers of his own disposition. The author seems to pitch his rhetoric to just such a Christian population situated in Judea/Palestine after some unspecified tumult involving the destruction of the Jerusalem Temple and the expatriation of some of the local Jewish population. This would date the text to sometime after 70 CE and, in all likelihood, after 135 CE, when Jerusalem's reestablishment as a Roman military colony effectively emptied the city of its Jews. Jones points to the author's doctored account of the death of James as one of several reasons to infer his use of the same lost chronicle of Hegesippus later to be cited by Eusebius.[168] In view of these and other diagnostic features, he dates the text to the late second century.

In view of these observations, we are left to ask what the Pseudo-Clementine source says about the conditions of Christian life to which its author speaks. Jones has proposed to read the text as an archetypical expression of Jewish Christian disdain for Paul and his antinomian gospel. As such, it would have functioned not as a companion to Acts but as a polemical rejoinder to that

---

[167] Koester (1989: 97–103), cites the author's insinuation of his community's permanent station in Judea as an early version of the aforementioned Pella tradition; see also Lüdemann (1989: 208–09). Yet the author of the Pseudo-Clementine source proceeds to track the migration of the Jerusalem Church after its stewardship by James not to the predominantly gentile city of Pella but to Jericho, a locale removed from Jerusalem but squarely within the borders of what was traditionally understood to comprise the Land of Israel (*Recog.* 1.71.5–6).

[168] F.S. Jones (1995: 142–45), referring to Eusebius, *Hist. eccl.* 2.23.3–18. Bourgel (2015) seems to overreach in reading the source as a political manifesto decrying both Bar Kokhba's failed revival of the Jewish sacrificial cult and the "paganization" of Judea that followed his rebellion.

book's exultant account of Paul's mission.[169] According to his reading, the author's endorsement of the Jewish law was meant as a targeted indictment of Paul. He thus depicts the apostle to the gentiles as an unrepentant persecutor of the Church whose reckless actions served to deter the leaders of the Jewish nation from willingly submitting to the gospel. The effect of his treatise is therefore that of a counternarrative to the book of Acts, presenting an alternative history of the early Church in which Paul's involvement marked the tragic decline of its original Jewish constitution rather than the increase of its fortunes among the nations.

I am not persuaded by that argument. The author of the text depicts Paul precisely as Paul depicted himself at the time of his initial engagement with the Church (cf. 1 Cor 15.9; Gal 1.13, 23; Phil 3.6). The fact that our text seems to afford him no chance for redemption might owe to its partial state of preservation.[170] We have no way of knowing whether the original text ended precisely where the author of the Recognitions ceases to utilize it. It is entirely conceivable that its narrative continued to recount Paul's missionary career in a positive light. Even excluding that possibility, one might observe that Paul's abuse of James serves the same constructive function as Stephen's martyrdom in the book of Acts. For if not for Paul's outburst, the apostles would not have left Jerusalem to pursue their mission among the nations. Only if one assumes that the author was opposed to that venture does his portrait of Paul seem unconditionally hostile. That is an assumption that cannot be sustained in view of his obvious approval of the gentile mission (*Recog.* 1.40.4, 1.42.1, 1.50.2).

Others have argued for the author's contact with contemporary Jews of non-Christian dispositions.[171] His depiction of the Pharisees as keepers of secret knowledge evokes the rabbinic concept of an oral Torah conceived by Moses and transmitted through the centuries alongside its written counterpart. By assigning that concept to the Pharisees of old, the author draws those erstwhile foes of the Church into a contemporary setting in which Jewish Christians saw themselves as peers of the rabbinic sages engaged in a common discourse of scriptural interpretation. Hence the author's account of Gamaliel, a figure likewise esteemed by the rabbis, as a friend of James, a fellow Christian, and a rare credit to his otherwise detested Pharisaic clique.[172] This reading would suggest

[169] So F.S. Jones (1995: 164–67; 1997: 242–43; 2005: 300–03); cf. Lüdemann (1989: 183–85); Reed (2003: 206–07).

[170] For similar concerns regarding the text's seemingly incomplete theological program, see Stanton (2007: 322).

[171] For the following, see especially Baumgarten (1992), and cf. F.S. Jones (2005: 324–35); Reed (2003: 205–06; 2008b: 290; 2008c: 193–94).

[172] As noted by Baumgarten (1992: 41–42), the Pseudo-Clementines preserve several notices indicating that some Pharisees and scribes were trustworthy while others were not; see, e.g., *Hom.* 3.70, 3.18, 11.28–29; *Recog.* 2.30.1, 6.11.2–3. I disagree with his argument that these notices speak to a healthy state of relations between their fourth-century authors and rabbinic Jews. They appear to me to be inferences based on the portrayal of Gamaliel in Acts and/or earlier

that the author, if not also his readers, was oriented toward a particular Jewish subculture quite at odds with the emerging Christian mainstream.

Again, I am not convinced. As noted in Chapter 2, the Pharisaic notion of a proprietary tradition of knowledge or, in Greek, a *paradosis*, is older than the rabbinic concept of oral Torah. And it was a concept known to early Christian readers.[173] Paul refers to it as an aspect of his former Pharisaic discipline (Gal 1.14). Matthew and Mark attack the sectarian concept as an invidious theological conceit (Matt 15.2–3, 6; Mark 7.3, 5, 8–9, 13). This is most likely the "tradition from Moses" which the author of our text diffidently assigns to the Pharisees and scribes (*Recog.* 1.54.7).[174] As for his flattering depiction of Gamaliel, the book of Acts provides all the information he would have needed to deduce that that man was not typical of his sect in respect to his moderate attitude toward the apostolic Church. That our author chose to embellish his source by depicting Gamaliel as a secret Christian seems irrelevant to the possibility that he knew that sage as a figure of high repute among the rabbis.

To be clear, I do not mean to imply that the author of the Pseudo-Clementine source was a vocal proponent of Paul's gospel nor completely oblivious to the nascent rabbinic movement. I simply believe that the arguments to the contrary are feeble. As for more constructive insights regarding the author's social location, I have little more to say. Like Matthew, he seems to speak to an audience consisting primarily of Jews. It would therefore appear that he predicated his account of the Church's earliest history on an understanding of the gospel not unlike Matthew's.[175] Yet like the evangelist, the author's endorsements of both the Jewish law and the gentile mission set no clear conditions as to the relationship between the two. Whether he considered gentile followers of Jesus bound to the legislation of the Torah is therefore impossible to determine.

In any case, it seems reasonable to conclude that the author of the Pseudo-Clementine source was a survivor. Long after the Church's founding Jewish demographic had been overtaken by gentiles, he confidently asserted his people's ancestral right to profess their faith in Jesus on their own terms. If what remains of his work does indeed bear witness to a Jewish Christian

documents of the Pseudo-Clementine literary tradition. Compare Reed (2003: 206, n. 64), who notes Baumgarten's tendency to homogenize disparate texts and redactional phases within that tradition.

[173] On the exploitation of this concept in early Christian exegesis of the New Testament, see Horbury (2010b: 3–6), and cf. Baumgarten (1987: 66–67).

[174] Due to the loss of the Greek text, whether it read *paradosis* for "tradition" is impossible to determine. The Syriac text reads *b'yad muše qabelu*, while the Latin text reads *ex moysis traditione*; cf. F.S. Jones (1995: 88).

[175] Of possible relevance here is Jones' reasonable inference that the original text was written under the name of Matthew the tax collector on the basis of the author's placement of that disciple at the head of an apostolic order copied from Matt 10.2–4 (*Recog.* 1.55.4); see F.S. Jones (1995: 140, 154–55). While it is appealing to imagine the Pseudo-Clementine source as a pseudepigraphic addendum to the Gospel of Matthew, I do not wish to overstate the significance of that possibility.

community in Palestine at the end of the second century, his is a testament of great significance toward the task of locating such individuals in the social world of the early rabbinic sages, if not necessarily in their intimate company.

CONSPECTUS: JEWS IN THE NEAR EASTERN CHURCHES

The evidences surveyed earlier do not add up to a cogent record of the early Church's Jewish demographic. But they do suggest some of its more notable features. Operating in western Syria and neighboring Judea/Palestine, Jewish followers of Jesus determined their own courses, sustaining typically Jewish modes of thought and behavior at least into the second century despite the efforts of many of their Christian contemporaries to distance their apostolic enterprise from the Jewish tradition. Presumably, their population was self-sustaining, drawing newcomers primarily from their own offspring as well as their families and friends. The catastrophic Jewish revolts against Rome likely affected their ability to attract gentile associates on a significant scale, effectively terminating the missionary element of their apostolic initiative. Yet over time, these Jewish Christians warmed to the prospect of cooperating with gentiles not given to Jewish lifestyles. Precisely how gentiles affiliated with Jewish Christian communities were to express their beliefs was likely a matter of negotiation on the individual level, to be determined by one's personal dispositions and capabilities.

I believe that my composite sketch of the early Jewish Christians improves upon that devised by F.C. Baur and the Tübingen School and taken up by Heinrich Graetz, James Parkes, and countless others since. According to my reading, the people ostensibly behind the Gospel of Matthew, the Didache, and the Pseudo-Clementine source were not locked in heated battle with Pauline Christians over the essence of their new religion. The Jewish Christians simply saw themselves as heirs of the apostolic mission to the Jews operating beyond the demographic footprint of Paul's evangelical instruction. That sense of historical right shielded them from the adversarial construction of Judaism increasingly prevalent in other corners of the Church. Nor did the Jewish Christians spurn their native religious and ethnic identities. Operating in locales home to sizable and diverse Jewish populations allowed them to function as Jews despite their ideological differences from other Jews. That they had misgivings about those of their countrymen who were antagonistic toward their number is only to be expected. But their malice was merely a function of their vulnerability.

What became of those folks one can only guess. The fact that some of their literary products were incorporated into the proto-orthodox Christian tradition suggests a tendency toward assimilation with the greater Christian population of the Near East over an indeterminate length of time.[176] It is also

---

[176] For an attempt to locate the Matthean and Didache communities in the subsequent evolutionary trajectory of Syrian Christianity, see Haar Romeny (2005: 13–33), and cf. Sim (1998: 289–97). On the survival of Jewish sensibilities, if not necessarily discrete Jewish identities, among

conceivable that persons of the type described stand behind the widespread patristic reports about the Ebionites (Aramaic: *ebyonayya,* "impoverished ones") and Nazarenes (Aramaic: *notzerayya,* "Christians"). Beginning with Irenaeus in the late second century, generations of Church Fathers would write of those reputed Christian sects in the interest of exposing their members as Jews. Though their reports rarely rise above the level of ill-informed rumor-mongering, they speak to the likelihood that Judaism did indeed remain a viable option for some Christians for quite some time.[177]

Of course, the patristic portraits of the Ebionites and Nazarenes are of deplorable heretics entertaining all manners of ideologies abhorrent to their critics. This makes it impossible to read those testimonies as fair or accurate representations of their practices and beliefs, much less of their alleged sectarian genealogies.[178] But some of the recurring features of the abstract polemic are suggestive. Ebionites and Nazarenes were charged with observing the laws of the Torah, principally the infamous triad of circumcision, Sabbath observance, and dietary restriction.[179] They were accused of asserting their ethnic identities as Jews and biological descendants of the nation of Israel.[180] More nefariously, they were denounced for not adhering to Paul's gospel.[181] And

the fourth-century authors of the Pseudo-Clementine tradition, see Reed (2008b: 291–97; 2008c: 203–07). A more conventional approach is assumed by F.S. Jones (2009, 339–46), who sees the disappearance of the Jewish Christians as a consequence of their marginalization by Christian and Jewish parties of greater persuasive power than their own.

[177] In other words, the misinformation of these patristic testimonies need not negate their values as indirect witnesses to the persistence of Jewish Christians beyond the first century. For complementary assessments, see Strecker (1971: 272–85), Klijn and Reinink (1973: 68–73); Carleton Paget (2010a: 24–33); Mimouni (2012: 76–81, 89–125).

[178] I thereby distinguish my reliance on these sources from the confidence typically invested in them by those proposing to describe the Ebionites and the Nazarenes as though those generic names refer to actual sects with distinctive histories, ideologies, and behavioral modalities. Recent studies of this impressionable variety include Pritz (1988: 19–82) and passim; Kaestli (1996); Boer (1988); Blanchetière (2001: 133–51) and passim; Häkkinen (2005); Luomanen 2005; 2007; 2012: 17–81) and passim; Bauckham (2003); Skarsaune (2007b); Broadhead (2010: 163–212). Compare Carleton Paget (2010b) for a judicious review of scholarship demonstrating the advantages and the fallacies of reading the patristic accounts of the Ebionites as genuine historical testimonies.

[179] On the Torah observance of the Ebionites, see Irenaeus, *Haer.* 1.26.2; Tertullian, *Praescr.* 32.3–5; Hippolytus, *Haer.* prol. 7.7–9, 7.34.1–2, 10.22.1; Origen, *Hom. Gen.* 3.5, *Comm. Matt.* 11.12, *Cels.* 2.1, 5.61; Eusebius, *Hist. eccl.* 3.27.1–6, 6.17; Epiphanius, *Pan.* 30.2.2, 30.17.5; Jerome, *Epist.* 112.13, 16, *Comm. Gal.* 5.3, *Comm. Isa.* 1.3, *Comm. Ezech.* 44.6–8; Augustine, *Epist.* 116.16, *Haer.* 10. On the Torah observance of the Nazarenes, see Epiphanius, *Pan.* 29.5.4, 29.7.5; Jerome, *Epist.* 112.13, *Comm. Isa.* 8.11, 8.19–22, *Comm. Ezech.* 16.16, *Comm. Jer.* 3.14–16; Augustine, *Bapt.* 7.1.1, *Faust.* 19.4, 7, *Cresc.* 1.31.36, *Epist.* 116.16, *Haer.* 9.

[180] On the ethnicities of the Ebionites, see Origen, *Princ.* 4.3.8; Jerome, *Comm. Isa.* 1.12. On the ethnicities of the Nazarenes, see Epiphanius, *Pan.* 29.5.4, 29.7.1, 29.9.1; Jerome, *Expl. Dan.* prol.

[181] On hostility toward Paul among the Ebionites, see Irenaeus, *Haer.* 1.26.2; Origen, *Cels.* 5.66. On hostility toward Paul among the Nazarenes, see Jerome, *Comm. Matt.* 12.2.

perhaps most tellingly, they were located in churches (and, of course, synagogues) throughout Syria, Palestine, and Arabia.[182] These qualities would well
describe the type of Christians documented in the Gospel of Matthew, the
Didache, or the Pseudo-Clementine source. It is therefore entirely plausible
that behind the heresiological name-calling lies the less provocative reality of
Christians isolated by circumstance from the Pauline tradition yet trained on a
gospel of their own, contemplating the life and teachings of Jesus in an objective framework uniquely attuned to their experiences as Jews.

To my mind, this simple observation is an apt starting point for our consideration of the actual people behind the early rabbinic invectives against
Christian *minim*. Lest we forget, the Church Fathers were not the only ones
who sought to marginalize Jewish Christians through rhetorical posturing. Yet
just as one must not place undue confidence in the documentary qualities of the
patristic evidence, one must proceed with caution when reading the commentaries of the early rabbis on those alleged Jewish miscreants. In view of these
methodological limitations, I will not venture to interpret the Jewish record in
light of the Christian. In other words, I will not attempt to divine the theologies
of the *minim* by appeal to the documents reviewed here, much less to the dubious patristic witnesses to the Ebionites and Nazarenes.[183] But considering the
likelihood that these fragmented testimonies are indicative at least of the general conditions of Jewish life in the churches of the Roman Near East, I shall
consider them valuable points of reference for the discussion of the rabbinic
evidence to follow in Chapter 4.

[182] On the geographical distribution of the Ebionites, see Eusebius, *Onom.* 172 s.v. Choba;
Epiphanius, *Pan.* 30.2.7–9, 30.18.1; Jerome, *Epist.* 112.13, *Sit.* 112 s.v. Choba. On the geographical distribution of the Nazarenes, see Epiphanius, *Pan.* 29.7.7–8; Jerome, *Epist.* 112.13,
Sit. 143 s.v. Nazareth, *Vir. ill.* 3.
[183] For efforts to correlate the Christian *minim* with Jewish Christian persons and groups attested
in early Christian texts, see, e.g., Bauckham (1990: 106–21); Baumgarten (1992: 39–41);
Kimelman (1999: 323–27); Saldarini (1998: 120–26); Jaffé (2005: 87–88). I am too cautious
to attempt the daring methodological leaps needed to justify the synthesis of the many and
diverse surviving evidences of Jewish Christian activity into a single, cohesive record.

4

Reading Christianity as a Jewish Heresy in Early Rabbinic Texts

In the preceding chapter, I tried to demonstrate how the idea of Christian identity arose from the efforts of its earliest proponents to define their new enterprise in reference to the idea of Jewish identity. The ensuing process of cultural
negotiation took place both within the Jewish collective and without, yield-
ing divergent modes of Christian thought and behavior for those disposed to
identify as Jews and those not so disposed. I submitted that the early rabbinic
sages were most likely acquainted with Christians of the former type, that is,
Jewish Christians. Documented primarily in Christian texts and reading traditions prone to obscure their Jewish identities, their story represents a lost chapter in the history of the Jewish people. Yet their story is of vital importance to
that history inasmuch as it supplies the information needed to reconstruct the
circumstances of the unique encounter impressed on the Jewish annals as the
initial meeting of Christian and Jew.

As I explained in the introduction, my account of that meeting will focus
on references to Christians as *minim*, or Jewish heretics, in the works of the
Tannaim, the rabbinic sages of the first and second centuries. I shall draw these
references from the Mishnah and the Tosefta, two related rabbinic anthologies
of the early third century. Presented as records of earlier Tannaitic teachings
relating to Jewish ritual laws and related narrative materials, these compilations
typically are classified under the generic rubric of the *halakhah*. Naturally, their
legislative discourses tend to speak to the particular cultural concerns of the
rabbis and their disciples. Yet despite their solipsistic rhetorical objectives, the
Mishnah and Tosefta describe a social world populated by Jews and gentiles
of all varieties who happened to inhabit Roman Palestine during the age when
the rabbinic movement took root there. That they speak to the existence of
Christians in that world speaks to the impetus of their rabbinic authors to
locate those individuals in relation to their own discipleship circles.[1]

---

[1] On the solipsistic or self-descriptive quality of classical rabbinic discourse, see S. Stern
(1994: 200–14), with discussion of *minim* as internal Jewish others at ibid. (109–12).

In the discussion to follow, I intend to show that those rabbis exhibited a distinct sense of uneasiness with Christianity, which they deemed one of many manifestations of Jewish cultural expression alien to their own sensibilities. While acknowledging that they did not assume a strict categorical distinction between Christian and Jew, I submit that they speak to the same developing sense of difference observed in the Gospel of Matthew, the Didache, and the Pseudo-Clementine source. I therefore shall argue that the distrustful attitudes of the rabbis mirrored those of their Christian contemporaries inclined to think and act as Jews. I thereby aim to establish the heuristic value of the earliest surviving Jewish witnesses to Christianity as testaments to a schism not yet resolved but certainly well underway.

READING FOR HISTORY IN THE MISHNAH AND TOSEFTA

Let us begin with a few words on our sources.[2] The Mishnah, Hebrew for "the repetition," is the fundamental document of the *halakhah*, the ancient tradition of Jewish scriptural interpretation relating to the laws of the Torah. According to tradition, the Mishnah was compiled by the Jewish Patriarch Rabbi Judah ha-Nasi, or Judah the Prince, during the early third century CE. The name of the treatise parallels the name of the *Tannaim*, Aramaic for "repeaters," a sobriquet referring to the idea that the rabbinic sages whose legal opinions Rabbi Judah recorded in the Mishnah were formerly preserved as teachings transmitted or repeated among the sages and their students in the oral medium. The Tosefta, Aramaic for "the addition," follows the style of the Mishnah and traditionally is thought to preserve Tannaitic teachings not chosen for inclusion in Rabbi Judah's text.

Until fairly recently, critical investigations into the contents and designs of these seminal rabbinic texts proceeded on the assumption that the conventional wisdom just described was more or less correct.[3] As a result, scholars tended to approach the Mishnah as though it was written or at least commissioned by Rabbi Judah for use as a binding code of law, a juridical textbook, or a classified register of his legislative research. Following the pioneering work of J.N. Epstein, these theories evolved to account for his hypothesis that some of the Mishnah's oral transcriptions previously circulated in alternate written forms preserved independently in the Tosefta and other classical rabbinic texts.[4]

---

[2] For comprehensive critical overviews of the Mishnah and Tosefta, see Strack and Stemberger (1996: 108–63); Kraemer (2006); Mandel (2006b).

[3] For the following, see Strack and Stemberger (1996: 124–39), and cf. Kraemer (2006: 299–300, 311–13). Notable defenses of the traditional ascription of the Mishnah to Rabbi Judah allowing for more nuanced interpretations of his method and design include Lieberman (1950: 83–99); Albeck (1959: 99–115); Halivni (1986: 43–47); Goldberg (1987a: 215–27); Elman (2004).

[4] Epstein (1948); see especially ibid. (2.697–706), for his influential theory that Rabbi Judah compiled the Mishnah on the basis of written study notes.

The Mishnah was thereby cast as more than a mere receptacle of Tannaitic oral traditions but also a work exhibiting limited but significant editorial input on Judah's part. The Tosefta, therefore, appeared to preserve inferior legal traditions that Rabbi Judah deemed unworthy of inclusion in his authoritative collection.[5]

The critical effort to describe the Mishnah's textual innovation reached its zenith in the work of Jacob Neusner. Eschewing its legendary association with Rabbi Judah, Neusner more incisively discarded the premise of retrieving authentic oral traditions from the Mishnah's redacted text.[6] According to his reading, the Mishnah's internal diagnostic features suggest that it was created by an anonymous cadre of late second-century rabbinic scholars responding to the failure of the Bar Kokhba rebellion. Their hopes for a restoration of the Temple put to rest, those authors conceived a philosophical Judaism predicated on ritual and ethical traditions that they deemed still viable in a post-Temple religious economy. In the process, they established the new scribal tradition eventually to yield the Mishnah. As for the Tosefta, Neusner argues that its ostensibly Tannaitic contents likewise were revised and arranged to form a rudimentary interpretive companion to the Mishnah anticipating the more elaborate commentaries of the Palestinian and Babylonian Talmuds.[7]

Where scholars following the traditional line had presumed to read the Mishnah as a generally reliable record of early rabbinic culture, Neusner challenged the prospect of mining its text for such historical data. In his view, the Mishnah outlines a religious system founded on the wisdom of the *Tannaim* but not necessarily speaking to their practices, beliefs, or social outlooks. To Neusner, the Mishnah speaks only to the sensibilities of its authors, who applied their sources to the novel discursive purpose of their philosophical program without specific regard for preserving their original forms or contexts. He therefore rejects the possibility of extracting from its pages authentic witnesses to the lives and times of the rabbinic sages quoted therein.[8] Although his reading of the Mishnah as a philosophical tract has won few supporters, Neusner's call for extreme methodological caution in utilizing its sources for historical study certainly put a damper on the efforts of those prone to accept those sources as genuine records of the rabbinic past that they purport to describe.

---

[5] See Strack and Stemberger (1996: 150–52), and cf. Lieberman (1950: 88–89); Goldberg (1987b: 283–84, 289–92, 293–95); Mandel (2006b: 316–21). Lieberman was exceptional among his contemporaries in treating the Tosefta as a record of Tannaitic sources independent of those preserved in the Mishnah, which investigative principle informed his monumental commentary on the work (Lieberman 1955–1988).

[6] Neusner outlines his theory of the Mishnah's origin and function most thoroughly in Neusner (1981a); see especially ibid. (122–26), on the circumstances of its composition. For an autobiographical account of Neusner's engagement of prior scholarship on the Mishnah, see Neusner (1981b).

[7] See, e.g., Neusner (1986: ix–x).

[8] See Neusner (1980) and cf. Neusner (1981a: 14–22).

More recently, however, Neusner's assertion of the Mishnah's redactional uniformity has come under fire by scholars critical of his denial of its oral composition history. Martin Jaffee and Elizabeth Shanks Alexander have shown that the Mishnah itself acknowledges both its oral and written redactional contexts in its use of literary forms native to those means of transmission.[9] To insist, therefore, on either of the two is to misrepresent an ancient mode of textual production equally invested in the recorded word and its oral performance. Consequently, one must not assume that a given textual lemma preserved in the Mishnah or, by association, the Tosefta, is traditional, invented, or synthetic without first considering all available internal and external indicators of its provenance.

Others have argued that the Tannaitic traditions preserved in the Mishnah and Tosefta were intentionally modified during their transmission. Independently of one another, Shamma Friedman and Judith Hauptman have explored the possibility that the Mishnah actually responds to the Tosefta in select instances of their convergence.[10] In their assessments, the earlier of the two compositions does not always exhibit the earliest extant versions of their common Tannaitic sources. In many cases, the Tosefta appears to preserve intact traditions later reworked by the editors of the Mishnah. That observation allows the contemporary reader to examine both documents for signs of dynamic textual development embedded within their redacted forms. In other words, it affords us the prerogative to utilize the Mishnah and Tosefta as annalistic records of rabbinic traditions predating the third century. Of course, bearing in mind Neusner's critique, one must not mistake that analytical license for an excuse to retreat to naïve historicism. Nevertheless, to recognize the Mishnah and Tosefta as documents cut from the same cloth permits one to subject their texts to the type of reductive literary analysis needed to read their traditions as witnesses to Jewish life and thought in Palestine during the age of the *Tannaim*.

Although the Mishnah and Tosefta are not the only rabbinic texts locating Christians in the social world of the *Tannaim*, they are the only texts that I believe to speak to that phenomenon from roughly contemporaneous perspectives. As I shall explain shortly, I do not wish to misrepresent the content and

---

[9] See Jaffee (2001: 100–25), on the Mishnah's reproductions of orally transmitted literary forms, lists, and mnemonic devices, features signaling the original oral-cultural milieu of its traditions, and E.S. Alexander (2006: 35–76), on its use of literary concepts, overarching structures, and mimetic phrasings, features signaling its design as a guide for the memorization of the *halakhah*.

[10] For the following, see S. Friedman (2002), especially ibid. (93–95) (cf. his summary treatment in S. Friedman 1999), as well as Hauptman (2005), with methodological comments, ibid. (17–24, 31–49). Where Friedman sees the received text of the Tosefta as a redacted supplement to the Mishnah incorporating select pre-Mishnaic materials, Hauptman sees it as an earlier, unedited version of the redacted Mishnah. The differences between their theories are immaterial to my investigation insofar as both acknowledge the Tosefta's inclusion of materials ostensibly attesting to the conditions of Jewish life in Palestine prior to the Mishnah's composition. For more traditional views on the relationship between the two texts less obligating to my historiographical agenda, see Strack and Stemberger (1996: 152–55); Mandel (2006b: 322–28).

tone of the rudimentary rabbinic construction of the Christian heresy by introducing anachronistic evidence originating in later Amoraic embellishments to
the Tannaitic record. Where relevant, however, I shall indicate where and how
that record was appropriated by subsequent rabbinic authors for novel application in their own more sophisticated commentaries on Christianity.

RECOVERING THE EARLY RABBINIC CONCEPT OF HERESY

Since scholars first began to consider rabbinic texts as records of the Christian
schism, efforts to describe the rabbinic construction of heresy often have proceeded on the basis of the medieval equation of *minut* with Christianity.[11] Yet
despite assuming the same basic premise, the results of those efforts were somewhat uneven. Those taking their cues from Moritz Friedländer's and Heinrich
Graetz's portraits of the *minim* as Gnostic Jews have construed them as mystical sages who traded in all manners of exotic theological currents abhorrent to the rabbis.[12] That those currents included Christian influences is taken
for granted. Others following the interpretive lines of Graetz and R. Travers
Herford have cast the *minim* as political dissidents.[13] Having witnessed the
fall of the Jewish state in 70 CE, those rogue Jews threw in their lots with the
fanatical Christian fringe celebrating Rome's triumph as the harbinger of a new
eschatological age. In time, the tensions between the Jewish masses and the dis-
affected few gave rise to the theological contest attested in the rabbinic polemic
against the *minim*. Still others have synthesized elements of both theories into
an eclectic portrait of the *minim* encompassing all individuals, whether Jew or
gentile, Gnostic or Christian or both, who entertained religious ideologies at
odds with those of the rabbis.[14]

The prevailing sense of uncertainty over the precise relationship between
minut and Christianity speaks to the ambiguity of the evidence at hand. As
I shall demonstrate forthwith, some of the most widely attested reports of
minut do indeed appear to allude to Christianity. Certain *minim*, for instance,
are characterized as followers of Jesus apt to invoke his name in the service of

[11] I mean to refer to the habit of medieval Jews to apply the category of *minut* exclusively to
Christians once the more variegated heresiological concerns of their ancient forebears had
faded from memory. On this development, see Langer (2012: 78–82). Also instructive is Teppler
(2007: 13–39), who traces the postclassical development of the terminology of *minut* on the
basis of its function in various medieval recensions of the *birkat ha-minim*.

[12] See especially Segal (1977: 3–29), who casts the *minim* as Gnostic Jews who selectively adopted
Christian ideas in their formation of the mystical tradition later to be expressed in the *Merkavah*
literature. In a similar vein, Janowitz (1998) depicts the *minim* as itinerant "holy men" and miracle workers whose populist ambitions placed them in direct competition with the rabbis.

[13] For examples of this commonplace approach, see Schiffman (1985: 51–67); Jaffé (2005: 88–92);
S.T. Katz (2006: 287–93); Teppler (2007: 164–83); Schremer (2010: 25–48; 2013).

[14] For the idea that the sages routinely applied the category of *minut* to opponents from without
the Jewish community, see, inter alia, Bacher (1899); Büchler (1956), especially ibid. (269);
Urbach (1981: 288–93); Rokeah (1982: 50–83); Simon (1986: 179–201).

teaching and healing.[15] One rabbinic statute classifies the gospels along with other heretical books as profane texts abusing the ineffable name of God.[16] In later texts, *minim* frequently are depicted as readers of the Hebrew Scriptures prone to challenge their rabbinic peers with contrarian passages concerning Israel's divine election.[17] As we have seen, this was a common preoccupation among early Christian exegetes seeking to demonstrate the Pauline notion that God appointed Israel not as a nation but as a community of faith.

No stretch of the imagination is required to identify the intended targets of those invectives as Christians. Yet in other cases, *minim* are described in terms bearing no clear Christian connotations. For instance, one may reasonably argue that the wide-ranging polemic against *minim* who recognized two powers in heaven subscribed to the same cosmic myths as certain Gnostic Christians without necessarily sharing their ideas about Jesus.[18] Similarly, accusations of their having misread the Hebrew Scriptures are just as likely to have been directed against Christian Jews as against any Jews who presumed to question the pedagogical authority of the rabbis.[19] To wit, while the rabbis railed against *minim* for distorting the word of God, they did not engage typically Christian exegetical strategies such as those used to prove Jesus' identity as the Messiah.[20] In several instances, *minim* are said to have maintained Jewish customs otherwise lost to the Christian tradition, such as the use of phylacteries (*tefillin*) during prayer and the practice of ritual slaughter (*shehitah*).[21] Occasionally, *minim* are shown harboring

[15] For the former characterization, see *t.Ḥullin* 2.24; *b.Avodah Zarah* 16b–17a; *Ecclestiastes Rabbah* 1.24, and for the latter, *t.Ḥullin* 2.22–23; *y.Shabbat* 14.4 (14d); *y.Avodah Zarah* 2.2 (40d–41a); *b.Avodah Zarah* 27b; *Ecclesiastes Rabbah* 1.24.

[16] Per the preferred reading of *gilyonim* as an approximation of the Greek *euangelia* or "gospels" in *t.Shabbat* 13.5; *t.Yadayim* 2.13; *y.Shabbat* 16.1 (15c); *b.Shabbat* 116a.

[17] See, e.g., *b.Pesaḥim* 87b; *b.Yoma* 56b; *b.Yevamot* 102b; *b.Sanhedrin* 39a; *b.Avodah Zarah* 4a. While the denial of Israel's election marks these *minim* as Christians only by inference, it seems likely that this apologetic stratagem alludes to the Church's appropriation of the title Israel. Compare the prototypical articulation of this argument in *Song of Songs Rabbah* 7.8, with discussion in S. Stern (1994: 49–50).

[18] On belief in two or more divine potentates as a trait of *minut*, see, e.g., *m.Sanhedrin* 4.5; *t.Sanhedrin* 8.7; *Mekhilta* Baḥodesh 5; *Sifra* Nedabah 2.5; *Sifre* Numbers 143; *y.Berakhot* 9.1 (12d–13a); *Genesis Rabbah* 8.9; *b.Sanhedrin* 38a-b; *b.Ḥullin* 87a. Although Segal (1977: 109–20) describes the *minim* implicated in this long-standing theological controversy as Jewish Christians operating under Gnostic influence, Ithamar Gruenwald points out that the cosmic dualism evident in these testimonies might have derived from Jewish folk traditions rather than Christian informants; see Gruenwald (1981).

[19] This principle is demonstrated in *b.Sanhedrin* 38b, where the exegetical impulses of the *min* are likened to those of the Jewish Epicurean (*apiqoros yisrael*), i.e., one who places the study of Greek philosophy before the study of the Torah; cf. *t.Shabbat* 13.5 and see discussion in Schiffman (1985: 43–44).

[20] In fact, the only clear evidence of direct rabbinic engagement with Christian literature focuses not on exegetical controversy but on Jesus' affirmative pronouncement on the Jewish law in Matt 5.17 (*b.Shabbat* 116a–b). On this Talmudic passage and its gently ribbing rhetoric, see Zellentin (2011: 137–66).

[21] See *m.Megillah* 4.8 (*tefillin*); *m.Ḥullin* 2.9, *t.Ḥullin* 2.18–19; *Sifre* Deuteronomy 126 (*shehitah*). One could make the argument that the *minim* in question in these cases are Jewish Christians,

ideologies fundamentally opposed to Christian doctrine, such as the worship of idols, denial of the concept of bodily resurrection, and denial of the afterlife.[22] In one particularly inflammatory instance, *minim* are implied to have denied the very existence of God.[23]

Taken on the whole, therefore, the rabbinic construction of heresy does not read like a targeted polemic against Christianity. Rather than singling them out for specific criticism, the rabbinic sages evidently saw Christians as part of an undifferentiated mass of Jews whose standards of practice and belief fell short of their own. As a result, to identify a unique anti-Christian strain amidst the expansive and often generalized polemical discourse is no simple task. But that challenge is not insurmountable. Recent studies on the origin and function of the category of *minut* have paved the way for constructive discussion of its sociorhetorical nuances. It will therefore be instructive to consider those efforts in order to demonstrate the merit of my own approach.

The first step in order to define the Christian quotient of the polemic against *minut* is to establish a diachronic framework for its development. In an important 1994 article, Richard Kalmin proposed to trace that development through contextual analysis of the fairly limited number of classical rabbinic passages explicitly equating *minut* with Christianity.[24] Locating those passages in successive stages in the evolution of rabbinic thought, he demonstrates how each seems to conform to the unique rhetorical conventions of its time and place. In the process, he illustrates a number of rhetorical tendencies distinguishing the attitudes of the *Tannaim* from those of the *Amoraim*. Whereas the former tend to impugn *minim* without explaining their alleged offenses, the latter often attempt to explain their deviant ideologies by forcing those alleged heretics of old into expository dialogues with their rabbinic contemporaries.[25]

Kalmin furthermore demonstrates a key disjunction between the Palestinian *Amoraim* and their Babylonian counterparts. As the former typically fashion their stories about *minim* from Tannaitic blueprints, they imply a plausible climate of conflict between the rabbis and their opponents. Babylonian authors, though often drawing on the same Tannaitic sources, generally depict those past confrontations in less realistic terms, straining the reader's credulity with exaggerated and sometimes patently incredible tales of sorcery

---

although the absence of any corroborating evidence to that effect would make the case difficult to prove.

[22] See *t.Hullin* 1.1, 2.20; *b.Hullin* 13a–b (idolatry); *b.Sanhedrin* 90b–91a (resurrection); *m.Berakhot* 9.5; *t.Berakhot* 6.21 (afterlife). To this list one might add a passage in *b.Sanhedrin* 99a depicting an exchange between the third-century Palestinian *Amora* Rabbi Abbahu and an anonymous *min* about when the Messiah will arrive, certainly an odd question for a Christian to entertain.

[23] *Sifre* Deuteronomy 320, comparing the *min* to the subjects of Psalm 14.1, "Fools say in their hearts, 'There is no God.'" This indictment is repeated in uncensored manuscripts of *b.Berakhot* 12b and *b.Yevamot* 63b.

[24] Kalmin (1994), summarized in Kalmin (1999: 68–74).

[25] Kalmin (1994: 160–62). For further examples of this phenomenon, see Miller (1993: 379–99).

and derring-do.[26] Consequently, one aiming to describe the rabbinic polemic against Christianity must account for its setting within a heresiological discourse that evolved over time and space into a narrative trope of no certain bearing on the circumstances of the actual encounter between Christian and Jew.

In identifying these distinct phases in its application, Kalmin suggests a more comprehensive theory of the evolution of the rhetoric of *minut*. What originated as a simple, though somewhat nebulous, stratagem of the *Tannaim* was extended by the *Amoraim* to apply to all manner of non-rabbinic Jewish behaviors and patterns of thought. Kalmin explains this disjunction in view of the disparate circumstances in which the rabbinic sages encountered Christianity. The *Tannaim*, he argues, styled themselves as leaders of a nation still recovering from their failed revolts against Rome. That they failed to single out Christians for special censure is entirely understandable given the inclement conditions of Christian life in Palestine during their days. By the third century, however, the danger of that erstwhile Jewish heresy was coming into greater focus. Thus did the *Amoraim* adjust their traditional polemic against *minut* to account for a Christianity more threatening to their people than the relatively benign sectarian enterprise witnessed by the *Tannaim*. That rhetorical trend continued unabated into the fourth century and thereafter as the Church gradually overtook the old religion of Rome, tightening its hold on the Empire's Jewish population in the process.[27]

Yet even as its anti-Christian undertones grew more pronounced in Palestine, the polemic against the *minim* underwent a different type of transformation among rabbinic readers beyond the Roman realm. Operating in the Sasanian Empire, the Babylonian *Amoraim* knew not of the sectarian divisions of Palestinian Jewry, much less of Christianity as a Jewish problem. The only Christians of whom they knew were gentiles, constituents of the indigenous churches of Mesopotamia.[28] Unlike their contemporaries in the west, those Christians were still an oppressed minority. To the eyes, therefore, of the Babylonian rabbis, the Christian *minim* of Palestinian lore seemed like fabulous creatures, bizarre scripture-quoting malcontents quite unlike any Jews with whom they were acquainted.[29] As a result, the Babylonian *Amoraim*

---

[26] Kalmin (1994: 163–65), who notes the tendency of Babylonian authors to depict *minim* as expert interpreters of the Torah. See further Bohak (2003), who notes that later rabbinic authors routinely depict their predecessors as having combatted the exegetical prowesses of *minim* by resorting to the very same supernatural forces supposedly marshaled by other of their heretical ilk.

[27] Kalmin (1994: 162–63).

[28] As noted by Kalmin (1994: 166), the uncertainty of the Babylonian sages over the ethnic dimension of the Tannaitic construction of *minut* is manifest in a pair of disputes recorded in the Babylonian Talmud over whether *minim* are to be considered Jews or gentiles with respect to the *halakhah* (b.Ḥullin 13a–b). I shall discuss this passage in Chapter 5.

[29] Per Kalmin (1994: 166), this seems to be the force of a claim ascribed in the Babylonian Talmud to the third-century *Amora* Rabbi Abbahu that the Palestinian sages had to hone their scriptural

typecast Christian *minim* along with the rest of their heretical kind as ineffectual pests bothersome to the Tannaitic sages but never legitimate contenders for their authority or popular influence.

Kalmin's observations have far-reaching consequences for the historical study of the *minim*. His departure from the traditional premise of construing *minut* as a static social distinction has helped set a course for a comprehensive critical reassessment of how rabbis of various places and times used the idea of heresy in their efforts to define themselves against other Jews, Christian or otherwise.[30] But that is not my purpose here. Since my interest is in the rabbinic response to Christianity, Kalmin's study is instructive in the following respect. According to his analysis, Amoraic reports of *Tannaim* dealing with Christians typically assume perspectives conditioned by social and historical factors alien to the world of the *Tannaim* themselves. As a result, only genuine Tannaitic witnesses to Christian *minim* can be said with reasonable certainty to speak to the circumstances in which the *Tannaim* actually encountered such individuals. To be clear, I do not mean to suggest that Amoraic texts have nothing to teach us about the ancient encounter between Christian and Jew.[31] But one must not presume them to represent reliable documentary records of the Tannaitic traditions that they appear to preserve.[32]

expertise for regular deployment against argumentative *minim* while their Babylonian counterparts had no such need (*b.Avodah Zarah* 4a). The factuality of this statement is questioned by Schremer (2005: 223–24), who sees it as an invention of the Talmud's anonymous editors of no bearing toward the actual presence of Jewish heretics in third-century Mesopotamia. While Schremer is correct to distinguish the story's narrative setting from its redactional setting, the likelihood that the passage was written much later than the era that it describes does not preclude the possibility of its accuracy as a recollection of the past state of affairs. Oddly, Schremer seems to contradict his own argument in Schremer (2010: 189, n. 48), where he asserts, "according to the Babylonian Talmud itself *minim* were almost unknown in Babylonia." My point is not that the Babylonian sages were disabused of the phenomenon of *minut* but merely that they knew not of Christian *minim*, i.e., Jewish Christians.

[30] For illustrations of this phenomenon, see Hayes (1998); Kalmin (2006: 87–101); P.S. Alexander (2007: 665–71); Burns (2012); Secunda (2013: 50–57).

[31] By way of contrast, one need only consider the Babylonian Talmud's comments on the festival "day of the *notzerim*" (uncensored manuscripts of *b.Avodah Zarah* 6a, 7b; *b.Ta'anit* 27b) and the forbidding "house of *nitzrefei*" (uncensored manuscripts of *b.Shabbat* 116a; *b.Eruvin* 79b–80a) along with its recurring polemic against Jesus the *notzeri* (uncensored manuscripts of *b.Berakhot* 17b; *b.Sotah* 47a; *b.Gittin* 57a; *b.Sanhedrin* 43a–b, 103a, 107b; *b.Avodah Zarah* 17a). Note that these Babylonian passages employ the common Aramaic term for Christians (*notzerim*) rather than the proprietary rabbinic term for Jewish Christians, i.e., *minim*. This suggests that the Babylonian *Amoraim* regarded their Christian neighbors not as heretical Jews but as persons of a social order entirely separate from their own. For comments to this effect, see Mimouni (1998: 232–42), although cf. Shaked (1995: 173–74), who detects possible "Judaeo-Christian" connotations in the rabbis' choice of language.

[32] The unfortunate tendency to read the contextually variegated rabbinic polemic against *minut* as a homogeneous heresiological discourse detracts from several recent studies proposing to document the early rabbinic response to Christianity, e.g., Basser (2000: 51–104); Jaffé (2005: 313–35); Teppler (2007: 297–347). While these authors claim to limit their discussions

In view of these considerations, it bears noting that the pool of Tannaitic evidence implicating Christians as *minim* is extremely small. Between the Mishnah and Tosefta, I count twenty-two passages referring to *minim* or *minut*.[33] The *midrashei halakhah*, compilations of Tannaitic legal exegesis closely related to the Mishnah and Tosefta, add ten additional passages to the tally.[34] But only four of these passages, all in the Tosefta, refer expressly to Christianity. Consequently, it will be difficult to say much at all about what the *Tannaim* thought of their Christian contemporaries without considering their rare comments on those individuals within the context of their more generalized polemic against heresy. Let us now turn to that task.

TANNAITIC HERESIOLOGY AND JEWISH IDENTITY

The word *min* literally translates as "variety" or "type." In the Hebrew Scriptures, it is typically used to connote a species of animal or grain. Its application to people of an ideological type does not appear in Hebrew literature prior to the rabbinic age. It therefore seems as though its heresiological usage originated among the rabbis. Precisely when, where, and how that happened is unclear. The only rabbinic text hinting at a specific provenance for the term is a passage in the Babylonian Talmud intimating its usage in the *birkat ha-minim* among the sages who assembled at Yavneh following the fall of Jerusalem in 70 CE.[35] But as I shall demonstrate subsequently, the credibility of that late Amoraic narrative is subject to question. Genuine Tannaitic allusions to *minim* and *minut* offer no specific insight as to its provenance beyond merely attesting to its use among the rabbinic collective at some point prior to the composition of the Mishnah and Tosefta. It therefore behooves us to consider a few current theories regarding the term's origin and semantic range before accounting for its application in those texts.

---

to Tannaitic evidence, they accept the historicity of the Amoraic witnesses to the activities of the *Tannaim* without question. That misstep makes their treatments difficult to defend against those of scholars willing to acknowledge that the *Amoraim* often embellished their received Tannaitic traditions concerning *minim* and even sometimes invented new "traditions" to serve their own discursive needs.

[33] The relevant passages are *m.Berakhot* 9.5; *m.Rosh Hashanah* 2.1; *m.Megillah* 4.8–9; *m.Sanhedrin* 4.5; *m.Hullin* 2.9; *m.Parah* 3.3; *m.Yadayim* 4.8; *t.Berakhot* 3.25, 6.21; *t.Shabbat* 13.5; *t.Kippurim* 2.10; *t.Megillah* 3.37; *t.Bava Metzi'a* 2.33; *t.Sanhedrin* 8.7; 13.4–5; *t.Hullin* 1.1, 2.18–19, 2.20–21, 2.22–23, 2.24; *t.Parah* 3.3; *t.Yadayim* 2.13. I exclude from this count *m.Berakhot* 5.3, which includes a reference to *minut* transposed from *m.Megillah* 4.9 in the Babylonian recension (*b.Berakhot* 34a; cf. *b.Megillah* 25a), *m.Sotah* 9.15, which includes a reference to *minut* interpolated from *y.Sotah* 9.6 (23b), and *t.Ta'anit* 1.10, which includes a passing reference to the *birkat ha-minim* only in Ms. Vienna Hebr. 20.

[34] The relevant passages are *Mekhilta* Bahodesh 5, Kaspa 3; *Sifra* Nedabah 2.5; *Sifre* Numbers 16, 115, 143; *Sifre* Deuteronomy 48, 126, 320, 331. I exclude from this count *Sifre* Numbers 112, for which uncensored manuscripts read Samaritans (*kutim*) for *minim*, and *Sifre* Deuteronomy 218, where some modern editors supply *min* against the manuscript evidence.

[35] I refer to *b.Berakhot* 28b–29a (cf. *b.Megillah* 17b).

In a 1996 article, Martin Goodman observed that early rabbinic texts tend to apply the category of *minut* to a purpose similar to that which the Church Fathers applied the category of *haeresis* or heresy, that is, as an indication of theological deviance from the proto-orthodox Christian mainstream.[36] He therefore posits that the rabbinic term originated from the corresponding Jewish usage of the terminology of *haeresis* as seen, for example, in the accounts of Flavius Josephus of the Pharisees, the Sadducees, and the Essenes. Consequently, the rabbinic invention of *minut* would appear to embody nothing but a Hebrew translation of a customary Jewish distinction applied to sectarian groups for some time prior to the foundation of the rabbinic movement. Whether that linguistic conversion was realized at Yavneh therefore would be immaterial to the question of how the rabbinic concept of heresy came to be.

Goodman's proposal seems correct to me. Given the impossibility of recovering the precise origin of the rabbinic terminology, to infer its allusion to the sectarian past to which the sages traced their own geneaologies is entirely reasonable. If we are to assume that the *Tannaim* devised their heresiological rhetoric to denounce the persistence of sectarian behaviors, it makes sense that the behaviors in question included those of sectarian groups formerly opposed to that to which the rabbis traced their own pedigree, namely the Pharisees.[37] I have argued elsewhere that one of the primary targets of the Tannaitic polemic against the *minim* were Essenes, or at least people sustaining Essenic practices following the general dissolution of the sect during the first Jewish revolt.[38] Other targets of the Tannaitic polemic included Sadducees, who are actually named as such independently of their functions as *minim*, and, of course, Christians.[39] Thus, despite the efforts of the early rabbinic sages to distance themselves from the divisive politics of sectarianism, they maintained an insular social objective quite in line with that of their Pharisaic forebears.[40]

The manifest continuity of the rabbinic concept of heresy with the pre-rabbinic Jewish concept of the same has yielded more far-reaching theories as to the precise origin and function of the former. One argument introduced by David Flusser traces the rabbinic construction to a common Jewish polemical discourse attested in the Dead Sea Scrolls.[41] A document known as *Miqtzat Ma'ase ha-Torah*, or "Some Works of the Law," refers to the Qumran

---

[36] Goodman (1996).

[37] Goodman (1996: 506–07). See also Goodman (1994).

[38] Burns (2006); cf. Goodman (1994: 353–55); Magness (2012: 69–74).

[39] On the functional equivalence of Sadducees and *minim* in rabbinic heresiology, see Goodman (1994: 349–50); Boyarin (2004: 58–63). Instone-Brewer (2003: 36–44), confuses the matter in inferring that the term *minut* originated as a Pharisaic indictment of Sadducees and only later was applied by the rabbis to heretics of other varieties.

[40] For this observation, see Goodman (1996: 508–09; 2009: 210–13), responding to S.J.D. Cohen (1984: 43–51).

[41] For the following, see Flusser (2007), followed largely by S.T. Katz (2006: 285–87); Marcus (2009: 540–48).

community as "we who have separated ourselves from the rest of the nation" (4QMMTᶜ [4Q398] frg. 14–21, ln. 7).[42] The Hebrew word for "we have separated" is *parshanu*, a form of the verbal root *prš*. This is the same lexeme underlying the Hebrew term for Pharisees, *perushim*. Some of the earliest surviving rabbinic references to *minim* categorize them alongside unnamed *perushim*, among whom Flusser submits were not only the most prominent self-professed separatists, the Pharisees, but also the Sadducees, the Essenes, the Christians, and untold other Jewish sectarians of the late Second Temple period.[43] The wording of the Qumran document thus indicates a pre-rabbinic provenance for the heresiological grouping of *minim* and *perushim*. Hence, the rabbinic concept of heresy was not a novel construction but a traditional mode of condemnation originally referring to Jewish sectarians of all varieties. The innovation of the *Tannaim* was merely to pare down its language to implicate *minim* alone, removing their revered Pharisaic predecessors from the generic polemical thread.

While I appreciate its ingenuity, I must say that I do not find this argument compelling. Flusser's case is based on a series of suppositions of progressively declining plausibility. While it is clear enough that the Qumran community saw themselves as separatists, one need not assume that they identified themselves accordingly to their sectarian competitors.[44] And while it is certainly appealing to believe that the rabbis were not so narrow-minded as to invent a new exclusionary rhetoric, one must not allow that apologetic impulse to guide one's interpretation of the evidence at hand. Since the text in question refers to neither *minim* nor *minut*, one cannot presume to assign those categories to the Qumran community, much less to other Jews of their age. While it is plausible

---

[42] On the character of this document as a statement of the Qumran community's sectarian legal order, see Fraade (2000), with comments on the author's account of his group's separation from the Jewish mainstream (ibid., 512–13).

[43] See especially Flusser (2007: 70–80). The rabbinic texts in question are *t.Berakhot* 3.25 (the so-called blessings of the *minim* and *perushim*) and *t.Sanhedrin* 13.4–5 (*minim* and *perushim* as accursed sinners). His dating of these traditions to a pre-rabbinic age depends on his original location of the latter Toseftan passage within *Seder Olam Rabbah*, a Talmudic chronology of debated provenance, on which see Strack and Stemberger (1996: 326–27). Flusser's dating of that work to the late Second Temple period relies on Milikowsky (1985–1986), to which compare now Milikowsky (2013: 1.228–29), for the relevant text (*Seder Olam* 3), and ibid. (2.66–72), for critical discussion. As I do not wish to engage Milikowsky's sophisticated textual analysis here, I shall say simply that Flusser's assessment of the text's pre-rabbinic origin relies on tendentious reasoning. Even ceding the possibility that the version of the passage in Seder Olam predates that of the Tosefta, to infer that their common indictment of "separatists" accidentally preserves an indictment of the Pharisees seems improbable. Compare, however, Schremer (2010: 57–61), who, though rejecting Flusser's dating scheme, accepts his identification of the sinners enumerated in Seder Olam and the Tosefta as the intended subjects of the blessings of the *minim* and *perushim* on the premise that the *Tannaim* considered heretics qua political dissidents as separatists by default.

[44] Compare Fraade (2000: 524–26), who reads the document's sectarian rhetoric as one pitched toward intramural pedagogy rather than extramural polemicizing.

that the *Tannaim* assimilated established modes of accounting for difference within the Jewish collective, to surmise that they passively imitated the polemical language of prior Jewish generations is simply not justifiable.

On the opposite end of the chronological spectrum is Daniel Boyarin's argument that the construction of *minut* was appropriated from Christians.[45] Given its function as a calque for the Greek *haeresis*, Boyarin suggests that the *Tannaim* conditioned their heresiological discourse as a functional analogue to the corresponding Christian discourse initiated by Justin Martyr in the mid-second century. Hence, according to his reading, the category of *minut* as inscribed on the early rabbinic record responses directly to Christianity even as it encompassed other modes of Jewish expression deemed just as unacceptable. It was not, then, the sages of Yavneh who invented the *minim* but, per Neusner, those of their later successors who compiled the Mishnah and Tosefta. Those early third-century scribes thus conditioned subsequent rabbinic practitioners of their rhetoric to view the Christian as a Jewish antitype just as Christians of their age had taken to judging the Jew a Christian antitype.

Although I find Boyarin's theory instructive as to the function of the Tannaitic category of *minut*, I am not satisfied by his methodology. The legendary quality of the Talmudic account of its Yavnean origin does not preclude the possibility that the invention of *minut* did indeed date to a relatively early stage in the history of the rabbinic movement. Should one accept that the Mishnah and Tosefta preserve authentic Tannaitic traditions, even if in irreversibly modified forms, there is no reason to assume a priori that those traditions did not originally include the allusions to *minut* presently inscribed upon their pages. Boyarin thus appears to assume an apologetic technique functionally similar to Flusser's, intimating that the rabbis devised their rhetoric of heresy on the basis of an existing mode of exclusionary discourse, albeit only once their Christian contemporaries prompted them to do so.[46]

To my mind, it seems best to assess the nature of the rabbinic construction of *minut* not in view of its obscure origin but in view of its function. I have already noted the tendency of the sages to apply the term *min* to Jews of ideological varieties different from their own yet literate in the Hebrew Scriptures and generally attentive to the laws of the Torah. In a recent study building upon these observations, Christine Hayes has demonstrated that the rabbis consistently assign *minim* a legal epistemology subtly but definitively branding them as heretics on account of their hermeneutical techniques.[47] The rabbis, she observes, normally assume a nominalist approach to developing the

45 For the following, see Boyarin (2004: 44–45, 54–58).
46 Note that Boyarin's deduction can be reversed with relative ease. F.S. Jones (2009: 333–39), suggests that Justin and his fellow Christians might have adopted their construction of heresy from the sectarian model as articulated in Jewish texts of the Second Temple era and channeled through Jewish Christian traditions such as that attested in Ps.-Clem. *Recog.* 1.53.5–54.1.
47 Hayes (2011).

halakhah, citing the preservation of existing ritual customs as the chief determinant of legislative innovation. In contradistinction to their own habits, the rabbis cast their opponents as realists, guided not by traditional concerns but by pragmatic concessions to the conditions in which the abstract principles of the law actually operate. Hence, Hayes argues, *minim*, along with Sadducees, Epicureans, and other alleged Jewish undesirables, typically are shown arguing with the sages over matters of applied scriptural interpretation. The purpose of their appearance in the rabbinic record is thus not merely to denounce them as wrongheaded. It is, rather, to instruct readers of its texts how to avoid reaching the same reckless conclusions as those who believe that they can correctly observe the laws of the Torah without the exegetical oversight of the rabbis.[48]

Hayes' considerate reading does not take the edge off of those instances where the rabbis appear to abuse their heretical opponents for no apparent reason. But it does support the premise of locating their heresiological objective in reference to that of their Pharisaic forebears. To the best of our knowledge, the Pharisees too assumed a nominalist legislative agenda, cultivating their sectarian *paradosis* by constantly adding new traditions to old. The Sadducees and Essenes, each to their own effect, prioritized legal reality to the maintenance of legal fiction.[49] That the earliest generations of rabbis preferred the Pharisaic method naturally explains their impetus to cast as heretics Jews who, though not necessarily sectarians by nature, read the Hebrew Scriptures like those one-time competitors of their intellectual forebears.

In view of these considerations, I believe that the most appropriate way to frame the question of who the original *minim* were is in terms of who the *Tannaim* wished them to be. Just like the Ebionites, the Nazarenes, and other alleged Christian heretics of the patristic record, the *minim* only existed as such in the imaginations of their detractors. Evidently, the early rabbinic sages wished to make heretics of Jews whom they deemed to operate in the same sectarian vein as the Sadducees of old. That the sages constructed their own insular sectarian objective in the process we may take for granted. But as with the Church Fathers, the prejudices of the rabbis must not interfere with our assessment of the people behind their disapproving rhetoric. While I therefore shall not presume to deduce the self-identities of the earliest *minim* on the basis of the Tannaitic record, I will attempt to exploit that record for some general observations as to where those individuals stood amidst the broader Jewish population of Roman Palestine.

Arguably the best place to establish a baseline conception of who precisely the *Tannaim* thought the *minim* were is a set of passages offering pronouncements on the eschatological fortunes of assorted non-rabbinic Jewish types.

---

[48] Hayes (2011: 139–44). See also Kahana (2006: 46–51), who accounts the engagement of the *Tannaim* with the exegetical habits of *minim* as an effect of early halakhic debates between the Pharisees and their sectarian detractors.

[49] For this observation, see D.R. Schwartz (1992a), followed by Hayes (2011: 120–33).

Appearing in alternate versions in the Mishnah and Tosefta (*m.Sanhedrin* 10.1–3; *t.Sanhedrin* 12.9–13.12), these texts appear to comprise the remnants of what was a single legal-exegetical unit before its selective incorporation into the previously mentioned compositions. In this case, the longer text preserved in the Tosefta appears to be the more original of the two.[50] It is also the only one to implicate *minim*. Amidst an involved theoretical discussion on the exercise of capital punishment in a Jewish tribunal setting, the text of the Tosefta pauses to consider the fates of those wrongdoers who seem to escape God's judgment on the earthly plane. The anonymous voice of the Tosefta thus speculates as to who from among the children of Israel shall be denied shares in the world to come. Immediately after discussing the "sinners of the nations" (*t.Sanhedrin* 13.2–4), the author enumerates the following "sinners of Israel" (*t.Sanhedrin* 13.4–5):

And as for the heretics, the apostates, the informants, the Epicureans, those who deny the Torah, those who separate themselves from the congregation, those who deny the resurrection of the dead, those who sin and cause others to sin like Jeroboam and Ahab, those who place their dead in the land of the living (cf. Ezek 32.23), and those who extend their hands toward the exalted, Gehenna is locked before them and there they are judged for generations to come, as it is written, *And they shall go out and look at the dead bodies of the people who have rebelled against me. For their worm shall not die, their fire shall not be quenched, and they shall be an abhorrence to all flesh* (Isa 66.24).[51]

Two elements of this passage offer key insights into the author's understanding of what defined the heretical *minim*. First and foremost is its exegetical framework. The scriptural proof text cited, the final verse of the book of Isaiah, refers to a future day when all the exiled of Israel would return to a Jerusalem littered by the corpses of those who had forsaken God's law (cf. Isa 66.17).[52] The Tosefta employs that terrifying prophetic image to implicate all sorts of Jewish contemporaries of the rabbis likewise thought to have transgressed God's law. Just earlier, these alleged sinners are accused of breaking the yoke of the covenant and misinterpreting the Torah (*t.Sanhedrin* 12.9; cf. *m.Sanhedrin* 10.1). The implication, therefore, is that heretics, apostates, and the others condemned here as "sinners of Israel" are nonetheless to be considered Jews in the basic sense of belonging to the same Israel as the rabbis themselves.[53] In other

---

[50] This would seem to account for the independent appearance of the Toseftan version in *Seder Olam* 3; cf. Milikowsky (2013: 2.66–67).

[51] Excerpted from *t.Sanhedrin* 13.5. The passage appears as a *baraita* or "external" (i.e., non-Mishnaic) Tannaitic tradition in *b.Rosh HaShanah* 17a, accompanied by Amoraic commentary immaterial to the present discussion.

[52] Isaiah's implication that those deceased offenders were bound by God's law naturally suggests that they too were Jews, i.e., of the number who remained in Jerusalem during the Babylonian Exile. See Blenkinsopp (2000–2003: 3.316–17).

[53] The Tosefta's implied contrast between deserving Jews and undeserving Jews might relate to the Mishnah's superscription affirming that all of Israel normally merit shares in the world to come (*m.Sanhedrin* 10.1); so S. Stern (1994: 30–31). Note, however, that this formula is lacking in Ms. Cambridge Add. 470 and Ms. Kaufmann A 50.

words, the text assumes the traditional ethnic distinction between Jew and gentile as a determinant of the former's categorical obligation to the rabbinic *halakhah*.[54] In this case, the condemnation of the dissenters in question has no conceivable practical ramification. But the author's explicit distinction of the offensive heretics, apostates, and so forth, from the offensive gentiles clearly establishes that individuals of the former order were supposed to be Jews.

No less significant than its intimation of the Jewish identity of the *minim* is the passage's taxonomic classification of *minut*. The author distinguishes heretics not only from sinful gentiles but also from other types of sinful Jews, such as scofflaws, dissidents, philosophers, libertarians, rabble-rousers, and necromancers. The distinction of *minim* amidst this veritable rogues gallery of malcontents suggests that the early rabbis had a very specific idea of who they were. The *minim* were not supposed to be apostates who chose to flout the authority of God and his Torah.[55] They were not informants apt to collude with the Roman authorities against the interests of their fellow Jews. They were not Epicureans who favored the wisdom of the Greeks over the wisdom of the rabbis. Simply put, the *minim* were in a class by themselves. To be clear, I do not mean to suggest that this categorical distinction was definitive. Later rabbinic writings show *minim* exhibiting traits typical of apostates, informants, Epicureans, and so forth.[56] Clearly, however, the author of our text judged *minim* sufficiently distinctive in their sinful ways to warrant their differentiation from those other detested types.

---

[54] While conventional wisdom dictates that the rabbinic sages were generally hostile toward gentiles qua idolators, careful consideration of their work suggests that they only expressed concern for gentiles insofar as they stood to interfere with the practice of the *halakhah* among Jews. For illustrations of this principle, see Fraade (1994: 147–50); Hayes (2002: 109–14). For a comprehensive study of the status of gentiles in Tannaitic texts, see Porton (1988), who concludes their occasional expressions of tension toward gentiles was an inevitable effect of the sages' efforts to construct exegetical rationales for the scriptural distinction between Israel and the nations (ibid., 285–88).

[55] See, e.g., *t.Horayot* 1.5, where the apostate (*meshumad*, literally "one who is destroyed") is described as a Jew who willfully violates the laws of the Torah, and *Sifra* Nedabah 2.3, where such persons are said to violate Israel's covenant with God (cf. *t.Sanhedrin* 12.9). On the rabbinic concept of apostasy, see S. Stern (1994: 106–09). Compare, however, Langer (2012: 48–53), who warns against reading the Tannaitic category to connote its subjects' wholesale rejection of the Torah. Though nominally different in respect to their motivations, the apostate and the heretic both function in rabbinic discourse as persons deemed to observe normal Jewish customs erratically.

[56] Compare Schiffman (1985: 41–49), who assumes the functional interchangeability of these categories. The abiding confusion in much of the secondary literature as to the independent functions of these distinctions (along with that of the *am ha-aretz*) appears to be a corollary of the uncertainty of the Babylonian *Amoraim* as to the precise grounds upon which the *Tannaim* conceived them. For like comments and examples, see S. Stern (1994: 120–23). See also Boyarin (2004: 197–200), citing a sequence in *b.Avodah Zarah* 26a–b, in which two Babylonian rabbis discussing the present Tannaitic passage are shown questioning the meaning of its distinction between heresy and apostasy.

Further testimony to the halakhic distinction between heretics and gentiles appears elsewhere in the Tosefta in a passage addressing the circumstances under which one may deliberately violate the sanctity of the Sabbath. The question is posed whether one may extinguish a fire, an action ordinarily forbidden on the Sabbath, in order to rescue a burning book provided that said book possesses certain sacred qualities (*t.Shabbat* 13.1–6).[57] Exploring several variations of this scenario, the anonymous author states that one may not violate the Sabbath in order to save "gospels" (*gilyonim*) and "books of heretics" (*sifrei minim*)" even if those books contain "memorials" (*ezkarot*) or vocalic representations of the Tetragrammaton, the ineffable name of God (*t.Shabbat* 13.5). I shall discuss the anti-Christian element of this ruling later in this chapter. What is notable for the moment is its intimation that the *Tannaim* knew *minim* to read and write in the same Hebrew scriptural medium that they practiced themselves. No less indicative of their Jewish identities are the following addenda to the *halakhah*:

Said Rabbi Tarfon: "May I lose my son! If such [books] were to come into my hands, I would burn them along with their memorials! Were a murderer pursuing me, I would sooner hide in a house of idolatry than one of their houses! For idolators do not recognize him (that is, God) while scoffing at him, whereas those guys actually do recognize him but scoff at him just the same! It is of them that the scripture says, *Behind the door and the doorpost you have set up your symbol* (Isa 57.8)."

Said Rabbi Ishmael: "Just as to make peace between a man and his wife God allows his name, which is written in holiness, to be blotted out with water (cf. Num 5.23), how much more so should books of heretics be blotted out,[58] which bring jealousy and hatred between Israel and their father in heaven! It is of them that the Scripture says, *Do I not hate those who hate you, O Lord? And do I not loathe those who rise up against you? I hate them with perfect hatred; I count them my enemies* (Ps 139.21–22)."[59]

Both Rabbi Tarfon and Rabbi Ishmael were active during the late first to early second century. The sentiments ascribed to them provide insight into the author's mindset as to how he wished his readers to remember the attitudes of these renowned Tannaitic sages toward the *minim*. The sharp words of Rabbi Tarfon are striking in their intimation of the theological disposition of the accused. The *minim*, he acknowledges, venerate the God of Israel. That explains his reference to Isaiah's fulmination against deviant Israelites.[60] Once

---

[57] More accurately, the question is not posed outright but can be surmised on the basis of the Tosefta's responses. The actual question is posed in the corresponding text of the Mishnah (*m. Shabbat* 16.1). The priority of the Tosefta's shorter version to that of the Mishnah has been demonstrated by S. Friedman (1993a).

[58] Ms. Erfurt (Berlin Or. fol. 1220) and Ms. London (British Library Add. 27296) read "burned," which makes sense but upsets the balance of Ishmael's analogy. My translation reflects Ms. Vienna Hebr. 20 and the editio princeps.

[59] Excerpted from *t.Shabbat* 13.5. For parallel texts citing the same material as a Tannaitic *baraita*, see *y.Shabbat* 16.1 (15c); *b.Shabbat* 116a.

[60] Specifically, the verse in Isaiah alludes to those whom the prophet alleges deserted God after the devastation of Jerusalem, employing the same verbal root for their (idolatrous) "symbol" (*zekher*)

again, the obvious implication here is that the *Tannaim* knew their heretics to identify as Jews. Precisely what made their habits of worship so repugnant to the rabbis is not said. But whatever the nature of their offense, the charge that *minim* somehow managed to serve the God of Israel in a fashion more deplorable than persons of no account to his worship is damning enough to indicate where the former were thought to have stood in the eyes of the text's author.

The words attributed to Rabbi Ishmael are no less suggestive. Seeking to prove that one need not prevent the destruction of heretical books inscribed with God's name, the sage alludes to the rite of *sotah*, a Pentateuchal ritual of divorce involving the deliberate erasure of the Tetragrammaton.[61] Following this exegetical demonstration is a peremptory allegation that *minim* cause strife between Israel and God. The force of the accompanying proof text is provided by the verses immediately preceding it in the Psalm: *O that you would kill the wicked, O God, and that the bloodthirsty would depart from me those who speak of you maliciously, and lift themselves up against you for evil!* (Ps 139.19–20). The words "speak of you maliciously" (*yomerukha li-mzima*) can be interpreted as "mention you for malice." So, apparently, does Ishmael intimate that those who mention God's name in heretical books are, in fact, enemies of God.[62] Though these imperious accusations are of little help in identifying the alleged heretics in question, they do suggest that those persons lived as Jews, that is, as members of the national collective to which the rabbis typically referred as Israel.

The common Tannaitic opinion of *minim* as moral inferiors to gentiles also finds expression in the arena of applied *halakhah*. This principle is illustrated

used in the Tosefta for the "memorials" to God. Compare Blenkinsopp (2000–2003: 3.160), who reads the symbol as an allusion to the lewd sign on the door of the verse's metaphorical prostitute, a play on the homonym *zakhor*, or "male."

[61] Notably, the sentiment behind Rabbi Ishmael's assessment that books of *minim* are not to be rescued on the Sabbath is expressed elsewhere in the Tannaitic tradition in another exegetical context. A passage in *Sifre* Numbers 16 cites the *sotah* ritual as the basis of an argument *a fortiori* that books of *minim* ought to be destroyed. To this end, Rabbi Ishmael (Ms. London [British Library Add. 16406]: Rabbi Shimon) opines that one should first blacken the "memorials" of God (i.e., erasing them by adding ink) before burning the remainder of the book, to which compare the position assigned to Rabbi Yose the Galilean later in *t.Shabbat* 13.5. Rabbi Akiva insists that the books should be burned entirely on account of the unholy intentions of their authors. The more nuanced exposition of the Sifre's version suggests its priority to the Tosefta. Yet the point of the *Sifre*'s author is not to impugn *minim* but to emphasize the flexibility of the *halakhah* in accommodating the transgressive act of the *sotah* ritual.

[62] A less specific application of this exegetical figure appears in the *Sifre* Deuteronomy 331 in reference to Moses' triumphant claim that God will take vengeance on his enemies (Deut 32.41). The anonymous author of the *midrash* anachronistically identifies those enemies as Samaritans and *minim*. Hammer (1985: 51), plausibly interprets this passage as an anti-Christian element of the *Sifre*'s more general commentary on the state of Palestinian Jewish society after the Bar Kokhba rebellion, although its formulaic indictment of the *minim* seems to me too vague to read with such precision.

at the beginning of an extended heresiological polemic preserved in the Tosefta (*t.Ḥullin* 2.18–24). The passage takes its point of departure from a law dictating that one slaughtering an animal in public should not drain its blood into a hole lest he appear to follow the ways of *minim*. Meats prepared in this obscure manner, the anonymous author thus concludes, are subject to the buyer's inspection (*t.Ḥullin* 2.19).[63] Although the precise scenario assumed here is difficult to pin down, the force of the ruling is unmistakable. "Heretical" butchers, despite their pretensions of upholding some standard of *kashrut*, are not to be trusted to prepare their meats according to the rabbinic standard. At this point, the Tosefta launches into the following screed:

> Meat found in the hands of a gentile is permitted for use. That found in the hands of a heretic is prohibited from use, as though it came from a house of idolatry. This is meat sacrificed to the dead, for they say that the slaughter of the heretic is idolatry, their bread is Samaritan bread,[64] their wine is an [idolatrous] libation, their fruits are not tithed, their books are books of sorcery, and their children are bastards. One should neither sell to them nor buy from them, neither take from them nor give to them. One should not teach their children trades and one should not receive healing from them, whether for financial recovery or for the recovery of lives.[65]

Clearly, the anonymous Tannaitic authorities cited in this passage did not mince words. Their indictment of the *minim* is illuminating in several respects. Firstly, the words of the Tosefta leave little doubt about the ill will of the *Tannaim* toward these individuals. Whereas they allow Jews to profit from butchered meat of unknown provenance obtained from a gentile, meat obtained from a *min* is tantamount to meat used in idolatrous worship and is therefore forbidden entirely.[66]

There is, of course, a paradox here. Why should the possibly idolatrous sacrifice of a heretic be more suspect than the definitely idolatrous sacrifice of a gentile? But prudent exegesis is not the author's point. His hyperbolic rhetoric is clear in the bevy of insults that he proceeds to heap upon the *minim*. Naturally, the more baseless of his allegations must be taken with a grain of

---

[63] The function of the hole is clarified in the Mishnah (*m.Ḥullin* 2.9; followed by *y.Kilayim* 9.1 [32a]; *b.Ḥullin* 41a–b), where it appears to indicate some sort of receptacle for collecting blood, although neither its mechanism nor the supposedly heretical connotations of its use receive further explanation.

[64] Samaritans occupied an anomalous space in the Tannaitic legal imagination similar to that of gentiles. For sources and discussion, see Porton (1988: 132–40).

[65] Excerpted from *t.Ḥullin* 2.20–21. Note the hyperbolic equation of heresy with idolatry. This was the source of the confusion among the Babylonian sages as to whether the *minim* in question were Jews or gentiles (*b.Ḥullin* 13b).

[66] The *halakhah* here renders meat obtained from a gentile "permitted for use" (*mutar be-hana'ah*), i.e., for resale as animal feed, to other gentiles, etc., although obviously prohibited for Jews to eat. In contrast, only meat prepared by a rabbinically sanctioned Jew is presumed *kosher* (*m. Ḥullin* 1.1; *t.Ḥullin* 1.1). On the rhetorical context of this seemingly unnecessary ruling, see Porton (1988: 227, n. 31).

salt. One must not assume that the individuals whom he construes as heretics actually indulged in idolatrous worship or routinely bore children out of wedlock.[67] But the other allegations are more telling. While casually acknowledging that *minim* regularly engage in commercial trade with their fellow Jews, the author indicts them as peddlers of magical remedies. To the minds of the *Tannaim*, magic was tantamount to theological fraud, exhibiting the practitioner's will to subvert the God-given laws of nature.[68] Not surprisingly, then, allegations of sorcery figure prominently in their construction of *minut*.[69] Although it would be unfair to say that the *Tannaim* genuinely supposed all *minim* to trade in the occult sciences, our author seems to issue a general accusation of their deceptive modus operandi. In this respect, he thus implies, *minim* were inestimably more dangerous than gentiles, who were at least candid about their disbelief.[70]

A more ruthless expression of the alleged deviance of the *minim* from the path of the *halakhah* appears elsewhere in the Tosefta. The ruling in question appears at the end of a collection of anonymous Tannaitic opinions on the legal responsibilities of the honorary trustee or one who happens upon another's lost or misplaced property (*t.Bava Metzi'a* 1–2). After drawing out the conversation to a suitable point of abstraction, the passage ends with a discussion of how one should prioritize the returning of lost items after having determined their rightful owners, that is, to his teacher before his father, to his father before his mother, to a man before a woman, and so forth (*t.Bava Metzi'a* 2.29–32).[71] Last in order are the following:

[67] Compare the other instances of seemingly arbitrary indictments of *minim* in the *midrashei halakhah*, i.e., *Mekhilta* Kaspa 3; *Sifre* Numbers 115; *Sifre* Deuteronomy 48, 320, 331.

[68] See Bohak (2008: 356–86), especially ibid. (357–59), on Tannaitic opinions on the legality of magical practice (e.g., *m.Sanhedrin* 6.4, 7, 11; *t.Sanhedrin* 11.5; *Sifre* Deuteronomy 171). That the *Tannaim* were generally wary of magical remedies is perhaps best exemplified in the Mishnah's programmatic ban of the practice which is likened to "the ways of the Amorites," i.e., foreign customs (*m.Shabbat* 10.6). See the extended tangent on said customs in *t.Shabbat* 6–7, with discussion in Berkowitz (2012: 96–100), and cf. Porton (1988: 33).

[69] This categorical rejection of magical practice belies a far more complex and more ambivalent halakhic discourse on magic that ultimately evolved to implicate *minim* as occultists. See in general Bohak (2003), and further, Bohak (2008: 398–401), on the subsequent rabbinic conflation of sorcery, heresy, and Christianity.

[70] That the litany of charges against the *minim* enumerated in this passage was rooted in the realities of their interactions with the early rabbis and their disciples is challenged by Schremer (2010: 69–86), who posits their origin in Jewish sectarian polemics of the Second Temple period; see especially ibid. (73–77). Even ceding to his reasoning, I find it untenable that the author of the Tosefta passage passively adopted his "laws of separation" (ibid., 76) from previous traditions without internalizing their spiteful rhetoric as they redirected it toward *minim*. I therefore am uneasy with Schremer's attempt to distinguish between the heresiological objective of the redacted text of the Tosefta and that of its theoretical source material (ibid., 77–78).

[71] The Mishnah presents a considerably shorter and arguably condensed version of this discussion (*m.Bava Metzi'a* 2.11). On the complicated relationship between the Mishnaic and Toseftan versions of tractate *Bava Metzi'a*, see S. Friedman (1999: 110–13).

As for gentiles, shepherds, and breeders of small cattle,[72] it makes no difference whether they are raised or lowered [in the order of the trustee's priorities]. But as for the heretics, the apostates, and the informants, they should be lowered and never raised.[73]

At first glance, the wording of this passage seems strange and ineffective. Upon closer inspection, however, the author appears to be having some lexical fun at the expense of the *minim* and their ilk. The measure of respect to be shown to gentiles and small-time stockmen is expressed with the formulation "they are neither raised nor lowered" (*lo ma'alin ve-lo moridin*). This is a common rabbinic legal phrase connoting the indifference of the *halakhah* roughly analogous to the contemporary American English idiom, "It could go either way."[74] In contrast, the measure of respect to be shown to the others enumerated in the passage is expressed with the negative inversion "they are lowered but not raised" (*moridin ve-lo ma'alin*). This novel expression was later understood by the Babylonian *Amoraim* to mean that heretics, apostates, and informants are not necessarily to be thrown into a pit, although under no circumstances are they to be rescued from a pit if discovered in that unfortunate state.[75] This explanation well captures the cruel spirit of the Tannaitic gibe. Once again, *minim*, along with apostates and informants, are treated as inferiors to gentiles, as though their value in the eyes of the *halakhah* somehow amounted to less than zero.[76]

In fairness, both of these legal rulings seem more puffery than practical. Certainly neither provides insight into the true designs of those whom the *Tannaim* indict as *minim*. What I find significant are their rhetorical assumptions. Considered in context, the insults read not as capricious smears but as

---

[72] Individuals who tend to and raise small cattle (i.e., goats, cows) are generally given short shrift by the *Tannaim*, presumably on account of their association with the poor and desperate; see, e.g., *m.Bava Qamma* 7.7; *t.Bava Qamma* 8.10–15, with comments in S.J.D. Cohen (1999b: 930–31).

[73] Excerpted from *t.Bava Metzi'a* 2.33. Parallel Babylonian texts (*b.Avodah Zarah* 26a–b; *b.Horayot* 11a) replace the typical Tannaitic term for apostate (*meshumad*) with the equivalent Amoraic epithet *mumar*, literally "one who is converted," employing a terminology developed as a means of distinguishing between the full-blown apostate and the so-called *mumar yisrael*, i.e., a Jew prone to observe some of the Torah's laws while neglecting others. See S. Stern (1994: 106–09). This emendation seems meant to serve the ensuing Amoraic discussion over the meaning of the halakhic distinction between an apostate and a heretic. Notably, the debate is resolved on appeal to a previously discussed Tannaitic passage (*t.Ḥullin* 2.20) in view of its intimation that *minim* are to be defined as those who eat carrion flesh and worship foreign gods with deliberate intent to violate God's law.

[74] For other instances of this Tannaitic formula, see *t.Demai* 5.2; *t.Ma'aser Sheni* 5.9. Why Schremer (2010: 61), claims that its meaning is "not entirely clear" is not entirely clear to me.

[75] This reading is implied in the Talmud's commentary on those unfortunate gentiles or stockmen found stuck in a pit. Per the Tannaitic directive, the *Amoraim* indicate that those individuals may be rescued for a fee in order to avoid incurring their ill will (*b.Avodah Zarah* 26a). As for *minim* et al., the consensus states that while one should not necessarily push them into a pit, neither should one extend one's self to keep them trapped in a pit once they have already fallen in (*b.Avodah Zarah* 26b).

[76] See Porton (1988: 99), for a complementary assessment.

expressions of legitimate fear among the sages for the spiritual wellbeing of their disciples.[77] Simply by calling them heretics, the authors of these passages meant to deter their dedicated readers from associating with those sketchy individuals. The *Tannaim*, in other words, sought to ostracize the *minim* by urging other Jews to avoid contact with them and, more perniciously, to judge them inferiors in the eyes of God. That exclusionary aspect of the early rabbinic construction of *minut* is perhaps best exemplified in the creation of the liturgical malediction later to be dubbed the *birkat ha-minim* (cf. *t.Berakhot* 3.25). But I do not wish to deal with the Tannaitic testimony to that elusive heresiological apparatus just yet. I shall return to the topic later in this chapter once I have established a suitable context against which to assess the possibility of its function as a response to Christianity.

Having thus accounted for the form of the early rabbinic construction of heresy, we may now consider its purpose. Why were the sages so fearful of those of their fellow Jews who read the Torah differently than they did? A passage in the Palestinian Talmud is perhaps illuminating here. Amidst a more elaborate exegetical digression on eschatological judgment, the following opinion is cited in the name of the third-century Palestinian sage Rabbi Yoḥanan: "Israel was not exiled until there had become twenty-four schools of heretics."[78] The reference to *minim* is a comment on the aforementioned Tannaitic condemnation of those individuals, which is cited earlier in the Talmudic passage. Utilizing the imagery of the Babylonian Exile, the rabbi evokes the memory of the more recent crises of displacement that resulted from the Jewish revolts against Rome. He recalls in mournful terms the sectarian rivalries that rent the fabric of Jewish society in the years leading up to those disasters. And yet, judging by his language, it would seem that Yoḥanan saw the social epidemic of centuries ago as a cause for concern even in his own day. To the minds of the rabbis, nothing less than the survival of the Jewish people was at stake in their ongoing struggle against *minut*.

To the *Tannaim* and the *Amoraim* alike, the *minim* were not mere peripheral voices of theological dissent. The tragedies that they believed had been brought upon their people by the divisive sectarian *haereseis* of a bygone era were constant reminders to the rabbis as they nurtured their own pietistic movement in what they saw as the spiritually wasted landscape of postwar Palestine. Yet to the limited extent that the rabbis acknowledged that they were still in competition with other would-be Jewish reformers for the hearts and minds of their people, they did so with the narrow and highly biased focus demanded of their own neo-sectarian initiative. The rare Christians who found their ways into the rhetorical crosshairs of the *Tannaim* represented just one Jewish type of the variety whom the latter believed stood to impede their own collective

---

[77] For similar comments, see Kalmin (1994: 162); Hayes (2007: 258–59); Janowitz (1998: 457–60).

[78] Excerpted from *y.Sanhedrin* 10.5 (29c); cf. *t.Sanhedrin* 13.5. For the following interpretation, compare Goodman (2000a: 213).

enterprise. Christianity, therefore, did play a role in their conception of *minut*, if only in the abstract sense that followers of Jesus were among those Jews whom they deemed fit to call heretics. But we must not overstate Christianity's impact on the shape of that construction or its underlying theology. As I shall now demonstrate, what the *Tannaim* actually knew about the Christians implicated in their polemic was not nearly so sophisticated.

As noted, amidst the litany of vague accusations against the *minim* preserved in the Tannaitic record are a few clearly identifying their subjects as Christians. Naturally, those passages have attracted much critical attention, not in the least among scholars eager to reinforce the once commonplace identification of *minut* and Christianity. Having already addressed the infeasibility of this approach, my interest here is not to discuss how these early witnesses to Christian *minim* figure into that anachronistic equation. While these particular texts certainly have influenced classical Jewish conceptions of the ancient *minim* in disproportion to the balance of the Tannaitic evidence, the *Tannaim* themselves left no indication that that was their intent. As a result, there is no reason to consider these passages more definitive of the early rabbinic construction of heresy than the many other passages in the Mishnah, the Tosefta, and the Tannaitic *midrashim* bearing no obvious anti-Christian overtones.[79]

My interest in revisiting these much-scrutinized passages is not to overemphasize their significance amidst the sea of rabbinic witnesses to *minim* and *minut*. I aim, rather, simply to account for the sociorhetorical functions of these texts within the broader heresiological discourse of the *Tannaim*, thereby accomplishing what I proposed in the introduction, namely to explain how and why the early rabbinic sages came to construe the Christian other in typically Jewish terms. I shall deal with the impact of this slanted perspective on subsequent rabbinic efforts to assess the differences between Christian and Jew in Chapter 5.

The first passage of interest appears in the Tosefta immediately following the aforementioned set of warnings against dealing with heretics in routine commercial exchange (*t.Ḥullin* 2.20–21). As noted, the concluding directive in that passage cautions the reader not to accept magical remedies from *minim*,

[79] I thereby distinguish my approach from those who would cite these passages as proof that the rabbinic category of *minut* referred principally to Christianity; compare, e.g., Schiffman (1985: 62–64, 69–73); Jaffé (2005: 117–312); Teppler (2007: 240–77, 286–93). I prefer to describe references to *minut* as having been directed against Christianity only where they unambiguously describe elements of Christian practice or belief. Lest the reader judge my approach overly cautious, compare Maier (1978: 130–92), and Maier (1982: 19–114), who attempts to dispel the patently anti-Christian rhetorical objectives of the following evidences. To my mind, Maier's forced readings betray a well-meaning but critically unfeasible apologetic agenda. See Schäfer (2007: 5–6), for a brief yet incisive critique of Maier's methodology.

signifying what apparently was a stereotypical association of heresy and sorcery. Following this advice, the text of the Tosefta provides the following illustrative anecdote:

> It happened that Rabbi Eleazar ben Damah was bitten by a snake. A certain Jacob of Kefar Sama came to heal him in the name of Jesus son of Pantira, but Rabbi Ishmael did not allow it. They told him, "You are not allowed [to receive him], Ben Damah." He responded, "I shall bring you proof that he may heal me." But there was no time to bring the proof before he died. Said Rabbi Ishmael, "Happy are you, Ben Damah, for you have departed in peace without violating the decree of the sages. For anyone who breaks the fence of the sages will suffer punishment in the end, as it says, *And whoever breaks through a wall will be bitten by a snake* (Eccl 10.8)."[80]

This is a disconcerting story. Given its position in the redacted text of the Tosefta, it seems clear that its intended function is to demonstrate the rationale behind the halakhic proscription of receiving aid from *minim*. The central figure in the story is the obscure early second-century sage Rabbi Eleazar ben Damah. The heretic is an otherwise unknown man named Jacob hailing from the fictitious locale of Kefar Sama (Aramaic for "Medicine Town"), shown here offering to cure the ailing rabbi by intoning the name of Jesus. The epithet "son of Pantira" alludes to a specious tale that circulated among early critics of Christianity alleging that Jesus of Nazareth was the illegitimate son of a Roman soldier named Panthera.[81]

The appearance of this smear does not help the credibility of the story. A real Christian healer would not likely have spoken of Jesus in such opprobrious terms. Rabbi Ishmael, nevertheless suspicious that the healer is a heretic, forbids Eleazar to see him. Despite a pathetic protest on Eleazar's part, Ishmael remains firm and allows Eleazar to die untreated. Afterwards, Ishmael assures himself through some abstract exegetical logic that his friend died in righteousness. Had Eleazar violated the decree (*gezerah*) of the sages, he reasons, he would have breached the fence (*gederah*) which the sages had erected to protect the laws of the Torah.[82] To that end, Ishmael adduces a scriptural proof text seemingly at odds with the events he has just witnessed, suggesting that Eleazar had in fact gone over the metaphorical fence of the

---

[80] Excerpted from *t.Ḥullin* 2.22–23. For parallel Amoraic texts, several of which deviate from the Tosefta on minor details, see *y.Avodah Zarah* 2.2 (40d–41a); *y.Shabbat* 14.4 (14d–15a); *b.Avodah Zarah* 27b; *Ecclesiastes Rabbah* 1.24 (cf. 7.39), with discussion in Schäfer (2007: 54). See also Schäfer (ibid., 138–39), for comparison of manuscript variants among the heavily redacted Talmudic versions.

[81] Further rabbinic references to the Panthera story appear in *t.Ḥullin* 2.24 and its parallels and in uncensored manuscripts of *b.Sanhedrin* 67a and 104b. The same disparaging story was known to the Greek critic Celsus, as attested in Origen, *Cels.* 1.28, 32, and to Eusebius, *Ecl. proph.* 3.10, who credits it to unnamed Jews. On the origins of this spurious legend and its function in rabbinic polemics against Christianity, see Schäfer (2007: 15–24).

[82] On this common rabbinic precautionary principle, see Goldin (1966); Schofer (2005: 74–75).

halakhah. Hence, apparently, God's decision to punish him by means of the deadly snakebite.[83]

Perhaps the most troubling aspect of the story is also its most suggestive. Despite their difference over the legitimacy of Jacob's technique, both rabbis appear convinced that it might actually work. The unfortunate Rabbi Eleazar makes it clear that he would accept the heretic's cure despite his Christian credentials. He even attempts to prove its permissibility before succumbing to the snake's venom. Rabbi Ishmael, though resolute about its prohibition, does not deny the possibility that the spell would have been effective. This presumed usefulness of Jesus' magical powers speaks to an important characteristic of Jacob's alleged heresy. Jesus was known for his curative capabilities. The gospels are replete with stories telling of his miraculous works on behalf of the blind, the lame, and even the dead. As early as the first century, therefore, that legendary aspect of his ministry had been appropriated by early Christian practitioners to become a defining attribute of their movement.[84]

Yet the supposedly miraculous properties of Jesus' name were as much a source of pride to his devotees as a source of disgrace to their detractors. The popular association between Jesus and the occult fueled criticism from Jews and gentiles eager to exploit this dubious aspect of Christian culture as an excuse to disparage the entire Christian enterprise.[85] This common polemical motif appears to underlie Rabbi Ishmael's hostility. By extension, moreover, one might surmise that the common anti-Christian polemic helped to shape the generic Tannaitic association of *minut* with sorcery attested in the Tosefta's preceding halakhic ruling. To be clear, I do not mean to suggest that the *Tannaim* supposed that all Christians practiced sorcery, nor that Christians were the only ones among the ranks of the *minim* thought to have done so.[86] That said, it seems reasonable to deduce that the *Tannaim* perceived sorcery,

[83] The apparent contradiction between the precautionary sense of the scriptural verse and the post-mortem condemnation of Rabbi Eliezer was noted by the *Amoraim*. In the Palestinian Talmud, the verse is read to indicate that Eleazar would be bitten again in the afterlife (*y.Avodah Zarah* 2.2 [40d–41a]; *y.Shabbat* 14.4 [14d–15a]). In the Babylonian Talmud, the snake of the verse is read metaphorically as "the snake of the rabbis" (*ḥewe de-rabanan*) embodied in the *halakhah*, suggesting that Eleazar would have been better off without Ishmael's help (*b.Avodah Zarah* 27b). See Schäfer (2007: 55–56).

[84] For the following, see M. Smith (1978), especially, ibid. (94–139), who provides copious evidence for the use of Jesus' name and literary reputation for healing in ancient Christian magical amulets. See also Schäfer (2007: 57–59), on corresponding Jewish incantation practices employing the name of God and other heavenly luminaries.

[85] On this common indictment, see M. Smith (1978: 21–80), especially ibid. (57–60), on the charges leveled by Celsus possibly with the aid of a Jewish informant (see, e.g., Origen, *Cels.* 1.38, 57, 68; 2.49–52).

[86] To the contrary, Stuart Miller has demonstrated the tendency of the *Amoraim* to describe wonder-working *minim* as individuals engaged in idolatrous gentile practices; see, e.g., *y.Sanhedrin* 7.19 (25d); *b.Sanhedrin* 65b, with discussion in Miller (1993: 381–85).

or at least magical healing, as a calling card of what they construed as the Christian heresy.

Other elements of the story are no less suggestive. That Jacob approaches Rabbi Eleazar of his own volition to offer his assistance speaks to the readiness of Jewish Christians to interact with other, non-Christian Jews, including those hostile to their number. In this case, Jacob seems to want to help Eleazar for no apparent personal gain beyond, perhaps, impressing the rabbis with the supernatural power of Jesus' name. Jacob, moreover, does not hide his Christian identity. Quite to the contrary, his open expression of his intent to cure Eleazar in the name of Jesus is crucial to his characterization. This alleged heretic is no outsider to the Jewish mainstream. He presumes to function as a Jew among other Jews, projecting the confidence of one who sees no essential conflict of interest between himself and the rabbis.

Even more impressive is the story's intimation that Rabbi Eleazar welcomes Jacob's intervention despite being aware of his Christian identity. Granted, Eleazar is in dire straits at the time of his overture. He really does need a miracle. From a purely emotional standpoint, his concession to heresy is completely understandable.[87] It is in the seemingly unfeeling reaction of Rabbi Ishmael that the severity of Eleazar's indiscretion is exposed. In intimating that Eleazar had broken the fence of the *halakhah* before the snake bit him, Ishmael appears to refer not to his friend's acceptance of the heretic's cure. Eleazar's transgression, rather, is his mere willingness to accept it, as shown in his futile effort to prove to Ishmael that, in fact, he was permitted to do so.[88] Although no less sensitive to Eleazar's suffering, Ishmael's response therefore seems justified in view of the preceding halakhic injunction. As a devout rabbinic sage, Eleazar presumably knew that he was not supposed to accept magical remedies from *minim*. But he wanted to do so regardless. Even at the risk of one's own life, the author thus seems to suggest, should one take care to steer clear of heretics, for merely to associate with their kind is to risk incurring the wrath of God.[89]

---

[87] I differ here from Boyarin (1999: 34–36), who sees Rabbis Eleazer's overture to the Christian *min* as more of a sympathetic gesture than a desperate grasp for survival. The intimation that Eleazar secretly identified with the unwelcome heretic seems a bit of a stretch considering Ishmael's concluding assessment that his friend died "happy" and "in peace." These sentiments would not be appropriate for a sage whom the author wished to portray as one who would appeal to the subjects of his censure.

[88] For a complementary reading, see Frenkel (2001: 102–04).

[89] For a similar interpretation of the story's legal-exegetical function, see Schremer (2010: 89–91). With respect to Schremer (ibid., 91) I would not infer that Eleazar was supposed to have known the contents of *t.Ḥullin* 2.20–21 in the form of a received, proto-rabbinic heresiology supposedly underlying that text. As far as the logic of the present passage is concerned, Eleazar should have known to stay away from *minim* simply by virtue of his characterization as a rabbi and a confidant of the more illustrious sage Rabbi Ishmael.

TEACHING IN THE NAME OF JESUS

Similar observations regarding the social profile of the Christian *minim* emerge from a Tannaitic story involving the late first-century sage Rabbi Eliezer ben Hyrcanus. The story appears immediately following the sad tale of Eleazar ben Damah as the final element of the Tosefta's extended digression on *minut*. The passage reads as follows:

It happened that Rabbi Eliezer was arrested for matters of heresy. They brought him to the stand for judgment. The governor said to him, "Could it be that an old man like you is involved in such affairs?" He answered, "I have faith in the judge." Though he was actually referring to his father in heaven (that is, God), the governor thought that [Eliezer] was speaking of none other than himself. He therefore told him, "Since I have your trust, it behooves me to admit that these gray hairs[90] might have been mistaken in these charges. *Dimissus!* You are set free."[91] After he was released from the stand, [Eliezer] was troubled that he had been arrested for matters of heresy. His disciples came to console him, but he would not receive them. Rabbi Akiva came and said to him, "Let me tell you something, my teacher, lest you remain troubled." "So tell me already," he replied. Said [Akiva], "Maybe one of those heretics told you a word of heresy and you enjoyed it." "By heaven," said [Eliezer], "you've reminded me! I was recently walking down the street in Sepphoris when I ran into a certain Jacob of Kefar Sekhanya. He did tell me a word of heresy in the name of Jesus son of Pantira[92] and I did enjoy it! That must be why I was arrested on charges of heresy, for I violated that which is written in the Torah: *Keep your path far from her and near not the entrance to her house, for she has brought down many victims* (Prov 5.8, 7.26)."[93]

The colorful characterizations of this passage have made it a favorite of scholars seeking to demonstrate the principle that the early rabbinic sages generally were unapprised of the distinction between the concepts of Jewish and

[90] I follow here the most common interpretation of the difficult term *ha-sevo*, which should appear as *ha-sevot* in the present grammatical construction. Maier (1978: 152–54), followed by Schäfer (2007: 43–44), reads the word as the plural verb *ha-sevu* ("those who were reclining"), which would indicate that Eliezer was charged for attending a symposium or meal. While that image is suggestive, it does not cohere with what follows, wherein Eliezer recalls his exchange with a Christian as having occurred during a chance encounter on the street. P.S. Alexander (2007: 661), prefers *yeshivot* as attested in the parallel text of *Ecclesiastes Rabbah* 1.24, which would indicate the governor's incredulity that such heretical affairs should occur in rabbinic academies. But this reading is supported neither by the text of the Tosefta nor the sense of the narrative.

[91] The governor's acquittal is recorded as *dimus*, an approximation of the Latin term provided, and repeated in Hebrew. On the use of Roman legal terminology in this passage, including the references to the judicial stand (*bēma*) and the governor (*hēgemon*), see Lieberman (1944: 19–24).

[92] The Talmudic version of the story (uncensored manuscripts of *b.Avodah Zarah* 16a–17a) features the common Aramaic term for Christian (*ha-notzeri*, "the Nazarene") in place of the spurious patronym "son of Pantira." For a comparison of alternate manuscript readings, see Schäfer (2007: 137–38).

[93] Excerpted from *t.Hullin* 2.24. For parallel Amoraic versions, see *b.Avodah Zarah* 16a–17a; *Ecclesiastes Rabbah* 1.24, with discussion in Schäfer (2007: 41–46).

Christian identity. The story begins with a swift sequence of actions whereby the hapless Rabbi Eliezer finds himself before a Roman tribunal on suspicion of his involvement in "matters of heresy" (*divrei minut*). Through a combination of wit and flattery, Eliezer manages to evade the charge leveled against him. Distraught, however, over why he had been suspected of heresy to begin with, the rabbi is consoled by his disciple Akiva, who guesses that his teacher might have taken in a passing "word of heresy" (*davar shel minut*) and forgotten about it. The elder rabbi is pleased to remember that he had indeed heard such a word spoken in the name of Jesus by one Jacob[94] of Kefar Sekhanya (Aramaic for "Danger Town")[95] while strolling through the Galilean city of Sepphoris. Eliezer thus concludes that this must have earned his ordeal on account of that transgression of the *halakhah*. To that end, he cites a synthetic scriptural proof text from Proverbs warning one to steer clear of the loose woman personified in that book as the antithesis of wisdom.[96] Since Eliezer had strayed from his route to converse with a heretic, so, he infers, did he deserve to be punished for erring from the true path of the Torah.[97]

As a historical set piece, the story works on several levels. The image of suspected Christians being arrested and put to trial before the Roman authorities clearly resonates with the early Christian martyrdom literature.[98] The intimation, moreover, that Rabbi Eliezer was afforded the chance to exculpate himself squares with the reports in those hagiographical texts of the due legal process afforded to Christian confessors prior to their sentencing. The persecution of

[94] Note that this Jacob bears the same name as the heretic of the preceding passage. The repetition of the name appears to reflect an obscure polemical trope perhaps attributable to the local fame of James (Greek: *iakōbos*), the brother of Jesus and the first prelate of the Palestinian church. To that end, it is possible that Jacob was a popular Christian name in the age of the *Tannaim* and is employed here in stereotypical fashion. I have no confidence in the inference of Bauckham (1990: 114–16), that this Jacob was meant to represent a historical personality of the same name, namely a distant cousin of Jesus descended from his youngest brother Judas.

[95] Although often identified with the historical village of Sikhnin (modern-day Sakhnin) in the Lower Galilee, the locale mentioned here seems to repeat the theme established by the fictitious "Kefar Sama" of the previous passage; cf. Miller (1993: 381, n. 16). Ms. London (British Library Add. 27296) reads *kefar hekhny'sama* ("Medicine Gathering Town") in what appears to be a textual corruption meant to correlate the two Jacobs.

[96] Note the corresponding exegetical motif comparing heresy to the loose woman of Proverbs in the pseudo-Tannaitic works *Avot of Rabbi Nathan* (A) 2 and *Avot of Rabbi Nathan* (B) 3. See also *Sifre* Numbers 115 for a similar rhetorical figure involving the proverbial wicked woman of Eccl 7.26.

[97] My usage of term "Torah" here corresponds with that of the Tosefta passage, indicating not the Pentateuch per se but the more diffuse "way of the Torah" that the rabbis associated with the figure of wisdom as depicted in the book of Proverbs. On this rabbinic idiom, see *Genesis Rabbah* 1.1, with discussion in D. Stern (1996: 27–28).

[98] On the thematic parallels between this story and early Christian martyr narratives, see Boyarin (1999: 26–30) and passim. My own reading of this passage is greatly indebted to Boyarin's masterful treatment. On the Roman tribunal as a dramatic set piece in Christian martyrologies, see Castelli (2007: 39–49).

Christians was an unfortunate fact of life in the Roman Empire during the age when the Mishnah and Tosefta were composed. Although the more systematic offensives which would characterize imperial policy toward Christians during the third and early fourth centuries were yet unknown to the *Tannaim* and their contemporaries, there is ample evidence for the occurrence of local persecutions throughout the Near Eastern region during the reigns of the emperors Septimius Severus (r. 193–211 CE) and Caracalla (r. 211–217 CE).[99] Although the writings of the *Tannaim* preserve no clear hints of even these isolated incidents, they provide sufficient evidence to indicate that the early rabbinic sages were well acquainted with the less salubrious aspects of the Roman civil procedure that sanctioned those fatal charades.[100]

In view of these observations, it is no coincidence that the author of the passage chose to frame this otherwise formulaic indictment of *minut* as an anti-Christian polemic. To our knowledge, Christianity would have been the only Jewish "heresy" of interest to a Roman government typically indifferent to the domestic politics of its provincial subjects. The alleged *min* of our story had to have been a Christian in order to provide the story a semblance of historicity. Even granting that its facts are impossible to verify, the story of Eliezer's near-martyrdom reads as a credible witness to how the *Tannaim* internalized the social divide between Jew and Christian already taking shape beyond Palestine's Jewish population.[101]

It is this tension between the internal and external dimensions of Jewish identity that drives the story's heresiological rhetoric. Despite its obvious anti-Christian pretense, the story's polemical edge is dulled by the author's failure to explain what was so objectionable about the word of Jesus spoken in his presence.[102] Evidently, it is not the message that concerns our author

[99] On the persecution of Christians under the Severan emperors, see Clarke (2005: 616–21). Of dubious relevance here is the assertion of the anonymous author of the late ancient biographical forgery known as the Augustan History, who states that Septimius Severus showed special favor to the Jews, even passing legislation explicitly distinguishing them from Christians (*Scriptores Historiae Augustae*, Septimius Severus 17.1). Although the Jews of Palestine generally did fare well during his reign, that the emperor would have personally interceded in their communal affairs seems improbable.

[100] See, e.g., *m.Avodah Zarah* 1.7, which regulates Jewish participation in the construction of edifices used in Roman juridical proceedings, and *t.Avodah Zarah* 2.7, which regulates attendance at said trials, with discussion in Burns (2007: 411–21).

[101] I differ here from Boyarin (1999: 31–32), who sees the story as a rabbinic meditation on an internal Jewish struggle between orthodoxy and heterodoxy. While concern for the preservation of traditional Jewish mores might be accounted as one of its thematic undercurrents, the story's blunt anti-Christian animus would seem to set its rhetoric in a time and place where the author reasonably could have assumed that his readers would identify with a Roman legal order objectifying the Christian as someone other than a Jew. For like comments, see Schäfer (2007: 48).

[102] This apparent oversight is resolved in the later Amoraic revisions to the story (*b.Avodah Zarah* 16a–17a; *Ecclesiastes Rabbah* 1.24), which define the unspecified "word" as either of two abstract halakhic opinions of no clear relevance to the anti-Christian thrust of the original Tannaitic text. See Schäfer (2007: 41–46).

but the medium. From his standpoint, Christianity had been forbidden, its proponents branded as atheists in the eyes of the Roman law. Being associated with Christians was bad for the Jews, no more so, one may presume, than in places where some of those Christians actually were Jews. Although the rabbis were by no means fans of the Roman government, they took full advantage of the fact that the Roman law protected their cultic rights.[103] Rabbi Eliezer's arrest alarms him not merely because he was mistaken by the local gentile authorities for a Christian, a person deemed illegitimate in the eyes of the secular authorities. What bothers him is his realization that he had been taken for a heretic, an illegitimate Jew, by the God whom he believes had orchestrated the whole sordid affair.[104] God, Eliezer knows, does not make mistakes. He therefore humbly concludes that he must have been in the wrong.

Rabbi Eliezer's submission to God's discipline notably echoes his earlier submission to the governor's judicial prerogative, if only in word, the author carefully notes, and not in fact. Where the renowned sage might reasonably have contested the charges leveled against him by both his earthly and heavenly judges, Eliezer thinks it wiser in each case to confess to his crime.[105] In this respect, his subsequent realization that he was indeed guilty of violating the *halakhah* recalls Ishmael's seemingly unfeeling response to his friend's death in the preceding narrative. Both sages through their respective ordeals come to appreciate that even fleeting, unsolicited contact with heresy is an affront to God. Their trying experiences thus seem to demonstrate the value of the

---

[103] This point is made to persuasive effect by Lapin (2012), who demonstrates the willingness of both the Tannaitic and Amoraic sages of Palestine to adapt the *halakhah* to function within the legislative limits of the Roman law; see especially his programmatic comments in ibid. (33–37). Boyarin (1999: 123), seems to neglect the story's positive depiction of the Roman government as an agency favorably disposed toward Rabbi Eliezer once the procedural mishap is corrected.

[104] This distinction seems lost on Schremer (2010: 92), who argues that Eliezer's brief conversation with Jacob had actually made the rabbi a heretic. This, he argues, is in contradistinction to Eleazar ben Damah, whose "blessed" demise he attributes to his having escaped the stigma of *minut* (ibid., 90). Accordingly, Eliezer, aware of his guilt, could not simply have professed his innocence of the governor's charge. Frankly, I have trouble seeing these as practical guides to avoiding a toxic ideology liable to infect all who come into contact with it. That is not how ideologies work. Their purpose, rather, is to warn readers in parabolic fashion that even the most casual association with heresy, intentional or not, will earn even the most devout Jew the reprimand of God.

[105] For an alternative suggestion as to why Eliezer does not simply deny the charges leveled against him, see Boyarin (1999: 97–101), who suggests that the rabbi did not wish to slander the name of Jesus and, by extension, his followers, by delegitimizing their beliefs. I am at a loss to discern any trace of the "irenic Torah conversation" that Boyarin sees in the rabbi's recollection (ibid., 28). While Eliezer makes it clear that his initial impression of Jacob was not unfavorable, I do not think it judicious to infer that he felt no guilt or contrition for his misdeed until after his arrest. His response to Rabbi Akiva suggests that Eliezer knew of Jesus and his heresy prior to his meeting with Jacob. In any case, Eliezer certainly does not appear to express esteem for Christianity in reckoning Jacob a *min*.

severe proscriptions against associating with heretics to which their stories are appended in the Tosefta.

Further to their common legal-exegetical agenda, the two stories include similar indications as to how the *Tannaim* related to Christians as Jews. Perhaps the most striking aspect of the story's social commentary is its implication that Christian *minim* so closely resemble rabbinic sages that the Roman officials who arrested Rabbi Eliezer mistook him for a heretic. Nor, for that matter, does Eliezer himself seem to have been capable of identifying his interlocutor as a heretic prior to the latter's allusion to Jesus. Judging by his later remarks, one would imagine that the rabbi would have avoided conversing with Jacob had he known the latter was, in fact, a Christian. As far as the narrative reveals, Jacob appeared to Eliezer as a typical Jew.[106] He approached Rabbi Eliezer as one eager to converse with Jewish sages not of his own Christian persuasion. He spoke learned words in the same idiom as those sages. He plied the wisdom of Jesus in a predominantly Jewish city.[107] All told, Jacob presented himself as a man wholly comfortable in his Jewish skin. That, the author implies, is precisely what made him so dangerous.

In the end, Rabbi Eliezer does not fault himself for having unintentionally exchanged words with a man whom he could not possibly have recognized as a Christian at the outset of their encounter. His transgression, as he sees it, is that he failed to repudiate Jacob's wisdom once he discovered its illicit source. In that passive act of acceptance, Eliezer finally realizes, he had tacitly validated the Christian heresy. From the author's standpoint, that inadvertent sin very nearly forced Eliezer onto the same destructive path as Eleazar ben Damah, who reportedly sealed his own fate by expressing his will to accept the unlawful remedy of a man whom he actually knew was a Christian. Rabbi Eliezer's reflection on the grounds for his arrest is thus meant to leave a powerful impression on the reader of the Tosefta as to just how cunningly Christian *minim* were believed to have operated in the social world of the *Tannaim*.

THE GOSPELS AND BOOKS OF HERETICS

The final text to be considered is the aforementioned *halakhah* addressing the sacred qualities of the gospels and other allegedly heretical books containing

---

[106] Compare Hezser (1997: 123–30), who argues that the sages generally did not distinguish themselves from other Jews in respect to their mode of dress. Evidently, they expected nothing different of Jewish Christians.

[107] Along with Tiberias, Sepphoris was one of the Galilee region's two major centers of Jewish population during the late ancient period. As such, it features prominently in rabbinic legal-exegetical discourse as a typical urban setting for the practice and regulation of the *halakhah*. The rabbinic traditions relating to Sepphoris have been studied extensively by Stuart Miller; see, inter alia, Miller (1984; 2006: 31–106). Per Miller (1993: 379–81), the Sepphorean setting of Rabbi Eliezer's encounter with Jacob seems meant to indicate that this particular *min* was a Jewish Christian as opposed to a gentile Christian.

the Tetragrammaton, the sacrosanct name of God. While this tightly worded legal tradition is not as illustrative as the more expansive narratives just discussed, its sociocultural rhetoric is nonetheless enlightening. Referring to the question of whether one may extinguish a fire on the Sabbath in order to save these volumes, the passage reads as follows:

> The gospels and books of heretics are not to be saved. They are, rather, to be left to burn in their places along with their memorials. Said Rabbi Yose the Galilean: On a weekday one should blacken[108] and conceal their memorials and burn what remains.[109]

The passage concludes with the hostile comments on the *minim* and their books ascribed to Rabbi Tarfon and Rabbi Ishmael cited earlier in this chapter. The precise articles of interest to this ruling have long been subjects of controversy. Until recently, the uncommon term for gospels (*gilyonim*) typically was rendered as "margins," referring to the blank areas surrounding the columns of written text on the pages of the heretical books in question. The latter books, in turn, were construed as otherwise normal Torah scrolls[110] or other Hebrew scriptural texts penned by *minim*.[111] That apologetic interpretation has since fallen out of favor. Both on linguistic grounds and on contextual

---

[108] My reading favors the dominant textual tradition of the Tosefta, which reads "blacken" (*qoder*), against Ms. Erfurt (Berlin Or. fol. 1220), which reads "read" (*qore*). The latter is likely a corruption or imprecise emendation of *qor'e* ("cut" or "tear"), as attested in the quotation of this tradition in the Palestinian Talmud (*y.Shabbat* 16.1 [15c]). The Babylonian Talmud (*b.Shabbat* 116a) and a related passage in *Sifre* Numbers 16 follow the dominant Tosefta tradition. For comments and further postclassical textual variants, see Lieberman (1955–1988: 3.207).

[109] Excerpted from *t.Shabbat* 13.5. For parallel Amoraic versions, see *y.Shabbat* 16.1 (15c); *b.Shabbat* 116a.

[110] The once commonplace identification of the anonymous "books" as Torah scrolls is supported by inference from a discussion in the Babylonian Talmud of such scrolls written by *minim* (*b. Gittin* 45b). Typically of their Babylonian context, the *Amoraim* seem confused by the halakhic distinction between *minim* and gentiles, ultimately reaching the incongruous conclusion that Torah scrolls written by gentiles are more acceptable than those written by *minim* (among other disreputable Jews). The basis of this discussion appears to be a garbled rendition of the present Tannaitic tradition explicitly identifying the "books of heretics" as Torah scrolls. The resulting Amoraic misrepresentation of the original Tannaitic ruling has since come to influence critical interpretation of the Tosefta; see, e.g., P.S. Alexander (1992: 13–15); Jaffé (2005: 282–86); S.T. Katz (2006: 279–80).

[111] That the books in question were presumed to represent sacred texts was based on a faulty inference from *t.Shabbat* 13.1 (cf. *m.Shabbat* 16.1; *m.Yadayim* 4.6), which introduces the topic at issue in the present ruling specifically in reference to "sacred writings" (*kitvei ha-qodesh*). The intimation that the allegedly heretical books at issue here were likewise presumed sacred is erroneous. As I shall discuss later, only their allusions to God are accorded such esteem. The ostensible critical justification for reading *gilyonim* as "margins" casts the term as a plural form of the Aramaic *gelayon*, literally "scroll," a term used by the *Tannaim* to indicate the blank portions bracketing the text of a document (cf. *m.Yadayim* 3.4; *t.Yadayim* 2.11). That is the meaning of *gilyonim* assumed in the Babylonian Talmud's discussion of the present *halakhah* (*b.Shabbat* 116a). For examples of this apologetic reading of the Tosefta, see Bacher (1899: 38–42); Herford (1903: 155–57); Kuhn (1964: 31–35); Urbach (1981: 290–91); Maier (1982: 30–69); Alon (1980–1984: 1.276); Teppler (2007: 252–57); Schremer (2010: 84–86).

grounds, the term *gilyonim* appears to be an approximate plural construction of *euangelion*, or "good message," the typical Greek term for a Christian gospel tract.[112] The passage's unnamed "books of heretics" are more difficult to pin down. Given their juxtaposition with Christian texts, one might read these as Christian books other than the gospels. On the other hand, one might also read them to indicate any books produced by *minim*, Christian or otherwise. The issue is insoluble.[113] What is clear, however, is that both types of books mentioned in the ruling are supposed to share certain traits rendering them equally repugnant in the eyes of the *halakhah*. The anonymous voice of the Tosefta dictates that those books, if found burning on the Sabbath, do not require rescuing by means of extinguishing the fire, an act which the *Tannaim* deemed to violate the sanctity of the Sabbath (cf. *m.Shabbat* 7.2). Another opinion is offered in the name of the second-century sage Rabbi Yose, who suggests that one should prevent the scenario envisioned in the original ruling by seizing those illicit books, censoring their memorials to God, storing the now illegible portions of the texts somewhere inaccessible to the general public, and burning the remainder of their pages.[114]

Given the limited information provided in the Tosefta, it is difficult to discern how the gospels were supposed to compare to other allegedly heretical books in the mind of the anonymous Tannaitic author. Clearly, he assumes that both sets of texts were presumed sacred by their readers. Hence their having

[112] This reading is supported by a passage excised from printed editions of the Babylonian Talmud featuring a conjectural Tannaitic exchange over whether a heretical book is properly to be called a "wretched scroll" (*aven gilyon*) or a "sinful scroll" (*avon gilyon*), both of which readings play on the Greek *euangelion* (uncensored manuscripts of *b.Shabbat* 116a). This exchange is followed by a thematically related narrative in which the first-century *Tanna* Rabban Gamaliel is shown quoting the Gospel of Matthew (*b.Shabbat* 116a–b; cf. Matt 5.17). The supplementary narrative appears in censored editions, although its relevance to the Tannaitic ruling on the *gilyonim* is obscured by the omission of the preceding exegetical figure. See Jaffé (2005: 247–51). Scholars favoring this pointedly anti-Christian interpretation of the Tosefta's ruling include Lieberman (1955–1988: 3.206–07); Schiffman (1985: 62–64); P.S. Alexander (1992: 5–11; 2007: 679–82); Boyarin (2004: 57–58); S.T. Katz (2006: 278–79) (although cf. S.T. Katz 1984: 46–62); Jaffé, ibid. (256–72).

[113] One approach has been to equate the *gilyonim* and "books of heretics," i.e., reading both terms in reference to Greco-Jewish books inscribed with Hebrew marginalia found in the possession of *minim*. This reading was introduced by Friedländer (1898: 81–89), who identified the heretical books as Gnostic treatises. See also Pines (1974: 206–09), who notes that the classical Syriac terms *gilyane* and *gilyone* refer to the New Testament book of Revelation, thus providing a semantic link between the Tosefta's *gilyonim* and noncanonical Jewish apocalyptic texts preserved in the Christian literary tradition. Boyarin (2004: 239), n. 113, cites Pines' observation as proof of a connection between the *gilyonim* and the gospels. I do not think that Pines' roundabout explanation is necessary to substantiate that connection.

[114] I use the term "pages" loosely. Given the conjectural nature of this ruling, it seems fruitless to speculate as to whether the illicit books in question were supposed to be written in parchment scrolls, which would demand that their allusions to God had to be excised (cf. *y.Shabbat* 16.1 [15c]) or in codices, in which case the leaves containing those allusions could be torn out individually.

been written in Hebrew, the holy tongue of the Jews, and hence their explicit allusions to Yahweh.[115] Yet despite emulating other sacred Jewish books in their compositional features, the rabbis did not consider those books intrinsically sacred. They did, however, deem sacred small portions of those books, namely the portions inscribed with the Tetragrammaton.[116] In other words, as far as the *Tannaim* were concerned, the problem with the gospels and other books of *minim* was that these texts, heretical though they were, were nevertheless significant in the eyes of the *halakhah*. As such, they merited inclusion in the Tosefta's discussion of the Sabbath law. Similar observations emerge from another less overtly critical Tannaitic reference to the gospels elsewhere in the Tosefta. Amidst a set of laws addressing which Hebrew books are to be considered intrinsically sacred (*t.Yadayim* 2.10–14; cf. *m.Yadayim* 3.3–5), the Tosefta reads:

> The gospels and books of heretics do not render one's hands impure. Books (sic) of Ben Sira and all books written thereafter do not render one's hands impure.[117]

The allusion to rendering one's hands impure is a metonymic reference to the halakhic status conferred upon an individual after touching a sacred object. By way of contrast, objects that do not render one's hands impure are considered profane, possessing no sure sacred qualities. Underlying this seemingly counterintuitive legal construction is an obscure ritual system not immediately relevant to the current discussion.[118] The force of the *halakhah* is that neither

[115] Although not stated outright, that the texts at issue in the Tosefta are presumed to be written in Hebrew may be inferred from its contrasting ruling that Aramaic translations of the Hebrew Scriptures (*targumim*) are also to be rescued from fire on the Sabbath and their damaged remains concealed (*t.Shabbat* 13.2; cf. *m.Shabbat* 16.1), which provides the same for translations into any language; see comments in S. Friedman (1993a: 318–22). See also *m.Yadayim* 4.5, which rules that only texts written in Assyrian characters, i.e., Aramaic square script, render one's hands impure by contact, suggesting that the *Tannaim* deemed intrinsically sacred only texts written in Hebrew or Aramaic (cf. Fraade 1992: 256). Note that a number of surviving fragments of ancient biblical and para-biblical manuscripts written in Greek feature the Tetragrammaton in transliteration, in Aramaic and archaic Hebrew script, and in other distinctive ways. For comments, see Kraft (2003: 66–67), with examples in nos. 8, 9, 13, 14, 19, 20, and 26.

[116] That the *Tannaim* considered the Tetragrammaton sacred irrespective of who wrote it may be inferred from the Tosefta's subsequent statement in the name of Rabbi Ishmael that God provides for his name to be "written in holiness" (*nikhtav be-kedushah*; *t.Shabbat* 13.5); cf. Rabbi Akiva's assertion in *Sifre* Numbers 16 that books of heretics are, by definition, not written in holiness and must be destroyed entirely. Note also that the *Tannaim* even considered whether the individual letters of God's name were to be considered sacred (they were not; see *t.Shabbat* 13.4; *t.Yadayim* 2.12).

[117] Excerpted from *t.Yadayim* 2.13.

[118] For further Tannaitic examples of this terminology, see *m.Eduyyot* 5.3; *m.Kelim* 15.6; *m.Yadayim* 4.6; *t.Bava Metzi'a* 5.8; *t.Yadayim* 3.19, with discussion of the poorly understood implications of these laws toward ancient Jewish sacred aesthetics in Goodman (1990). For a more probative discussion, see S. Friedman (1993b), who traces it to a long disused Israelite ritual order regulating the transference of purity between animate and inanimate bodies.

the gospels, nor heretical books, nor the apocryphal book of Ben Sira, nor any books written after Ben Sira's time (that is, the early second century BCE) are to be considered inherently sacred. In its present redacted context, the ruling gives no indication that the *Tannaim* considered those books specifically impure or otherwise sacrilegious but merely that they were not comparable to older, more established components of the formative Jewish scriptural canon.[119] As if to demonstrate that principle, the Tosefta proceeds to discuss the status of Song of Songs and Ecclesiastes, books which the rabbis ultimately did accept as sacred (*t.Yadayim* 2.14; cf. *m.Yadayim* 3.5).

The juxtaposition of these two passages erases any doubt as to why the author of the passage preserved in tractate *Shabbat* should have presumed the gospels sacred to begin with. It also illuminates the rationale behind Rabbi Yose's judgment that only select portions of the illicit books should be removed from circulation. The physical articles themselves were not supposed to be unholy. On the contrary, the sacred portions of their texts deserve the same degree of care that the *Tannaim* reserved for perfectly acceptable books no longer fit for use.[120] Once the portions containing the name of God are removed, what remains of such books possesses no inherently sacred qualities. Only those profane, distinctively heretical remains should be destroyed outright.

Obviously, Rabbi Yose's dismissive stance on books sacred to Christians and other non-rabbinic Jews does not make for a pleasant image. Simply to acknowledge the casual tone of his ruling does not relieve its sting. In fact, given the typical lack of specificity exhibited in the Tannaitic polemic against *minut*, the Tosefta's indictment of the Christian gospels seems too pointed simply to write off as a matter of rhetorical convention. Scholars thus have pondered whether the passage's reference to Christian Scriptures reflects concern

---

[119] In declining to characterize this Tannaitic trope as a contribution to a formal process of canonization, I distinguish my position from that of Leiman (1976), who submits that the contents of the Jewish Bible were by the late first century generally understood to include all books currently in that canon except for those interrogated by the *Tannaim* with respect to whether they defile one's hands upon contact. To wit, he argues, the book of Ben Sira, though popular among the rabbis, was deemed too late and too far removed from the prophetic tradition to qualify as biblical; see ibid. (92–102). Although I can offer no better explanation as to why Ben Sira ultimately was neglected where other books of debated sacred quality were not, I would not infer that the Tannaitic tradition at issue speaks to that process of deliberation. It hardly needs to be said that the rabbis would never have considered the gospels or other allegedly heretical books as viable candidates for inclusion among their sacred scriptures. Leiman's attempt, ibid. (118–19), to explain this particular Tannaitic ruling as a precautionary measure against efforts by Jews wishing to expand the biblical canon under Christian influence is implausible, to say the least.

[120] That is, sacred books damaged by fire or by regular wear and tear (*m.Shabbat* 9.6, 16.1; cf. *t.Shabbat* 13.2–3) and nonsacred books damaged by fire (*t.Shabbat* 3.4); see S. Friedman (1993a: 323–24), on the halakhic background of this ancient precedent to the medieval Jewish custom of maintaining formal repositories (*genizot*) for such purposes.

among the *Tannaim* over the popular dissemination of gospel tracts written in Hebrew and Aramaic. The early Church Fathers knew of such translations of the canonical gospels. As I mentioned in Chapter 3, allusions to these texts often refer to Hebrew editions of the Gospel of Matthew.[121] Other notices actually quote from a synthetic text (or texts) called the Gospel of the Hebrews, which reportedly circulated among Ebionites, Nazarenes, and other alleged Christian heretics reputed to exhibit Jewish tendencies.[122] These witnesses leave little doubt about the availability of gospel texts written in the same scribal medium practiced by the rabbis. One might therefore conclude that the early rabbinic sages were wary of their disciples obtaining such texts and mistakenly believing them to be holy on account of their superficial resemblances to what they considered genuinely sacred Jewish books.[123] That would explain why they singled out Christian gospels for specific criticism among the other unnamed heretical texts accompanying their citations in the Tosefta.

While I do not question the possibility that the *Tannaim* knew of such "Jewish" gospel texts, I am uncertain whether they would have seen a need to warn their disciples against mistaking those books for sacred. In fact, neither of the Tosefta's rulings alluding to the gospels says anything about reading them. I believe that there is a simpler explanation for the Tosefta's critique. Just prior to the ruling regarding the ritual statuses of gospels and heretical books, the anonymous voice of the Tosefta rules that the unmarked margins of sacred books render one's hands impure when touched (*t. Yadayim* 2.11; cf. *m. Yadayim* 3.4). The term used for margins is the singular form of the Aramaic *gelayon*, literally "scroll." Per my prior comments, that is the term often submitted as that underlying the plural *gilyonim*, which, according to the Tosefta's subsequent ruling, are not supposed to render one's hands impure (*t. Yadayim* 2.11).

I find it difficult to imagine that the author of the Tosefta would have preserved two contradictory rulings in such close proximity.[124] The only reasonable explanation is that the singular *gelayon* and the plural *gilyonim* were not meant to refer to the same article. It seems, rather, that the juxtaposition of the two

---

[121] Note that the patristic reports are immaterial to the Hebrew translation of Matthew included in the *Even Boḥan*, a polemical work of the fourteenth-century Spanish Jewish philosopher Shem-Tov ben Isaac ibn Shaprut. Although the origins of this unique text are obscure, its emulation of the Latin idiom and its use of common medieval anti-Christian tropes locate its composition well past the age of the *Tannaim*. For like comments, see Horbury (1983).

[122] The relevant testimonies and textual fragments, too numerous to catalogue here, are collected in Klijn (1992). See also Luomanen (2012: 83–144); Mimouni (2012: 175–91, 220–33).

[123] This speculative argument is pursued to disconcerting effect by Jaffé (2005: 300–12). For more reserved comments of this order, compare Carleton Paget (2005: 208–10).

[124] One might posit that the plural *gilyonim* was meant to modify the "books of heretics" alongside which they are cited in *t. Yadayim* 2.13, rendering the phrase as "the margins of the books of heretics." This reading is generally assumed by those who would deny the anti-Christian sentiment of the ruling in *t. Shabbat* 13.5. This reading, however, is supported neither by the syntax of the Tosefta passages nor any of its corresponding Amoraic versions.

distinct terms was meant to be understood as a pun exploiting the phonetic sim-
ilarity of the Aramaic term *gelayon* and the Greek term *euangelion*.[125] The mild
anti-Christian sentiment thereby expressed in the ruling seems meant to lend an
amusing quality to an otherwise formulaic halakhic indictment of heresy. The
resulting grouping of "the gospels and books of heretics" thus was incorporated
into the passage involving the rescuing of burning books as a stock polemical
motif. Once removed, however, from its original legal-exegetical context, the
effect of the pun is lost. As a result, the indictment of the gospels in the Tosefta's
Sabbath legislation seems more vicious than clever. Yet the anti-Christian barb
is only incidental to the more generic heresiological application of its secondary
usage. Hence the absence of the gospels or any clear anti-Christian animus from
the ensuing commentary on the *minim* and their books.[126]

In the final analysis, therefore, it seems as though the Tosefta's indictment
of the gospels is little more than a perfunctory expression of hostility toward
Christian *minim*. Beyond its plausible intimation that those particular heretics
read books written in a conventional Jewish medium, the Tosefta reveals nothing about their social or cultural orientations. One might infer that the presumption of the *Tannaim* to deny the sacred qualities of their gospel treatises
speaks to their knowledge that the subjects of their dissent did consider their
books holy. But that observation would hardly be unique to the Jewish milieu
in which those particular Christians evidently operated.

Nevertheless, that the *Tannaim* thought to implicate the Christian Scriptures
in their polemic against heresy is a remarkable statement of their heresiological
intent. Amidst their efforts to explain how the so-called *minim* stood to challenge their own pedagogical authority, the early rabbis recognized that among
those alleged miscreants were Christians spreading their gospel through the
written medium. Worse yet, their illicit books stood to project the same com-
manding aura as other Jewish books that the sages deemed genuinely sacred.
Consequently, the dissemination of Christian literature represented no less a
danger to the rabbis and their disciples than the clandestine operation of the
Christian healers and teachers in their midst. To their minds, the written word
simply presented the unsuspecting Jew another route toward the same tragic
end that the rabbis believed was due to all heretics and their kind.

THE *BIRKAT HA-MINIM*

Having addressed the few Tannaitic references to heresy explicitly implicating
Christians, I am now ready to discuss the one most often adduced by scholars

---

[125] For a complementary reading of the parallel text in *b.Shabbat* 116a-b, see Zellentin
(2011: 151–52). For general comments on this common rabbinic exegetical technique, see
Hasan-Rokem (2007).
[126] Note that the anti-gospel angle is entirely absent in the ruling's homiletic exposition in *Sifre
Numbers* 16.

as evidence of a coordinated rabbinic response to Christianity. The *birkat ha-minim* receives mention in the Tosefta, albeit with no accompanying explanation of its origin, its function, or the subjects of its censure (*t.Berakhot* 3.25). As I shall explain, I believe that all we can reasonably deduce from this passing notice is that the *Tannaim* were aware of such a blessing. Nevertheless, I would be remiss not to offer a more formidable rebuttal to the still prevalent misconception that the *birkat ha-minim* was designed as a formal means of banishing Christians from Jewish society.[127] In what follows, I shall attempt to chart the genesis of that popular theory as a function of what I shall demonstrate is a procedurally flawed and highly tendentious reading of the evidences at issue. I thereby shall clear the air for my own assessment of the original Tannaitic *birkat ha-minim* as a generic heresiological measure of incidental significance to my investigation.

Let us begin with the attestations to the *birkat ha-minim* in the classical rabbinic library. The lone secure reference to the blessing preserved in the Tannaitic literary record appears in the Tosefta at the end of a long list of directions regarding the proper recitation of the *Amidah*, a liturgical cycle likely of rabbinic design comprising a fixed sequence of benedictions (*t.Berakhot* 3.1–25).[128] It reads as follows:

The eighteen blessings dictated by the sages correspond with the eighteen memorials (that is, allusions to God) in [the Psalm], *Ascribe to the Lord, O heavenly beings* (Ps 29.1). The one regarding heretics is included in the one regarding separatists,[129] the one regarding proselytes is included in the one regarding the elderly, and the one regarding

---

[127] Cf. Langer (2012: 4–6). Langer carefully and considerately documents the development of this perception as a function of Jewish and Christian understandings of the blessing throughout her book, which must now be considered the authoritative critical study on the *birkat ha-minim*. Though an impressive effort, the recent contribution of Teppler (2007) is too laden with false assumptions, methodological missteps, and inadequate documentation to offer much more than an impressionistic defense of the traditional view of the blessing's anti-Christian design.

[128] The Mishnah's treatment of the *Amidah* (*m.Berakhot* 4.1–5.5) varies considerably both in its contents and its order of presentation. For comparative analysis, see Houtman (1996: 1.101–06).

[129] Per my prior comments, I read the text's *perushim* literally as "separatists" rather than the more difficult "Pharisees." That the *Tannaim* saw themselves as inheritors of the Pharisees makes it unlikely that they would have endorsed a prayer aligning that sect with their detested *minim*. For like comments, see, e.g., Lieberman (1955–1988: 1.54); Baumgarten (1983: 422–23); S.J.D. Cohen (1984: 38–39). I am not persuaded by Schremer (2010: 57–68), who argues that the text's *minim* and *perushim* refer to the same group, the former having earned their heretical reputation for their pro-Roman political leanings. In addition to the present passage, Schremer (ibid., 61–62) bases his argument on the aforementioned *t.Bava Metzi'a* 2.33 and an opaque passage in *t.Megillah* 3.37 alleging that *minim* separate themselves from their nation much as the Israelites distanced themselves from Moses during the golden calf incident (*t.Megillah* 3.37). To my mind, the notion that the *minim* were supposed to be equivalent to the *perushim* is at odds with the plain sense of the Tosefta's ruling. One wonders why the *Tannaim* would have developed both a *birkat ha-minim* and a *birkat ha-perushim* if both terms referred to the same type of person.

David is included in the one regarding Jerusalem. Should they recite any of these on its own, they nevertheless fulfill their obligation.[130]

The anonymous author of the Tosefta acknowledges that the tally of supplementary blessings included in the cycle in his own day exceeded the eighteen originally ordained by the *Tannaim*. This presents a problem inasmuch as Psalm 29, the scriptural text that he believes to sanction the pronouncement of God's name in each blessing, provides for only eighteen such utterances. He therefore attempts to rationalize this seeming discrepancy by explaining that three of the blessings current in his day are in fact extensions of three other blessings of earlier provenance. In other words, he counts six blessings as three, thereby bringing his tally of twenty-one pronouncements of God's name down to the original eighteen of the Psalm. Nevertheless, he asserts, should one mistakenly pronounce unique benedictions for any of the six blessings listed earlier, that individual will have fulfilled his ritual obligation.

Read in isolation, the Tosefta passage does not reveal anything of substance about the original *birkat ha-minim* beyond the mere fact of its existence and its thematic connection with another, now lost blessing concerning unspecified separatists. One can therefore safely deduce that the so-called "blessing of the heretics" was meant from its outset to function more like a curse. As to the specific features of the malediction, the Tosefta is silent. Given, therefore, that this is the one and only reference to the blessing preserved in the literature of the *Tannaim*, one simply cannot use this passage to determine its original function or design without the aid of inferential reasoning and undisciplined speculation.[131]

In fact, the greater part of the speculation of this order has pivoted on a related Amoraic account of the origin of the *birkat ha-minim* recorded in the Babylonian Talmud. The story appears amidst a lengthy commentary on the Mishnah's prescriptions for the *Amidah* liturgy. The question is posed as to how the eighteen blessings originally mandated by the *Tannaim* have since increased to nineteen, which is to say the original eighteen plus the *birkat ha-minim*. The answer, attributed to the third-century *Amora* Rabbi Levi, is that the *birkat ha-minim* was added to the *Amidah* at Yavneh, that is, shortly after the institution of the original eighteen benedictions.[132] Following several

---

[130] Excerpted from *t.Berakhot* 3.25. This tradition appears nowhere else in the classical rabbinic literary corpus, although it is paraphrased in *y.Berakhot* 4.3 (8a), on which see below.

[131] In other words, the passage's mere mention of the *birkat ha-minim* affords the reader no evidentiary basis from which to deduce its origin, its wording, or its intended purpose. Compare the adventurous theories of the blessing's prehistory offered by Flusser (2007: 84–113); Instone-Brewer (2003: 33–36); Marcus (2009: 540–48).

[132] Of related interest here is the question of whether the classic form of the *Amidah* cycle was indeed produced by the sages of Yavneh or, alternatively, was merely affirmed by those sages on the basis of an existing liturgical cycle. For the former, traditional position, see Heinemann (1977: 218–29), and for the latter, moderately revisionist position, see Fleischer (1989–1990: 433–35). From a methodological standpoint, I favor Heinemann's empirical

proposed exegetical justifications for the addition, the anonymous voice of the Talmud offers the following anecdote:

Our rabbis taught: Shimon the Linener arranged the eighteen blessings according to their order before Rabban Gamaliel in Yavneh. Rabban Gamaliel asked the sages, "Is there anyone who knows how to compose a blessing of the heretics?" Samuel the Small arose and composed it. The next year he forgot it and he contemplated for two or three hours, but they did not remove him [from the pulpit]. Why did they not remove him? For did not Rabbi Judah say in the name of Rav, "Should one make a mistake [while reciting] any other blessing they do not remove him, but for the blessing of the heretics they do remove him lest we suspect that perhaps he is a heretic." It was different for Samuel the Small because he was the one who composed it.[133]

According to this account, the original eighteen blessings of the *Amidah* were composed at Yavneh by the obscure sage Shimon the Linener under the direction of the illustrious Rabban Gamaliel, a grandson of the Gamaliel mentioned in the New Testament. Sometime later, the author reports, Rabban Gamaliel called for the composition of a "blessing of the heretics" to be appended to the original liturgical cycle. His request is fulfilled by one Samuel the Small. Sometime after that, Samuel happened to be leading an assembly in prayer when he forgot the words of his own composition, stalling for several hours as he tried to remember them. The question is therefore posed as to why Samuel was not simply asked to retire from the pulpit, the procedure typically to be followed in that situation. The answer provided is that Samuel's rabbinic colleagues did not wish to give anyone in attendance the wrong impression that his silence was deliberate. Although one normally would attract suspicion for refusing to recite the *birkat ha-minim*, this was patently not the case with Samuel. Lest, however, his colleagues were to cast doubt over Samuel's commitment to the rabbinic way, they correctly inferred he simply had forgotten the words to his own blessing.

As is often the case with Talmudic narratives, it is difficult to say whether the events reported here were meant to be understood as historical facts or well-meaning fictions. In this case, however, the story's literary form clearly follows its exegetical function as an explanation of how the *birkat ha-minim* came to be affixed in the *Amidah* cycle even as other additional blessings mentioned in the Tosefta passage had fallen from common usage.[134] The explanation

approach. But I demur from his reading of the present Talmudic passage as an accurate historical record (cf. Heinemann, ibid., 13).

[133] Excerpted from *b.Berakhot* 28b–29a; cf. *b.Megillah* 17b for a partial parallel. Note that the censored text appearing in standard printed editions of the Babylonian Talmud reads Sadducees (*tzadoqim*) for *minim*. The original reading upon which I draw here appears in Ms. Paris Heb. 671. Compare Ms. Florence II.1.7, where *minim* is emended to *malshinim* ("slanderers"), which term eventually would supplant the more volatile "heretics" in numerous liturgical traditions. On this development, see Langer (2012: 61–63).

[134] Specifically, the blessings cited in the Tosefta regarding separatists, proselytes, and the elderly were lost to the *Amidah* liturgy by the time of the Talmud's composition. The resulting count of

supplied, namely that the *birkat ha-minim* was sanctioned by the same rabbinic authority figure who commissioned the original eighteen blessings, is
achieved through a deft synthesis of two earlier, originally unrelated Amoraic
narrative traditions ostensibly supporting that conjecture. Both of those narratives are preserved in the Palestinian Talmud in the tractate *Berakhot*. The first
reads as follows:

> Said Rav Huna: If someone tells you that the [blessings of the *Amidah*] are seventeen,
> tell him that the sages in Yavneh already fixed the one regarding heretics. Rabbi Eleazar
> ben Rabbi Yose objected in the presence of Rabbi Yose: But it is written, *the God of
> glory thunders* (Ps 29.3). [Rabbi Yose] replied: But it has been taught that the one
> regarding heretics and the one regarding separatists are included in [the blessing] "… he
> who casts down the proud," the one regarding the elderly and the one regarding pros-
> elytes in [the blessing] "… the refuge for the righteous," and the one regarding David in
> [the blessing] "… he who builds Jerusalem."[135]

Discussing the number of blessings in the *Amidah* cycle, the anonymous
voice of the Talmud alludes to a friendly debate between the third-century
Amoraim Rav Huna, Rabbi Eleazar ben Yose, and his father, Rabbi Yose, the
same debate later to be revisited in the Babylonian Talmud. Rav Huna insists
there are eighteen blessings including the *birkat ha-minim,* which was established, he notably claims, by "the sages in Yavneh." Hence, according to his
count, the *birkat ha-minim* actually was one of the original eighteen blessings. Rabbi Eleazar affirms the count of nineteen. Yet he maintains that the
birkat ha-minim was indeed a later addition, albeit one sanctioned by the same
scriptural passage used by Yavnean sages to authorize the original eighteen.
Applying some exegetical sleight of hand, he adds to the Psalm's tally of eighteen explicit allusions to Yahweh one inexplicit allusion utilizing the generic
Hebrew term for God (*el*). Finally, Rabbi Yose appeals to the Tannaitic tradition preserved in the Tosefta, counting only eighteen blessings in view of the
earlier Tannaitic teaching that the *birkat ha-minim* is to be counted as part of
what he knew as the blessing against sinners, which concludes with the formula "he who casts down the proud."

Read on its own, the Talmud appears to preserve a straightforward debate
between three Amoraic sages over the exegetical justification whereby the
Tannaim incorporated the *birkat ha-minim* into the *Amidah* liturgy. Like its
parallel version in the Tosefta, the Tannaitic tradition cited by Rabbi Yose

---

nineteen blessings, including the *birkat ha-minim* as an independent blessing, informs the order
of the prayer in common use to this day.

[135] Excerpted from *y.Berakhot* 4.3 (8a); cf. *y.Ta'anit* 2.2 (65c) for parallel text. A Genizah fragment
of the *Ta'anit* version features Rabbi Ḥiyya in place of Rav Huna; see Ginzberg (1909: 173),
transcribed from Oxford Ms. Heb. f. 34, fol. 1. Note that Yose actually misquotes the Tannaitic
tradition recorded in *t.Berakhot* 3.25, replacing "separatists" (*perushim*) with "sinners"
(*posh'im*). Whether the alternate wording reflects a deliberately emended Amoraic version of
the now lost blessing or is simply a defective Talmudic tradition is impossible to say.

provides no clear insight into the wording or function of the supplementary blessing. The key innovation here is Rav Huna's unqualified but uncontested assertion that both the *Amidah* and the *birkat ha-minim* were instituted at Yavneh.[136] This, then, is the earliest documented witness to the blessing's Yavnean origin. But we must bear in mind the obscure quality of Rav Huna's testimony as we consider the other Palestinian narrative tradition behind the Babylonian account.[137] That passage reads as follows:

Samuel the Small went before the [Torah] ark and forgot the end of [the blessing] "… he who casts down the proud." He paused and contemplated [the words]. They told him: The sages did not design it like that.[138]

This passage briefly recounts an incident when the sage Samuel the Small, leading an assembly in prayer, forgot the words to the blessing of the *Amidah* concluding with the formula "he who casts down the proud." After spending some time trying to remember the words, Samuel is let off the hook by his fellow worshippers, who playfully tell him that the prayer, which, as the reader presumably knows, alludes to heretics and separatists, was not meant to impugn a man of his estimable character. In other words, they poke fun at Samuel by implying that his hesitation signaled their colleague's fear of revealing himself as a sinner of the order he had just denounced.

It is easy to see how the details of these two brief Palestinian stories were combined to form the more elaborate Babylonian narrative. The impetus of the Babylonian author to locate the composition of the *birkat ha-minim* at Yavneh comes directly from the words assigned to Rav Huna. His implication of Rabban Gamaliel, the legendary dean of the Yavnean sages, represents a plausible inference as to who would have been the rabbinic authority most likely to sanction that pointed malediction. As the leading rabbi of his generation, he further inferred, Gamaliel would most likely have been the one to authorize the *Amidah* itself, which, following the logic of the Tannaitic tradition and the ensuing Amoraic exposition, must have predated the addition of the *birkat ha-minim*. His implication of Samuel the Small as the author of the *birkat ha-minim* is based on the originally unrelated report of that sage's confusion over the wording to the blessing ending with "he who casts down the proud." This, of course, is the same blessing associated in the first story with

---

[136] Note that Rav Huna, though no stranger to the Palestinian *Amoraim*, was the principal of the rabbinic academy of Sura in Babylonia. If the ascription of the Palestinian Talmud is accurate, it might have been he who transmitted the legend of the blessing's Yavnean authorship to the east, thereby providing a traditional basis for the contrived account of its authorship in the Babylonian Talmud. I thank Christine Hayes for this insight.

[137] An anonymous statement in the Byzantine-era midrashic compilation *Numbers Rabbah* 18.21 likewise locates the authorship of the blessing at Yavneh, albeit in terms obviously borrowed from the Palestinian Talmud.

[138] Excerpted from *y.Berakhot* 5.3 (9c). That Samuel should have been relieved from his leadership of the service on account of his hesitation follows the ruling of *m.Berakhot* 5.3.

the *birkat ha-minim*. Read in light of the earlier passage, one might easily con-clude that Samuel had forgotten the words to the *birkat ha-minim*.

But why does the Babylonian author think that Samuel the Small actually wrote the *birkat ha-minim*? That conclusion pivots on his interpretation of the phrase, "The sages did not design it like that" (*lo shi'aru ḥakhamim kakh*). The Babylonian author misreads these words as, "The sages did not design it as you did" (*lo shi'aru ḥakhamim kekha*), exploiting a vocalic ambiguity in the last word of the Aramaic phrase. This alternative reading thus implies that the blessing ending with the formula "he who casts down the proud" once existed in two versions, namely the original version and an emended version composed by Samuel himself. In view, therefore, of the Tannaitic tradition characterizing the *birkat ha-minim* as a supplement to the original blessing, the Babylonian author reasoned that Samuel's contribution was to add a reference to *minim*. Like the original blessing, he further assumed, Samuel's revised edition would have been authorized by Rabban Gamaliel. Hence his conclusion that the blessing that he knew as the *birkat ha-minim* was, in fact, composed by Samuel the Small at Yavneh upon Gamaliel's request not long after the composition of the original *Amidah* liturgy.

What we have, therefore, in the Babylonian Talmud is not a genuine Tannaitic tradition. It is, rather, an invented Tannaitic narrative attempting to reconstruct the origin of the *birkat ha-minim* through synthetic exegesis of several independent Palestinian traditions speaking not to the circumstances of its origin but merely to its place in the *Amidah* liturgy. Although the compos-ite quality of the Babylonian narrative does not preclude its historicity, neither does it instill great confidence in that possibility. Rav Huna's unsubstantiated claim notwithstanding, we are left with no firm basis on which to trace the authorship of the *birkat ha-minim* to any specific place or time, much less to Yavnean sages of the late first century. That observation naturally upends the possibility of citing the Talmudic narrative as a corroborating witness to the blessing's proposed anti-Christian design.[139]

But that record represents just one element of an interpretive plan less eas-ily undone. That the originally generic *birkat ha-minim* evolved over time to

---

[139] My observation here is not new. The historicity of the Talmudic tale has been challenged by several scholars of analytical temperaments complementing my own; see, e.g., Schäfer (1975: 55–56); Stemberger (1977: 15–16; 2012b: 76–83); Kimelman (1981: 226–28); Langer (2012: 18–26). More incisive in his critique is Boyarin, who submits that there was no *birkat ha-minim* prior to its citation by the author of the Tosefta in the third century; see Boyarin (2004: 67–71; 2012b: 92–95, 98–100). While I agree with Boyarin's assessment of the fictive quality of the Babylonian narrative, I am less sure of his characterization of the tale as an attempt on the part of the Babylonian sages to impose a mythic orthodox façade on early his-tory of the rabbinic movement. At the very least, it seems clear that the Palestinian *Amoraim* traced the *birkat ha-minim* to Yavneh before the invention of the Babylonian tale, which sug-gests that there might be more to the possibility of its Yavnean origin than Boyarin cares to acknowledge. For a corresponding critique, see Langer, ibid. (33–35).

target Christians is beyond question. Medieval Jewish and Christian commentators certainly and correctly understood the blessing to have served that purpose in their own times.[140] In fact, fragments of actual medieval prayer books recovered from the Cairo Genizah offer unmistakable proof that multiple versions of the *birkat ha-minim* once included specific reference to Christians. A representative example exhibiting the pertinent depreciatory formula reads as follows:

For the apostates may there be no hope and may the wicked kingdom be uprooted swiftly in our days. And may the Christians and the heretics perish immediately. May they be erased from the book of life and may they not be inscribed with the righteous. Blessed are you, God, who casts down the proud.[141]

The phrase "the Christians and the heretics" refers to *notzerim* and *minim*, indicating a functional correspondence between the two subjects of censure while nevertheless assuming a categorical distinction between them. According to Ruth Langer, examples from the Genizah exhibiting this formula preserve liturgical traditions traceable to Palestine and Babylonia no earlier than the ninth century.[142] Although it is impossible to determine on the basis of these fragments when this emended formula entered the Jewish vernacular in the east, Langer plausibly infers that it would not have been until well after the rise of Islam during the seventh century. One would assume, she argues, that only Jews living under Muslim rule would have felt secure enough in their surroundings actually to commit to writing deprecations of the "wicked kingdom," a traditional rabbinic epithet for Rome now evidently applied to the Byzantine Empire along with its Christian constituents.[143]

And yet, other evidence suggests that the blessing's explicit implication of Christians was older than that. A number of patristic witnesses suggest that Jews were in the habit of cursing Christians in their synagogue liturgies as early as the second century.[144] While these notices do not necessarily imply their authors' knowledge of the *birkat ha-minim*, two exceptional Christian witnesses suggest otherwise. In his account of the alleged Nazarene sect, the late fourth-century Church Father Epiphanius asserts that the Jews pronounce curses against those alleged Christian heretics in their synagogues three times

[140] See Langer (2012: 66–101).
[141] Excerpted from Cairo Genizah fragment T-S K 27.33, as reproduced in Langer (2012: 188). See Langer, ibid. (187–93), for a complete inventory of texts featuring this formula.
[142] Langer (2012: 6, 41–42), and ibid. (42–45), on the origins of the various liturgical innovations exhibited in the Genizah versions of the *Amidah*.
[143] Langer (2012: 40–65), especially ibid. (55–57).
[144] I refer to Justin Martyr and Origen, each of whom accused Jews of cursing Christians in their synagogues without exhibiting specific knowledge of a liturgical apparatus facilitating such behavior. See Justin, *Dial.* 16, 47, 96, 137, with further references to Jewish abuse, ibid. (93, 95, 108, 123, 133); Origen, *Hom. Jer.* 8.12, 12.31, *Hom. Ps.* 2.8, and cf. Origen, *Cels.* 2.29. These passages exemplify a common early Christian polemical trope utilizing "the synagogue" as a metonym for Jews, on which see Lieu (2003); Rutgers (2010).

a day.[145] This is clearly an allusion to the rabbinic *Amidah* cycle, albeit somewhat confused by Epiphanius' mistaken belief that the Hebrew term *notzerim*
referred to a specific order of Christian sectarians rather than to Christians
in general. Epiphanius' younger contemporary Jerome more pointedly alleges
that the "Pharisees" of his own day curse the Nazarenes under the name
minaei, that is, *minim*.[146] Elsewhere, he claims more plausibly that the Jews
curse all Christians under the name Nazarenes.[147] These testimonies, however
obscure their sources, seem to suggest that some Jews living under Roman rule
informally had taken to implicating Christians in the *birkat ha-minim* not long
after the onset of the Empire's Christianization.

Although indications of the blessing's anti-Christian polemical thrust are
absent from the classical rabbinic sources on its evolution, the mere fact of
their existence has fueled much speculation as to whether the *birkat ha-minim*
was designed to target Christians from the outset. In other words, scholars
aiming to characterize the original Tannaitic *birkat ha-minim* as a tool for
combatting Jewish Christians have sought to read its subsequent history of
anti-Christian application back into the rabbinic literary record. This ostensibly would allow us to discern traces of a coordinated Jewish offensive against
Christianity as early as the late first century, the putative date of the blessing's
institution at Yavneh. That very assumption underlies the influential thesis of
J. Louis Martyn that the *birkat ha-minim* lies behind the Gospel of John's seminal polemic against "the synagogue" as a site of hostility toward Christians.[148]
If so, it stands to reason that the *birkat ha-minim*, however subtly at first,
played a decisive role in alienating subsequent generations of Jewish Christians
from a mainstream Jewish collective growing progressively more open to rabbinic influence over time.[149]

While it should be clear by now that the evidence at our disposal does not
support this tenuous line of reasoning, it remains to explain how the questionable premise of tracing the anti-Christian aspect of the *birkat ha-minim*
back to the first century entered the critical conversation to begin with. To the
best of my knowledge, the first to introduce the *birkat ha-minim* into modern scholarship on the Christian schism was Heinrich Graetz, who referred

---

[145] Epiphanius, *Pan.* 29.9.2, with comments in Thornton (1987: 422–23).

[146] Jerome, *Epist.* 112.13, with comments in Thornton (1987: 423–24). I shall say more about
Jerome's testimony in Chapter 5.

[147] Jerome, *Comm. Am.* 1.11–12, *Comm. Isa.* 5.18–19, 49.7, 52.4–6, with comments in Thornton
(1987: 424–25).

[148] Martyn (2003: 46–66), with reference to the *birkat ha-minim*, ibid. (56–65). The relevant passages in the gospel are John 9.22, 12.42, 16.2.

[149] So Martyn (2003: 166). Martyn's reading of the *birkat ha-minim* as a first-century liturgical
reform with a global Jewish reach has been debunked by Johannine scholars attentive to the
poor documentary quality of the rabbinic record. See, e.g., Lieu (2003: 195–97); Reinhartz
(2006: 288–92). Marcus (2009: 523–33), dubiously defends Martyn's position by attempting
to reconstruct blessing's ostensible first-century form with the aid of materials from Qumran.

to the Talmudic account of its origin in the fourth volume of his *Geschichte der Juden*, published in 1853. To Graetz, the invention of the *birkat ha-minim* represented a chance to turn the table on the baldly anti-Jewish perspective on Christian origins developed by F.C. Baur and his followers. Conveniently, the Yavneh legend coincided with the first-century timeline of the decisive rift between Jewish Christians and Pauline Christians proposed by Baur. Reading the *birkat ha-minim* as a counterpoint to Paul's supposed rejection of Judaism, Graetz wrote with admiration of the rabbinic luminaries who assembled at Yavneh to set a new course for their ailing nation by enacting a series of binding religious reforms.[150] To this end, Graetz read the *birkat ha-minim* as a formal ban against Christianity designed to protect the hobbled Jewish nation.[151]

Though following a traditional line of Jewish interpretation, Graetz was the first modern critical commentator to present the *birkat ha-minim* as a targeted effort of the Yavnean sages to combat Christian influence among their fellow Jews. His theory came to wider attention upon its endorsement by the Protestant theologian Emil Schürer in his influential *Geschichte der jüdischen Volkes*, published between 1886 and 1890. Schürer was the first to supplement Graetz's theory with reference to the patristic witnesses, thereby lending credence to his predecessor's unverified inference that the *birkat ha-minim* was not only composed at Yavneh but disseminated by the sages for implementation in synagogues far and wide.[152] These and other ostensible Christian witnesses to the *birkat ha-minim* were subsequently validated by the Jewish scholar Samuel Krauss, whose landmark 1892–1894 study of patristic allusions to Jews and Judaism further served to introduce Graetz's theory into Anglo-American scholarship.[153]

The idea that the *birkat ha-minim* was meant to combat Christianity gained further ground upon the 1898 publication by Solomon Schechter of what would be the first in a series of medieval recensions of the *Amidah* recovered from the Cairo Genizah.[154] In due course, these manuscripts were determined to

[150] Although popularized by Graetz, the idea of an authoritative rabbinic council or synod at Yavneh already appears in Spinoza's annotations to his *Tractatus Theologico-Politicus* (1677). For the relevant text, see Israel (2007: 369–70). On the possible link between Spinoza and Graetz, see Aune (1991).

[151] Graetz (1853–1875, 4.104–106; 1891–1898: 2.379–80). Graetz's unequivocally anti-Christian characterization of the *birkat ha-minim* quickly gained traction to become the de facto word on the blessing's origin in Judaic scholarship for a long time to follow. On this development, see Heinemann (1977: 225–26), and cf. Kuhn (1950: 18–21); Gevaryahu (1958–1959); Petuchowski (1974); Fleischer (1989–1990: 435–37).

[152] Schürer first endorsed Graetz's theory in the first edition of his *Geschichte*, Schürer (1886–1890: 2.386), with reference to the patristic evidence, ibid. (386–87, n. 164).

[153] Krauss (1892: 130–34). Note Krauss' prescient theory that the original wording of the *birkat ha-minim* included explicit reference to *notzerim* in view of the accounts of Epiphanius and Jerome (ibid., 131–32).

[154] The first published Genizah text of the *Amidah* appeared in Schechter (1898), followed by Marmorstein (1924–1925).

preserve Palestinian and Babylonian versions of the *birkat ha-minim* long lost
to history. Along with the previously attested allusion to the Roman Empire,
the novel juxtaposition of the terms *notzerim* and *minim* seemed to confirm
Graetz's intimation that the intended function of the prayer was to purge the
synagogues of the rabbinic sages of all Christians, whether of Jewish or gentile
origin. That this formula preserved the original wording of the prayer as sanctioned by Rabban Gamaliel and subsequently preserved in the rabbinic tradition was casually assumed by scholars following Schechter's lead.[155] But the
absence of corroborating evidence within the rabbinic literary record meant
that Graetz's theory would remain untested and, by definition, unproven.

Yet the mere semblance of proof seen in the Genizah texts proved enough
to vindicate Graetz's theory amidst an emerging scholarly discourse predicated
on reading the Christian schism in view of its Jewish social context. So did
R. Travers Herford adhere to Graetz's reading.[156] And so did James Parkes
in his influential parting of the ways narrative.[157] At the end of the first century, Parkes confidently states, "emissaries of the Jewish Patriarch in Palestine"
were dispatched by the Yavnean sages to Jewish communities throughout the
Mediterranean region bearing instructions for a "daily cursing of Christ in
the synagogues."[158] Directed against Christians still presuming to live as Jews,
the *birkat ha-minim* represented a statement of "official Judaism ... that the
presence of these people could not be tolerated."[159] The authors of the blessing, Parkes dubiously asserts, "knew the teaching of Paul, and condemned it
utterly."[160] They therefore created the *birkat ha-minim* as a means of telling
followers of Jesus that their ideas about the Messiah and the Torah would
have no place in their forthcoming plans for Jewish orthodoxy. The rabbis thus
closed the door on Christianity just as their orthodox Christian peers were
beginning to realize the same need with respect to Judaism.

Needless to say, the evidence surveyed here does not support Parkes' theory. Yet
the proliferation of his account of the Chirstian schism has served to propagate
Graetz's tendentious reading of the *birkat ha-minim* among scholars willing to
overlook its empirical shortcomings.[161] Others skeptical of the Talmudic narrative

---

[155] Notable early contributors to the revised theory of the blessing's anti-Christian design include
Emil Schürer in the revised edition of his *Geschichte* (Schürer 1901–1909: 2.543–44); Kohler
(1924: 390–91, 401–02); Mann (1925: 296, 306); Finkelstein (1925–1926: 19).

[156] Herford (1903: 125–37).

[157] Parkes (1934: 77–81).

[158] Parkes (1934: 79).

[159] Parkes (1934: 78).

[160] Parkes (1934: 77).

[161] See, inter alia, Alon (1980–1984: 1.288–90, 305–07); Ben-Chorin (1980); N. Cohen
(1983–1984); Flusser (1988: 637–43); Pritz (1988: 102–07); Matsunaga (1992); J.T. Sanders
(1993: 58–61); Henshke (1999); Horrell (2000: 151–52); Porter and Pearson (2000: 45–46);
Blanchetière (2001: 277–82); Tomson (2003: 14–18); Dunn (2006: 312); P.S. Alexander
(1992: 6–11; 2007: 671–77); Teppler (2007: 9–29); Klink (2009); Marcus (2009: 548–51);
Mimouni (2012: 133–57).

have nonetheless cited the vague patristic witnesses to the cursing of Christians in synagogues as proof of the blessing's gradual diffusion among the Jewish communities of the Near East prior to the fourth century.[162] Others still have rightly recognized the *birkat ha-minim* as a red herring, that is, a false lead offering no clear means of access to its form or its heresiological function prior to a relatively late stage in its textual development.[163] I place myself in the last camp. As far as I am concerned, it is untenable to imagine that the sages who assembled at Yavneh, still reeling from the loss of the Temple, possessed the foresight and organizational capacity to implement a decisive Jewish ban against Christianity. While I am willing to cede the possibility raised in both the Palestinian and Babylonian Talmuds that the *birkat ha-minim* actually did originate at Yavneh, I must conclude that the surviving evidence of its earliest phases of development is not strong enough to support any firm conclusions regarding its original design.[164]

The Genizah evidence is not especially helpful here. Though it offers fascinating insight into the medieval reception of the blessing, the textual witnesses in question offer no firm basis of evidence on which to argue for or against Schechter's inference regarding the wording of the original Tannaitic composition. The fact, moreover, that those recensions employ both the terms *notzerim* and *minim* suggests that whoever first added the former to the liturgy did not assume a unilateral equation of *minut* with Christianity per Graetz's reading. Efforts to distinguish between the original Yavnean blessing's Jewish Christians (*minim*) and the evolved version's gentile and Jewish Christians (*notzerim* and *minim*) are frustrated by the faulty premise of accounting the Nazarenes of patristic lore as a genuine sectarian faction.[165] We are therefore left with the

---

[162] See, inter alia, Horbury (1982); Overman (1990: 48–56); Joubert (1993); Wilson (1995: 179–83); van der Horst (1998); Carleton Paget (1999: 772–74); Vana (2001); Bobichon (2003); Mayo (2006).

[163] For the characterization of the *birkat ha-minim* as a red herring in New Testament research, see Meeks (1985: 102–03), and cf. Boyarin (2004: 68), in reference to Justin's calumnies against the Jews. More substantial statements to this effect include Kimelman (1981: 228–44); Maier (1982: 130–41); S.T. Katz (1984: 48–53) (cf. S.T. Katz 2006: 271–76); Thornton (1987: 429–31); Boyarin (2012b: 100–03); Langer (2012: 26–33); Stemberger (2012: 84–86).

[164] Cf. S.J.D. Cohen (2014: 248–54), whose negative conclusions regarding the usefulness of the rabbinic testimonies to the blessing as demonstrations of its anti-Christian design are consonant with my own.

[165] The *birkat ha-minim*, in other words, though designed at Yavneh to target Jewish Christians, later evolved to target both Jewish and gentile Christians. For this proposal, see Schiffman (1985: 53–61); van der Horst (1998: 123–24); Jaffé (2005: 410–16); Broadhead (2010: 290–96). This reasoning is hinted at by Kimelman (1981: 232–44), who distinguishes between the *minim* (heretical Jews), the *notzerim* of the medieval *Amidah* liturgy (Jewish Christians), and the Nazarenes of Christian record (heretical gentile Christians). The *notzerim*, he argues, were not the same as the gentile Christian Nazarenes to whom the Babylonian Talmud alludes as *natzerim*. Kimelman achieves this dubious effect by exploiting the orthographical variance between the Genizah texts and the Talmudic text, the former reading *nwṣrym* and the latter *nṣrym* without the vocalic *waw*. In view of the foregoing considerations, I find neither Kimelman's strained argument nor its more straightforward variation especially persuasive.

cautious, if perhaps unsatisfying, conclusion that we simply do not know when, where, or by whose hands the *birkat ha-minim* came to implicate Christians alongside the generic heretical targets of its original formulation.

Let us therefore conclude by considering the function of that elusive original blessing. The intimation in the Babylonian Talmud that the prayer was thought to function as a shibboleth for rousing heretics from the synagogue seems plausible in retrospect. But it would be a mistake to assume that the mere inclusion of such a blessing in the *Amidah* liturgy implies that the alleged heretics targeted in its formula were in the habit of joining the rabbinic sages in prayer. Returning to the Tosefta, it would seem unreasonable to assume that those whom the *Tannaim* chided as separatists regularly associated with them. We must therefore assume no different of the *minim* with whom the sages grouped those anonymous social misfits. In other words, one need not stare one's adversary in the face to know that he or she exists. We must bear in mind, moreover, that the *Amidah* liturgy was composed in the first place as a solemn supplication before God, not an occasion for disruptive sectarian politicking.

In the end, all we can say for certain about the original malediction is that its author and, presumably, its audience deemed its allegedly heretical subjects fit for censure in their own private ritual conventicles. That some of those subjects were Christians we may take for granted. But what effect, if any, the *birkat ha-minim* had upon those Christians we simply cannot tell. Given, however, the silence of both the Jewish and Christian literary records on the matter of its efficacy, it seems reasonable to surmise that the invention of the *birkat ha-minim* accomplished very little by way of actually driving Christians from Palestinian Jewish society. Consequently, I see no need to press the question of its relevance to my investigation any further.

CONSPECTUS: CHRISTIANS IN PALESTINIAN JEWISH SOCIETY

As a function of the broader Tannaitic discourse on heresy, the targeted indictments of Christians preserved in the Tosefta and subsequent rabbinic texts contribute to a distinct impression of just who the early rabbinic sages thought those people were. The Christians with whom they were acquainted were, in the first place, Jews. In other words, they were active players in the lives of the same Galilean Jewish communities frequented by the sages and their disciples. These Jewish Christians apparently revered Jesus as a teacher and a healer, conferring upon his name a measure of authority that the rabbis deemed worthy only of God himself. Some were literate folks who saw themselves peers of the rabbis rather than antagonists to their number. Perhaps most notably, they casually expressed their Christian identities even in their decidedly Jewish cultural environs. As such, they were difficult to distinguish from other Jews on the basis of their outward appearances alone.

In view of these considerations, it seems fair to conclude that Christianity was integral to the early rabbinic construction of heresy, if no more quantifiably than any of the other more obscure sectarian ideologies categorized under the generic rubric of *minut*. But the refusal of the *Tannaim* to engage the Christians in their midst renders their portrait of those individuals incomplete. If not for their passing reference to Jesus and the gospels, their indictments of Christianity could apply to any of the hapless Jews ensnared in their heresiological net. The early rabbis did not acknowledge Christianity's basic theological tenets, such its recognition of Jesus as the Messiah or the Son of God. Although aware that the Roman authorities had outlawed Christianity, they appear neither to have known nor cared why that was the case. Perhaps most significantly, they seem completely unaware of the state of the Christian enterprise beyond their local Jewish communities. By the time the seeds of the rabbinic movement were planted, the Church's gentile demographic likely had already eclipsed its Jewish demographic, conditioning the greater part of the Christian population to abstain from following the laws of the Torah. That there were gentiles elsewhere in the world laying claim to the name of Israel left no clear impression on the *Tannaim*. Consequently, the sense of mutual alienation between Christian and Jew sadly taking hold beyond their field of vision played no discernable role in shaping their common perception of the Christian other as a fellow Jew, a detestable Jew, to be sure, but a Jew nonetheless.

That the earliest rabbinic sages saw the Christian as a type of Jew was not a deliberate subversion of the proto-orthodox Christian view of Judaism. Given how little the *Tannaim* cared to learn about the Christians in their own communities, I find it improbable that they would have acquainted themselves with the heresiological posturing of Christian theologians operating beyond their local frame of reference. The *Tannaim* characterized the Christian as a Jew because the only Christians whom they knew actually were Jews. Yet the impetus of those sages to mark Christians as heretics speaks to a vague sense of apprehension about the strange new kind of Jewish identity that the latter appeared to espouse. What the rabbis, therefore, discerned as the first sign of the Christian schism was not a dramatic rupture but subtle, almost imperceptible cultural evolution specific to their Galilean milieu. Allowing them their own theological conceits, one would not expect them to have responded to the situation any differently than they did.

5

Shifting Demographics and the Making of a Schism

In Chapter 4, I presented the Tannaitic literary record as a time capsule attesting to the activity of Christians within Palestinian Jewish society between the late first and early third centuries. Its image of the Christian as a vaguely subversive Jewish heretic coheres with that presented in Christian texts of its age alluding to followers of Jesus given to Jewish lifestyles yet at odds with other Jews hostile toward their number. The net effect of these complementary portraits is that of a separation between Christian Jew and non-Christian Jew predicated more on suspicion than on matters of theological disagreement. My aim in this, the final chapter of my study, is to consider how that mutual sense of distrust developed after the age of the *Tannaim* to take on the aspect of an irreparable schism by the turn of the fifth century. That process, I shall argue, served to reify a divide between Christian and Jew already centuries in the making.

RABBINIC REINVENTION IN THE SEVERAN AGE

The early decades of the third century were high times for the people of the Near East.[1] In 194 CE, the recently confirmed Roman emperor Septimius Severus had put down a rebellion in Syria spearheaded by the province's governor and royal contender Pescennius Niger.[2] Over the following year, Severus established a large imperial presence in that province, using it as a base of operations for retaliatory expeditions against the vassal states of Rome's eastern frontier whose leaders had supported Niger. The emperor returned to Syria in 197 to embark on a major offensive against the declining Parthian Empire

---

[1] For the following history of the Severan dynasty, compare the more methodical overview of Campbell (2005). On the eastern affairs of the Severan emperors, see Millar (1993: 118–26); Sartre (2005: 135–36).

[2] On Niger's revolt and Severus' response, see Birley (1999: 108–20).

of Persia, ultimately seizing a large swath of territory that was to become the remade Roman province of Mesopotamia. Before leaving the region in early 198, Severus named as his co-emperor his son Marcus Aurelius Severus Antoninus, better known by his nickname Caracalla, born ten years earlier to the elder Severus' Syrian wife Julia Domna. Their joint rule was extended in 209 to Severus' and Julia's second son Publius Septimius Geta. The death of their father early in 211 left charge of the Empire to two men of Syrian descent beholden to a matriarch with powerful connections in the aristocratic courts of the Near East.[3] Once Caracalla executed his brother Geta later in that year, he alone was left to uphold an imperial line that would extend to his Syrian-born maternal cousins Elagabalus (r. 218–222) and Alexander Severus (r. 222–235).

The Severan age brought newfound prosperity to the province of Syria. Throughout Severus' time there, the cities and peoples of his wife's homeland who had proven loyal to the emperor during his showdown with Niger benefited tremendously from their imperial largesse. Aiming to preempt another power grab, Severus doubled Syria's administrative infrastructure by splitting the rebellious province in two.[4] Roads were built and defenses strengthened to ward off further trouble in Rome's eastern hinterlands. Remote towns and villages were elevated to new heights of civic status. Money flowed into the public coffers as streams of military personnel made their ways to the Parthian front. Grand temples to the gods of the Near Eastern cults were erected in tribute to the royal family. Following Caracalla's assumption of the throne, the new emperor made the unprecedented decision to extend the courtesy of citizenship to all of Rome's freeborn subjects. The Antonine Constitution of 212 (or thereabout) placed innumerable masses of people throughout the Roman realm under a common standard of civil law, a move long overdue for an Empire whose leadership and vitality were no longer to be found among its financially ailing patrician class.[5]

In the thick of these developments were the Jews.[6] Their province having been incorporated into Syria in 135, the people of Palestine naturally benefitted

---

[3] On Julia Domna, see Birley (1999: 68–80). The daughter of the high priest of the cult of Baal at Emesa, she was uniquely positioned to ply her family's influences in the eastern Roman vassal states holding the Empire's line against the Parthians.

[4] See Millar (1993: 122–23); Birley (1999: 114). Note that the establishment of new provinces of Syria Coele, whose local administrators had supported Severus, and Syria Phoenice, whose leaders had supported Niger, likely contributed to the ensuing imperial investments in Palestine, whose leaders now found themselves geographically cut off from their fellow Severan loyalists.

[5] I provide the date conventionally proposed for the Antonine Constitution with the caveat that the precise details of its design and implementation are lost to history. On the fragmentary evidence attesting to the edict and the contemporary scholarly debates over their interpretation, see Hekster (2008: 45–55).

[6] For the following, see Millar (1993: 374–77), and cf. Sartre (2005: 155); Lapin (2012: 28–29). Instructive but less reliable are the more elaborate accounts of Smallwood (1981: 487–506), and Oppenheimer (2005), who rely heavily on rabbinic and Greco-Roman texts of questionable documentary quality.

from the policies of the Severan emperors. A number of localities in the region were elevated in civic status during Septimius Severus' residency in the east. The Jews in particular reportedly earned the patronage of the royal family for supporting Severus during his contest with Niger.[7] A new law enacted by Severus and Caracalla granted Jews the right to serve on municipal councils without undertaking the sacrificial liturgies normally required of those offices.[8] Those Jews who wished to avoid such offensive ritual duties out of respect for the Torah were thereby permitted to enter civic politics, collaborating with their gentile neighbors and their less observant Jewish brethren on equal footing.[9] Moreover, Caracalla's citizenship reform affected the Jews as it did all other onetime foreigners who constituted the greater part of the Empire's vast population base. Though of little practical impact on their everyday lives, the Antonine Constitution afforded the Jews the knowledge that they possessed the same legal rights as everyone else, enabling them to see themselves as true members of the Roman society in which they lived.[10]

---

[7] Our information on the Jews' support for Severus is murky, consisting chiefly of a series of confused statements in the Augustan History suggesting that the emperor allowed Caracalla to hold a triumphal procession in Judea (sic) in reference to a disturbance at the Samaritan city of Flavia Neapolis; see *Scriptores Historiae Augustae*, Septimius Severus 14.6, 16.7, 17.1, Pescennius Niger 7.9, 9.5. The nature of the conflagration is clarified by Jerome, who refers to a war during Severus' reign involving Jews and Samaritans (Jerome, *Chron.* s.a. 197 CE: *iudaicum et samariticum bellum motum*). Jerome thus seems to indicate a struggle not between Jews and Samaritans per se but between supporters of the two Roman legions stationed in Palestine at the time of the Syrian war, namely the VI Ferrata, based in Kefar Otnay in northern Palestine, and the X Fretensis, based in Aelia Capitolina in central Palestine. Where the Jews perforce would have aided their local soldiers in their efforts on behalf of Severus, the Samaritans would have aided theirs in their efforts on behalf of Niger. In other words, it was simply the luck of the draw that Jews were the ones who ultimately found themselves on the winning side of the conflict. Of possible relevance here are two hopelessly obscure passages in the Babylonian Talmud suggesting that the late second-century *Tannaim* Rabbi Eleazar ben Shimon and Rabbi Ishmael aided Roman troops on the hunt for local brigands in the Galilee (*b.Bava Metzi'a* 83b–84a); cf. Smallwood (1981: 489); Birley (1999: 135).

[8] The relevant legislation is cited in the Digest of Justinian by Modestinus (*Dig.* 27.1.16.6) and Ulpian (*Dig.* 50.2.3.3). For texts and discussion, see Linder (1987: 103–07, 110–13) (nos. 2 and 4).

[9] Goodman (1983: 128–34), correctly observes that Jews likely served on city councils in Sepphoris and Tiberias prior to the passage of the Severan legislation. But in attempting to downplay the novelty of reform (ibid., 129), he overlooks the possibility that those Jews willingly performed the public liturgies, offering sacrifices to the gods of Rome against the laws of the Torah, as persons of the sort whom the *Tannaim* pegged as apostates. My point here is that the Severan reform opened the curial offices to Jews unwilling to violate their ancestral customs, e.g., adherents to the rabbinic *halakhah*. On the contributions of Jews to the typically Hellenistic political apparatuses of these Galilean cities, see Belayche (2001: 85–95), who regrettably assumes a misleading disjunction between Judaism and Greco-Roman paganism as mutually exclusive religious systems.

[10] Note that the entitlement of citizenship, though prized by many of its new recipients, was essentially meaningless as a mark of legal privilege by the turn of the third century, having been subordinated in practice by the social distinction between the landed upper class or, in Latin, the *honestiores*, and the impoverished underclass, the *humiliores*. See Garnsey (2004: 135–40).

The political developments of the Severan age left only faint impressions on the culture of the rabbinic sages.[11] Long distrustful of Rome, the rabbis took to the new political order with caution. As far as their literature indicates, they generally did not choose to avail themselves of the opportunities for civic engagement newly open to Jews of their devout kind.[12] That would have entailed commitments of time better spent studying the Torah and monetary resources better spent on causes less frivolous than public expenditures. Nor did they celebrate their newly acquired rights of citizenship, rights that one must imagine they accepted with some ambivalence.[13] But the beneficence of the Severan emperors would be the catalyst of two developments of major significance to the rabbinic movement, namely the establishment of the Jewish Patriarchate and the codification of the Mishnah. To be clear, I do not mean to suggest that these developments were expressly sanctioned by the Roman government, at least not at first. But it seems reasonable to surmise that they were facilitated by the favorable, though by no means exceptional, treatment extended to their Jewish subjects by the early Severan emperors.[14] Let us therefore briefly address those developments before considering their impact on the emerging divisions between those within Near Eastern Jewish society inclined to measure their loyalties to God independently of their loyalties to their fellow Jews.

The office of the Jewish Patriarch is a well-attested but poorly understood institution during the period under consideration.[15] Whereas rabbinic literary

---

[11] By "faint" I mean that the rabbis generally did not acknowledge the Severan reforms as such. They were, however, attentive to their effects on administrative and legal procedures impacting their lives and the lives of their fellow Jews. For this observation, see Applebaum (1989); Oppenheimer (2005: 171–76).

[12] Hezser (1997: 273–75), lists an obscure "Rabbi Shimon the Councilman" as an exception (*y. Pesaḥim* 4.1 [30c]; *y. Ta'anit* 4.2 [67d]), along with a certain Rabbi Naḥman, who is said to have been forced to serve on a civic council against his will (*y. Bava Batra* 9.4 [17a]). As Hezser, ibid., demonstrates, the *Amoraim* generally sought to avoid these duties in order to avoid the heavy monetary obligations that came with the curial office.

[13] The *Amoraim* seem to have acknowledged the citizenship reform indirectly in reference to what they perceived as the unfortunate right of their fellow Jews to seek adjudication before Roman tribunals over civil disputes otherwise permissible for arbitration in their own courts. See *y. Megillah* 3.2 (74a), with discussion in Lapin (2012: 117–18).

[14] In this respect, I agree in principle with Applebaum (1989: 148–49), and Millar (1993: 383), each of whom points to the Severan reforms as likely factors in the advancement of the rabbinic movement and its related institutions. Cf. Sartre (2005: 328–30), who invests too much confidence in the documentary quality of the rabbinic record.

[15] The following overview is informed by a number of studies on the institution of the Patriarchate, of which I shall list just a few that I have found especially helpful. For an all-inclusive overview of said evidence, see L.I. Levine (1996). For comments focusing on the rabbinic literary sources, see L.I. Levine (1989: 134–91); Goodblatt (1994: 176–231); Hezser (1997: 405–49); Lapin (2012: 52–55), and, on the non-rabbinic literary sources, Stemberger (2000: 230–68). For a comprehensive treatment accounting for all the available evidences, see M. Jacobs (1995), who offers a minimalist reading of the Patriarchate's influence in view of the poor documentary quality of the rabbinic record. For a more positivistic but no less careful interpretation acknowledging the office's vital but limited operation prior to its recognition by Rome in the fourth century, see Sivertsev (2002).

traditions trace its history to the late Second Temple period, extra-rabbinic evidence for the Patriarch's recognition as an official liaison between the Jewish community and the Roman administration does not appear until the late fourth century.[16] We therefore must rely primarily on the opaque rabbinic record to assess the office's function and responsibilities during the intervening years.

By most critical accounts, the Patriarchate did not begin its evolution into an official arm of the Jewish community until the Severan age. It was likely around the turn of the third century that Rabbi Judah ha-Nasi achieved limited executive recognition for what previously had been an informal private agency serving the needs of Jews wanting for access to their Roman overseers.[17] The Patriarchs who succeeded Judah evidently continued to style themselves as rabbis, although their working relationships with proponents of the rabbinic movement varied.[18] In general, however, the *Amoraim* identified with the Patriarchs, supporting the heirs of their revered Rabbi Judah and receiving their support in return. In their quaint imaginations, the Patriarchs were as close to the seat of the Roman government as Jews of their persuasion possibly could get. That perception is perhaps best exemplified in a novel rabbinic narrative motif casting Judah as a friend and advisor to a Severan emperor called Antoninus.[19] Although the rabbi's personal acquaintanceship with Caracalla is unlikely, the stories in question suggest that subsequent generations of sages recalled Judah as having cultivated good relations with local Roman authority figures who represented the emperor in Palestine.

By the middle of the third century, what once was a private office had begun its evolution into a public office.[20] The tombs of the Patriarchs in the Galilean

[16] That the Patriarchate originated during the Second Temple period in the judicial council known as the Sanhedrin (Greek: *synedrion*) is the contention of Goodblatt (1994: 131–75), stressing Judah ha-Nasi's descent from the house of the Pharisaic leader Gamaliel, whom the rabbis depicted as the head of that assembly. See also S. Stern (2003), who similarly argues that Judah merely initiated the transformation of what was a traditional rabbinic seat of authority into a public office. Compare, however, Goodman (1983: 111–18), M. Jacobs (1995: 99–123), and Sivertsev (2002: 40–52), who see Judah's recollection as a Patriarch in classical rabbinic texts as an anachronistic reflection of the official recognition only to be achieved by his successors.

[17] My characterization of the early Patriarchate as a private institution meaningful to Jews but of no account to the Roman government follows Sivertsev (2002); see especially ibid. (117–31).

[18] On the occurrence of tension between the Patriarchs and the rabbis, see L.I. Levine (1989: 186–91); Hezser (1997): 429–35. S. Schwartz (2001: 110–19), posits that the Patriarchate, though originally a rabbinic institution, grew estranged from the rabbinic movement over time as its officers assumed populist political stances.

[19] The earliest examples of this literary motif appear in the third-century *midrash* Mekhilta of Rabbi Ishmael (*Mekhilta* Beshallaḥ 1, 2, Shirata 2, 6; cf. *Mekhilta of Rabbi Shimon bar Yoḥai* Beshallaḥ 21.6, Shirata 28.2). For a thorough analysis of these and subsequent exemplars, see M. Jacobs (1995: 125–54). Jacobs (ibid., 153–54) fairly judges accounts as fables and their "Antoninus" as a stock character of no specific relation to any of the several Roman emperors who bore that name. Yet it seems reasonable to surmise that the initial choice of that name was meant to evoke positive memories of an actual Severan emperor or emperors whose royal titles included the cognomen Antoninus. For this observation, see A. Appelbaum (2010: 234–35).

[20] For the following, compare Sivertsev (2002: 187–96).

town of Beth She'arim attest to the emergence of a local Jewish aristocracy revolving around the descendants of Rabbi Judah and drawing supporters of diverse cultural persuasions from throughout Palestine and the Near Eastern Diaspora.[21] That impression corroborates a rabbinic record likewise indicating that Judah's successors, though sympathetic to the aims of the *Amoraim*, served constituencies not exclusively beholden to rabbinic standards.

Yet although many Jews saw the Patriarchs as important communal functionaries, their actual responsibilities remained quite limited. Perhaps their most significant efforts in the early decades of their operation were their fundraising initiatives. Diverse literary and epigraphic evidences indicate that the Patriarchs and their agents traversed the Diaspora collecting charitable donations for the upkeep of Jewish communal institutions in Palestine.[22] Their resulting disbursements made the Patriarchs formidable public players in those localities whose residents stood to benefit from their patronage.

More significant to the *Amoraim* than their charity was the authorization of the Patriarchs to appoint local judicial agents. The Antonine Constitution afforded Rome's new citizens the right to seek adjudication over matters once left to private mediation outside the Roman legal system.[23] In order to aid the mass absorption of those former foreigners into that system following the passage of Caracalla's reform, Roman jurists took to recognizing that any local legislative custom (Latin: *consuetudo*) not expressly offensive to Rome's own civil statutes was to be considered legally binding. That allowed government agents not necessarily versed in the fine points of Roman law to serve as arbitrators on behalf of litigants wishing to exercise their newly acquired legal rights as citizens. Evidently, the Patriarchs were granted exclusive license to appoint such agents on behalf of Jews who desired to resolve their civil disputes according to their *consuetudo*, that is, the legislation of the Torah.[24]

---

[21] On the epigraphic evidence from Beth She'arim and its implications for the Patriarchate's orbit of influence, see Rajak (1998); L.I. Levine (2005). Of the twenty-five individuals whose inscriptions denote their foreign origins, twenty-one came from Syria, including nine from Palmyra and others from locales such as Antioch, Beirut, Sidon, and Tyre. Of the remaining four, two came from Arabia and one from Parthia. The final one was a native of Caesarea who had since relocated to Pamphylia in Asia Minor. Among these are a number named as priests, synagogue leaders, and other communal functionaries, suggesting that the Patriarchate's influence reached even further into the lives of their local constituencies. For the relevant inscriptions, see Mazar (1973: 197–207); Schwabe and Lifshitz (1974: 217–22). On the cultural values of these individuals, see Peppard (2007).

[22] For the relevant evidences, see L.I. Levine (1996: 6, 11, 12–16). S. Schwartz (2001: 113–15), plausibly submits the Patriarchs functioned primarily as fundraisers prior to the third century. Sivertsev (2002: 161–83), seems to reach too far in arguing that the funds they collected were used to establish private facilities for the rabbis.

[23] On the ramifications of Caracalla's citizenship reform toward Roman judicial practice, see Ando (2011: 19–22).

[24] On the Patriarchal appointment of judges, rabbinic and otherwise, see Lapin (2012: 83–87), and compare L.I. Levine (1989: 167–70); Hezser (1997: 475–80); S. Schwartz (2001: 115–16). See also Sivertsev (2002: 140–60), whose discussion of those private rabbinic tribunals frequently touches on the Patriarchal regulation thereof.

While the practice of arbitration was not new to the *Amoraim*, they apparently saw in the empowerment of the Patriarchs a chance to implement their *halakhah* on a scale larger than their predecessors had. They therefore lobbied the Patriarchs for judicial appointments in the Galilee and further afield in Palestine, Syria, and Arabia.[25] Styling themselves as experts in the interpretation of the Torah, the early *Amoraim* thus managed to extend their legislative reach beyond their still fairly small discipleship circles and into the general Jewish public.

Of course, their influence in the public arena remained quite limited. As subordinates to the Romans, the rabbis and other Patriarchal judicial appointees could only try civil suits between Jewish litigants who voluntarily submitted to them.[26] They could not enact new legislation nor try criminal cases. Their rulings, moreover, were ever subject to review by higher judicial authorities within their local administrative hierarchies.[27] Yet despite these limitations, the rabbis took full advantage of their newfound opportunities to put the *halakhah* into practice. In that respect, they saw those Patriarchs favorably disposed toward their number not merely as benefactors and political allies but as fellow sages supportive of their movement's long-standing efforts to set their fellow Jews in line with the Torah and, to their minds, closer to God.[28]

Closely linked to this development was the composition of the Mishnah. While the traditional assignment of its authorship to Judah ha-Nasi is wanting for material proof, nor have we firm evidence to indicate that the ascription is inaccurate.[29] That said, the treatise presently known as the Mishnah likely

[25] On the activities of rabbinic judicial appointees in Syria and Arabia, see Roth-Gerson (2001: 49–50); Sartre (2005: 322–24). Also instructive is the discussion of Edrei and Mendels (2007: 102–14), on rabbinic perceptions of cultural commonality between the Jewish populations of Palestine and the Near Eastern Diaspora.

[26] For this crucial observation, see Lapin (2012: 113–19). In this respect, the judicial authority assumed by the *Amoraim* was of no qualitative difference than that assumed by the *Tannaim*. The later rabbis merely believed that they possessed greater authority than their predecessors on account of the Roman government's de facto authorization of the *halakhah* as an acceptable standard of Jewish practice (cf. ibid., 119–23). On the routine practice of nonbinding arbitration of civil disputes in the later Roman Empire, see Harries (1999: 175–84).

[27] See Linder (1987: 114–17) (no. 5), for an imperial edict to this effect apparently addressed to a Jewish arbitrator. The relative impotency of their judicial prerogatives apparently was a sore spot among the Palestinian *Amoraim*, who naturally did not care to acknowledge the powerlessness of the *halakhah* relative to the more persuasive force of Rome's civil codes. For comments to this effect, see S. Schwartz (2010: 118–29).

[28] For a similar assessment of the theological motivations of the rabbis to participate in the Roman judicial system, see Dohrmann (2013: 71–75). On the desire of the early *Amoraim* to introduce the *halakhah* to the "common" Jews whom the *Tannaim* called the *am ha-aretz*, see Miller (2006), especially ibid. (446–66), for programmatic conclusions. Lapin (2012: 33–37), is correct to qualify the apparent advancement of the rabbinic movement during the third and fourth centuries by emphasizing the demographic minority and social inferiority of the rabbis even within Palestinian Jewish society in that era. But as he demonstrates throughout his study, the early *Amoraim* assumed a sense of juridical privilege exceeding that which they actually possessed.

[29] For the following, compare Strack and Stemberger (1996: 124–26).

should not be attributed to Judah himself, as its precise form would remain fluid for some time following Judah's day.[30] Nor should we assume that the initial compilation of the Mishnah registered among the Jewish masses. The Mishnah and, subsequently, the Tosefta and the *midrashei halakhah* were produced by rabbis and for rabbis, their contents at first just as obscure to the general Jewish public as the oral traditions upon which their authors drew.[31]

Nevertheless, it seems clear that something significant happened during Rabbi Judah's age that compelled the sages to deem the "repeated" legislative opinions of their movement's past as an authoritative and closed body of knowledge. This decision likely reflected the need of the first *Amoraim* to compile a record of the *halakhah* for use in settings beyond their study halls. One of those settings was likely the tribunal. While the contents of the Mishnah are not uniformly applicable in the arena of civil procedure, they include plenty of materials useful in that context, including rulings on contracts, estates, torts, and so forth. Those subjects would have fallen under the broad Roman category of *consuetudo*, meaning that rabbinic arbitrators would have been free to apply their received Tannaitic legal opinions to their own judicial deliberations. The need for written records of those rulings would have been obvious. Consequently, it was likely in response to that need that the text of the Mishnah as we know it began to take shape.[32]

If only indirectly, the favorable policies of the Severan emperors thus profoundly influenced the direction of the rabbinic movement. Augmenting the organic growth of their discipleship communities, the willingness of the Roman authorities to accommodate the needs of Torah-observant Jews allowed the rabbis and their followers to come out of their shells. With their tentative entry onto the public stage, the first generations of *Amoraim* began what in time would evolve into a mass movement. Where the *Tannaim* had cultivated their wisdom through intimate pedagogical relationships with their students, their

---

[30] In other words, the Mishnah and its constituent traditions remained open to interpretive debate among the very same rabbinic sages who presumed to transcribe them. On this phenomenon, see E.S. Alexander (2006: 77–83), who sees the exegetical discussions of the *Amoraim* preserved in the two Talmuds as evidence of the Mishnah's continued oral cultural medium of transmission. Compare Jaffee (2001: 132–40), on the formation of the Palestinian Talmud, and further, ibid. (140–51), on Amoraic narrative traditions upholding the enduring value of the spoken word as the preferred medium for the communication of Torah despite the availability of written documents.

[31] To wit, the efforts of the *Amoraim* to implement the *halakhah* beyond their discipleship circles did not lead to the democratization of their legislative means. To the minds of the sages, the study of the Torah was best left to persons of their rare commitment and particular type of expertise. For like comments, see Hirshman (2009: 17–30).

[32] Per Strack and Stemberger (1996: 173–75), a number of scholars have argued that the earliest surviving evidence for the reception of the Mishnah is preserved in the tractate of the Palestinian Talmud known as *Neziqin* ("Damages"), a commentary on the massive collection of Tannaitic civil legislation comprising the Mishnaic tractates of *Bava Qamma*, *Bava Metzi'a*, and *Bava Batra*.

successors disseminated the *halakhah* among Jewish populations and through communicative channels hitherto untapped. To be clear, it would take more than a century for the rabbis even to begin to achieve measurable influence over the Jewish masses. But the developments of the early third century helped the sages of that era grow more expressive and arguably more confident about their potential to reach those masses. The sense of entitlement that they acquired through the passive agency of the Roman government fueled a sense of popular resolve more ambitious than that of their movement's past.

However tentatively at first, the *Amoraim* asserted themselves amidst those of their fellow Jews from whom their predecessors had shied away. Unfortunately, that created problems for those of their new Jewish contacts whom the *Tannaim* had vilified. Rabbinic texts of the third and fourth centuries are replete with accounts of popular disregard and disdain for the sages.[33] One must imagine that among their detractors were Jews of the varieties whom their predecessors knew as apostates, informers, Epicureans, and, of course, heretics. In what follows, I shall show that the public debut of the *Amoraim* was not well received among those of their fellow Jews liable to take exception to their received anti-Christian prejudices. I thereby shall argue that the minor advancements achieved by the rabbis during the early third century helped to realize the alienation of the Jewish Christians from a general Jewish population that now seemed distressingly acquiescent to those prejudices.

ORIGEN

The Church Father Origen was one of the most influential Christian thinkers of his age. Born in Alexandria in the late second century, he visited the city of Caesarea Maritima on Palestine's northern coast around 215 CE, later to take up residence there around 232 until his death around 254. An industrious writer on all things Christian, Origen was also something of an iconoclast. His choice to settle in what was at the time a remote and fairly undeveloped outpost of the Roman Church was driven in part by doctrinal disagreement with his ecclesiastical superiors in Egypt.[34] But Origen made Caesarea his own, establishing a major theological library there and introducing a tradition of exegetical scholarship that would in time elevate Palestine's most urbane city to a position of considerable importance on the emerging map of Christian orthodoxy.[35]

---

[33] So, e.g., L.I. Levine (1989: 117–27); Hezser (1997: 119–23). Compare, however, Miller (2006: 301–87), who shows that the Palestinian *Amoraim* often attempted to accommodate "common" Jews and their existing legal habits in their efforts to adapt the Tannaitic *halakhah* for the sake of its judicial application among the general Jewish populace.

[34] On the fractured state of the Church in Palestine prior to Origen's arrival, see Irshai (2006: 91–129). Irshai (ibid., 130–36) accounts Origen's relocation to Caesarea as a transformative event for the region's Christian population.

[35] On Origen's literary and academic initiatives in Caesarea, see McGuckin (1992a). Compare, however, Lapin (1996) for a more reserved assessment of the scale of Origen's renowned

A rare eyewitness to the life of the Church in third-century Palestine, Origen also attests to local developments beyond the walls of his Christian community. As Palestine's provincial capital, Caesarea was a city teeming with Romans, Greeks, Syrians, and Jews of every cultural persuasion.[36] It was a place where Christians could operate in relative safety simply by blending in with the crowd. Naturally, Origen labored to sustain the strictly Pauline Christian doctrine that he brought with him from Egypt. But that did not keep him from acknowledging those members of his congregation in Caesarea who seemed to entertain theological designs at odds with his own. Nor was Origen oblivious to the affairs of the thriving Jewish population in the cities and towns of the Galilee to the east of Caesarea. Consequently, his occasional comments on those who identified with both the Christian and Jewish camps offer valuable insight into how those individuals related to the proto-orthodox Christian mainstream recently gaining ground in their local environment.

Origen's relationship with the Jewish people defies simple definition. One expects that he frequently encountered Jews during his years in Caesarea. Many have thus read his frequent allusions to Jews and Judaism as signs of his regular interaction with members of the local Jewish community, a community which included rabbis and other learned individuals trading in the same exegetical currents informing his own commentaries on the Hebrew Scriptures.[37] Yet Origen rarely indicates sustained contact with Jews or exposure to Jewish texts or ideas not previously taken up in Christian discourse. Origen, in other words, did not deal with Jews as much as he thought with Jews, exploiting his limited knowledge of Judaism as a means of demonstrating what he saw as its philosophical inferiority to Christianity.[38] That he frequently engaged Jewish theology during his time in Caesarea seems best attributed to his apologetic efforts on behalf of Christian audiences still struggling to achieve legitimacy within a local social order more favorably disposed toward Jews.

Yet Origen was not oblivious to the realities of Jewish life. His first visit to Caesarea coincided with the initial ascent of the Jewish Patriarchate to public prominence. On two occasions in his early writings, he refers to that office in antagonistic terms. In his treatise *On First Principles*, Origen refers

exegetical school in view of corresponding rabbinic evidences on the conditions of Jewish scriptural learning in Caesarea and elsewhere in Palestine.

[36] On cultural diversity of Caesarea's population during the late ancient period, see Holum (1998), and on the city's Jewish population, L.I. Levine (1975: 61–106).

[37] Most notable here is de Lange (1976), whose comparative exegetical approach has informed many subsequent studies emphasizing the frequent affinities between the scriptural readings of Origen and the rabbis. My more guarded approach reflects the critiques of those who have emphasized Origen's unambiguous rejection of what he perceived as the excessively literal exegetical approaches of the Jews in favor of his preferred allegorical approach; see, e.g., Visotzky (1988a: 258–62); McGuckin (1992b).

[38] For like comments, see A.S. Jacobs (2004: 60–67); Drake (2013: 38–58). For a complementary overview of Origen's highly tendentious interfaces with Jewish exegesis, see Martens (2012: 135–48).

to a prophecy of Hosea foretelling an age when Israel would have no king or prince (Hos 3.4). Though claiming that that day had come to pass, he derisively asserts that some Jews of his own day believe that a prince of the royal line of Judah still presides over their people as the Ethnarch or "national leader" and, moreover, that his descendants would remain in power until the arrival of their Messiah.[39]

Elsewhere, in a letter addressed to the Christian chronographer Sextus Julius Africanus, Origen refers to the Ethnarch in even more abusive terms. Referring to the scriptural tale of Susannah, Africanus had questioned how Jews exiled in Babylon would have attained the judicial authority to sentence the book's heroine to death.[40] Origen replies that the Jews regularly pay their subjugators for the right to hold private tribunals. So, he claims, the Jewish Ethnarch of his own day pays the Romans for the right to judge his subjects in accord with the Torah, his judicial delegates even condemning alleged violators to death in violation of Rome's criminal codes. He thereby maintains the credibility of Susannah's reported mistreatment by the Jewish elders.[41]

Scholars have rightly pointed to Origen's testimony as proof that the public emergence of the Jewish Patriarchate was no mere fantasy of the rabbis.[42] His use of the term Ethnarch seems to suggest that the office known to the rabbis as that of the *nasi*, the prince, had not yet attained wide recognition as the Patriarchate.[43] But his accounts leave no doubt as to the subject of his dissent. He describes the unnamed Ethnarch of whom he had heard as a royal

---

[39] Origen, *Princ.* 4.1.3. Whether the unnamed individual in question actually styled himself as an heir to the long vacant throne of Judah is unclear. It is possible that Origen merely plays on the name of Judah ha-Nasi or that of his namesake grandson and Patriarchal successor, whom the *Amoraim* called Judah Nesiah. For further comments, see Goodblatt (1994: 169–70); Sivertsev (2002: 77–78).

[40] Africanus' letter evidently posed a series of questions related to the story of Susannah included in the Greek text of Daniel but lacking in the Hebrew version (LXX Dan 13.1–64). On Origen's response, see Drake (2013: 59–77).

[41] Origen, *Ep. Afr.* 14 (cf. LXX Dan 13.41). Although the contemporary Jewish judges to whom Origen refers certainly did not possess the right to levy capital punishment, he might allude here to the fact that the rabbinic sages of his day entertained lively theoretical discussions of the criminal code of the Pentateuch; see, e.g., the Tannaitic traditions preserved in the Mishnaic and Toseftan tractates *Sanhedrin* and *Makkot* and their corresponding commentaries in the Palestinian Talmud. On this subject, see Berkowitz (2005), with reference to Origen's slanderous charge at ibid. (12–13). See also Origen, *Comm. Rom.* 6.7.11, where he states that the Jews do not possess the right of capital punishment, a prerogative which he correctly assigns exclusively to the Roman tribunal.

[42] See, e.g., L.I. Levine (1996: 21–23); S. Schwartz (2001: 113–14); Lapin (2012: 23–25).

[43] Whether Origen knew the office in question by any formal name is unclear. The Greek term *ethnarchēs* alludes to a ceremonial title assumed by certain Hasmonean and Herodian kings, and his subsequent claim that the Jews pay a half-shekel to Rome alludes to the long abolished punitive tax levied against the Jews after the first revolt. In other words, Origen describes the office in deliberately stereotypical terms. See M. Jacobs (1995: 232–34). Compare Origen, *Sel. Ps.* prol., where he applies the term *patriarchēs* to a Jewish sage of no evident relation to the communal office later associated with that title.

pretender. He acknowledges, however libelously, that the Ethnarch appoints judges to preside over private Jewish courts. Perhaps correctly, he infers that the Ethnarch earned his credentials with the Romans through bribery. Origen's assessment of the Ethnarch's communal role and responsibilities thus corresponds with what the rabbinic sages of his day assigned to the Patriarchs. In that respect, Origen's words are telling of his distrust of those Jews prone to place the rule of the Torah before the rule of Rome. One can only imagine whether he knew those Jews to be equally distrustful of those of their countrymen whom they suspected of placing the rule of Jesus before the rule of the Torah.

Evidently, it was not until Origen's later residency in Caesarea that he learned of the rabbis. In the introduction to his commentary on Song of Songs, he acknowledges, "It is to be observed among the Hebrews ... their custom that all the scriptures are told to the youngsters by teachers and sages along with what they call the *deuterōseis*."[44] Preserved in a fourth-century Latin translation, the text utilizes Origen's original Greek term for the secondary scriptural teachings circulating in his day under the guise of the "repeated" exegetical traditions of the *Tannaim*. He thus appears to refer specifically to the rabbinic sages, using a term specific to their intellectual milieu.[45] While his benign reference here speaks only to a fleeting knowledge of their culture, his testimony is no less valuable a witness to the emerging public presence of the rabbinic movement in Palestine during his lifetime.

To Origen, the Jews operating just outside the doors of his church were a sketchy crowd. Their leaders aligned themselves with a Roman administration still officially intolerant of Christians. Their teachers disseminated scriptural knowledge of dubious authority. As far as Origen was concerned, the Jews of third-century Palestine were synonymous with the insidious Pharisees and scribes whom the evangelists had accused of stealing the key to the kingdom of heaven by demanding that all of Israel follow the laws of the Torah.[46] Reading those laws literally, the Jews stood to undermine the uncompromising strategy of allegorical interpretation that Origen had brought with him from Alexandria. He therefore had every reason to keep his distance from his Jewish neighbors and, moreover, to urge his fellow Christians to do the same.

Yet in assuming an a priori distinction between Christian and Jew, Origen turned a blind eye to the situation of his own church. Throughout his scriptural homilies and commentaries, he indicates that certain members of his congregation observed the Jewish law. They observed the Jewish Sabbath, attending the

---

[44] Excerpted from Origen, *Comm. Cant.* prol. Origen proceeds to invoke a series of theologically challenging scriptural passages allegedly withheld by the Jewish sages to all but mature students. This custom is echoed in a Tannaitic tradition cited in *m.Ḥagigah* 2.1 and *t.Ḥagigah* 2.1.

[45] On the use of the terms *deuterōseis*, *deuterōsis* (*Mishnah*), and *deuterōtai* (*Tannaim*) in patristic texts, see Kamesar (1994: 62–64) and passim; Horbury (2010b: 6–10).

[46] For comments to this effect, see Origen, *Comm. Matt.* 16.15, referring to Matt 23.13 and Luke 11.52.

synagogue on Saturday and the church on Sunday.[47] They observed the Jewish festivals of Passover and Yom Kippur.[48] Like the reviled Pharisees of old, they washed their hands before eating.[49] Although Origen does not say so explicitly, he thereby indicates that some of the Christians whom he knew to frequent his church in Caesarea were Jewish Christians.

To be clear, Origen was well aware of the phenomenon that he appears inadvertently to document. Elsewhere, he reprimands the Ebionites in terms evoking Irenaeus' original tirade against those so-called heretics.[50] He even maliciously infers that those infamous falsifiers of the gospel identified primarily as Jews, only infiltrating the Church in order to corrupt gentile Christians.[51] Yet whether deliberately or not, Origen did not associate those rumored Jewish Christians with the actual specimens who attended his sermons.[52]

What Origen did not grasp, or perhaps did not care to acknowledge, was the unique history of the Christian population whose number he had joined. Origen arrived in Palestine determined to find what he believed Paul had deemed excessively Jewish modes of thought and behavior abhorrent to proper Christian living. Evidently, he paid no mind to the possibility that some of his fellow worshippers had been raised on gospel traditions encouraging them to maintain their ancestral Jewish identities. The most renowned Christian scholar ever to preach in Palestine up to his time thus presented what was to some in his new hometown the alarming news that they could not attain the spiritual perfection assured by Jesus as long as they continued to live as Jews. Neither their ethnic backgrounds nor their honest intentions mattered to Origen. To his mind, keeping the would-be Ebionites in his very own church from falling victim to that heresy was an essential pastoral need.

---

[47] Origen, *Hom. Lev.* 5.8.3, *Hom. Jer.* 12.13.1, *Sel. Exod.* 12.46.

[48] Origen, *Hom. Jer.* 12.13.1 (Passover), *Hom. Lev.* 10.2.1, *Hom. Jer.* 12.13.2 (Yom Kippur).

[49] Origen, *Comm. Matt.* 11.8.

[50] Origen, *Cels.* 5.66, *Comm. Matt.* 11.12, 15.14, 16.12, *Comm. ser. Matt.* 79, *Hom. Gen.* 3.5, *Hom. Luc.* 17, *Princ.* 4.3.8. My reading of Origen's comments on the Ebionites follows Klijn and Reinink (1973: 23–25), who conclude that he drew his account from Irenaeus and his own inference of the sect's reliance on an apocryphal "Gospel of the Hebrews" that he had seen in Alexandria (cf. Origen, *Comm. Jo.* 2.12, *Comm. Matt.* 15.14, *Hom. Jer.* 15.4). On attempts to read his testimony as a witness to a genuine "Ebionite" sect, see Carleton Paget (2010b: 328–29) with notes ad loc., although compare the author's skeptical assessment of this approach at ibid. (342). I am not impressed by the effort of Mimouni (2012: 105–13), to extrapolate early evidence of the Nazarene sect from Origen's patently confused inference of two distinct orders of Ebionites divided over the doctrine of Jesus' virgin birth (Origen, *Cels.* 5.61, 66).

[51] Origen, *Cels.* 2.1, 5.61; cf. Origen, *Comm. Matt.* 11.12, 16.12.

[52] Cf. Martens (2012: 148–56), who reads Origen's representation of "Ebionite" exegesis as an extension of his negative comments on the "Jewish believers in Jesus" (ibid., 150) in his congregation. While I agree that Origen applied the same hostile sentiment to both polemical aims, I find it improbable that he would have let the heretical designs of persons in his own church pass without notice. That he simply did not presume to cast those well-meaning but misinformed individuals in the ghastly mold of the Ebionites seems a more reasonable explanation of his apparent oversight.

222 Shifting Demographics and the Making of a Schism

Origen's arrival in Caesarea thus signaled a turning point for those Christians in the region previously inclined to identify as Jews. While we must not assume that his polarizing stance on Judaism spread through the local churches immediately on his arrival, one surmises that the influx of proto-orthodox Christian intellectuals whom Origen attracted to Palestine helped transform the region's Christian demographic over the subsequent decades.[53] Already put out by increasingly vocal critics among their fellow Jews, the Jewish Christians now found themselves facing pressure from both sides. The ambiguous conceptual territory that their ancestors and spiritual forebears had occupied for two hundred years was beginning to shrink. As a result, the dividing line between Judaism and Christianity long recognized outside of their communities grew difficult to ignore.

THE DIDASCALIA APOSTOLORUM

The Didascalia Apostolorum, or "The Teaching of the Twelve Apostles and the Holy Disciples of the Savior," is the earliest surviving example of an ancient Christian literary tradition known as the Church Order.[54] Loosely based on the Didache, the Didascalia presents a far more developed set of ritual instructions and accompanying exegetical demonstrations principally concerned with regulating liturgical practices and ecclesiastical appointments. Though ascribed to the book's namesake apostles, the book seems to speak to a Christian population more evolved than that described in the Didache, albeit not yet to the point of proto-orthodox doctrinal conformity. Likely composed in Greek, it is preserved intact only in a fourth-century Syriac translation and in a fragmentary Latin translation of uncertain provenance. These diagnostic features suggest that the Didascalia was written for the benefit of a culturally heterogeneous Christian community in western Syria during the mid-to-late third century.[55]

Notable for my purpose is the Didascalia's anti-Jewish polemic, which is concentrated in its closing chapters. The major elements of the polemic include a traditional condemnation of the Jews for their complicity in the persecution of Jesus, a traditional condemnation of Judaism as a Christian heresy, and, finally, a decidedly nontraditional condemnation of a Jewish standard of ritual

---

[53] On local ecclesiastical developments after Origen's time, see Irshai (2006: 136–37). For a more thoroughgoing account of the Palestinian church's subsequent orthodox transformation, see Markschies (2006).
[54] For the following, see Vööbus (1979: 2.*23–*30), and, more succinctly, Stewart-Sykes (2009: 3–5). My characterization of the Didascalia as the earliest example of its genre follows Mueller (2007: 356–58), who argues that the Didache, despite serving as a model for later ecclesial orders, was not designed for that purpose.
[55] On the Didascalia's provenance, see Vööbus (1979: 2.*23), who prefers the earlier end of this range, and compare Stewart-Sykes (2009: 49–55), who prefers the later end, positing its continuous textual development into the fourth century.

practice that the author calls the second legislation. The Syriac term used here is *tenyan namusa*, literally "the repeated law," which appears to represent the Greek *deuterōsis*.[56] The author evinces scanty knowledge of the content of the second legislation, speaking vaguely of Sabbath regulations not expressly decreed in the Pentateuch and, more substantively, of purity regulations of the same secondary order.[57] Naturally, the author's use of the rabbinic terminology suggests his proximity to Jewish persons practicing those traditions. Yet his purpose here is not to indict those Jews per se. What he finds distressing is that members of his own community have been practicing these elements of the second legislation against the advice of the gospel.

Where early commentators read the book's apparent anti-rabbinic sentiment as a symptom of the author's general distaste for Jews, more recent scholarship has judged the author's rhetorical aim as an internecine polemic of reformist design.[58] The author, accordingly, would appear to have imbued his otherwise conventional ecclesial handbook with a screed against the second legislation in order to instruct his readers to desist from acting like Jews. The Didascalia thus appears to document a Christian community in the process of breaking away from the Jewish society with which some of its members were prone to identify. Those Jewish Christians, moreover, appear to have aligned themselves with other Jews deferent to the *Tannaim* and their "repeated" legal traditions. To that end, one scholar has proposed to describe the Didascalia as a "Mishnah for the disciples of Jesus," a functional Christian analogue to the code of Tannaitic law making inroads among Syria's Jewish population thanks to the expanding judiciary efforts of the *Amoraim*.[59]

Yet while the rabbinic *halakhah* apparently had found its way into his frame of reference, it seems unlikely that the author of the Didascalia would have felt

[56] The Syriac *tenyan namusa* appears in the Latin text as *deuterosis legis* and simply as *deuterōsis* in the parallel Greek text of the Apostolic Constitutions, which incorporates elements of the lost original text of the Didascalia (*Const. ap.* 1.6.3, 2.5.4, 6.22.4). The polemic against the second legislation appears chiefly in *Did. apost.* 26 (Vööbus: 1.241–65/2.223–48; Stewart-Sykes: 6.15.1–6.23.8). Note that all subsequent references to the text of the Didascalia will follow Vööbus' edition and translation. I provide corresponding citations of Stewart-Sykes' edition for ease of reference.

[57] On the Sabbath, see *Did. apost.* 21 (Vööbus: 1.216–17/2.200-01; Stewart-Sykes: 5.20.1–5) and 26 (Vööbus: 1.251–53/2.233–36; Stewart-Sykes: 6.18.11–18), and on ritual purity, *Did. apost.* 26 (Vööbus: 1.256–63/2.239–45; Stewart-Sykes: 251–57). The latter topic, which chiefly addresses the practice of menstrual purification rites or, in Jewish terms, the laws of *niddah*, is treated at length by Fonrobert (2000: 166–209).

[58] So, e.g., Strecker (1971: 244–57); Fonrobert (2000: 166–72); Stewart-Sykes (2009: 69–73). For the older position, see Marmorstein (1935: 230–33); Hayman (1985: 425–26); Simon (1986: 88–90). Vööbus (1979: 2.*43–*67), obviates the question by declining to associate the text's calls for liturgical and ritual reform with Jewish practice.

[59] Fonrobert (2001). For a puzzling response, see Ekenberg (2007: 649–53), who acknowledges the likelihood that the book's author and some of his audience were of Jewish descent while denying their participation in the Jewish rites targeted in the book's polemic against the second legislation.

obliged to respond to the still obscure legislative apparatus of the Mishnah. As noted, the Mishnah would not achieve currency outside of rabbinic scribal circles until well after its composition. Moreover, the Didascalia's transitory account of the second legislation exhibits only a vague awareness of the many and intricate Tannaitic legal traditions actually recorded in the Mishnah. In fact, the author construes as "secondary" all Jewish customs exceeding the Ten Commandments.[60] Consequently, his polemic against the Jewish heresy targets ritual practices predating the *halakhah* and sometimes not even clearly distinguishable as Jewish.[61] As for the Didascalia's function, the comparison to the Mishnah falters on our ignorance of how that composition was meant to function beyond the realm of applied Torah study. It therefore seems more reasonable to describe the Christian treatise not principally in reference to its anti-Jewish content but simply as an ecclesial order in the exegetical tradition of the Didache.[62]

But if the Didascalia does not respond directly to the Mishnah, we are left to explain its polemical prodding. What compelled its author to inscribe his pointed attack on the second legislation upon an otherwise formulaic record of ecclesial rules? Here one might consider the setting of the Didascalia's composition. In a recent study, Alistair Stewart-Sykes proposed to distinguish three distinct layers of editorial activity in the text.[63] The basic layer, he argues, comprising the main of the book's instruction, was free or relatively free of anti-Jewish animus. The second layer, which Stewart-Sykes assigns to a "deuterotic" redactor, added to that instruction an exhortation against the second legislation, which he implies had come to the attention of his readership community since the creation of the previous layer.[64] The third, which Stewart-Sykes

---

[60] This broad definition is spelled out in the book's initial citation of the second legislation in *Did. apost.* 2 (Vööbus: 1.18–19/2.15–16; Stewart-Sykes: 1.6.7–12) prior to its elaboration in *Did. apost.* 26 (Vööbus: 1.241–43/2.223–25; Stewart-Sykes: 6.15.1–4).

[61] So, for instance, is the author's polemic against "Jewish" ritual purification diluted by his defense of Christian baptism, on which see Reed (2012: 244–47). Stewart-Sykes (2009: 69–72), likewise points out the allegedly Jewish liturgical preoccupations decried in chapter twenty-one are actually more typical of Christian ascetics and Quartodecimans, Christians who observed the Pascha or the Easter festival in accordance with the Jewish liturgical calendar; see, e.g., *Did. apost.* 21 (Vööbus: 1.212/2.196; Stewart-Sykes: 5.17.2), where the book's gentile addressees are told not to schedule the Pascha to coincide with the Passover rite in the manner of the "believing Hebrews" (*ebraye mhaymne*) in their company.

[62] In other words, the Didascalia exhibits exegetical tendencies paralleling those of the Mishnah yet founded in earlier Christian literary traditions. For like assessments, see Mueller (2007: 349–56); Stewart-Sykes (2009: 32–33).

[63] For the following, see Stewart-Sykes (2009: 22–44). For a complementary, albeit more tentative, reading of the changes in local Christian practice implied in the book's variegated heresiology, see Vööbus (1979: 2.*64–*67).

[64] Stewart-Sykes (2009: 25–29), referring primarily to *Did. apost.* 26. References to the second legislation earlier in the book would therefore be emendations to what were originally generic indictments of the Jewish law; see *Did. apost.* 2 (Vööbus: 1.18–19/2.15–16; Stewart-Sykes: 1.6.7–12), 4 (Vööbus: 1.56/2.47; Stewart-Sykes: 2.5.4), 9 (Vööbus: 1.112/2.107; Stewart-Sykes: 2.34.7), 19 (Vööbus: 1.190/2.172; Stewart-Sykes: 5.5.3), and 24 (Vööbus: 1.231/2.214; Stewart-Sykes: 6.11.2).

assigns to an "apostolic" redactor, embellished the polemic of his predecessor to suggest that both the first and second legislations of the Jews were declared obsolete at the apostolic council in Jerusalem recounted in Acts 15.[65] Thenceforth, he asserts, all Jewish rites were deemed heretical and unfit for Christian practice.

Although Stewart-Sykes' source-critical approach is wanting for material support, I find his impetus to read the Didascalia as the product of a dynamic textual tradition quite reasonable. Although we cannot ascertain who contributed to the present text, simply to acknowledge the likelihood that it had more than a single author invites the reader to discern in the Didascalia's variegated discourses evidence of equally varied rhetorical objectives. For my purpose, it is helpful to posit that the author of the material on the second legislation surreptitiously grafted his polemic onto an existing textual tradition in response to recent developments in the life of his community. Likewise, it is helpful to suppose that another author representing a distinctly proto-orthodox perspective presumed to rewrite the relatively mild polemic of his predecessor to denigrate Judaism on the whole. While we must not assume the empirical legitimacy of these inferences, we may nevertheless consider their potential advantages toward explaining the Didascalia's outwardly uneven commentary on the Jews and their customs.

The apostolic pretense of the Didascalia provides its unequivocally Jewish narrative voice.[66] Given that the apostles of Jesus were Jews, it naturally follows that a historically conscientious author or authors writing in their names would presume to speak in a voice inured to Jewish cultural conventions. This technique is manifest in a few instances where the narrator refers to the apostolic collective as having come from "the people," that is, the Jews, as opposed to "the nations," that is, the gentiles.[67] Of course, it is impossible to say whether the book's actual author or authors counted themselves as Jews. But that possibility is at least raised by the narrator's clear distinction between those of his addressees who came to the Church as Jews and those who came as gentiles.[68]

---

[65] Stewart-Sykes (2009: 22–25), referring to *Did. apost.* 24 (Vööbus: 1.231–38/2.214–19; Stewart-Sykes: 6.11.1–6.13.1), and further (ibid., 33–44) on the same proposed redactor's anti-Jewish embellishment of the anti-Quartodeciman polemic in *Did. apost.* 21 (Vööbus: 1.203–18/2.184–202; Stewart-Sykes: 5.10.1–5.20.12).

[66] On the literary conceit of the Didascalia and its relation to the book's Jewish heresiological objective, see Fonrobert (2001: 489–91).

[67] For the juxtaposition of "the people" and "the nations," see, e.g., *Did. apost.* 15 (Vööbus: 1.159/2.145; Stewart-Sykes: 3.6.2), 19 (Vööbus: 1.190/2.172; Stewart-Sykes: 5.5.3). See also *Did. apost.* 13 (Vööbus: 1.150/2.136; Stewart-Sykes: 2.60.3) on the relative value of the term "Jew" as applied to Jewish persons of questionable integrity.

[68] For addresses directed toward gentile readers, see *Did. apost.* 21 (Vööbus: 1.208–10/2.192–94; Stewart-Sykes: 5.14.22–5.15.4); 24 (Vööbus: 1.237–38/2.218–19; Stewart-Sykes: 6.11.15). For addresses directed toward Jewish readers, see *Did. apost.* 26 (Vööbus: 1.248/2.230, 1.251/2.233; Stewart-Sykes: 6.17.6, 6.18.11). For a unified address of both ethnic constituencies, see *Did. apost.* 26 (Vööbus: 1.249/2.231; Stewart-Sykes: 6.18.4). On the mixed ethnic makeup of the book's readership community, see Fonrobert (2001: 491–502).

The narrator applies these ethnic distinctions without further justification. It therefore stands to reason that the book's intended audience likewise presumed to distinguish between the Jews and the gentiles in their number. This would explain the narrator's observation of what he sees as troublesome Jewish ritual observance among certain members of his own community. If this reading is correct, the function of the Didascalia's overarching anti-Jewish polemic would merit a threefold characterization. Firstly, it denigrates Judaism in general. Secondly, it seeks to deter Jewish Christians from sustaining their Jewish ritual habits. Finally, it seeks to deter their gentile associates from imitating Jewish Christians. Each of these rhetorical objectives thus informs the anti-rabbinic animus evidently expressed in the book's polemic against the second legislation.

The first major element of the book's polemic against the Jews is fairly pedestrian. In chapter twenty-one, the narrator retells the passion narrative in a manner highlighting the complicity of the Jews. The Jewish people, he asserts, destroyed themselves by refusing to heed the call of Jesus and conspiring to murder him.[69] While certainly no trivial charge, it reflects a common Christian polemic. The narrator goes on in chapter twenty-three to describe the Jews as heretics abandoned by God, stripped of their Temple, and prodded by Satan to torment the apostles.[70] Again, this is boilerplate stuff.

Not until the twenty-fourth chapter does the narrator's traditional polemical line lead to the Didascalia's readership community. That chapter presents an elaborate scriptural pastiche of the apostolic council held in Jerusalem following the row between Peter and Paul in Antioch.[71] Drawing primarily on Acts 15, the narrator uniquely infers that the root of the controversy was not whether gentiles had to be circumcised in accord with the legislation of the Torah but, rather, whether Jews had to abide by the second legislation. The resolution of James thus served to release Jewish followers of Jesus from the heavy yoke of the second legislation. Consequently, the narrator implies, the Jewish heresy originated not merely in the Jewish people's rejection of Jesus but also in their rejection of the apostolic decree enjoining them to practice their Jewish identities more liberally.[72]

This imaginative interpretation of the Christian scriptural record sees the Didascalia draw the first-century controversy over Paul's gospel into the narrator's contemporary frame of reference. What in fact had been a debate over the relevance of the laws of the Torah for gentile followers of Jesus is reconceived

---

[69] See especially *Did. apost.* 21 (Vööbus: 1.210–11/2.194–95; Stewart-Sykes: 5.15.5–5.16.7).
[70] See especially *Did. apost.* 23 (Vööbus: 1.226/2.208–09, 1.227–28/2.210–11, 1.229/2.212; Stewart-Sykes: 6.5.4, 6.6.7, 6.8.1).
[71] For the following, see *Did. apost.* 24 (Vööbus: 1.231–38/2.214–19; Stewart-Sykes: 6.11.1–6.13.1).
[72] Compare *Did. apost.* 23 (Vööbus: 1.230–31/2.213; Stewart-Sykes: 6.10.1–5), where the arch-heretics Simon Magus and Cleobius are said to have regarded all of the Torah and the Prophets as one universal law, thereby justifying the conflation of the law and the second legislation in *Did. apost.* 24 and 26.

here as a referendum on the rabbinic *halakhah*. This doctored memory leads the narrator to the book's ultimate exposition of the second legislation, a subject previously mentioned only in passing. The book's account of the second legislation in chapter twenty-six begins with a defense of the Decalogue, here construed as the first and only true law.[73] It was that law, the narrator claims, that Jesus claimed to uphold in the Sermon on the Mount when he asserted that he would not erase one *iota* from the Torah (Matt 5.17–18). *Iota* is the tenth letter of the Greek alphabet and the first letter in the name of Jesus (Greek: *iēsous*). Hence, the narrator argues, the Ten Commandments signify the gospel and remain compulsory for Christians.[74] But the Christian law, he continues, is light and easy, free of taxing dietary restrictions and abominable sacrificial obligations. Nor does it mandate the painful procedure of circumcision. It is therefore a law accessible to all who choose to avail themselves of the saving grace of Jesus.

But not so the second legislation.[75] That arduous code, the narrator avers, was laid upon the Jews as a punishment for the sin of the golden calf (Exod 32).[76] Seeing that his people were not ready to receive his liberal statutes, God imposed heavier laws, laws that would keep the Jewish nation in a state of constant sinfulness until the arrival of the Messiah. And yet, when their Messiah arrived in the person of Jesus, they failed to grasp his salvific fulfillment of the law. Instead, they stubbornly chose to remain under the penalty of the second legislation despite its abrogation in the vain hope of achieving perfection through its obsolete ritual ordinances. His Christian readers, the narrator therefore implies, should not follow the Jews in their error. Both Jew and gentile, he asserts, must look for moral guidance in the first law, the Decalogue, but shun the second legislation that keeps the nonbelieving Jew blinded and bound. There must be no compromise between those who venerate Jesus and those who cursed themselves by rejecting his gospel.[77]

The Didascalia's account of the second legislation subtly evokes the words of Paul in his letter to the Galatians, who likewise speaks of the Torah's legislation

[73] For the following, see *Did. apost.* 26 (Vööbus: 1.241–43/2.223–25; Stewart-Sykes: 6.15.1–4), which is followed by a middling attempt to subordinate those rites practiced before the revelation at Mount Sinai such as circumcision and animal sacrifice (Vööbus: 1.243–44/2.225–26; Stewart-Sykes: 6.16.1–4).

[74] For the Decalogue as binding legislation for Christians, compare Ps.-Clem. *Recog.* 1.35.2. Note as well *Leviticus Rabbah* 19.2, for a possibly related rabbinic exegetical figure on the legislative symbolism of the *iota* (Hebrew: *yod*), with discussion in Visotzky (2003: 165).

[75] For the following, see *Did. apost.* 26 (Vööbus: 1.244–51/2.226–33; Stewart-Sykes: 6.16.5–10).

[76] For the Torah as a punishment, compare Ps.-Clem. *Recog.* 1.36.1, referring more broadly to Israel's corruption in Egypt. Compare *Leviticus Rabbah* 27.8, for a possibly related defensive stratagem blaming the golden calf incident on Egyptian refugees traveling with the Israelites. Per Visotzky (2003: 164–65), this might be an attempt to combat anti-Jewish accusations of the order expressed in the Didascalia.

[77] See especially *Did. apost.* 26 (Vööbus: 1.254/2.237, 1.264/2.246; Stewart-Sykes: 6.19.3–5, 6.23.4).

as a temporary punitive measure since abrogated by Jesus (cf. Gal 3.19–29). But its defense of the Decalogue adds a new fold to that traditional argument. For in distinguishing some of the Jewish law as worthy of Christian practice, the text adds nuance to Paul's categorical rejection of that law. However inadvertently, the narrator gives voice to a living Jewish tradition within his church, a tradition of dedication to the Torah comparable, if not commensurate, with that known among other Jews of his day as the *halakhah*.[78] He therefore argues that the second legislation, supposedly embodied in the *halakhah*, is not suited for Christian practice on the very same epistemological grounds on which the apostles were thought to have nullified the legislation of the Torah. Not content, however, to rely on Paul's logic, the narrator turns to an unlikely supporting witness, namely the Roman government. The passage in question bears quoting in full. Referring to the abrogation of the second legislation, the narrator asserts:

And [God] showed this not merely by himself, but he also worked through the Romans. He destroyed the Temple, he caused the altar to be still, he abolished the sacrifices, and he abrogated all the commands and bonds of the second legislation. For the Romans too observe the law, but from the second legislation they abstain. That is why their power is strong. You, therefore, who today prefer to be under the second legislation while the Romans are ruling, you cannot actually accomplish anything inscribed in the second legislation. For neither can you stone sinners, nor execute those who venerate idols, nor keep watch over the sacrifices, nor perform the libations or the sprinklings for the heifer. In fact, you can neither fulfill nor maintain anything inscribed in the second legislation.[79]

Here, as in his earlier commentary on the Jews, the narrator betrays the Didascalia's literary conceit by referring to the events of 70 CE in the past tense. The idea that God punished the Jews by allowing the Romans to destroy the Jerusalem Temple speaks to a theological argument already attested in the New Testament. But the intimation that the Romans observe the law of God, that is, the Decalogue, is unprecedented. The strength of Rome, the narrator asserts, rests on God's favor toward a nation manifestly more powerful than the Jews, a nation whose judicial purview exceeds that of the Torah, all the more so that of the second legislation. For the Jews, he observes, are able neither to perform their cultic rites nor to try criminal cases in accord with their delusional second legislation.

---

[78] Note the corresponding Amoraic construction of *minut* as a mode of Jewish ritual observance attentive to the Ten Commandments to the exclusion of all other Pentateuchal legislation in *y.Berakhot* 5.3 (9c) (cf. *b.Berakhot* 12a). This definition of heresy is specific to the Talmud's exegetical application and must not be taken as a certain allusion to Christianity, much less to the legal rationale of the Didascalia. It simply indicates that the *Amoraim* deemed selective observance of the Torah's laws unacceptable for Jews. See Hayes (2011: 142).

[79] Excerpted from *Did. apost.* 26 (Vööbus: 1.253–54/2.236; Stewart-Sykes: 6.19.1–2).

But can it really be that the Romans abide by God's original laws? The text goes on to explain that they do:

It is inscribed in the law, *You shall not murder* (Exod 29.13). And anyone who does commit murder is condemned in accord with the law of the Romans and, therefore, comes under the law.[80]

In other words, the narrator contends, the Romans follow the law of God unwittingly. Tactfully choosing one of the Ten Commandments that obviously corresponded with a basic Roman civil statute, he claims that the Romans observe those ordinances as a matter of course. Hence, he concludes, all people who happen to live under Roman rule already observe the law of God whether they know it or not. This argument appears to echo an incidental statement of Origen, who similarly observes that the Romans had arrogated the authority of the Jewish law with respect to the criminal codes of the Pentateuch.[81] The Didascalia reframes that basically sound observation in reference to the second legislation, which, the narrator claims, is impossible for Jews to observe to perfection while living among the gentiles.[82]

Further defying his apostolic pretense, the narrator indicates that certain Jews of his day presumed to practice the second legislation in accord with the laws of Rome. That, he asserts, simply cannot be done. For the authority of the Roman law prohibits the Jews from meting out the criminal judgments prescribed in the second legislation for those who would violate the Ten Commandments. God, in other words, dispatched the Romans not only to punish the Jews but also to ensure the regulation of the Jewish law among all persons living under their rule. Those Jews who assert the primacy of the second legislation thus deny the preeminence of the Roman law, a position both empirically false and politically inopportune. Lest his readers incur the wrath of a Roman government still officially intolerant of Christians, the narrator suggests that they would do best to fall in line with their imperial overseers.

Even if the rabbinic sages preferred to imagine otherwise, the Tannaitic legislative traditions that they endeavored to implement in their private tribunals were of no specific interest to the Roman supervisors who passively allowed those judiciaries to be held. It therefore seems as though the narrator of the Didascalia introduces the looming specter of Rome in order to frighten his readers into submission. Whether this technique was effective is doubtful. Only the most naïve ancient reader possibly could have believed that the heathenish Romans observed the Ten Commandments, much less obliviously. Yet the author of this astonishing endorsement clearly saw in Rome a persuasive force

---

[80] Excerpted from *Did. apost.* 26 (ed. Vööbus: 1.254/2.237; Stewart-Sykes: 6.19.5).
[81] See Origen, *Comm. Rom.* 6.7.11. A similar argument not specifically alluding to the supersessory force of the Roman law appears in Eusebius, *Dem. ev.* 1.3.
[82] See *Did. apost.* 26 (Vööbus: 1.254/2.236–37; Stewart-Sykes: 6.19.3), and compare Paul's similarly disparaging comment on the impossibility of strict adherence to the Jewish law in Gal 3.10.

potentially more effective than his own. That he thought to discourage his readers from adhering to the second legislation suggests that some members of his local church were doing precisely that.

In view of the book's earlier comments on the Jewish heresy, it is attractive to follow Stewart-Sykes in tracing a linear evolution of thought within the Didascalia's pages. One might thereby discern the gradual transformation of its readership community from an original state of casual obedience to the Jewish law to one of tension with the Jewish law and, finally, to one of outright rejection of the Jewish law. While this reconstruction is by no means secure, it seems sufficiently clear that the book assumes alternating vantage points on the sacred quality of the Jewish law in its acknowledgement of its two qualitatively disparate stages of revelation. Again, if we are to read the Didascalia's "second legislation" as a byword for the rabbinic *halakhah*, it would seem that the author responsible for the polemic knew fairly little about the substance of his subject of dissent. But he clearly knew enough to exploit the *halakhah* for its reputedly burdensome ritual obligations and its manifest inferiority to the law of Rome.

Yet despite its endorsement of the Decalogue, one must not mistake the Didascalia's nod to the Jewish law for an endorsement of Jewish practice. The Ten Commandments are presented here not as elements of the Jewish law but as the entirety of the Christian law prescribed by Jesus and confirmed by his apostles. In this respect, the book's heresiology is no less imperious than those of the many early Christian theologians who cast the Jewish people as illegitimate claimants to the name and legacy of Israel. The Didascalia speaks to the compromised situation of a localized readership community hemmed in by the proto-orthodox Christianity advocated by the likes of Origen and the proto-orthodox Judaism promoted by their rabbinic contemporaries. Its bias notwithstanding, the book thus offers a rare glimpse into the internal politics of a Jewish Christian population gently but inexorably being squeezed out of existence.

THE PALESTINIAN TALMUD

The first of the two great Amoraic commentaries on the Mishnah, the Palestinian Talmud documents the evolution of the rabbinic movement in its age of emergence from relative obscurity among the Jewish population of Palestine and its environs.[83] Traditionally known by the geographical misnomer *Talmud Yerushalmi* or the Jerusalem Talmud, the sizable compendium likely was assembled during the last decades of the fourth century at one or more of the

---

[83] On the origins of the Palestinian Talmud, see the appropriately cautious comments of Jaffee (2001: 126–28); Lapin (2012: 60–62). A fuller account detailing traditional and modern theories of the text's composition and character appears in Strack and Stemberger (1996: 164–80).

rabbinic academies established in the Galilee region with the aid of the Jewish Patriarchs.[84] The precise circumstances of the Palestinian Talmud's composition are woefully lacking for documentation, an effect of its general neglect during the Middle Ages in favor of the later and more expansive *Talmud Bavli*, or the Babylonian Talmud. With this development, the earlier Talmud largely receded from the agendas of those scholars of the *halakhah* most likely to entertain antiquarian interest in the history of its text.

That the Palestinian Talmud was meant to function as a companion to the Mishnah is reasonably clear in view of its structural correspondence with the earlier document. The greater part of its content, moreover, resumes the Mishnah's legislative agenda by presenting further Tannaitic legal traditions and more recent Amoraic traditions in dialogue with the Mishnaic text. Often, the *Amoraim* are shown debating how best to interpret the legislative precedents of the *Tannaim* in contemporaneous judicial settings, thus lending the Talmud's exposition of the *halakhah* the quality of case law, if not its formal resemblance to that still inchoate technical medium.[85] But the Talmud also preserves extensive narrative materials or *aggadah* used to illustrate principles of law and ethics in a parabolic fashion seldom seen in the Mishnah. The net effect lends the Talmud the quality of a vast repository of rabbinic knowledge not clearly designed for any specific utility beyond aiding study of the Mishnah.

Although its interpretation incurs the same methodological liabilities as other texts of the classical rabbinic library, the Palestinian Talmud stands as the primary source of historical data on Jewish life and thought in Palestine during the third and fourth centuries. In this respect, it is a potentially valuable witness to the social location of the local Christian population documented in earlier rabbinic texts as *minim*. Yet the Talmud offers surprisingly little concrete information on the continuing operation of Christians in and near Palestinian Jewish society during an age when one would expect the rabbis to have intensified their opposition toward such individuals.[86] Instead, it presents a portrait of a rabbinic collective gradually becoming aware that the rhetorical advantage over the Christian other assumed by their predecessors was no more. What the *Tannaim* once derided as an indistinct symptom of heresy thus evolved before the eyes of the *Amoraim* into a cultural force less easily written off.

[84] On the development of the Palestinian rabbinic academies in the late fourth century and the reliance of their leaders on the Patriarchs, see Stemberger (2000: 269–75), with comments on the provenance of the Palestinian Talmud, ibid. (289–97). See also S. Schwartz (2010: 110–12), for a more reserved assessment along similar lines.

[85] On this aspect of the Talmud's legislative program, see Lapin (2012: 109–13). Also instructive here is Hezser (1998), who is perhaps too confident in inferring the Talmud's emulation of contemporary Roman legislative compilations of the variety later to be utilized for the Code of Justinian.

[86] For this observation, see Goodman (2000b), responding to Neusner (1987: 65–80), who discerns traces of an anti-Christian Messianic ideology in the Talmud's eschatological outlook.

Minim do not appear frequently amidst the Talmud's legislative materials. That does not mean that such individuals were not present in the social world behind its composition. Narrative portions of the Talmud suggest that the sages of the Amoraic era continued to encounter scripturally literate Jews inclined to challenge their authority.[87] But the Talmud's halakhic debates focus on matters of practical ritual and judiciary concern to the rabbis, their disciples, and their families. Presumably, Jews whom the *Amoraim* knew as heretics would not regularly have sought their expertise. As a result, the sectarian anxieties of the *Tannaim* were not apropos of the Talmud's modus operandi.[88] To the extent that the *Amoraim* did account for *minim* in their expositions of the *halakhah*, it was largely in reference to received traditions. Thus, for example, the Talmud cites the aforementioned Tannaitic tradition forbidding the rescue of gospels and other heretical books found burning on the Sabbath.[89] But it records no Amoraic commentary on that ruling. This is likely due to its outlandish practical implications. That any reasonable person should have consulted a rabbi over whether to salvage a book in the process of being consumed by flames is simply implausible. The *Amoraim* thus evidently did not deem that unrealistic Tannaitic statute worthy of exegetical elaboration.

Scholars searching for traces of sound Jewish knowledge of Christianity in the Palestinian Talmud have looked beyond its allusions to *minut*. Thus, for instance, an abstract polemical statement attributed to the third-century sage Rabbi Abbahu has been taken as an indictment of Christian Trinitarian theology. Commenting on the prophetic pretensions of Balaam, Abbahu declares:

Should someone tell you, "I am a god," he is a liar. "I am the Son of Man," he will regret it in the end. "For I shall go up to heaven," he has said it, but he shall not do it (cf. Num 23.19).[90]

The allusion to a divine aspirant assuming the persona of Daniel's eschatological "Son of Man" certainly resonates with Christian beliefs about Jesus

---

[87] See, e.g., *y.Berakhot* 1.8 (3c), 5.4 (9c), 9.1 (12d–13b). Visotzky has argued that the extended rebuttal of *minut* at *y.Berakhot* 9.1 (12d–13b) addresses aspects of Christian theology amidst other subjects; see Visotzky (1988b; 2008). While I find this reading plausible, the proposed Trinitarian connotations would seem too vague to allow an accurate diagnosis of the alleged heresy at issue. For a complementary assessment, see Schäfer (2012: 42–54).

[88] So Lapin (2012: 112). Compare, however, John Chrysostom, *Adv. Jud.* 1.3.4–5, on the appearance of a Christian before a Jewish tribunal in Antioch on the pretext of making an oath, with discussion in Wilken (1983: 79–80). On the operation of a Jewish, if not necessarily rabbinic, court in Antioch, see also *y.Sanhedrin* 3.2 (21a).

[89] I refer to the tradition cited in *t.Shabbat* 13.5, which appears in alternate form in *y.Shabbat* 16.1 (15c).

[90] Excerpted from *y.Ta'anit* 2.1/24 (65b). On this passage as a covert allusion to Jesus, see, e.g., Graetz (1853–1875: 4.309; 1891–1898: 2.539); Herford (1903: 62–63); Lauterbach (1951: 545–51); L.I. Levine (1975: 83–84); Segal (1977: 213–14, n. 87); Irshai (1982); Schäfer (2007: 107–09).

(cf. Dan 7.13–14). But one has to wonder what sort of Christian practitioner would dare to claim Jesus' singular Messianic credentials for himself. Abbahu's words, moreover, contain no hint of the sophisticated Christological doctrines expounded by Origen and his intellectual heirs. It therefore seems more likely that the rabbi's indictment is directed toward mystical poseurs versed in the language of the ancient Jewish apocalyptic treatises so abhorred by the rabbis.[91] Those individuals might well have included Christians. But the wording of the indictment is altogether too vague to justify its characterization as an argument against Christianity per se.

Another Talmudic passage cited to similar effect is an eschatological prophecy foretelling the fall of Rome. Ascribed to the third-century sage Rav Huna, the oracle refers to the figure of Esau in what appears to be one of the earliest documented examples of a widely attested Byzantine-era rabbinic exegetical motif associating the duplicitous brother of Jacob with the Roman Empire.[92] God, Huna avers, will cast down Esau in the world to come when the latter shall dare to don a *tallit*, a Jewish prayer shawl, and assume a seat in heaven.[93] The intimation here that the Romans pretend to be Jews has been interpreted in view of early Christian claims to the identity and soteriological privilege of the nation of Israel. Rav Huna, however, is said to impugn Esau not for trying to keep his righteous brother Jacob from his due place alongside God but, rather, for trying to pass himself off as righteous as well. He therefore implies no harmful intent against the Jews on Esau's part.[94] While arguably critical of the Romans for their undeserved sense of moral superiority, the passage exhibits no certain knowledge of the Christian theological conceit of supersessionism. It is therefore unlikely that the Talmudic passage signals a premonition of the Church's yet unrealized imperialistic future.

In fact, the Palestinian Talmud includes only one original passage expressly addressing Christianity. It is modeled on the Tannaitic narrative involving Rabbi Eleazar ben Damah and the healer Jacob of Kefar Sama, which appears

---

[91] This reading is supported by a seemingly related tradition in *Genesis Rabbah* 25.1, where Rabbi Abbahu is shown debating unspecified *minim* over the authenticity of Enoch's legendary translation into heaven; see comments in Burns (2014: 210–11). Maier (1978: 76–82), typically denies the passage's reference to Jesus, although I find his inference of its anti-Roman thrust no more tenable.

[92] The exegetical equation of Esau and/or Edom with Rome would become a mainstay of the rabbinic polemic against Christianity during the Byzantine era. For illustrations to this effect, see Yuval (2006: 1–30). Although Yuval (ibid., 19–20) plausibly submits that the Talmudic passage in question is the earliest known example of this trope, that its figurative portrait of Rome implies a Christian Rome does not necessarily follow.

[93] The passage appears in *y.Nedarim* 3.12 (38a). For the following interpretation, see, e.g., Herford (1903: 210–11); Simon (1986: 187–88); Boyarin (1999: 3–4); P.S. Alexander (2007: 697–98).

[94] For similar comments, see Schremer (2010: 219–20, n. 9), who proposes to associate the Talmudic passage to a recurring early rabbinic fantasy involving Romans who wish to study the Torah alongside the sages.

alongside the Amoraic tale in the Talmudic text.[95] Referring to the third-century sage Rabbi Joshua ben Levi, the story reads as follows:

His grandson was choking. A certain man came and whispered to him something in the name of Jesus son of Pandera. He recovered. When [the healer] was leaving, [Rabbi Joshua] asked him, "What did you whisper to him?" He told him such-and-such a word. [Rabbi Joshua] responded, "He would have been better off not hearing that word and dying!" And so it was for him, *Like an error that came from the mouth of a ruler* (Eccl 10.5).[96]

The typically terse wording of the Talmudic text leaves much to the imagination. Clearly, however, the stakes of the polemic have been raised since the tale's initial appearance in the rabbinic record. This time, the threat of Christianity is more invasive. Not only does the Christian healer manage to fool Rabbi Joshua into allowing him to work his illicit magic, but, much to the rabbi's chagrin, the spell actually works. Worse still, when Joshua flippantly remarks that his grandson would have been better off dead than cured by a Christian, the boy dies instantly. Acknowledging by way of Ecclesiastes the danger of words spoken out of turn, the rabbi's speech is thus shown to be just as powerful as the Christian's.[97] But the rabbi's counteroffensive is by no means satisfying. For in the end, Joshua is left to suffer the tragic outcome of their encounter while the healer sustains only a reprimand.[98]

Compared to its Tannaitic prototype, the Amoraic story suggests that the rabbinic fear of the Christian other grew more acute with the passage of time. Yet something more subtle appears to be at issue here. Whereas in the earlier tale Rabbi Ishmael manages to shield the dying Rabbi Eleazar from the scourge of heresy, in the later version Rabbi Joshua fails to accomplish as much. Whereas Eleazar, moreover, in his desperation nearly agrees to accept Jacob's illicit remedy, Rabbi Joshua's grandson shows no such intent. The boy exercises no agency at all in receiving either the healer's spell or his grandfather's untimely retort. The image of a Christian healer forcibly subjecting a Jewish innocent to his toxic medicine thus seems to speak to a different kind of

---

[95] I refer to the aforementioned narrative preserved in *t.Ḥullin* 2.22–23, and paralleled in *y.Avodah Zarah* 2.2 (40d–41a) and *y.Shabbat* 14.4 (14d–15a).

[96] Excerpted from *y.Avodah Zarah* 2.2 (40d), to which compare *y.Shabbat* 14.4 (14d) and *Ecclesiastes Rabbah* 10.6. I favor the version in tractate *Avodah Zarah* in view of its superior orthography. See Schäfer (2007: 139), for a comparison of the texts in question.

[97] For this observation, compare Bohak (2003: 275), who cites this passage in reference to Rabbi Joshua ben Levi's reputation for having used sorcery to combat heretics as attested in an independent narrative in *b.Avodah Zarah* 4a–b (ibid., 272–75). Bohak seems to have the literary relationship between the two traditions out of order. It is more likely that the author of the Babylonian story deduced his impression of Rabbi Joshua's propensity to best *minim* through magic on the basis of the earlier Palestinian tradition.

[98] Compare Schäfer (2007: 60–62), who suggests that the Talmudic story is meant to exemplify the rabbinic moral principle that magical practice, though sometimes effective, is nonetheless an affront to God. See also P.S. Alexander (2007: 694–95), for like comments.

Christianity than that which figured in the original story, a Christianity more powerful than the easily neutralized heresy of old.[99]

A clue to the Amoraic story's rhetorical function is its setting amidst a collection of materials relating to the Mishnah's ruling that a Jew must not receive healing from a gentile.[100] Appearing immediately before the story is a series of opinions excluding from the halakhic stricture the consultation of professional physicians employing legitimate medical techniques. The implication of the ensuing narrative is that the Christian healer in question is a gentile utilizing what the sages naturally deemed an illegitimate technique. This reading is supported by the text. Where the Tannaitic story, at least in its Toseftan recension, associates its healer with *minut*, the Amoraic story intimates no such connection.[101] The Christian portrayed here is thus not presented as a heretical Jew. He is presented as a meddling outsider whose assumption of a Jewish persona causes a flustered Rabbi Joshua to send his own grandchild to the grave. This is a Christian more dangerous than the type known to the *Tannaim*. This is a Christian who can resist the censure of the rabbis without consequence, who can create havoc for the Jew by sheer force of will. In short, this Christian belongs not to the world of the *Tannaim* but to that of their successors who witnessed the early stages of his ascent to power.

The *Amoraim* were not oblivious to the relationship between the new gentile religion and the erstwhile Jewish heresy memorialized in the literature of the *Tannaim*. Perhaps the Talmud's most famous acknowledgment of that history appears in a prophecy ascribed to Rabbi Eliezer ben Hyrcanus, the subject of the aforementioned Tannaitic narrative set during Rome's initial persecution of the Christians in Palestine. Amidst a number of ominous signs to portend the coming of the Messiah, Eliezer predicts that "the kingdom will turn to heresy."[102] Although no further information is given as to the identity of the

[99] Kalmin (1994: 162), suggests that the story shows a certain degree of rabbinic receptivity to Christianity in its intimation that Rabbi Joshua should have accepted the healer's help rather than doom his grandson to death. While I agree that the Amoraic story speaks to a more nuanced view of Christianity than its Tannaitic prototype, I disagree with Kalmin's interpretation of that nuance. In citing the version of the story in tractate *Shabbat*, Kalmin neglects its relation to the series of debates over healing amidst which it appears in tractate *Avodah Zarah*. To read the story as a minor moral concession to Christianity is to miss its point with respect to the legitimacy of medical magic.

[100] See *m.Avodah Zarah* 2.2, and cf. *y.Avodah Zarah* 2.2 (40d–41a).

[101] In other words, while the Tannaitic tale does not actually call Jacob a heretic, its setting in the Tosefta amidst a collection of materials relating to *minim* and *minut* implies that identification (cf. *t.Hullin* 2.18–24).

[102] See *y.Sotah* 9.6 (23b), paralleled in *b.Sotah* 49b, *b.Sanhedrin* 97a, and *Song of Songs Rabbah* 2.33, where the statement is attributed to various other rabbinic authorities. An alternate version of the Talmudic passage is appended to the end of the Mishnaic tractate *Sotah* in several medieval manuscripts and in the editio princeps, although its Amoraic provenance is clearly indicated by its Aramaic language, which stands in contrast to the Mishnah's typical Hebrew idiom (*m.Sotah* 9.15); for comments see Epstein (1948: 2.976).

kingdom or the heresy, it seems reasonable to surmise that the rabbi's words refer to Constantine's legalization of Christianity in 313 CE and the dramatic changes in Rome's religious order that took place over the following decades. The passage thus appears to depict Rabbi Eliezer foretelling a nightmare scenario in which the Christians, once the common enemies of the Romans and the rabbis, would ascend to the very top of the imperial order. Its words thus elicit the pathos of a rabbinic collective subjected to an unexpected and agonizing role reversal with those whom their forerunners indifferently maligned as heretics.[103]

In reality, the kingdom did not turn to Christianity quite so suddenly. Constantine's edict was just the beginning of a long and complicated process whereby Rome's ruling elite gradually took to the new religion. It would take centuries for the effects of that process to diffuse among the Empire's masses. The Jews of Palestine sustained these developments in unique ways.[104] Churches and shrines were erected by order of the imperial administration. Christian pilgrims from all corners of the map began trickling into their land to see the sites where they believed their saints had walked. By the end of the fourth century, laws were enacted restricting the rights of the Jews to exercise the civic freedoms that they had enjoyed since the Severan age. The office of the Patriarchate was gradually stripped of its power. The practice of Judaism was subjected to unprecedented governmental regulation. Slowly but surely, the oppressed became the oppressors. The Jews had only to stand by helplessly and watch.

Rabbi Eliezer's clairvoyance notwithstanding, the *Amoraim* processed the news just as slowly as it dawned on them.[105] Evidence elsewhere in the Palestinian Talmud suggests that the old rabbinic understanding of Christianity as a Jewish heresy gradually ceded to a more current sensibility. Two unique Talmudic passages set amidst a series of halakhic responses to governmental coercion indicate that some of the latest contributors to the Talmud were sufficiently aware of the difference between Christian and Jew not to make the mistake of confusing the two categories.[106] The first passage raises the question of

---

[103] For like comments, see Boyarin (2004: 220), although cf. Schremer (2010: 121–26), who expresses due skepticism over the likelihood that the authors of the Talmud would have possessed the foresight to predict of the Roman Empire's turn to Christianity beyond the higher echelons of its political and social orders.

[104] On the following, see Stemberger (2000: 22–120), and, more succinctly, S. Schwartz (2001: 179–202). The laws restricting the rights of the Jews enacted by Constantine and his successors, too many to list here, are discussed in detail by Linder (1987).

[105] On the transformation of the Palestinian rabbinic polemic against Christianity from an inward-looking heresiological discourse to an outward-looking defensive stratagem, see, e.g., Irshai (2012: 20–27); Lapin (2012: 132–44); Levinson (2013). Compare, however, S. Schwartz (2003: 197–201), for a more reserved assessment of Christianity's impact on rabbinic thought in the early Byzantine era.

[106] The passages in question appear within a *sugya* or textual sequence referencing Ursicinus, a Roman official known to have been active in Palestine during the 350's and the latest securely datable historical personality attested in the Palestinian Talmud. On this sequence,

whether gentiles must sanctify the name of God, a rabbinic euphemism for surrendering one's life for the sake of one's principles or, in contemporary terms, to submit to martyrdom. Responding in the negative, two Amoraic authorities offer scriptural proof texts to the effect of demonstrating that the halakhic injunction against profaning the name of Yahweh applies only to the nation of Israel, that is, to the Jews.[107]

Since the rabbis generally did not assume that gentiles were obliged to the *halakhah*, their exemption of the latter from the onus of the Jewish martyr is only to be expected. What is remarkable is that the question was raised to begin with. Clearly, the rabbinic authorities cited in the passage knew of gentiles professing belief in the God of Israel and suffering for it at the hands of the Roman government. The scenario envisioned thus suggests the tragic spectacle of Christian martyrdom, a phenomenon that swept through Palestine in the years preceding Constantine's accession to the throne.[108] Yet the Christians in question are not characterized as *minim*. They are simply called *goyim*, gentiles. The Talmud thus attests to the knowledge of certain *Amoraim* that those of whom they had heard were being killed with the name of God on their lips were not Jews at all. This observation adds nuance to the Talmud's concomitant allegation of Rome's turn to heresy, implying that the heresy in question had already taken root beyond Palestine's Jewish population.

Immediately following that passage is another involving the subject of ethnic boundaries. A parable tells of Rabbi Abba bar Zemina, who worked in Rome as a tailor in the employ of an Aramean gentleman.[109] The man presents Rabbi Abba with a *neveleh*, that is, the carcass of an animal not slaughtered according to the laws of *kashrut*. He instructs the rabbi to eat it. When he refuses, the Aramean threatens to kill him unless he tastes the meat. Abba tells his master to do as he sees fit. Finally, the Aramean relents, telling the abused Rabbi Abba that he was wise to refuse the unclean food, for, as he puts it, "One is either a Jewish Jew or an Aramean Aramean" (*o yehudai yehudai o aramai aramai*).

---

which appears in alternate forms in *y.Shevi'it* 4.2 (35a–b) and *y.Sanhedrin* 3.6 (21b), see Lapin (2012: 144–49), to whose treatment I am indebted.

[107] Notably, the verses adduced here (Lev 22.32; 2 Kgs 5.18) refer to violations of the Pentateuchal proscription against idolatry, perhaps implying a categorical distinction between the foreign theological designs of the gentiles in question and the innately Jewish designs of the *minim*.

[108] I refer to the sporadic persecution of Palestine's Christian populace during the reign of Diocletian and his imperial coregents between 303 and 311 CE, attested by Eusebius in his hagiographic treatise *De martyribus Palaestinae* ("On the Martyrs of Palestine"). On the realities behind the tragic histories documented in this work and elsewhere in Eusebius' oeuvre, see Barnes (1981: 148–63).

[109] The identification of Rabbi Abba's master as an Aramean is doubly significant. That ethnic distinction appears in the Torah as a principal marker of difference for the Israelites (Deut 26.5). Moreover, the Aramaic term for Aramean, *aramai*, is phonetically and orthographically similar to the standard Aramaic term for Roman, *romai*, thus lending the characterization of Abba's cruel master a subtle anti-Roman undertone matching the story's setting. For a similar example of rabbinic wordplay, see *Leviticus Rabbah* 23.1, with discussion in Berkowitz (2012: 117–18).

The lesson of the story is subtle but incisive. The Aramean, a gentile, recognizes the traditional ethnic categories that set him apart from Rabbi Abba. A Jew, he therefore asserts, should not violate his principles lest he surrender his Jewish identity. Applying the converse argument to the preceding halakhic exchange, the Talmud thus suggests that gentiles ought not to surrender their assigned places in Yahweh's economy by pretending to be Jews. We thus find here an allusive statement to the effect that the *Amoraim* knew of certain powerful gentiles in faraway Rome entertaining designs to erase the traditional ethnic distinction between gentile and Jew. That sort of thinking, the author seems to say, is not advisable. Gentiles should not put themselves at risk of offending the God of Israel by worshipping him in their strange new ways. Nor, for that matter, should Jews submit to their Roman superiors pressuring them to violate the will of God by doing as the gentiles do.[110]

These passages indicate that the same Amoraic commentators who sustained their people's memories of Christianity's Jewish roots also knew of its more recent severence from those roots. The Talmud's intimation that the Roman Empire had turned to *minut* therefore must be taken not as a sign of confusion over the nature Rome's new religion but, rather, as a pronouncement that its lifespan as a Jewish heresy had reached its end. As seen in the story of Rabbi Joshua ben Levi, the Christian other had relinquished his Jewish identity by the time of the Talmud's composition. He still had the capacity to look like a Jew and sound like a Jew. But he was not a Jew. He was an Aramean, a Roman, a gentile. Depending on the circumstance, he could be a sympathetic figure or an agent of malice. But in either case, the gentile Christian was not of the same constitution as the Jewish Christian of yesteryear.

What became of the Jewish Christians seems not to have concerned the *Amoraim*. It is possible that the rabbis of the third and fourth centuries maintained the vague suspicion of their predecessors as to the designs of those individuals without singling them out amidst the number of so-called *minim* still operating in their midst. But the evidence surveyed earlier suggests that those *Amoraim* who lived to see the beginning of Christianity's transformation into the new religion of Rome knew of its reputed heretical pedigree. Assuming that those sages were acquainted with persons in their own communities who aligned themselves with the new regime, I see no reason why they should have refrained from exploiting that knowledge by resuming the heresiological polemic of their Tannaitic predecessors.

---

[110] The passage actually ends with a statement attributed to the fourth-century sage Rabbi Mana chastising Rabbi Abba for nearly having given his life to avoid a relatively trivial offense, citing an earlier discussion in the Talmudic sequence advocating self-sacrifice only for sake of violations of the Pentateuchal statutes forbidding idolatry, sexual impropriety, and murder. Per Lapin (2012: 148), Mana's prudent halakhic assessment does not detract from the exemplary quality of the story to which it refers.

To my mind, a simpler explanation would be that the *Amoraim* no longer saw Jewish Christians as credible threats. Origen and the Didascalia indicate that the middle of the third century was an unsettling time for Jewish Christians in Palestine and its surrounding areas. The increased presence of agents of the Roman Church amidst a Christian demographic traditionally obliging to their ethnic proclivities would have put the Jewish Christians a tough spot. Coupled with the emerging rabbinic support base among the region's Jewish population, the pull of doctrinal conformity with what they now realized was the Christian majority proved too strong for some to resist. Over time, assimilation diminished their numbers. They stopped attending synagogues. They stopped schooling their children in the ways of their ancestors. Thus, by the time the *Amoraim* began to compile the Palestinian Talmud in the late fourth century, the Jewish Christians no longer operated on a scale sufficient to warrant their attention.

Of course, it is difficult to base such positive conclusions on an argument from silence. Neither the Jewish nor the Christian record actually documents the disappearance of the Jewish Christians as such. Yet it is no less apparent that something happened between the beginning of the third century and the end of the fourth to render the old rabbinic polemic against Christian *minim* obsolete. That the *Amoraim* saw Constantine's conversion as a major turning point in the evolution of the Christian enterprise is clear enough, even if they failed to acknowledge that event in explicit terms. Yet even if the authors of the Palestinian Talmud had yet to face the full effect of Rome's turn to Christianity, it seems reasonable to conclude that they knew enough to comprehend that the Church's break from its Jewish past was a foregone conclusion.

A POSTMORTEM: JEROME ON THE NAZARENES

As the *Amoraim* of Palestine assembled their Talmudic magnum opus, the famed Christian scholar Jerome of Stridon settled into a hermitage near Bethlehem.[111] The well-traveled monk arrived in Palestine late in the year 385 and would remain there until his death in 419. The years intervening were a time of immense literary output for Jerome. In Palestine, he produced the Latin translations of the Hebrew Scriptures to be adopted as the Vulgate or the common text of the Old Testament. He produced Latin translations of key Christian treatises written in Greek and original scriptural commentaries imbued with his unique exegetical expertise. In addition, Jerome conducted correspondences with Christian notables elsewhere in the Roman Empire seeking his opinions on matters of global doctrinal significance. Jerome had been born into world where Christianity was not only legal, but regulated by

---

[111] On Jerome's life and literary activity in Palestine, see Williams (2008: 281–301), to whose chronology I adhere in the discussion to follow.

bishops empowered by Rome's imperial administration to dictate its practice among a public increasingly drawn to the religion now favored by their ruling class. An ardent observer of ecclesial politics prior to his monastic withdrawal, he continued to monitor the affairs of the Church from afar.

Although the Christianization of the Empire was by no means a fait accompli by the time he arrived in Palestine, the region's Christian population was sufficiently beholden to Rome for Jerome to proceed on the assumption of its orthodox character. Unlike Origen before him, he saw no need to establish boundaries of thought and practice between Christian and Jew beyond those already enforced by the law of Rome. In fact, Jerome made no secret of his association with Jews, whom he knew to possess the linguistic and exegetical skills he needed to achieve his mastery of the Hebrew Scriptures.[112] Having previously spent time in Syria, he had studied with Christians of Jewish descent, recent converts eager to share their exotic knowledge of Hebrew philology. In Palestine, Jerome interacted not only with Christians versed in Jewish matters but also with actual Jews willing discuss their sacred books with gentiles. Jerome applied himself to know Judaism as a living phenomenon rather than merely as an antiquated theological stereotype. He thus exhibits in his later writings a measure of contemporary Jewish knowledge surpassing his patristic peers.[113]

But Jerome was no Judaic savant.[114] Despite his occasional references to *deuterōtai* and their *deuterōsis*, he shows scant familiarity with the rabbinic culture supposedly signified by those terms. His Jewish contacts were thus apparently of the common variety, men literate in the Hebrew Scriptures but only vaguely aware of the rabbinic sages and their *halakhah*.[115] Furthermore, much of his supposedly "Jewish" narrative exegesis appears to derive from the works of earlier Christian authors likewise purporting to speak for the Jews.[116] Finally, much of Jerome's commentary on Judaism refers not to actual Jews but to "Judaizers" (Latin: *iudaizantes*), that is, orthodox Christians who

---

[112] The most comprehensive study to date on Jerome's relationships with Jews is Newman (1997). See ibid. (112–22), on his consultations with Jewish teachers and Christian teachers of Jewish descent. See also Williams (2008: 221–31).

[113] For corresponding assessments, see Kamesar (1994: 65–67); Newman (1997: 192–206).

[114] For the following conservative estimate of the extent of Jerome's Judaic knowledge, see Stemberger (1993); Newman (1997: 98–103); S. Schwartz (2002: 61–65).

[115] That notwithstanding Jerome's claim to have known an actual *deuterōtēs* or *Tanna* hailing from Lydda in Jerome, *Comm. Habac.* 1.2.578. Whether the individual in question identified himself with this outdated rabbinic sobriquet is unclear. Elsewhere, Jerome appears to describe the same man simply as a teacher (Latin: *praeceptor*; see Jerome, *Prologus in libro Iob de hebraeo translato* 20). It therefore seems reasonable to infer that Jerome surreptitiously applied the anachronistic terminology to his Jewish contact unaware of its obsolescence.

[116] For this observation, see Bardy (1934), and, more recently, Stemberger (1993: 355–59). Compare, however, the reappraisals of Newman (1997: 103–11), and Williams (2008: 226–31), who reasonably surmise that Jerome acquired his Jewish knowledge from a combination of written and oral sources.

believed that the Jerusalem Temple would be restored upon the second coming of the Messiah.[117] Jerome sought to confound advocates of that premillennialist eschatology by deriding them as would-be heretics eager to revert to the cultic habits of the Jews. He thereby displays a profound lack of understanding as to how Palestine's Jewish population had evolved in their practices and beliefs since the fall of the Second Temple. One therefore wonders how extensively Jerome cared to acquaint himself with his Jewish neighbors beyond his efforts to lay hold of their rare scriptural knowledge.[118]

In view of these concerns, some have questioned Jerome's sincerity as a seeker of Jewish wisdom. Andrew Jacobs has interpreted Jerome's interfaces with the Jews of Palestine as a means of contemporizing the scriptural stereotype of the Jew espoused by his patristic predecessors, subjecting that old rhetorical bogeyman to the new language of Christian imperialism.[119] Megan Hale Williams suggests that Jerome's submission to his Hebrew teachers was an ascetic affectation meant to enhance the effect of his mastery of the Jewish knowledge that he had lowered himself to obtain.[120] I agree in principle with both these theories. Jerome could not help but to envisage a Church assured of its victory over Judaism. In view of the political reality of his day, the Christian interpreter had no longer to fear the Jew's superior scriptural knowledge. Although humble his demeanor, Jerome acquired that knowledge in the name of an unassailable Christian exegetical enterprise. The actual Jews behind his unusually well stocked arsenal of scriptural information are thus, in a sense, no more realistic than the figurative Jew of his traditional theological polemic.

Jerome's readiness to use the Jew as a rhetorical foil illuminates his occasional comments on Jewish Christians. As noted, Jerome was not above accusing his fellow Christians of Judaizing tendencies. But he also knew of Christians who reportedly acted upon those tendencies, engaging in Jewish behaviors anathematic to the orthodox Church. Naturally, Jerome had little patience for those heretical sorts. But he did not hesitate to deploy them where they could be useful. One revealing example of that habit appears in a letter of 404 CE addressed to Augustine, the bishop of Hippo Regius in North Africa. Augustine had previously written to Jerome inquiring about his understanding of the dispute between Peter and Paul recounted in the latter's epistle to the

---

[117] See, e.g., Jerome, *Comm. Zach.* 14.9, where he calls Judaizers "not Jews who are made Christians but Christians who are made Jews" (*non iudaei christiani sed christiani iudaei fiant*). On Jerome's stereotypical representation of Judaism in his polemics against the Christians in question, see Newman (2001), especially ibid. (440–44), on his apparent lack of familiarity with contemporary Jewish ritual culture. Compare, however, Kinzig (2003), who argues that Jerome's account of "Judaizing" eschatology and its practical implication reflect firsthand knowledge of the beliefs of actual Jewish Christians, specifically those of the Nazarene variety.

[118] For similar conclusions, see Stemberger (1993: 360–64); Newman (1997: 188); Schwartz (2002: 64–65).

[119] A.S. Jacobs (2004: 67–83).

[120] Williams (2008: 231).

Galatians (Gal 2.11–14).[121] In his commentary on that book, Jerome had asked why Peter would have enjoined his fellow Christians in Antioch to observe Jewish rites. Did the founder of the Roman Church not accept Paul's teaching on the law? Unwilling to cede that possibility, Jerome asserted that Peter merely feigned opposition to Paul. Their dispute, in other words, was staged. Peter knew that Jesus had removed the yoke of the law per Paul's argument. He thus assumed the false position only to provide Paul a pretext on which to demonstrate the truth of his gospel to the Antiochenes.[122]

Augustine, however, begged to differ. He knew that the apostles had been born and raised as Jews. Accordingly, he reasoned that the question of whether to uphold the Jewish law had been a legitimate topic of debate in the first-century Church. Paul had reported the facts accurately. Jerome, he therefore chides the monk, should not have distorted those facts for the sake of imposing his orthodox agenda upon the biblical text.[123]

Yet what Augustine meant as a corrective to Jerome's exegetical approach the latter took as an indictment of his motives. Jerome thus acerbically protests that if Christians of Jewish descent were to observe the Jewish law, they would induce the entire Church into the heresy of Cerinthus and Ebion.[124] As to the ills of that heresy, he relates:

And what shall I say about the Ebionites, who pretend to be Christians? There is today a heresy among the Jews throughout all the synagogues of the East, namely that of the *minim*. It is cursed by the Pharisees to this very day. Commonly called Nazarenes, they believe in Christ, the Son of God born to the Virgin Mary, whom they say suffered and was resurrected under Pontius Pilate, and in whom we also believe. But while they wish to be both Jews and Christians, they are neither Jews nor Christians.[125]

---

[121] For the following, see Fredriksen (2008: 235–39), and cf. Newman (2001: 429–34). What motivated Augustine's communique was not his desire to rehash the dispute between Peter and Paul but to relate to Jerome the danger of undermining the authority of the scriptures by misreading them to support one's theological agenda. For comments to this effect, see, Fredriksen (2008: 186–87), and, more extensively, Hennings (1994: 218–64); Fürst (1999: 45–87).

[122] The offending commentary appears in Jerome, *Comm. Gal.* 2.11–13. Jerome, *Epist.* 112.6, claims to have derived his reading from Origen, although none of the latter's surviving writings speaks directly to Jerome's purpose. Fürst (1999: 26–29), suggests that Jerome meant to refer to Origen's exegetical methods rather than to a specific example of his predecessor's exegesis.

[123] See Augustine, *Epist.* 28.3–5 (=Jerome, *Epist.* 56.3–5), 40.4–7 (=Jerome, *Epist.* 67.4–7).

[124] Jerome, *Epist.* 112.13 (=Augustine, *Epist.* 75.13). Cerinthus was the alleged founder of an old Gnostic heresy recently accounted as Jewish by Jerome's contemporary Epiphanius (*Pan.* 28.1.3), while the plainly contrived figure of "Ebion" had been pegged as the originator of the Ebionite heresy by Tertullian (*Praescr.* 10.8, 33.5, 11, *Virg.* 6.1, *Carn. Chr.* 18.1, 24.2), Origen (*Comm. Rom.* 3.11.2), and Epiphanius (*Pan.* 30.1.1, 2.1–8, 3.1, 13.1, 14.6, 15.3, 17.1, 3, 5, 18.1, 33.3), among others. For Jerome's pairing of Cerinthus and Ebion, cf. Epiphanius, *Pan.* 31.2.1, 51.2.3, 6.7, 10.4. On the spurious Jewish characterization of Cerinthus, see Klijn and Reinink (1973: 8–9), and on the invention of Ebion (ibid., 21–22).

[125] Excerpted from Jerome, *Epist.* 112.13 (=Augustine, *Epist.* 75.13). For the dating of the letter to 404 CE, see Williams (2008: 297).

Forgoing for the moment their polemical pretext, Jerome's comments are notable in several respects. As noted in Chapter 4, he appears to refer to the *birkat ha-minim*, specifically to a form of that benediction indicting heretics and Christians on separate accounts.[126] It is conceivable that Jerome based his knowledge of the *birkat ha-minim* on the testimony of his onetime mentor Epiphanius.[127] Clearly, however, he possessed enough unique information to improve on his friend's account, providing the Hebrew term by which he knew the "Pharisees" to impugn their heretical adversaries. Yet he repeats the error of Epiphanius in accounting the *notzerim* targeted by those men as members of a peculiar Christian sect, assimilating his predecessor's novel construction of the Nazarene heresy. Jerome thus fails to grasp that the *birkat ha-minim* had evolved by his day to implicate all Christians under the generic category *notzerim*.[128] Nevertheless, he manages to reach the unprecedented conclusion that the various "Jewish" heresies with which he was acquainted all spoke to the same phenomenon of persons wishing to identify as Jews and as Christians simultaneously.[129] He thus infers that the Ebionites and Nazarenes cited by his predecessors were synonymous with the *minim* of rabbinic lore. Jerome certainly is correct here, even if he does misrepresent the generic heresiological implication of the rabbinic epithet.

In assigning the *birkat ha-minim* to the Pharisees, Jerome establishes another equivalency linking that long gone Jewish sect to their putative heirs, the rabbis. He thus insinuates that the rabbis had by the early fifth century achieved sufficient recognition among their fellow Jews to assume leadership roles in the synagogues of Palestine and its environs. That claim is mirrored in in another of Jerome's epistles dated to 407 CE, in which he claims that the Pharisees of his day include "sages" (Greek: *sophoi*; Latin: *sapientes*) who preach in the synagogues the *deuterōseis* of their masters Akiva, Shimon, and Hillel.[130] Commenting on the Gospel of Matthew, Jerome's claim of the popular respect commanded by those sages must be considered hyperbolic. His intent obviously is to malign them like the domineering Pharisees of Matthew's account. In fact, the rabbis to whom he alludes were not as widely esteemed as Jerome

[126] See Newman (1997: 138–45). Jerome appears to cite the *birkat ha-minim* in less specific terms in Jerome, *Comm. Am.* 1.11–12, *Comm. Isa.* 5.18–19, 49.7, 52.4–6.

[127] Epiphanius, *Pan.* 29.9.2. On Jerome's acquaintance with Epiphanius, see Williams (2008: 40, 42, 50, 63, 98). On their shared knowledge of contemporary Judaism, see Lössl (2002), with reference to their comments on the *birkat ha-minim* (ibid., 418–19).

[128] This despite Jerome's note in his translation of Eusebius' *Onomasticon* that all Christians were once abusively called Nazarenes; see Jerome, *Sit.* 143 s.v. Nazareth, and cf. Acts 24.5.

[129] For an earlier example of this equation implicating only the Ebionites and Nazarenes, see Jerome, *Comm. Matt*, 12.13, which Williams (2008: 292), dates to 398 CE.

[130] Jerome, *Epist.* 121.10, referring to Matt 5.1–11. For the dating of the letter to 407 CE, see Williams (2008: 298). Newman (1997: 49–51), plausibly argues that the Greek terminology which Jerome provides in his Latin text (*hoi sophoi deuterōsin*, "the sages repeat …") replicates a formal pattern of rabbinic speech used to signify Tannaitic traditions (cf. Hebrew: *shanu ḥakhamim*; Aramaic: *tanu rabbanan*).

needed them to be in order to validate his analogy.[131] Even, therefore, acknowledging Jerome's sound knowledge of the content of the *birkat ha-minim*, it is impossible to say whether that proprietary rabbinic liturgical apparatus actually had achieved the level of currency that he tells Augustine it had.

Jerome's casual conflation of Judaism's past and present naturally casts doubt on the precision of his Jewish heresiology. Writing to Augustine, Jerome states that Ebionites and Nazarenes continue to worship alongside the "Pharisees" even in their own day. That statement is difficult to reconcile with the roughly contemporaneous record of the Palestinian Talmud, which provides no evidence for the appearance of Christian *minim*, nor indeed of any *minim*, in synagogues frequented by the *Amoraim*. Nor does the Talmud offer any indication that *Amoraim* actually utilized the *birkat ha-minim* for what Jerome supposes was its purpose of cursing the heretics in their company. His inference of the continual operation of Christians in Jewish society is thus wanting for credibility.

Yet Jerome's impression of that phenomenon was not likely based on his own observation. As noted, most of what he presumed to know about Jews and Judaism came from books and informants. In order, therefore, to assess the critical value of his testimony, we must consider his sources. A passage in Jerome's commentary on the book of Isaiah is instructive here. Written a few years after his correspondence with Augustine, Jerome's commentary is notable for his consultation of an apocryphal gospel tract allegedly of Nazarene provenance.[132] That volume, he reports, was his own translation of a Hebrew edition of the Gospel of Matthew which he had come across, evidently a work of the type elsewhere attested as the Gospel of the Hebrews. Why Jerome presumed to associate the tract with the Nazarenes is not entirely clear.[133] One can

---

[131] So S. Schwartz (2002: 64–65), although cf. S.J.D. Cohen (1997: 104–05), and Lapin (2012: 158), who read Jerome's testimony to indicate his witness to the early elevation of the rabbis to popular influence in Palestine.

[132] See Jerome, *Comm. Isa.* prol., 8.11–15, 8.19–22, 9.1, 11.1–3, 29.17–21, 31.6–9, 40.9–11, and cf. Jerome, *Comm. Matt.* 23.25, with critical discussion in Klijn (1992: 16–19). Klijn's analysis is predicated on his earlier study, Klijn (1972), where he argues that Jerome's source was not a gospel tract but a Jewish Christian commentary on Isaiah featuring cross-references to Matthew's gospel; see especially ibid. (252–55). Klijn observes that Jerome's quotations include passages from Isaiah not actually cited in the gospel and, more importantly, that his genuine quotations from the so-called Nazarene gospel exhibit no clear signs of its heretical tendency. Ergo, he contends, Jerome possessed a fairly orthodox version of Matthew written in Hebrew or Aramaic and a Nazarene commentary on Isaiah written in Aramaic. See also Luomanen (2012: 103–19), who follows Klijn in his minimalist reconstruction of the so-called Nazarene gospel. While I find Klijn's proposal worthy of consideration, I cannot endorse it. To my mind, Jerome seems to acknowledge not two separate documents but, rather, an expanded version of the Gospel of Matthew written in Hebrew or Aramaic and incorporating the exegetical glosses absent from its canonical version.

[133] Compare Jerome, *Comm. Matt.* 12.13 and *Vir. ill.* 3, where he refers to the Hebrew text of Matthew as the original edition of Matthew's implicitly orthodox gospel. See also Jerome, *Comm. Eph.* 5.4, *Comm. Ezech.* 16.13, 18.5–9, *Comm. Matt.* 2.5, 6.11, 12.12, 27.16, 27.51, *Comm. Mich.* 7.6, *Epist.* 20.5, *Pelag.* 3.2, *Tract. Ps.* 135, and *Vir. ill.* 2, where he appears to refer

only assume that he relied on Epiphanius, who likewise ascribed those alleged heretics a Hebrew version of Matthew's gospel.[134]

In any case, Jerome utilized the so-called Nazarene gospel's exegetical citations of Isaiah as aids for his own careful philological exposition of the original Hebrew text of that ancient prophetic book. Among those citations is a particularly suggestive passage on Isaiah 8.14, which reads, *He shall be a as sanctuary, but a stone of stumbling and a rock of slipping for both houses of Israel, a trap and a snare for those who dwell in Jerusalem.* The original Hebrew verse speaks to the ascent of King Hezekiah, whom Isaiah foretold would right the listing ships of the kingdoms of Judah and Israel. But the Nazarenes, says Jerome, interpret the verse's "two houses of Israel" differently:

The Nazarenes, who accept Christ in such a way as not to desist from observing the old laws, explain the two houses as the two households of Shammai and Hillel, from whom originated the scribes and the Pharisees. Akiva, who took over their school, is called the teacher of Aquila the proselyte, and after him came Meir, who was succeeded by Yoḥanan ben Zakkai, followed by Eliezer [ben Hyrcanus], Tarfon, Yose the Galilean, and, up to the capture of Jerusalem, Joshua [ben Ḥananiah]. Then Shammai and Hillel came from Judea not long before the Lord was born. The name of the first means 'he who scatters'[135] and of the second 'the unholy one'[136] because the one scattered and [the other] defiled the precepts of the law by his traditions and *deuterōseis*. And these are the two houses who did not accept the savior, who has become to them ruin and shame.[137]

Assuming that Jerome accurately represents his source here, one would have to describe as tendentious the exegetical logic on which the author bases his reading of Isaiah's prophecy. The accompanying register of rabbinic notables is no more coherent, exhibiting a haphazard sequence of persons and events irreconcilable with the Jewish sources attesting to the lives of those men.[138]

---

to the same volume as the Gospel of the Hebrews. On the common subject of these assorted testimonies, see Klijn (1992: 17–18).

[134] See Epiphanius, *Pan.* 29.9.4. Jerome, *Vir. ill.* 3, claims that he consulted a copy of the Nazarene gospel obtained in the Syrian city of Beroea (modern-day Aleppo), although he does not indicate whether he acquired it from actual Nazarenes. It is possible that that volume was the same as the one that he claims to have found in the scholastic library of Caesarea; cf. Jerome, *Pelag.* 3.2. With respect to Lössl (2002: 422–23), it is possible that Jerome's location of Jewish Christians in Beroea reflects firsthand knowledge gleaned during his stay in the nearby town of Chalcis. But I find it more likely that he surreptitiously assigned the Hebrew gospel to that city in view Epiphanius' claim that there were Nazarenes there (*Pan.* 29.7.7).

[135] The implication is that the name Shammai derives from the Aramaic root *šmm*, meaning to "scatter" or "become desolate."

[136] The implication is that the name Hillel derives from the Aramaic root *ḥwl*, meaning to "defile" or "profane."

[137] Excerpted from Jerome, *Comm. Isa.* 8.11–15. See Klijn (1972: 243–44).

[138] Newman (1997: 72–74), gamely attempts to restore a semblance of chronological order on the premise of identifying the passage's "capture of Jerusalem" with the end of the Bar Kokhba rebellion in 135 CE. I find it more reasonable to infer that the author simply did not have his facts straight.

Nevertheless, the author manages to make the point that he considered the renowned first-century BCE Pharisaic masters Hillel and Shammai disreputable influences on their people. To his mind, therefore, the arrival of Jesus shortly after their age marked a point of disjunction between the author's group and those of his fellow Jews beholden to the *Tannaim*.

Yet it seems clear that this assessment was made in hindsight. That the author knew the names of Tannaitic sages active through the mid-second century suggests a certain measure of familiarity with what was to that point in time still a quite insular rabbinic collective. One might therefore surmise that he speaks to the memories of a Christian community still apt to keep up with the rabbinic sages for quite some time following the founding of the apostolic mission. But the relationship between the author's group and their fellow Jews must have soured by the time the rabbinic sages began to commit their repeated traditions to writing, if not earlier.[139] He thus determined that Hillel and Shammai, in his anachronistic reconstruction the founders of the rabbinic discipline, somehow had foreseen the need to deter their Jewish followers from accepting Jesus as their agent of salvation.[140]

Such was the nature of Jerome's knowledge of the Nazarenes, at least insofar as he wished to document their Jewish pedigrees. Let us therefore now revisit Jerome's earlier comments on the persistence of those alleged heretics and their Ebionite confrères.[141] While I would not deny that Jerome actually dealt with Christians given to Jewish practices, his claim to Augustine that Ebionites and Nazarenes still existed in their day cannot be substantiated.[142] Jerome's knowledge of those heretical types seems to derive from earlier Christian literature, especially the writings of Epiphanius, along with a smattering of traditional theological prejudices against the Jews and more current, if secondhand,

---

[139] In other words, the Christian group's association with the disciples of the *Tannaim* seems to have ended before the beginning of the third century. For like comments, see S. Schwartz (2002: 61–62). Contrary to Klijn (1972: 249–51), the plural *deuterōseis* cited should not necessarily be taken to refer to the singular composition known as the Mishnah (cf. Schwartz, 2002: 64–65).

[140] The implication that the author regarded the legislative activity of the *Tannaim* deleterious only in hindsight is expressed more clearly in another citation in Jerome's commentary stating that the *deuterōtai* already had expended their efforts to keep their people bound to the Jewish law; see Jerome, *Comm. Isa.* 29.17–21, and cf. ibid. (8.19–22, 9.1). Luomanen (2012: 76), constructively likens the author's seemingly recent change of heart regarding the validity of the law to the similarly orthodox posture expressed in the Didascalia in reference to the second legislation.

[141] Klijn (1992: 19), observes that Jerome seems to have abandoned his earlier equation of the Ebionites and Nazarenes by the time he composed his scriptural commentaries, perhaps realizing that the latter were not really all that unorthodox. That may be, but Jerome's apparent reassessment of his language does not reverse his earlier claim to Augustine that Ebionites and Nazarenes continued to operate in their age.

[142] Which is not to say that they made no impression on Augustine, who mimics Jerome's language on the Nazarenes in his reply; see Augustine, *Epist.* 82.16 (=Jerome, *Epist.* 116.16), and cf. Augustine, *Faust.* 19.4.

information about the state of Jewish culture in early fifth-century Palestine.[143] On that last count, Jerome's knowledge of the *birkat ha-minim* is undoubtedly exceptional. But it is far from perfect. His inference that those who recited the benediction meant to target specific Christian heretics is entirely off base. His assumption, moreover, that those heretics were actually present in the synagogues where the *birkat ha-minim* was recited seems contrived at best.

What Jerome actually knew about the Nazarenes is obscured by his orthodox fanaticism. It appears as though the persons whom he reflexively cast as heretics in the Ebionite mold were nothing more than orthodox Christians mindful of their Jewish lineage. To the extent that those Christians sustained memory of their Jewish past, they appear to have put that past behind them long before Jerome's lifetime. The schism, as it were, between their ancestors and their fellow Jews seems to have occurred during the age of the *Tannaim* or shortly thereafter. After that point and for reasons unknown, those men and women of old ceased to observe the Jewish law. One assumes that they began to migrate toward the proto-orthodox Church at roughly the same time. Whether Epiphanius was correct to suspect that some of their descendants continued to practice Jewish rites into the late fourth century is impossible to say. Yet it seems reasonably clear that his "Nazarene" heresy was misconceived.

Jerome's casual endorsement of his mentor's error is belied by his own research. The people whose gospel Jerome believed he had read were not Nazarenes at all, at least not as Epiphanius had imagined those heretical monstrosities.[144] They were *notzerayya*, normal Christians who happened to speak Aramaic. Their sectarian visage was an illusion, a testimonial to their memory that their predecessors once defined themselves as Jews. The only offense committed by those ancestors was not having embraced Paul's gospel quite as quickly as had other Christians of their age. Despite, therefore, Jerome's claim that the Nazarenes and, by extension, the Ebionites continued to plague the Church in his own day, he inadvertently speaks to the fact that those heretical apparitions had vanished ages ago. Just like the authors of the Palestinian Talmud, Jerome saw the schism between Christian and Jew as one already decided. That he thought to impugn those who refused to see the situation as he did does not necessarily signify that he knew such individuals to exist in his day.

---

[143] I demur here from the otherwise instructive treatment of Mimouni (2012: 114–25), who proceeds on the unfounded assumption that Jerome possessed firsthand knowledge of those whom he pegged as Ebionites and Nazarenes on the basis of his personal encounters with Jewish Christians in Palestine.

[144] For a similarly skeptical assessment, see Kinzig (2007: 486–87), who questions whether the Nazarenes ever were a formally organized group. Luomanen (2012: 76–77), quixotically questions whether the persons whom Jerome presumed to know as Nazarenes actually were Jewish despite confirming that aspect of their characterization in Epiphanius' account of their sect (ibid., 65–66).

NEW REALITIES AND CONFLICTED MEMORIES

Between the beginning of the third and the end of the fourth century, developments in the lives of Jews and Christians in the Roman Near East yielded a gradual and variegated process of shifting allegiances for those who once presumed, as Jerome put it, to be both Jews and Christians. Where that seemed a feasible option for some during roughly the first one hundred and fifty years of the Christian enterprise, its viability was compromised by the empowerment of a local Jewish population increasingly able to practice their identities without fear of reprisal from those outside their group. Meanwhile, the arrival of a decidedly foreign brand of Christianity sensitized that group's Christian element to the need for alignment with the Roman Church. The unexpected turn of events sparked by Constantine's legalization of Christianity served to establish a universal standard of orthodoxy not obliging to "Jewish" Christians. The distinction between Christian and Jew long acknowledged in other quarters was thereby finally imposed upon what was perhaps the last population on earth to grasp its implications.

The sundry evidences surveyed in this chapter do not add up to a complete picture of what happened to effectuate that outcome. They offer only passing glances at a complex process of mutual disaffection involving generations of Christians, Jews, and those caught between those evolving demographics. But those evidences seem to point to the following scenario. The minor social advancements achieved by Palestine's Torah-observant Jews during the early third century emboldened the proponents of the rabbinic movement to begin publicizing their efforts among the general Jewish population of their region. The initial efforts of the rabbinic sages to disseminate their *halakhah* were probably of negligible impact owing to the limited extent of their jurisdiction as well as their competition with other local authorities, both Jewish and Roman, who stood to impede their reformist ambitions. Nevertheless, the mere appearance of their empowerment served to drive a wedge between those Jews prone to accede to the conservative agenda of the rabbis and those apt to resist that agenda.

Among the latter were Jews who also identified as Christians. The literature of the early rabbinic sages includes legislation demeaning to those individuals. Their construction of *minut* made it difficult for those implicated in its heresiological rhetoric to support the rabbis once they began to disseminate the teachings of the *Tannaim* more widely than the *Tannaim* themselves had. Christians were therefore among those Jews who chose to avoid rabbis and their disciples during the age of the *Amoraim*. Yet as those alleged *minim* receded from the social horizons of the rabbis, a new kind of Christian began to enter their frame of view. These new Christians, however, were of a different sort than those known to the *Tannaim*. Despite their resemblances to the *minim* of old, these Christians were of no account to the *halakhah*. They were Christians of the sort whom Origen wished to find in Caesarea, Christians who, at most, sustained memories of their Jewish roots in the fashion of the author of the Didascalia Apostolorum. Gradually, willingly, these Christians acquiesced to the Pauline gospel that their ancestors had understood to apply only to gentiles. In their discreet withdrawal from Jewish society, a schism was born.

Meanwhile, focusing their attentions on the needs of their own willing constituents, the Amoraic sages of Palestine opted to remain aloof of the affairs of their Christian neighbors. They thereby declined to bear witness to the final resolution of the Christian schism as it unfolded. Only when faced with the disturbing news that the Christians in their midst no longer wished to be known as Jews did the rabbis and their followers come to appreciate that a decisive rupture had occurred. In time, the sectarian division that they recalled as a minor nuisance to their forebears took on the aspect of an event of major significance.¹⁴⁵ The quaint *minim* thus became frozen in rabbinic memory, nagging reminders of a former age when the Jew could still disparage the Christian other without fear of reprisal.¹⁴⁶ The new Christian demanded a new understanding of his modus operandi as a gentile and a representative of a Roman state no longer obliging to the rights of its Jewish subjects.

My investigation finds a fitting conclusion in the Babylonian Talmud. Having already sampled this work in the introduction to this study, I shall say now only that it resembles the Palestinian Talmud in its form while expanding the content base of its predecessor to include exegetical traditions of Babylonian and Palestinian *Amoraim* through the end of the fifth century CE. Its present text, however, appears to have been composed by successive generations of Babylonian editors organizing and embellishing their received Amoraic materials over the course of the sixth through seventh centuries, and perhaps later still.¹⁴⁷ The second Talmud's rhetorical objective is thus fixed squarely in Sasanian Mesopotamia, a land governed by Iranian potentates bound to traditional Zoroastrian culture, albeit with an abiding interest in the conditions of Jewish life under Byzantine rule in Palestine.

A passage in the Babylonian Talmud pertinent to my account appears in a short textual sequence or *sugya* referring to a ruling in the Mishnah regarding the use of meat obtained from a gentile butcher (*m.Ḥullin* 1.1).¹⁴⁸ As shown in Chapter 4,

---

¹⁴⁵ On the complex rabbinic internalization and response to the onset of Christian imperialism, see, e.g., S. Schwartz (2001: 263–74); Schremer (2010: 121–41); Sivertsev (2011: 9–44). See also Langer (2012: 55–57), on the addition of anti-imperial formulas to the *birkat ha-minim* during the late ancient period.

¹⁴⁶ I refer to the fact that later Amoraic depictions of *minim*, Christians and otherwise, typically portray them in conversation with earlier rabbinic sages as opposed to contemporary personalities. For this observation, see Kalmin (1994: 163–67).

¹⁴⁷ On the Babylonian sages and their scribal executors, see Rubenstein (2007: 66–73). For a more detailed overview of the Babylonian Talmud's text and history, see Strack and Stemberger (1996: 190–215).

¹⁴⁸ For the following, see *b.Ḥullin* 13a–b. My citations reflect the uncensored text of Ms. Munich Cod. Hebr. 95, which reads "gentile(s)" (*nokhri/nokhrim/umot/goyim*) for the Vilna edition's

the *Tannaim* ruled such meat unacceptable for Jews to eat but permissible to resell or otherwise put to profitable use.[149] The Talmud's commentary begins with a statement ascribed to the late third-century Babylonian *Amora* Rabbi Ammi, who relates the Mishnah's ruling to the Tannaitic statement recorded in the Tosefta regarding meat obtained from a heretic, a *min*. That meat, the *Tannaim* ruled, is not permitted for Jewish use in any capacity, as one must be suspect of its having been prepared in conjunction with an idolatrous sacrifice (cf. *t.Ḥullin* 1.1, 2.20). Rabbi Ammi thus correctly concludes that the *Tannaim* deemed Jewish heretics more likely than gentiles to trade in foodstuffs categorically unfit for use by those who abide by the *halakhah*.

Having thus introduced the topic of *minut* to the conversation, the anonymous voice of the Talmud poses a disconcerting question. According to the Mishnah, a Jew may derive benefit from meat slaughtered by a gentile. But what if that gentile happens to be a *min*? The Talmud proceeds to quote Rabbi Ammi's contemporary Rav Naḥman, who credits his teacher Rabbah bar Abbuha as having programmatically stated, "There are no heretics among the gentiles." To this claim, the Talmud adduces a challenge in the aforementioned Tannaitic legislation likening the heretic's sacrificial offering to idolatry. It thus proposes to emend Rabbah's statement to read, "The majority of gentiles are not heretics." In support of this recommendation, the Talmud quotes the Palestinian *Amora* Rabbi Yoḥanan, who is said to have discharged gentiles outside of the Land of Israel from the Pentateuchal definition of idolatry on the grounds that they merely maintain the cultic habits of their ancestors.

The passage ends with an exchange between two fourth-century Babylonian sages regarding the practical ramifications of distinguishing certain gentiles as *minim*, the details of which are immaterial to our discussion.[150] What is remarkable is the line of thought prompting that question. The very possibility that a gentile should be counted as a *min* would have seemed unfathomable to the Palestinian sages who devised that heresiological category. That the

---

"(nations of) star worshipper(s)" (*oved kokhavim/ovdei kokhavim/umot ovdei kokhavim*). The latter epithet, a value-neutral term originally referring devotees of indigenous Mesopotamian cults, is regularly used in censored editions of the Talmud to soften unqualified expressions of ethnic bias. But the correction is misapplied here as the Tannaitic tradition at issue actually favors gentiles over *minim*. For the pertinent textual variants, see Rabbinovicz (1868–1897: 16.11b–12a).

[149] On the context of this ruling and its Talmudic expositions, see Hayes (2002: 218–19), who observes its typical construction of the gentile as a neutral party in view of the *halakhah*.

[150] To summarize, Rav Joseph bar Minyomi and Rav Ukva bar Ḥama adduce a series of Tannaitic rulings involving *minim*, questioning whether identifying the heretics in question as gentiles would affect the application of those laws (cf. *t.Hullin* 1.1, 2.20, *t.Bava Metzi'a* 2.33). They conclude that the only ruling in need of revision would be a prohibition of Temple priests to accept sacrificial offerings from *minim* on the grounds that they ordinarily would be permitted to receive certain such tributes from gentiles (cf. *t.Kippurim* 2.10). If, therefore, a known *min* were to bring an animal for sacrifice at the Jerusalem Temple, the priest would have to ascertain that said *min* is a bona fide gentile heretic rather than an apostate Jew.

unknown Babylonian scribe who arranged this sequence thought to raise that interpretive possibility is without precedent. It therefore appears as though that scribal editor was not entirely sure of the term's range of meaning, that despite knowing of Rav Naḥman's denial of the possibility that a gentile could be a *min*. Referring, rather, to Rabbi Ammi's tradition, he seems to mistake the hyperbolic tone of the Tannaitic polemic to indicate that the Jews whom the early rabbinic sages callously compared to idolaters actually were idolaters inasmuch as they practiced forbidden sacrificial rites. The editor's desire to articulate a middle position between his two conflicting sources is perfectly reasonable. But in concluding that most gentiles are not *minim*, he naturally implies that some are. That raises the question as to what kind of anomalous Jew/gentile hybrid he has in mind here.

The tradition credited to Rabbi Yoḥanan is suggestive. Speaking from within the traditional borders of *Eretz Yisrael*, Yoḥanan asserts that gentiles living beyond those borders are not to be counted as idolaters and, consequently, not to be implicated as such in the eyes of the *halakhah*. His rationale is easily inferred. Having not been acculturated to the worship of Yahweh, their veneration of other gods cannot be said to offend Yahweh.[151] But Yoḥanan's failure to extend the same courtesy to gentiles residing in Palestine suggests that he held those folks to a different standard. Those gentiles, he seems to say, should know better than to worship gods other than Yahweh. Whether by virtue of their Israelite roots or by their casual exposure to Jewish practice, they should know that the God of Israel is the only deity worthy of their devotion. As a result, the rabbi implies, gentiles living in Palestine should be deemed willful violators of God's law and approached with caution by Jews beholden to that law.

Yoḥanan's words provide no specific insight into the cultic predilections of the gentiles to whom he refers. But the Talmud's editor has an idea. By drawing the rabbi's statement into conversation with the Tannaitic screed against the *minim*, the editor subtly speaks to what he sees as a crucial difference between his gentile neighbors in Babylonia and those whom he knows to reside in Palestine. For according to Yoḥanan's logic, it must be among the latter where the idolatrous heretics adduced by Rabbi Ammi are to be found. In other words, the editor deduces that the non-Jewish population of Byzantine Palestine includes certain individuals liable to be recognized as heretics. We can be reasonably certain that the persons in question are Christians. Yet where the sages of old casually accounted those Christians as errant Jews, our editor knows that the language of *minut* no longer signified what it once had. Without

---

[151] Compare Goldenberg (1998: 89), who reads Yoḥanan's statement as an attempt to "finesse" the Torah's prejudicial identification of gentiles as idolaters. Although Yoḥanan's intent might well have been to establish a legal loophole allowing for Jewish cooperation with gentiles, that is certainly not the purpose to which his words are applied in the Talmudic text.

question or comment, he applies the old Tannaitic term for Jewish heretics to persons of no account to his God and of no standing among his people.

And so a new image of the Christian other was forged. Henceforth, leading Jewish minds were to know the Christian as one bound to the Jew not by kinship or ethnicity but by a contested principle of belief. The Christian heretic thus was refashioned in Jewish discourse as an apostate, his religion just another variety of the idolatry one would expect to find among the gentiles.[152] As for his Jewish past, that too was updated to match his current persona. So we meet in the Talmud the Jesus of Christian veneration reimagined as an unruly Pharisaic disciple likely to make rude comments about women and to worship bricks. To the minds of its authors, sheltered in Babylonia from the bigoted regime harassing their colleagues in Palestine, the misguided young man from Nazareth was just the first of untold numbers of Jewish souls enticed to apostasy by the strange Torah now preached in his name. "That is why," said the master, "Jesus the Nazarene practiced magic, deceiving Israel and leading them astray."[153] That was the memory of the Christian schism to be inscribed on the collective consciousness of the Jewish people for what would prove a long time to follow.[154] I imagine that the real story would have seemed far too incredible for many of them to accept.

---

[152] This equation is confirmed in the Babylonians Talmud's lone explicit reference to Christianity as a typically gentile vocation. The Mishnah records a statement in the name of Rabbi Ishmael forbidding commerce with gentiles ("star worshippers" in censored texts of *b.Avodah Zarah* 2a) for three days before and after their festivals so as to avoid inadvertently selling one an article for use in idolatrous worship (*m.Avodah Zarah* 1.2). Referring to this opinion, the obscure Babylonian *Amora* Rav Taḥlifa bar Abdimi quotes his predecessor Samuel of Nehardea as having observed that Ishmael would have categorically forbidden trade with Christians in view of the fact that those particular gentiles celebrate a festival on a weekly basis, i.e., on Sunday, the Christian Sabbath (uncensored manuscripts of *b.Avodah Zarah* 6a, 7b, reading *notzerim/notzeri* or "[the festival of the] Christians" for the Vilna edition's *yom eḥad* or "[the festival of the] first day;" for relevant textual variants, see Rabbinovicz [1868–1897: 10.15, 17]). Doubly obscured in most modern editions of the Talmud, Samuel's casual inference appears to be the first known rabbinic testimony to the effect of describing Christianity according to its own terms.

[153] Excerpted from *b.Sanhedrin* 107b and *b.Sotah* 47a, uncensored manuscripts.

[154] On the image of Christianity as a type of idolatry (Hebrew: *avodah zarah*) in postclassical Jewish thought, see Korn (2012: 195–204), who notes than many of the medieval and early modern rabbinic authorities who elected to adhere to the Talmud's characterization of Christianity as a heresy restricted its stigma to would-be Jewish practitioners while acknowledging its advantage as a morally superior choice for gentiles.

Epilogue

The ancient rabbis had an apt parable about memory. A man was walking on the road and was attacked by a wolf. But he survived. So he went and told the story of the wolf. Then he was attacked by a lion. He survived that bout as well. So he forgot about the story of the wolf and told the story of the lion. Later still, the man was attacked by a snake. But, again, he was spared. So he forgot about the stories of the wolf and the lion and proceeded to tell the story of the snake. So it is for the people of Israel. The experiences of our most recent hardships cause us continually to forget the trials of old, if not necessarily completely.[1]

Although I do not mean to liken the Church to a vicious animal, I find this parable apropos of Christianity's impact on the Jewish people in the classical age. Already bitten by Egypt, Assyria, Babylon, Greece, and Rome, their encounters with the Christian kingdoms of Rome and Byzantium were just the latest in a series of dramatic sagas of calamity and perseverance. The Jews were well equipped to confront their latest challenge in stride, ever confident that the danger posed by the wolf someday would be trivialized by the danger of the lion, the danger of the lion by that of the snake, and so forth. Inevitably, the commitment of those old memories to the archives demanded consolidation. Thus was the Christian schism casually relegated to the relatively trivial status it occupied in Jewish historical memory prior to the modern era. A disjunction of tremendous ideological and social complexity that unfolded over great expanses of time and space was condensed into a concise event, an act of apostasy commenced and concluded by Jesus. The rest of the details were inconsequential. For the most part, the Jews compelled to endure the consequences of the schism needed only to know that their faith was the truth and Christianity

---

[1] The parable appears in *t.Berakhot* 1.13 and is repeated in *y.Berakhot* 1.9 (4a) and *b.Berakhot* 13a. See also *Mekhilta* Pisḥa 16, where an abbreviated version is ascribed to the first-century sage Rabbi Shimon bar Yoḥai, and cf. *Mekhilta of Rabbi Shimon bar Yoḥai* 34.3.

the heresy in order to steel their wills against those who would have had them believe otherwise.

Left upon the Jewish historical record as a result of this defensive mentality was but a faint and highly tendentious impression of how the difference between Christian and Jew came to be. But the lurid tales of the Talmud and the *Toledot Yeshu* raised questions that could only be ignored for so long. Of what significance is it to Jews that Jesus and his disciples were of their nation? How did Paul justify his conviction that that nation no longer constituted what it once had? Is it possible for gentiles to claim membership in the people of Israel on grounds different from Jews? Might the Christian transcend his or her heretical assignment to become a friend of the Jew and a partner in theological dialogue? Questions like these consumed early Christian thinkers mindful of the Church's Jewish roots. But they are frustratingly absent from the writings of the Jewish sages who lived through the history in question.

I hope to have shown in these pages that the questions those sages neglected to ask are not impossible for the modern reader to interrogate. Barring the discovery of further evidence, we will never know precisely what the authors of Judaism's earliest recollections of Christianity knew about the phenomenon that they presumed to describe. But careful consideration of the materials in our possession suggests that that initial meeting of Christian and Jew was less a contest of exclusive theological truths than a match of wits between two parties equally unsure of what truly set one apart from the other. That their subsequent efforts to define their respective groups against one another would obscure the common ground beneath their feet was perhaps inevitable. Yet that must not discourage us from seeking to recover that lost ground, to answer those questions about the relationship between Christianity and Judaism once considered too dangerous for either Christian or Jew to ask. Should we hope to overcome the misgivings of those of our predecessors who wished to efface that common ground, we must strive to remember what the authors of the Christian schism so diligently labored to forget.

References

Albeck, Ch. (1959) *Introduction to the Mishnah* [Hebrew]. Jerusalem: Bialik Institute.

Albertz, R. (1994) *A History of Israelite Religion in the Old Testament Period, Vol. 2: From the Exile to the Maccabees.* Louisville, KY: Westminster John Knox.

Alexander, E.S. (2006) *Transmitting Mishnah: The Shaping Influence of Oral Tradition.* Cambridge: Cambridge University Press.

Alexander, P.S. (1992) "'The Parting of the Ways' from the Perspective of Rabbinic Judaism," in *Jews and Christians: The Parting of the Ways, A.D. 70 to 135,* ed. J.D.G. Dunn. Tübingen: Mohr (Siebeck): 1–25.

(2007) "Jewish Believers in Early Rabbinic Literature (2nd to 5th Centuries)," in *Jewish Believers in Jesus: The Early Centuries,* ed. O. Skarsaune and R. Hvalvik. Peabody, MA: Hendrickson: 659–709.

(2010) "Using Rabbinic Literature as a Source for the History of Late-Roman Palestine: Problems and Issues," in *Rabbinic Texts and the History of Late-Roman Palestine,* ed. M. Goodman and P.S. Alexander. London: British Academy: 7–24.

Alon, G. (1980–1984) *The Jews in Their Land in the Talmudic Age (70–640 C.E.),* trans. and ed. G. Levi. 2 Vols. Jerusalem: Magnes.

Ando, C. (2008) *The Matter of the Gods: Religion and the Roman Empire.* Berkeley, CA: University of California Press.

(2011) *Law, Language, and Empire in the Roman Tradition.* Philadelphia, PA: University of Pennsylvania Press.

Appelbaum, A. (2010) *The Rabbis' King-Parables: Midrash from the Third-Century Roman Empire.* Piscataway, NJ: Gorgias.

Applebaum, S. (1989) "Syria-Palaestina as a Province of the Severan Empire," in S. Applebaum, *Judaea in Hellenistic and Roman Times: Historical and Archaeological Essays.* Leiden: Brill: 143–54.

Arnal, W.E. (2005) *The Symbolic Jesus: Historical Scholarship, Judaism and the Construction of Contemporary Identity.* London: Equinox.

Assmann, J. (2011) *Cultural Memory and Early Civilization: Writing, Remembrance, and Political Imagination.* Cambridge: Cambridge University Press.

Audet, J.-P. (1996) "Literary and Doctrinal Affinities of the 'Manual of Discipline'," in *The Didache in Modern Research,* ed. J.A. Draper. Leiden: Brill: 129–47.

Aune, D.E. (1991) "On the Origins of the 'Council of Javneh' Myth," *Journal of Biblical Literature* 110: 491–93.

Avi-Yonah, M. (1976) *The Jews of Palestine: A Political History from the Bar Kokhba War to the Arab Conquest.* Oxford: Blackwell.

Bacher, W. (1899) "Le mot 'Minim' dans le Talmud: Désigne-t-il quelquefois des chrétiens?," *Revue des Études Juives* 38: 38–46.

Bainbridge, W.S. (1997) *The Sociology of Religious Movements.* London: Routledge.

Bakhos, C. (2006) *Ishmael on the Border: Rabbinic Portrayals of the First Arab.* Albany: State University of New York Press.

Bammel, E. (1966–1967) "Christian Origins in Jewish Tradition," *New Testament Studies* 13: 317–35.

Bar-Asher, M. (2002) "Il y avait à Suse un homme juif," *Revue des Études Juives* 161: 227–31.

Barclay, J.M.G. (1995) "Paul among Diaspora Jews: Anomaly or Apostate?," *Journal for the Study of the New Testament* 60: 89–120.

  (1996) "'Do We Undermine the Law?': A Study of Romans 14.1–15.6," in *Paul and the Mosaic Law: The Third Durham-Tübingen Research Symposium on Earliest Christianity and Judaism (Durham, September, 1994),* ed. J.D.G. Dunn. Tübingen: Mohr (Siebeck): 287–308.

Bardy, G. (1934) "Saint Jérôme et ses maîtres hébreux," *Revue bénédictine* 46: 145–64.

Barnes, T.D. (1981) *Constantine and Eusebius.* Cambridge, MA: Harvard University Press.

Baron, S.W. (1952–1983) *A Social and Religious History of the Jews.* 18 Vols., 2nd edn. New York, NY: Columbia University Press.

Basser, H.W. (2000) *Studies in Exegesis: Christian Critiques of Jewish Law and Rabbinic Responses, 70–300 C.E.* Leiden: Brill.

Bauckham, R. (1990) *Jude and the Relatives of Jesus in the Early Church.* Edinburgh: T&T Clark.

  (1995) "James and the Jerusalem Church," in *The Book of Acts in Its Palestinian Setting,* ed. R. Bauckham. Grand Rapids, MI: Eerdmans: 415–80.

  (2003) "The Origin of the Ebionites," in *The Image of the Judaeo-Christians in Ancient Jewish and Christian Literature,* ed. P.J. Tomson and D. Lambers-Petry. Tübingen: Mohr Siebeck: 162–81.

  (2005) "James, Peter, and the Gentiles," in *The Missions of James, Peter, and Paul: Tensions in Early Christianity,* ed. B. Chilton and C.A. Evans. Leiden: Brill: 91–142.

Bauer, W. (1971) *Orthodoxy and Heresy in Earliest Christianity,* trans. and ed. R.A. Kraft and G. Krodel. Philadelphia, PA: Fortress.

Baumgarten, A.I. (1983) "The Name of the Pharisees," *Journal of Biblical Literature* 102: 411–28.

  (1987) "The Pharisaic *Paradosis,*" *Harvard Theological Review* 80: 63–77.

  (1992) "Literary Evidence for Jewish Christianity in the Galilee," in *The Galilee in Late Antiquity,* ed. L.I. Levine. New York, NY: Jewish Theological Seminary of America: 39–50.

  (1997) *The Flourishing of Jewish Sects in the Maccabean Era: An Interpretation.* Leiden: Brill.

Baur, F.C. (1831a) *De Ebionitarum origine et doctrine, ab Essenis repetenda.* Tübingen: Hopferi de l'Orme.

(1831b) "Die Christuspartei in der korinthischen Gemeinde, der Gegensatz des petrinischen und paulinischen Christenthums in der ältesten Kirche, der Apostel Petrus in Rom," *Tübinger Zeitschrift für Theologie* 4: 61–206.

(1845) *Paulus, der Apostel Jesu Christi. Sein Leben und Wirken, seine Briefe und seine Lehre.* Stuttgart: Bechet & Müller.

(1853) *Christenthum und die christliche Kirche der drei ersten Jahrhunderte.* Tübingen: Fues.

Beard, M., J. North, and S. Price (1998) *Religions of Rome, Vol. 1: A History.* Cambridge: Cambridge University Press.

Becker, A.H. (2003) "Beyond the Spatial and Temporal Limes: Questioning the 'Parting of the Ways' Outside the Roman Empire," in *The Ways that Never Parted*, ed. A.H. Becker and A.Y. Reed. Tübingen: Mohr Siebeck: 373–92.

Ben-Chorin, S. (1980) "Die Ketzerformel," in S. Ben-Chorin, *Betendes Judentum: Die Liturgie der Synagoge.* Tübingen: Mohr: 83–99.

(2001) *Brother Jesus: The Nazarene through Jewish Eyes*, trans. J.S. Klein and M. Reinhart. Athens, GA: University of Georgia Press.

Belayche, N. (2001) *Iudaea-Palaestina: The Pagan Cults in Roman Palestine (Second to Fourth Century).* Tübingen: Mohr Siebeck.

Berger, D. (1998) "On the Uses of History in Medieval Jewish Polemic against Christianity: The Quest for the Historical Jesus," in *Jewish History and Jewish Memory: Essays in Honor of Yosef Hayim Yerushalmi*, ed. E. Carlebach, J.M. Efron, and D.N. Myers. Hanover, NH: Brandeis University Press: 25–39.

Berkowitz, B.A. (2005) *Execution and Invention: Death Penalty Discourse in Early Rabbinic and Christian Cultures.* Oxford: Oxford University Press.

(2012) *Defining Jewish Difference: From Antiquity to the Present.* Cambridge: Cambridge University Press.

Betz, H.D. (1995) *The Sermon on the Mount: A Commentary on the Sermon on the Mount, including the Sermon on the Plain (Matthew 5:3–7:27 and Luke 6:20–49).* Minneapolis, MN: Fortress.

Biale, D. (1999) "Counter-History and Jewish Polemics Against Christianity: The *Sefer toldot yeshu* and the *Sefer zerubavel*," *Jewish Social Studies* 6: 131–45.

Bickerman, E.J. (1979) *The God of the Maccabees: Studies on the Meaning and Origin of the Maccabean Revolt*, trans. H.R. Moehring. Leiden: Brill.

Birley, A.R. (1999) *Septimius Severus: The African Emperor.* Rev. ed. London: Routledge.

Blanchetière, F. (2001) *Enquête sur les racines juives du mouvement chrétien (30–135).* Paris: Cerf.

Blenkinsopp, J. (2000–2003) *Isaiah: A New Translation with Introduction and Commentary.* 3 Vols. New York, NY: Doubleday.

(2001) "Was the Pentateuch the Civic and Religious Constitution of the Jewish Ethnos in the Persian Period?" in *Persia and Torah: The Theory of Imperial Authorization of the Pentateuch*, ed. J.W. Watts. Atlanta, GA: Society of Biblical Literature: 41–62.

(2009) *Judaism, the First Phase: The Place of Ezra and Nehemiah in the Origins of Judaism.* Grand Rapids, MI: Eerdmans.

Bobichon, P. (2003) "Persécutions, calomnies, 'Birkat ha-Minim' et émissaires juifs de propagande antichrétienne dans les écrits de Justin Martyr," *Revue des Études Juives* 162: 403–19.

Boccaccini, G. (1991) *Middle Judaism: Jewish Thought, 300 B.C.E. to 200 C.E.* Minneapolis, MN: Fortress.

Bockmuehl, M. (2000) *Jewish Law in Gentile Churches: Halakhah and the Beginning of Christian Public Ethics.* Edinburgh: T&T Clark.

Boer, M.C. de (1998) "The Nazoreans: Living at the Boundary of Judaism and Christianity," in *Tolerance and Intolerance in Early Judaism and Christianity*, ed. G.M. Stanton and G.G. Stroumsa. Cambridge: Cambridge University Press: 239–62.

Bohak, G. (2002) "Ethnic Continuity in the Jewish Diaspora in Antiquity," in *Jews in the Hellenistic and Roman Cities*, ed. J.R. Bartlett. London: Routledge: 175–92.

(2003) "Magical Means for Handling *Minim* in Rabbinic Literature," in *The Image of the Judaeo-Christians in Ancient Jewish and Christian Literature*, ed. P.J. Tomson and D. Lambers-Petry. Tübingen: Mohr Siebeck: 267–79.

(2008) *Ancient Jewish Magic: A History.* Cambridge: Cambridge University Press.

Bourgel, J. (2015) "Reconnaissances 1.27–71, ou la réponse d'un groupe judéo-chrétirn du Judée au désastre du soulèvement de Bar-Kokhba," *New Testament Studies* 61: 30–49.

Boustan (Abusch), R.S. (2003) "Negotiating Difference: Genital Mutilation in Roman Slave Law and the History of the Bar Kokhba Revolt," in *The Bar Kokhba War Reconsidered*, ed. P. Schäfer. Tübingen: Mohr Siebeck: 71–91.

Boyarin, D. (1994) *A Radical Jew: Paul and the Politics of Identity.* Berkeley, CA: University of California Press.

(1999) *Dying for God: Martyrdom and the Making of Christianity and Judaism.* Stanford, CA: Stanford University Press.

(2004) *Border Lines: The Partition of Judaeo-Christianity.* Philadelphia, PA: University of Pennsylvania Press.

(2009) "Rethinking Jewish Christianity: An Argument for Dismantling a Dubious Category (to Which Is Appended a Correction of My *Border Lines*)," *Jewish Quarterly Review* 99: 7–36.

(2012a) *The Jewish Gospels: The Story of the Jewish Christ.* New York, NY: New Press.

(2012b) "Once Again *Birkat Hamminim* Revisited," in *La croisée des chemins revisitée: Quand l' "Église" et la "Synagogue" se sont-elles distinguées? Actes du colloques de Tours 18–19 juin 2010*, ed. S.C. Mimouni and B. Pouderon. Paris: Cerf: 91–105.

Boys, M.C. (2000) *Has God Only One Blessing? Judaism as a Source of Christian Self-Understanding.* New York, NY: Paulist.

Brenner, M. (2010) *Prophets of the Past: Interpreters of Jewish History*, trans. S. Rendall. Princeton, NJ: Princeton University Press.

Broadhead, E.K. (2010) *Jewish Ways of Following Jesus: Redrawing the Religious Map of Antiquity.* Tübingen: Mohr Siebeck.

Brown, R.E., and J.P. Meier (1983) *Antioch and Rome: New Testament Cradles of Catholic Christianity.* New York, NY: Paulist.

Büchler, A. (1956) "The Minim of Sepphoris and Tiberias in the Second and Third Centuries," in *Studies in Jewish History: The Adolf Büchler Memorial Volume*, ed. I. Brodie and J. Rabbinowitz. London: Oxford University Press: 245–74.

Buell, D.K. (2005) *Why This New Race: Ethnic Reasoning in Early Christianity.* New York, NY: Columbia University Press.

Burns, J.E. (2006) "Essene Sectarianism and Social Differentiation in Judaea after 70 C.E.," *Harvard Theological Review* 99: 247–74.

(2007) "The Archaeology of Rabbinic Literature and the Study of Jewish-Christian Relations in Late Antiquity: A Methodological Evaluation," in *Religion, Ethnicity, and Identity in Ancient Galilee: A Region in Transition*, ed. J. Zangenberg, H.W. Attridge, and D.B. Martin. Tübingen: Mohr Siebeck: 403–24.

(2012) "The Relocation of Heresy in a Late Ancient Midrash, or: When in Rome, Do as the Romans Do," *Jewish Studies Quarterly* 19: 129–47.

(2014) "The Watchers Traditions in Targum and Midrash," in *The Watchers in Jewish and Christian Traditions*, ed. A.K. Harkins, K. Coblentz Bautch, and J.C. Endres. Minneapolis, MN: Fortress: 199–216.

Byrskog, S. (1994) *Jesus the Only Teacher: Didactic Authority and Transmission in Ancient Israel, Ancient Judaism and the Matthean Community*. Stockholm: Almqvist & Wiksell.

Cameron, Al. (2011) *The Last Pagans of Rome*. Oxford: Oxford University Press.

Cameron, Av. (2003) "Jews and Heretics: A Category Error?," in *The Ways that Never Parted*, ed. A.H. Becker and A.Y. Reed. Tübingen: Mohr Siebeck: 345–60.

Campbell, B. (2005) "The Severan Dynasty," in *The Cambridge Ancient History, Vol. 12: The Crisis of Empire, A.D. 193–337*, ed. A.K. Bowman, P. Garnsey, and A. Cameron. 2nd edn. Cambridge: Cambridge University Press: 1–27.

Carleton Paget, J. (1999) "Jewish Christianity," in *The Cambridge History of Judaism, Vol. 3: The Early Roman Period*, ed. W. Horbury, W.D. Davies, and J. Sturdy. Cambridge: Cambridge University Press: 731–75.

(2001) "Some Observations on Josephus and Christianity," *Journal of Theological Studies* 52: 539–624.

(2005) "The Four among Jews," in *The Written Gospel*, ed. M. Bockmuehl and D.A. Hagner. Cambridge: Cambridge University Press: 205–21.

(2007) "The Definition of the Terms *Jewish Christian* and *Jewish Christianity* in the History of Research," in *Jewish Believers in Jesus: The Early Centuries*, ed. O. Skarsaune and R. Hvalvik. Peabody, MA: Hendrickson: 22–52.

(2010a) *Jews, Christians and Jewish Christians in Antiquity*. Tübingen: Mohr Siebeck.

(2010b) "The Ebionites in Recent Research." in J. Carleton Paget, *Jews, Christians and Jewish Christians in Antiquity*. Tübingen: Mohr Siebeck: 325–79.

Carr, D.M. (2011) *The Formation of the Hebrew Bible: A New Reconstruction*. Oxford: Oxford University Press.

Castelli, E.A. (2007) *Martyrdom and Memory: Early Christian Culture Making*. New York, NY: Columbia University Press.

Carter, W. (2007) "Matthew's Gospel: Jewish Christianity, Christian Judaism, or Neither?," in *Jewish Christianity Reconsidered: Rethinking Ancient Groups and Texts*, ed. M. Jackson-McCabe. Minneapolis, MN: Fortress: 155–79.

Catchpole, D.R. (1971) *The Trial of Jesus: A Study in the Gospels and Jewish Historiography from 1770 to the Present Day*. Leiden: Brill.

Chaunu, P. (1978) *Histoire quantitative, histoire sérielle*. Paris: Colin.

Chazan, R. (1988) "The Condemnation of the Talmud Reconsidered (1239–1248)," *Proceedings of the American Academy of Jewish Research* 55: 11–30.

(1999) "The Hebrew Report on the Trial of the Talmud: Information and Consolation," in *Le brûlement du Talmud à Paris, 1242–1244*, ed. G. Dahan. Paris: Cerf: 79–93.

(2004) *Fashioning Jewish Identity in Medieval Western Christendom*. Cambridge: Cambridge University Press.

Clarke, G. (2005) "Third-Century Christianity," in *The Cambridge Ancient History, Vol. 12: The Crisis of Empire, A.D. 193–337*, ed. A.K. Bowman, P. Garnsey, and A. Cameron. 2nd edn. Cambridge: Cambridge University Press: 589–671.

Cohen, G.D. (1967) *A Critical Edition with a Translation and Notes of the Book of Tradition (Sefer Ha-Qabbalah) by Abraham ibn Daud*. Philadelphia, PA: Jewish Publication Society of America.

Cohen, J. (1982) *The Friars and the Jews: The Evolution of Medieval Anti-Judaism*. Ithaca, NY: Cornell University Press.

Cohen, N. (1983–1984) "What Did Shmu'el Hakatan Innovate in the *Birkhat Haminim?*" [Hebrew], *Sinai* 94: 57–70.

Cohen, S.J.D. (1984) "The Significance of Yavneh: Pharisees, Rabbis, and the End of Jewish Sectarianism," *Hebrew Union College Annual* 55: 27–53.

(1986) "The Political and Social History of the Jews in Greco-Roman Antiquity: The State of the Question," in *Early Judaism and Its Modern Interpreters*, ed. R.A. Kraft and G.W.E. Nickelsburg. Atlanta, GA: Scholars: 31–56.

(1997) "Were Pharisees and Rabbis the Leaders of Communal Prayer and Torah Study in Antiquity? The Evidence of the New Testament, Josephus, and the Church Fathers," in *The Evolution of the Synagogue: Problems and Progress*, ed. H.C. Kee and L.H. Cohick. Harrisburg, PA: Trinity International: 85–105.

(1999a) *The Beginnings of Jewishness: Boundaries, Varieties, Uncertainties*. Berkeley, CA: University of California Press.

(1999b) "The Rabbi in Second-Century Jewish Society," in *The Cambridge History of Judaism, Vol. 3: The Early Roman Period*, ed. W. Horbury, W.D. Davies, and J. Sturdy. Cambridge: Cambridge University Press: 922–90.

(2005) *Why Aren't Jewish Women Circumcised? Gender and Covenant in Judaism*. Berkeley, CA: University of California Press.

(2014) *From the Maccabees to the Mishnah*. 3rd edn. Louisville, KY: Westminster John Knox.

Cohn, N.S. (2013) *The Memory of the Temple and the Making of the Rabbis*. Philadelphia, PA: University of Pennsylvania Press.

Collins, J.J. (1985) "A Symbol of Otherness: Circumcision and Salvation in the First Century," in *"To See Ourselves as Others See Us": Christians, Jews, "Others" in Late Antiquity*, ed. J. Neusner and E.S. Frerichs. Chico, CA: Scholars: 163–86.

(1998) *The Apocalyptic Imagination: An Introduction to Jewish Apocalyptic Literature*. 2nd edn. Grand Rapids, MI: Eerdmans.

(2000) *Between Athens and Jerusalem: Jewish Identity in the Hellenistic Diaspora*. 2nd edn. Grand Rapids, MI: Eerdmans.

(2001) "Cult and Culture: The Limits of Hellenization in Judea," in *Hellenism in the Land of Israel*, ed. J.J. Collins and G.E. Sterling. Notre Dame, IN: University of Notre Dame Press: 38–61.

(2005) "Hellenistic Judaism in Recent Scholarship," in J.J. Collins, *Jewish Cult and Hellenistic Culture: Essays on the Jewish Encounter with Hellenism and Roman Rule*. Leiden: Brill: 1–20.

(2009) *Beyond the Qumran Community: The Sectarian Movement of the Dead Sea Scrolls*. Grand Rapids, MI: Eerdmans.

Colpe, C. (1987) "Das deutsche Wort 'Judenchristen' und ihm entsprechende historische Sachverhalte," in *Gilgul: Essays on Transformation, Revelation and Permanence in the History of Religions, dedicated to R. J. Zvi Werblowsky*, ed. S. Shaked, D. Shulman, and G.G. Stroumsa. Leiden: Brill: 50–68.

Cowley, A.E. (1923) *Aramaic Papyri of the Fifth Century B.C.* Oxford: Clarendon.

Crown, A.D. (2004) "Judaism and Christianity: The Parting of the Ways," in *When Judaism and Christianity Began: Essays in Memory of Anthony J. Saldarini, Vol. 2: Judaism and Christianity in the Beginning*, ed. A.J. Avery-Peck, D.J. Harrington, and J. Neusner. Leiden: Brill: 545–62.

Cuvillier, É. (2009) "Torah Observance and Radicalization in the First Gospel. Matthew and First-Century Judaism: A Contribution to the Debate," *New Testament Studies* 55: 144–59.

Daniélou, J. (1958) *Théologie du judéo-christianisme*. Paris: Desclée.

Deines, R. (2004) *Die Gerechtigkeit der Tora im Reich des Messias: Mt 5,13–20 als Schlüsseltext der matthäischen Theologie*. Tübingen: Mohr Siebeck.

(2008) "Not the Law but the Messiah: Law and Righteousness in the Gospel of Matthew – An Ongoing Debate," in *Built upon the Rock: Studies in the Gospel of Matthew*, ed. D.M. Gurtner and J. Nolland. Grand Rapids, MI: Eerdmans: 53–84.

De Lange, N.R.M. (1976) *Origen and the Jews: Studies in Jewish-Christian Relations in Third-Century Palestine*. Cambridge: Cambridge University Press.

(1998) "James Parkes: A Centenary Lecture," in *Cultures of Ambivalence and Contempt: Studies in Jewish-Non-Jewish Relations. Essays in Honour of the Centenary of the Birth of James Parkes*, ed. S. Jones, T. Kushner, and S. Pearce. London: Vallentine Mitchell: 31–49.

Del Verme, M. (2004) *Didache and Judaism: Jewish Roots of an Ancient Christian-Jewish Work*. New York, NY: T&T Clark.

Destro, A. and M. Pesce (2012) "From Jesus Movement to Christianity: A Model for the Interpretation, Cohabitation and Separation of Jews and Christians," in *La croisée des chemins revisitée: Quand l' "Église" et la "Synagogue" se sont-elles distinguées? Actes du colloques de Tours 18–19 juin 2010*, ed. S.C. Mimouni and B. Pouderon. Paris: Cerf: 21–49.

Deutsch, Y. (2011) "The Second Life of the Life of Jesus: Christian Reception of the *Toledot Yeshu*," in *Toledot Yeshu ("The Life Story of Jesus") Revisited*, ed. P. Schäfer, M. Meerson, and Y. Deutsch. Tübingen: Mohr Siebeck: 283–95.

Doering, L. (1999) *Schabbat: Sabbathalacha und -praxis im antiken Judentum und Urchristentum*. Tübingen: Mohr Siebeck.

(2010) "Sabbath Laws in the New Testament Gospels," in *The New Testament and Rabbinic Literature*, ed. R. Bieringer, F. García Martínez, D. Pollefeyt, and P.J. Tomson. Leiden: Brill: 207–53.

Dohrmann, N.B. (2013) "Law and Imperial Idioms: Rabbinic Legalism in the Roman World," in *Jews, Christians, and the Roman Empire: The Poetics of Power in Late Antiquity*, ed. N.B. Dohrmann and A.Y. Reed. Philadelphia, PA: University of Pennsylvania Press: 63–78.

Doran, R. (1981) *Temple Propaganda: The Purpose and Character of 2 Maccabees*. Washington, DC: Catholic Biblical Association of America.

(1990) "Jason's Gymnasion," in *Of Scribes and Scrolls: Studies on the Hebrew Bible, Intertestamental Judaism, and Christian Origins presented to John Strugnell on the Occasion of His Sixtieth Birthday*, ed. H.W. Attridge, J.J. Collins, and T.H. Tobin. Lanham, MD: University Press of America: 99–109.

(2001) "The High Cost of a Good Education," in *Hellenism in the Land of Israel*, ed. J.J. Collins and G.E. Sterling. Notre Dame, IN: University of Notre Dame Press: 94–115.

(2011) "The Persecution of Judeans by Antiochus IV: The Significance of 'Ancestral Laws'," in *The "Other" in Second Temple Judaism: Essays in Honor of John J. Collins*, ed. D.C. Harlow, K. Martin Hogan, M. Goff, and J.S. Kaminsky. Grand Rapids, MI: Eerdmans: 423–33.

(2012) *2 Maccabees: A Critical Commentary*. Minneapolis, MN: Fortress.

Drake, S. (2013) *Slandering the Jew: Sexuality and Difference in Early Christian Texts*. Philadelphia, PA: University of Pennsylvania Press.

Draper, J.A. (1996a) "Christian Self-Definition against the 'Hypocrites' in Didache VIII," in *The Didache in Modern Research*, ed. J.A. Draper. Leiden: Brill: 223–43.

(1996b) "The Didache in Modern Research: An Overview," in *The Didache in Modern Research*, ed. J.A. Draper. Leiden: Brill: 1–42.

(1996c) "Torah and Troublesome Apostles in the *Didache* Community," in *The Didache in Modern Research*, ed. J.A. Draper. Leiden: Brill: 340–63.

(2003) "A Continuing Enigma: The 'Yoke of the Lord' in Didache 6.2-3 and Early Jewish-Christian Relations," in *The Image of the Judaeo-Christians in Ancient Jewish and Christian Literature*, ed. P.J. Tomson and D. Lambers-Petry. Tübingen: Mohr Siebeck: 106–23.

(2005) "Do the Didache and Matthew Reflect an 'Irrevocable Parting of the Ways' with Judaism?," in *Matthew and the Didache: Two Documents from the Same Jewish-Christian Milieu?*, ed. H. van de Sandt. Assen: Van Gorcum: 217–41.

(2007) "The Holy Vine of David Made Known to the Gentiles through God's Servant Jesus: 'Christian Judaism' in the *Didache*," in *Jewish Christianity Reconsidered: Rethinking Ancient Groups and Texts*, ed. M. Jackson-McCabe. Minneapolis, MN: Fortress: 257–83.

Dunn, J.D.G. (1983) "The New Perspective on Paul," *Bulletin of the John Rylands University Library of Manchester* 65: 95–122.

(1990) "The Theology of Galatians," in J.D.G. Dunn, *Jesus, Paul and the Law: Studies in Mark and Galatians*. London: SPCK: 242–64.

ed. (1992a) *Jews and Christians: The Parting of the Ways, A.D. 70 to 135. The Second Durham-Tübingen Research Symposium on Earliest Christianity and Judaism (Durham, September, 1989)*. Tübingen: Mohr (Siebeck).

(1992b) "The Question of Anti-Semitism in the New Testament Writings of the Period," in *Jews and Christians: The Parting of the Ways, A.D. 70 to 135. The Second Durham-Tübingen Research Symposium on Earliest Christianity and Judaism (Durham, September, 1989)*, ed. J.D.G. Dunn. Tübingen: Mohr (Siebeck): 177–211.

(2006) *The Partings of the Ways between Christianity and Judaism and their Significance for the Character of Christianity*. 2nd edn. London: SCM.

(2008) *The New Perspective on Paul*. Rev. ed. Grand Rapids, MI: Eerdmans.

Eastman, D.L. (2011) *Paul the Martyr: The Cult of the Apostle in the Latin West*. Atlanta, GA: Society of Biblical Literature.

Eckhardt, B., ed. (2012) *Jewish Identity and Politics between the Maccabees and Bar Kokhba: Groups, Normativity, and Rituals*. Leiden: Brill.

Edrei, A., and D. Mendels (2007) "A Split Jewish Diaspora: Its Dramatic Consequences," *Journal for the Study of the Pseudepigrapha* 16: 91–137.

Eisenbaum, P. (2005) "Paul, Polemics, and the Problem of Essentialism," *Biblical Interpretation* 13: 224–38.

Ekenberg, A. (2007) "Evidence for Jewish Believers in 'Church Orders' and Liturgical Texts," in *Jewish Believers in Jesus: The Early Centuries*, ed. O. Skarsaune and R. Hvalvik. Peabody, MA: Hendrickson: 640–58.

Eliav, Y.Z. (2005) *God's Mountain: The Temple Mount in Time, Place, and Memory*. Baltimore, MD: Johns Hopkins University Press.

(2009) "Secularism, Hellenism, and Rabbis in Antiquity," in *Religion or Ethnicity? Jewish Identities in Evolution*, ed. Z. Gitelman. New Brunswick, NJ: Rutgers University Press: 7–23.

Elliott, N. (2011) "Romans," in *The Oxford Encyclopedia of the Books of the Bible*, ed. M.D. Coogan. 2 Vols. Oxford: Oxford University Press: 2.271–79.

Elman, Y. (2004) "Order, Sequence, and Selection: The Mishnah's Anthological Choices," in *The Anthology in Jewish Literature*, ed. D. Stern. Oxford: Oxford University Press: 53–80.

Elukin, J.M. (1998) "A New Essenism: Heinrich Graetz and Mysticism," *Journal of the History of Ideas* 59: 135–48.

Epstein, J.N. (1948) *Introduction to the Mishnaic Text* [Hebrew]. 2 Vols. Jerusalem: Magnes.

Eshel, H. (2008) "The Changing Notion of the Enemy and Its Impact on the Pesharim," in H. Eshel, *The Dead Sea Scrolls and the Hasmonean State*. Grand Rapids, Mich.: Eerdmans: 163–79.

Evans, C.A. (2000) "Root Causes of the Jewish-Christian Rift from Jesus to Justin," in *Christian-Jewish Relations through the Centuries*, ed. S.E. Porter and B.W.R. Pearson. Sheffield: Sheffield Academic: 20–35.

Feldman, L.H. (1993) *Jew and Gentile in the Ancient World: Attitudes and Interactions from Alexander to Justinian*. Princeton, NJ: Princeton University Press.

Fine, S. (1999) "Non-Jews in the Synagogues of Late-Antique Palestine: Rabbinic and Archeological Evidence," in *Jews, Christians, and Polytheists in the Ancient Synagogue: Cultural Interaction during the Greco-Roman Period*, ed. S. Fine. London: Routledge: 224–42.

Finkelstein, L. (1925–1926) "The Development of the Amidah," *Jewish Quarterly Review* 16: 1–43, 127–70.

Firestone, R. (2012) *Holy War in Judaism: The Fall and Rise of a Controversial Idea*. Oxford: Oxford University Press.

Fishman, T. (2011) *Becoming the People of the Talmud: Oral Torah as Written Tradition in Medieval Jewish Cultures*. Philadelphia, PA: University of Pennsylvania Press.

Fleischer, E. (1989–1990) "On the Beginnings of Jewish Obligatory Prayer" [Hebrew], *Tarbiz* 59: 397–441.

Flusser, D. (1988) "The Jewish-Christian Schism," in D. Flusser, *Judaism and the Origins of Christianity*, Jerusalem: Magnes: 617–44.

(2007) "4QMMT and the Benediction against the *Minim*," in idem, *Judaism of the Second Temple Period*, Vol. 1: *Qumran and Apocalypticism*, trans. A. Yadin. Grand Rapids, MI: Eerdmans: 70–118.

Foakes Jackson, F.J., ed. (1912) *The Parting of the Roads: Studies in the Development of Judaism and Early Christianity*. London: Arnold.

Fonrobert, C.E. (2000) *Menstrual Purity: Rabbinic and Christian Reconstructions of Biblical Gender*. Stanford, CA: Stanford University Press.

(2001) "The *Didascalia Apostolorum*: A Mishnah for the Disciples of Jesus," *Journal of Early Christian Studies* 9: 483–509.

Foster, P. (2004) *Community, Law and Mission in Matthew's Gospel*. Tübingen: Mohr Siebeck.

Foucault, M. (1972) *The Archaeology of Knowledge and the Discourse on Language*, trans. A.M. Sheridan Smith. New York, NY: Pantheon.

Fraade, S.D. (1992) "Rabbinic Views on the Practice of Targum, and Multilingualism in the Jewish Galilee of the Third-Sixth Centuries," in *The Galilee in Late Antiquity*, ed. L.I. Levine. New York, NY: Jewish Theological Seminary of America: 253–86.

(1994) "Navigating the Anomalous: Non-Jews at the Intersection of Early Rabbinic Law and Narrative," in *The Other in Jewish Thought and History: Constructions of Jewish Culture and Identity*, ed. L.J. Silberstein and R.L. Cohn. New York, NY: New York University Press: 145–65.

(2000) "To Whom It May Concern: 4QMMT and Its Addressee(s)," *Revue de Qumran* 19: 507–26.

(2007) "Rabbinic Polysemy and Pluralism Revisited: Between Praxis and Thematization," *AJS Review* 31: 1–40.

(2009) "The Temple as a Marker of Jewish Identity before and after 70 CE: The Role of the Holy Vessels in Rabbinic Memory and Imagination," in *Jewish Identities in Antiquity: Studies in Memory of Menahem Stern*, ed. L.I. Levine and D.R. Schwartz. Tübingen: Mohr Siebeck: 237–65.

(2011) *Legal Fictions: Studies of Law and Narrative in the Discursive Worlds of Ancient Jewish Sectarians and Sages*. Leiden: Brill.

Fredriksen, P. (2003) "What 'Parting of the Ways'? Jews, Gentiles and the Ancient Mediterranean City," in *The Ways that Never Parted*, ed. A.H. Becker and A.Y. Reed. Tübingen: Mohr Siebeck: 35–63.

(2008) *Augustine and the Jews: A Christian Defense of Jews and Judaism*. New York, NY: Doubleday.

Fredriksen, P., and O. Irshai. (2006) "Christian Anti-Judaism: Polemics and Policies," in *The Cambridge History of Judaism, Vol. 4: The Late Roman-Rabbinic Period*, ed. S.T. Katz. Cambridge: Cambridge University Press: 977–1034.

Fredriksen, P., and A. Reinhartz, eds. (2002) *Jesus, Judaism and Christian Anti-Judaism: Reading the New Testament after the Holocaust*. Louisville, KY: Westminster John Knox.

Frenkel, Y. (2001) *The Aggadic Narrative: Harmony of Form and Content* [Hebrew]. Tel-Aviv: ha-Kibbutz ha-Meuhad.

Frey, J., D.R. Schwartz, and S. Gripentrog, eds. (2007) *Jewish Identity in the Greco-Roman World/Jüdische Identität in der griechisch-römischen Welt*. Leiden: Brill.

Freyne, S. (1985) "Vilifying the Other and Defining the Self: Matthew's and John's Anti-Jewish Polemic in Focus," in *"To See Ourselves as Others See Us": Christians, Jews, "Others" in Late Antiquity*, ed. J. Neusner and E.S. Frerichs. Chico, CA: Scholars: 117–43.

(2004) *Jesus, a Jewish Galilean: A New Reading of the Jesus-Story*. London: T&T Clark.

Friedländer, M. (1898) *Vorchristliche jüdischen Gnosticismus*. Göttingen: Vandenhoeck & Ruprecht.

Friedman, J., J.C. Hoff, and R. Chazan. *The Trial of the Talmud: Paris, 1240*. Toronto, ON: Pontifical Institute of Mediaeval Studies.

Friedman, S. (1993a) "The Ancient Tosefta: On the Parallel Development of the Mishnah and the Tosefta (a): All the Sanctified Writings (Sabbath 16:1)" [Hebrew], *Tarbiz* 62: 313–38.

(1993b) "The Holy Scriptures Defile the Hands: The Transformation of a Biblical Concept in Rabbinic Theology," in *Minhah Le-Nahum: Biblical and Other Studies Presented to Nahum M. Sarna in Honour of His 70th Birthday*, ed. M. Brettler and M. Fishbane. Sheffield: JSOT: 117–32.

(1999) "The Primacy of Tosefta to Mishnah in Synoptic Parallels," in *Introducing Tosefta: Textual, Intratextual and Intertextual Studies*, ed. H. Fox and T. Meacham. Hoboken, NJ: Ktav: 99–121.

(2002) *The Ancient Tosefta, Pesaḥ Rishon: Synoptic Parallels of Mishnah and Tosefta Analyzed with a Methodological Introduction* [Hebrew]. Ramat-Gan: Bar-Ilan University Press.

Frymer-Kensky, T., D. Novak, P. Ochs, D.F. Sandmel, and M.A. Signer, eds. (2000) *Christianity in Jewish Terms*. Boulder, CO: Westview.

Funkenstein, A. (1993) *Perceptions of Jewish History*. Berkeley, CA: University of California Press.

Fürst, A. (1999) *Augustins Briefwechsel mit Hieronymus*. Münster: Aschendorffsche.

Gager, J.G. (1975) *Kingdom and Community: The Social World of Early Christianity*. Englewood Cliffs, NJ: Prentice-Hall.

(1986) "Jews, Gentiles, and Synagogues in the Book of Acts," *Harvard Theological Review* 79: 91–99.

(1993) "The Parting of the Ways: A View from the Perspective of Early Christianity: 'A Christian Perspective'," in *Interwoven Destinies: Jews and Christians Through the Ages*, ed. E.J. Fisher. New York, NY: Paulist: 62–73.

(2000) *Reinventing Paul*. Oxford: Oxford University Press.

Gale, A.M. (2005) *Redefining Ancient Borders: The Jewish Scribal Framework of Matthew's Gospel*. New York, NY: T&T Clark.

Garnsey, P. (2004) "Roman Citizenship and Roman Law in the Late Empire," in *Approaching Late Antiquity: The Transformation from Early to Late Empire*, ed. S. Swain and M. Edwards. Oxford: Oxford University Press: 133–55.

Garsoïan, N.G., trans. (1989) *The Epic Histories Attributed to P'awstos Buzand (Buzandaran Patmuk'iwnk')*. Cambridge, MA: Harvard University Press.

Gaston, L. (1987) *Paul and the Torah*. Vancouver, BC: University of British Columbia Press.

Geiger, A. (1864–1871) *Das Judenthum und seine Geschichte*. 3 Vols. Breslau: Schletter.

Geiger, J. (2002a) "The Hasmonaeans and Hellenistic Succession," *Journal of Jewish Studies* 53: 1–17.

(2002b) "Language, Culture and Identity in Ancient Palestine," in *Greek Romans and Roman Greeks: Studies in Cultural Interactions*, ed. E.N. Ostenfeld. Aarhus: Aarhus University Press: 233–46.

Geller, M.J. (1977) "Jesus' Theurgic Powers: Parallels in the Talmud and Incantation Bowls," *Journal of Jewish Studies* 28: 141–55.

Gerdmar, A. (2009) *Roots of Theological Anti-Semitism: German Biblical Interpretation and the Jews, from Herder and Semler to Kittel and Bultmann*. Leiden: Brill.

Gero, S. (1994) "The Stern Master and His Wayward Disciple: A 'Jesus' Story in the Talmud and in Christian Hagiography," *Journal for the Study of Judaism* 25: 287–311.

Gevaryahu, H.M.I. (1958–1959) "Birkat ha-Minim" [Hebrew], *Sinai* 44: 367–76.

Ginzberg, L. (1909) *Yerushalmi Fragments from the Genizah*, Vol. 1 [Hebrew]. New York, NY: Jewish Theolgical Seminary of America.

Gitelman, Z., ed. (2009) *Religion or Ethnicity? Jewish Identities in Evolution*. New Brunswick, NJ: Rutgers University Press.

Goldberg, A. (1987a) "The Mishna: A Study Book of Halakha," in *The Literature of the Sages, First Part: Oral Tora, Halakha, Mishna, Tosefta, Talmud, External Tractates*, ed. S. Safrai. Assen: Van Gorcum: 211–62.

(1987b) "The Tosefta: Companion to the Mishna," in *The Literature of the Sages, First Part: Oral Tora, Halakha, Mishna, Tosefta, Talmud, External Tractates*, ed. S. Safrai. Assen: Van Gorcum: 283–302.

Goldenberg, R. (1998) *The Nations That Know Thee Not: Ancient Jewish Attitudes toward Other Religions*. New York, NY: New York University Press.

(2006) "The Destruction of the Jerusalem Temple: Its Meaning and Its Consequences," in *The Cambridge History of Judaism, Vol. 4: The Late Roman-Rabbinic Period*, ed. S.T. Katz. Cambridge: Cambridge University Press: 191–205.

Goldin, J. (1966) "The End of Ecclesiastes: Literal Exegesis and Its Transformation," in *Biblical Motifs: Origins and Transformations*, ed. A. Altmann. Cambridge, MA: Harvard University Press: 135–58.

Goldschmidt, D., ed. (1971) *Seder Rav Amram Gaon* [Hebrew]. Jerusalem: Mosad ha-Rav Kook.

Goodblatt, D. (1994) *The Monarchic Principle: Studies in Jewish Self-Government in Antiquity*. Tübingen: Mohr (Siebeck).

(2006) *Elements of Ancient Jewish Nationalism*. Cambridge: Cambridge University Press.

(2012) "Varieties of Identity in Late Second Temple Judah (200 B.C.E.-135 C.E.)," in *Jewish Identity and Politics between the Maccabees and Bar Kokhba: Groups, Normativity, and Rituals*, ed. B. Eckhardt. Leiden: Brill: 11–27.

Goodman, M. (1983) *State and Society in Roman Galilee, A.D. 132–212*. Totowa, NJ: Rowman & Allanheld

(1987) *The Ruling Class of Judaea: The Origins of the Jewish Revolt against Rome, A.D. 66–70*. Cambridge: Cambridge University Press.

(1989) "Nerva, the *Fiscus Judaicus* and Jewish Identity," *Journal of Roman Studies* 79: 40–44.

(1990) "Sacred Scripture and 'Defiling the Hands'," *Journal of Theological Studies* 41: 99–107.

(1992) "Diaspora Reactions to the Destruction of the Temple," in *Jews and Christians: The Parting of the Ways, A.D. 70–135. The Second Durham-Tübingen Research Symposium on Earliest Christianity and Judaism (Durham, September, 1989)*, ed. J.D.G. Dunn. Tübingen: Mohr (Siebeck): 27–38.

(1994) "Sadducees and Essenes after 70 CE," in *Crossing the Boundaries: Essays in Biblical Interpretation in Honor of Michael D. Goulder*, ed. S.E. Porter, P. Joyce, and D.E. Orton. Leiden: Brill: 347–56.

(1996) "The Function of Minim in Early Rabbinic Judaism," in *Geschichte-Tradition-Reflexion: Festschrift für Martin Hengel zum 70. Geburtstag*, ed. H. Cancik, H. Lichtenberger, and P. Schäfer, Vol. 1: *Judentum*, ed. P. Schäfer. 3 Vols. Tübingen: Mohr (Siebeck): 501–10.

(2000a) "Josephus and Variety in First-Century Judaism," in *Proceedings of the Israel Academy of Sciences and Humanities VII.6*. Jerusalem: Israel Academy of Sciences and Humanities: 201–13

(2000b) "Palestinian Rabbis and the Conversion of Constantine to Christianity," in *The Talmud Yerushalmi and Graeco-Roman Culture*, Vol. 2, ed. P. Schäfer and C. Hezser. Tübingen: Mohr Siebeck: 1–9.

(2007) *Rome and Jerusalem: The Clash of Ancient Civilizations.* New York, NY: Knopf.

(2009) "Religious Variety and the Temple in the Late Second Temple Period and Its Aftermath," *Journal of Jewish Studies* 60: 202–13.

Grabbe, L.L. (1999) "Israel's Historical Reality after the Exile," in *The Crisis of Israelite Religion: Transformation of Religious Tradition in Exilic and Post-Exilic Times*, ed. B. Becking and M.C.A. Korpel. Leiden: Brill: 9–32.

Graetz, H. (1846) *Gnosticismus und Judenthum.* Krotoschin: Monasch.

(1853–1875) *Geschichte der Juden von den ältesten Zeiten bis auf die Gegenwart, aus den Quellen neu bearbeitet.* 11 Vols. Leipzig: Leiner.

(1891–1898) *History of the Jews: From the Earliest Times to the Present Day*, trans. B. Löwy. 6 Vols. Philadelphia, PA: Jewish Publication Society of America.

Gruen, E.S. (1998) *Heritage and Hellenism: The Reinvention of Jewish Tradition.* Berkeley, CA: University of California Press.

(2002) *Diaspora: Jews amidst Greeks and Romans.* Cambridge, MA: Harvard University Press.

Gruenwald, I. (1981) "The Problem of the Anti-Gnostic Polemic in Rabbinic Literature," in *Studies in Gnosticism and Hellenistic Religions Presented to Gilles Quispel on the Occasion of His 65th Birthday*, ed. R. Van den Broek and M.J. Vermaseren. Leiden: Brill: 171–89.

Gurtner, D.M. (2008) "Matthew's Theology of the Temple and the 'Parting of the Ways': Christian Origins and the First Gospel," in *Built upon the Rock: Studies in the Gospel of Matthew*, ed. D.M. Gurtner and J. Nolland. Grand Rapids, MI: Eerdmans: 128–53.

Haar Romeny, Bas ter. (2005) "Hypotheses on the Development of Judaism and Christianity in Syria in the Period after 70 C.E.," in *Matthew and the Didache: Two Documents from the Same Jewish-Christian Milieu?*, ed. H. van de Sandt. Assen: Van Gorcum: 13–33.

Hadas-Lebel, M. (2006) *Jerusalem against Rome*, trans. R. Fréchet. Leuven: Peeters.

Hagner, D.A. (2003) "Matthew: Apostate, Reformer, Revolutionary?," *New Testament Studies* 49: 193–209.

(2012) "Another Look at 'The Parting of the Ways'," in *Earliest Christian History: History, Literature, and Theology. Essays from the Tyndale Fellowship in Honor of Martin Hengel*, ed. M.F. Bird and J. Maston. Tübingen: Mohr Siebeck: 381–427.

Häkkinen, S. (2005) "Ebionites," in *A Companion to Second-Century Christian 'Heretics'*, ed. A. Marjanen and P. Luomanen. Leiden: Brill: 247–78.

Halbwachs, M. (1992) *On Collective Memory*, trans. L.A. Coser. Chicago, IL: University of Chicago Press.

Halivni, D.W. (1986) *Midrash, Mishnah, and Gemara: The Jewish Predilection for Justified Law.* Cambridge, MA: Harvard University Press.

Hall, J.M. (2002) *Hellenicity: Between Ethnicity and Culture.* Chicago, IL: University of Chicago Press.

Hammer, R. (1985) "A Rabbinic Response to the Post Bar Kochba Era: The Sifre to Ha-azinu," *Proceedings of the American Academy of Jewish Research* 52: 37–53.

Hanson, P.D. (1979) *The Dawn of Apocalyptic: The Historical and Sociological Roots of Apocalyptic Eschatology.* Rev. ed. Philadelphia, PA: Fortress.

Hare, D.R.A. (2000) "How Jewish Is the Gospel of Matthew?," *Catholic Biblical Quarterly* 62: 264–77.

Harnack, A. von (1909–1920) *Lehrbuch der Dogmengeschichte.* 3 Vols. 4th edn. Tübingen: Mohr.

Harries, J. (1999) *Law and Empire in Late Antiquity.* Cambridge: Cambridge University Press.

Harris, H. (1975) *The Tübingen School.* Oxford: Clarendon.

Harris, J.R. (1891) *The Apology of Aristides on Behalf of the Christians.* Cambridge: Cambridge University Press.

Harvey, G. (1996) *The True Israel: Uses of the Names Jew, Hebrew and Israel in Ancient Jewish and Early Christian Literature.* Leiden: Brill.

Hasan-Rokem, G. (2007) "An Almost Invisible Presence: Multilingual Puns in Rabbinic Literature," in *The Cambridge Companion to the Talmud and Rabbinic Literature,* ed. C.E. Fonrobert and M.S. Jaffee. Cambridge: Cambridge University Press: 222–39.

Hauptman, J. (2005) *Rereading the Mishnah: A New Approach to Ancient Jewish Texts.* Tübingen: Mohr Siebeck.

Hayes, C. (1998) "Displaced Self-Perceptions: The Deployment of *Mînîm* and Romans in B. Sanhedrin 90b–91a," in *Religious and Ethnic Communities in Later Roman Palestine,* ed. H. Lapin. College Park, MD: University Press of Maryland: 249–89.

(2002) *Gentile Impurities and Jewish Identities: Intermarriage and Conversion from the Bible to the Talmud.* Oxford: Oxford University Press.

(2007) "The 'Other' in Rabbinic Literature," in *The Cambridge Companion to the Talmud and Rabbinic Literature,* ed. C.E. Fonrobert and M.S. Jaffee. Cambridge: Cambridge University Press: 243–69.

(2011) "Legal Realism and the Fashioning of Sectarians in Jewish Antiquity," in *Sects and Sectarianism in Jewish History,* ed. S. Stern. Leiden: Brill: 119–46.

Hayman, A.P. (1985) "The Image of the Jew in Syriac Anti-Jewish Polemical Literature," in *"To See Ourselves as Others See Us": Christians, Jews, "Others" in Late Antiquity,* ed. J. Neusner and E.S. Frerichs. Chico, CA: Scholars: 423–41.

Heinemann, J. (1977) *Prayer in the Talmud: Forms and Patterns,* trans. R.S. Sarason. Berlin: De Gruyter.

Hekster, O. (2008) *Rome and Its Empire, AD 193–284.* Edinburgh: Edinburgh University Press.

Hengel, M. (1974) *Judaism and Hellenism: Studies in Their Encounter in Palestine During the Early Hellenistic Period,* trans. J. Bowden. 2 Vols. Philadelphia, PA: Fortress.

(2002) "Paul in Arabia," *Bulletin for Biblical Research* 12: 47–66.

Hengel, M., and A.M. Schwemer (1997) *Paul between Damascus and Antioch: The Unknown Years,* trans. J. Bowden. Louisville, KY: Westminster John Knox.

Hengel, M., and R. Deines (1995) "E. P. Sanders' 'Common Judaism', Jesus, and the Pharisees," *Journal of Theological Studies* 46: 1–70.

Hennings, R. (1994) *Der Briefwechsel zwischen Augustinus und Hieronymus und ihr Streit um den Kanon des alten Testaments und die Auslegung von Gal. 2, 11–14.* Leiden: Brill.

Henshke, D. (1999) "Parashat ha-Ibbur and the Blessing of the Apostates" [Hebrew], in *From Qumran to Cairo: Studies in the History of Prayer*, ed. J. Tabory. Jerusalem: Orḥot: 75–102

Herford, R.T. (1903) *Christianity in Talmud and Midrash*. London: Williams & Norgate.

Heschel, S. (1998) *Abraham Geiger and the Jewish Jesus*. Chicago, IL: University of Chicago Press.

Hess, J.M. (2002) *Germans, Jews and the Claims of Modernity*. New Haven, CT: Yale University Press.

Hezser, C. (1997) *The Social Structure of the Rabbinic Movement in Roman Palestine*. Tübingen: Mohr Siebeck.

  (1998) "The Codification of Legal Knowledge in Late Antiquity: The Talmud Yerushalmi and Roman Law Codes," in *The Talmud Yerushalmi and Graeco-Roman Culture*, Vol. 1, ed. P. Schäfer. Tübingen: Mohr Siebeck: 581–641.

Himmelfarb, M. (1993) "The Parting of the Ways Reconsidered: Diversity in Judaism and Jewish-Christian Relations in the Roman Empire: 'A Jewish Perspective'," in *Interwoven Destinies: Jews and Christians Through the Ages*, ed. E.J. Fisher. New York, NY: Paulist: 47–61

  (1998) "Judaism and Hellenism in 2 Maccabees," *Poetics Today* 19: 19–40.

  (2006) *A Kingdom of Priests: Ancestry and Merit in Ancient Judaism*. Philadelphia, PA: University of Pennsylvania Press.

Hirshman, M. (2009) *The Stabilization of Rabbinic Culture, 100 C.E.–350 C.E.: Texts on Education and Their Late Antique Context*. Oxford: Oxford University Press.

Holum, K.G. (1998) "Identity and the Late Antique City: The Case of Caesarea," in *Religious and Ethnic Communities in Later Roman Palestine*, ed. H. Lapin. College Park, MD: University Press of Maryland: 157–77.

Honigman, S. (2014) *Tales of High Priests and Taxes: The Books of the Maccabees and the Judean Rebellion against Antiochus IV*. Berkeley, CA: University of California Press.

Hopkins, K. (1998) "Christian Number and Its Implications," *Journal of Early Christian Studies* 6: 185–226.

Horbury, W. (1982) "The Benediction of the *Minim* and Early Jewish-Christian Controversy," *Journal of Theological Studies* 33: 19–61.

  (1983) "The Hebrew Text of Matthew in Shem Tob ibn Shaprut's *Eben Bohan*," *Sefarad* 43: 221–37.

  (1985) "Extirpation and Excommunication," *Vetus Testamentum* 35: 13–38.

  (2006) "Beginnings of Christianity in the Holy Land," in *Christians and Christianity in the Holy Land: From the Origins to the Latin Kingdoms*, ed. O. Limor and G.G. Stroumsa. Turnhout: Brepols: 7–89.

  (2010a) "Rabbinic Perceptions of Christianity and the History of Roman Palestine," in *Rabbinic Texts and the History of Late-Roman Palestine*, ed. M. Goodman and P.S. Alexander. London: British Academy: 353–76.

  (2010b) "The New Testament and Rabbinic Study: A Historical Sketch," in *The New Testament and Rabbinic Literature*, ed. R. Bieringer, F. García Martínez, D. Pollefeyt, and P.J. Tomson. Leiden: Brill: 1–40.

Horrell, D.G. (2000) "Early Jewish Christianity," in *The Early Christian World*, ed. P.F. Esler. 2 Vols. London: Routledge: 1.136–67.

Hort, F.J.A. (1894) *Judaistic Christianity: A Course of Lectures*. London: Macmillan.

Houtman, A. (1996) *Mishnah and Tosefta: A Synoptic Comparison of the Tractates Berakhot and Shebiit*. 2 Vols. Tübingen: Mohr (Siebeck).

Iggers, G.G. (1997) *Historiography in the Twentieth Century: From Scientific Objectivity to the Postmodern Challenge*. Hanover, NH: Wesleyan University Press

Instone-Brewer, D. (2003) "The Eighteen Benedictions and the *Minim* before 70 CE," *Journal of Theological Studies* 54: 25–44.

Irshai, O. (1982) "Rabbi Abbahu Said: If a Man Should Say to You 'I Am a God,' He is a Liar" [Hebrew], *Zion* 47: 173–77.

(2006) "From Oblivion to Fame: The History of the Palestinian Church (135–303 CE)," in *Christians and Christianity in the Holy Land: From the Origins to the Latin Kingdoms*, ed. O. Limor and G.G. Stroumsa. Turnhout: Brepols: 91–139.

(2012) "Confronting a Christian Empire: Jewish Life and Culture in the World of Early Byzantium," in *Jews in Byzantium: Dialectics of Minority and Majority Cultures*, ed. R. Bonfil, O. Irshai, G.G. Stroumsa, and R. Talgam. Leiden: Brill: 17–64.

Isaac, B. (1998) "Roman Colonies in Judaea: The Foundation of Aelia Capitolina," in B. Isaac, *The Near East under Roman Rule: Selected Papers*. Leiden: Brill: 87–108.

Israel, J., ed. (2007) *Benedict de Spinoza: Theological-Political Treatise*, trans. M. Silverthorne and J. Israel. Cambridge: Cambridge University Press.

Jackson-McCabe, M. (2007) "What's in a Name? The Problem of 'Jewish Christianity'," in *Jewish Christianity Reconsidered: Rethinking Ancient Groups and Texts*, ed. M. Jackson-McCabe. Minneapolis, MN: Fortress: 7–38.

Jacobs, A.S. (2004) *Remains of the Jews: The Holy Land and Christian Empire in Late Antiquity*. Stanford, CA: Stanford University Press.

(2012) *Christ Circumcised: A Study in Early Christian History and Difference*. Philadelphia, PA: University of Pennsylvania Press.

Jacobs, M. (1995) *Die Institution des jüdischen Patriarchen: Eine quellen- und traditionskritische Studie zur Geschichte der Juden in der Spätantike*. Tübingen: Mohr (Siebeck).

Jaffé, D. (2003) "Jésus dans le Talmud: Le texte sur Josué ben Parahyah et son disciple Jésus réexaminé," *Pardès* 35: 79–92.

(2005) *Le judaïsme et l'avènement du christianisme: Orthodoxie et hétérodoxie dans la littérature talmudique Iᵉʳ-IIᵉ siècle*. Paris: Cerf.

Jaffee, M.S. (2001) *Torah in the Mouth: Writing and Oral Tradition in Palestinian Judaism, 200 BCE-400 CE*. Oxford: Oxford University Press.

Janowitz, N. (1998) "Rabbis and Their Opponents: The Construction of the 'Min' in Rabbinic Anecdotes," *Journal of Early Christian Studies* 6: 449–62.

(2000) "Rethinking Jewish Identity in Late Antiquity," in *Ethnicity and Culture in Late Antiquity*, ed. S. Mitchell and G. Greatrex. London: Duckworth: 205–19.

Jefford, C.N. (2001) "Conflict at Antioch: Ignatius and the *Didache* at Odds," *Studia Patristica* 36: 262–69.

Jenkins, K. (1991) *Re-thinking History*. London: Routledge.

Johnson, A.P. (2006) *Ethnicity and Argument in Eusebius' Praeparatio Evangelica*. Oxford: Oxford University Press.

Johnson Hodge, C. (2007) *If Sons, Then Heirs: A Study of Kinship and Ethnicity in the Letters of Paul*. Oxford: Oxford University Press.

Jones, F.S. (1995) *An Ancient Jewish Christian Source on the History of Christianity: Pseudo-Clementine Recognitions 1.27–71*. Atlanta, GA: Scholars.

(1997) "An Ancient Jewish Christian Rejoinder to Luke's Acts of the Apostles: Pseudo-Clementine Recognitions 1.27–71," *Semeia* 80: 223–45.

(2005) "Jewish Christianity of the Pseudo-Clementines," in *A Companion to Second-Century Christian 'Heretics'*, ed. A. Marjanen and P. Luomanen. Leiden: Brill: 314–34.

(2007) "The Pseudo-Clementines," in *Jewish Christianity Reconsidered: Rethinking Ancient Groups and Texts*, ed. Matt Jackson-McCabe. Minneapolis, MN: Fortress: 285–304.

(2009) "Jewish Christians as Heresiologists and as a Heresy," *Rivista di Storia del Cristianesimo* 6: 333–47.

(2012a) "From Toland to Baur: Tracks of the History of Research into Jewish Christianity," in *The Rediscovery of Jewish Christianity: From Toland to Baur*, ed. F.S. Jones. Atlanta, GA: Society of Biblical Literature: 123–36.

(2012b) "Introduction to the *Pseudo-Clementines*," in F.S. Jones, *Pseudoclementina Elchasaiticaque inter Judaeochristiana: Collected Studies*. Leuven: Peeters: 7–49.

Jones, S. (1997) *The Archaeology of Ethnicity: Constructing Identities in the Past and Present*. London: Routledge.

(1998) "Identities in Practice: Towards an Archaeological Perspective on Jewish Identity in Antiquity," in *Jewish Local Patriotism and Self-Identification in the Graeco-Roman Period*, ed. S. Jones and S. Pearce. Sheffield: Sheffield Academic: 29–49.

Joubert, S.J. (1993) "A Bone of Contention in Recent Scholarship: The 'Birkat Ha-Minim' and the Separation of the Church and Synagogue in the First Century A.D.," *Neotestamentica* 27: 351–63.

Kaestli, J.-D. (1996) "Où en est le débat sur le judéo-christianisme?," in *Le déchirement: Juifs et chrétiens au premier siècle*, ed. D. Marguerat. Geneva: Labor et Fides: 243–72.

Kahana, M.I. (2006) "The Halakhic Midrashim," in *The Literature of the Sages, Second Part: Midrash and Targum, Liturgy, Poetry, Mysticism, Contracts, Inscriptions, Ancient Science and the Languages of Rabbinic Literature*, ed. S. Safrai, Z. Safrai, J. Schwartz, and P.J. Tomson. Assen: Van Gorcum: 3–105.

Kalmin, R. (1994) "Christians and Heretics in Rabbinic Literature of Late Antiquity," *Harvard Theological Review* 87: 155–69.

(1999) *The Sage in Jewish Society of Late Antiquity*. London: Routledge.

(2006) *Jewish Babylonia between Persia and Roman Palestine*. Oxford: Oxford University Press.

Kamesar, A. (1994) "The Evaluation of the Narrative Aggada in Greek and Latin Patristic Literature," *Journal of Theological Studies* 45: 37–71.

Kaminsky, J.S. (2007) *Yet I Loved Jacob: Reclaiming the Biblical Concept of Election*. Nashville, TN: Abingdon.

Kartveit, M. (2009) *The Origin of the Samaritans*. Leiden: Brill.

Kasher, A. (1988) *Jews, Idumaeans, and Ancient Arabs: Relations of the Jews in Eretz-Israel with the Nations of the Frontier and the Desert during the Hellenistic and Roman Era (332 BCE-70 CE)*. Tübingen: Mohr (Siebeck).

(1990) *Jews and Hellenistic Cities in Eretz-Israel: Relations of the Jews in Eretz-Israel with the Hellenistic Cities during the Second Temple Period (332 BCE-70 CE)*. Tübingen: Mohr (Siebeck).

Katz, J. (1973) *Out of the Ghetto: The Social Background of Jewish Emancipation, 1770–1870*. Cambridge, MA: Harvard University Press.

Katz, S.T. (1984) "Issues in the Separation of Judaism and Christianity after 70 C.E.: A Reconsideration," *Journal of Biblical Literature* 103: 43–76.

(2006) "The Rabbinic Response to Christianity," in *The Cambridge History of Judaism, Vol. 4: The Late Roman-Rabbinic Period*, ed. S.T. Katz. Cambridge: Cambridge University Press: 259–98.

Kaye, B.N. (1984) "Lightfoot and Baur on Early Christianity," *Novum Testamentum* 26: 193–224.

Kee, H.C. (1992) "The Jews in Acts," in *Diaspora Jews and Judaism: Essays in Honor of, and in Dialogue with, A. Thomas Kraabel*, ed. J.A. Overman and R.S. McLennan. Atlanta, GA: Scholars: 183–95.

Kimelman, R. (1981) "*Birkat Ha-Minim* and the Lack of Evidence for an Anti-Christian Jewish Prayer in Late Antiquity," in *Jewish and Christian Self-Definition, Vol. 2: Aspects of Judaism in the Graeco-Roman Period*, ed. E.P. Sanders, A.I. Baumgarten, and A. Mendelson. Philadelphia, PA: Fortress: 226–44.

(1999) "Identifying Jews and Christians in Roman Syria-Palestine," in *Galilee through the Centuries: Confluence of Cultures*, ed. E.M. Meyers. Winona Lake, IN: Eisenbrauns: 301–33.

Kinzig, W. (1991) "'Non-Separation': Closeness and Co-operation between Jews and Christians in the Fourth Century," *Vigiliae Christianae* 45: 27–53.

(2003) "Jewish and 'Judaizing' Eschatologies in Jerome," in *Jewish Culture and Society under the Christian Roman Empire*, ed. R. Kalmin and S. Schwartz. Leuven: Peeters: 409–29.

(2007) "The Nazoraeans," in *Jewish Believers in Jesus: The Early Centuries*, ed. O. Skarsaune and R. Hvalvik. Peabody, MA: Hendrickson: 463–87.

Klausner, J. (1925) *Jesus of Nazareth: His Life, Times, and Teaching*, trans. H. Danby. New York, NY: Macmillan.

Klawans, J. (2006) *Purity, Sacrifice, and the Temple: Symbolism and Supersessionism in the Study of Ancient Judaism*. Oxford: Oxford University Press.

(2012) *Josephus and the Theologies of Ancient Judaism*. Oxford: Oxford University Press.

Klijn, A.F.J. (1972) "Jerome's Quotations from a Nazoraean Interpretation of Isaiah," *Recherches de Science Religieuse* 60: 241–55.

(1973) "The Study of Jewish Christianity," *New Testament Studies* 20: 419–31.

(1992) *Jewish-Christian Gospel Tradition*. Leiden: Brill.

Klijn, A.F.J., and G.J. Reinink (1973) *Patristic Evidence for Jewish-Christian Sects*. Leiden: Brill.

Klink, E.W., III. (2009) "Expulsion from the Synagogue? Rethinking a Johannine Anachronism," *Tyndale Bulletin* 59: 99–118.

Knowles, M.D. (2006) *Centrality Practiced: Jerusalem in the Religious Practice of Yehud and the Diaspora in the Persian Period*. Atlanta, GA: Society of Biblical Literature.

Koester, C. (1989) "The Origin and Significance of the Flight to Pella Tradition," *Catholic Biblical Quarterly* 51: 90–106.

Kogan, M.S. (2008) *Opening the Covenant: A Jewish Theology of Christianity*. Oxford: Oxford University Press.

Kohler, K. (1924) "The Origin and Composition of the Eighteen Benedictions with a Translation of the Corresponding Essene Prayers in the Apostolic Constitutions," *Hebrew Union College Annual* 1: 387–425.

Korn, E. (2012) "Rethinking Christianity: Rabbinic Positions and Possibilities," in *Jewish Theology and World Religions*, ed. A. Goshen-Gottstein and E. Korn. Oxford: Littman Library of Jewish Civilization: 189–233.

Kraemer, D. (2006) "The Mishnah," in *The Cambridge History of Judaism, Vol. 4: The Late Roman-Rabbinic Period*, ed. S.T. Katz. Cambridge: Cambridge University Press: 299–315.

Kraft, R.A. (1972) "In Search of 'Jewish Christianity' and Its 'Theology': Problems of Definition and Methodology," *Recherches de Science Religieuse* 60: 81–92.

(2003) "The 'Textual Mechanics' of Early Jewish LXX/OG Papyri and Fragments," in *The Bible as Book: The Transmission of the Greek Text*, ed. S. McKendrick and O.A. O'Sullivan. London: British Library: 51–72.

Krauss, S. (1892) "The Jews in the Works of the Church Fathers," *Jewish Quarterly Review* (old series) 5: 122–57.

Krauss, S., and W. Horbury, ed. and rev. (1995) *The Jewish-Christian Controversy from the Earliest Times to 1789, Vol. I: History*. Tübingen: Mohr (Siebeck).

Kuhn, K.G. (1950) *Achtzehngebet und Vaterunser und der Reim*. Tübingen: Mohr.

(1964) "Giljonim und Sifre Minim," in *Judentum, Urchristentum, Kirche: Festschrift für Joachim Jeremias*, ed. W. Eltester. 2nd edn. Berlin: Töpelmann: 24–61.

Laible, H. (1893) "Jesus Christ in the Talmud," in *Jesus Christ in the Talmud, Midrash, Zohar, and the Liturgy of the Synagogue: Texts and Translations*, trans. A.W. Streane and ed. G.H. Dalman. Cambridge: Deighton, Bell: 1–98

Lampe, G.W.H. (1984) "A.D. 70 in Christian Reflection," in *Jesus and the Politics of His Day*, ed. E. Bammel and C.F.D. Moule. Cambridge: Cambridge University Press: 153–71.

Lampe, P. (2003) *From Paul to Valentinus: Christians at Rome in the First Two Centuries*, trans. M. Steinhauser and ed. M.D. Johnson. Minneapolis, MN: Fortress.

Langer, R. (2012) *Cursing the Christians? A History of the Birkat Haminim*. Oxford: Oxford University Press.

Langton, D.R. (2010) *The Apostle Paul in the Jewish Imagination: A Study in Modern Jewish-Christian Relations*. Cambridge: Cambridge University Press.

Lapin, H. (1996) "Jewish and Christian Academies in Roman Palestine: Some Preliminary Observations," in *Caesarea Maritima: A Retrospective after Two Millennia*, ed. A. Raban and K.G. Holum. Leiden: Brill: 496–512.

(2012) *Rabbis as Romans: The Rabbinic Movement in Palestine, 100–400 CE*. Oxford: Oxford University Press.

Lauterbach, J.Z. (1951) "Jesus in the Talmud," in J.Z. Lauterbach, *Rabbinic Essays*. Cincinnati, OH: Hebrew Union College Press: 473–570.

Le Roy Ladurie, E. (1979) *The Territory of the Historian*, trans. B. Reynolds and S. Reynolds. Chicago, IL: University of Chicago Press.

Lee, K.-J. (2011) *The Authority and Authorization of Torah in the Persian Period*. Leuven: Peeters.

Leiman, S.Z. (1976) *The Canonization of Hebrew Scripture: The Talmudic and Midrashic Evidence*. Hamden, CT: Connecticut Academy of Arts and Sciences.

Levene, D. (2003) *A Corpus of Magic Bowls: Incantation Texts in Jewish Aramaic from Late Antiquity*. London: Kegan Paul.

Lévinas, E. (1969) *Totality and Infinity: An Essay on Exteriority*, trans. A. Lingis. Pittsburgh, PA: Duquesne University Press.

(1998) *Otherwise than Being or Beyond Essence*, trans. A. Lingis. Pittsburgh, PA: Duquesne University Press.

Levine, A.-J. (1988) *The Social and Ethnic Dimensions of Matthean Social History: "Go Nowhere among the Gentiles ..." (Matt.10:5b).* Lewiston, NY: Mellen.

Levine, A.-J., and M.Z. Brettler, eds. (2011) *The Jewish Annotated New Testament.* Oxford: Oxford University Press.

Levine, L.I. (1975) *Caesarea under Roman Rule.* Leiden: Brill.

　(1989) *The Rabbinic Class of Roman Palestine in Late Antiquity.* Jerusalem: Yad Ben-Zvi.

　(1996) "The Status of the Patriarch in the Third and Fourth Centuries: Sources and Methodology," *Journal of Jewish Studies* 47: 1–32.

　(1998) *Judaism and Hellenism in Antiquity: Conflict or Confluence?* Seattle, WA: University of Washington Press.

　(2005) "Bet Še'arim in Its Patriarchal Context," in *"The Words of a Wise Man's Mouth Are Gracious" (Qoh 10,12): Festschrift for Günter Stemberger on the Occasion of His 65th Birthday,* ed. M. Perani. Berlin: De Gruyter: 197–225.

Levine, L.I., and D.R. Schwartz, eds. (2009) *Jewish Identities in Antiquity: Studies in Memory of Menahem Stern.* Tübingen: Mohr Siebeck.

Levinson, J. (2013) "There is No Place Like Home: Rabbinic Responses to the Christianization of Palestine," in *Jews, Christians, and the Roman Empire: The Poetics of Power in Late Antiquity,* ed. N.B. Dohrmann and A.Y. Reed. Philadelphia, PA: University of Pennsylvania Press: 99–120.

Lieberman, S. (1944) "Roman Legal Institutions in Early Rabbinics and in the Acta Martyrum," *Jewish Quarterly Review* 35: 1–57.

　(1955–1988) *Tosefta ki-Fshuta: A Comprehensive Commentary on the Tosefta.* 10 Vols. New York, NY: Jewish Theological Seminary of America.

　(1950) *Hellenism in Jewish Palestine: Studies in the Literary Transmission, Beliefs and Manners of Palestine in the I Century B.C.E.-IV Century C.E.* New York, NY: Jewish Theological Seminary of America.

Liebeschuetz, W. (2001) "The Influence of Judaism among Non-Jews in the Imperial Period," *Journal of Jewish Studies* 52: 235–52.

Lieu, J.M. (1994) "The Parting of the Ways: Theological Construct or Historical Reality?," *Journal for the Study of the New Testament* 56: 101–19.

　(1996) *Image and Reality: The Jews in the World of the Christians in the Second Century.* Edinburgh: T&T Clark.

　(1998) "Accusations of Jewish Persecution in Early Christian Sources, with Particular Reference to Justin Martyr and the *Martyrdom of Polycarp,*" in *Tolerance and Intolerance in Early Judaism and Christianity,* ed. G.M. Stanton and G.G. Stroumsa. Cambridge: Cambridge University Press: 279–95.

　(2003) "The Synagogue and the Separation of the Christians," in *The Ancient Synagogue from Its Origins until 200 C.E.: Papers Presented at an International Conference at Lund University, October 14–17, 2001,* ed. B. Olsson and M. Zetterholm. Stockholm: Almqvist & Wiksell: 189–207.

　(2004) *Christian Identity in the Jewish and Graeco-Roman World.* Oxford: Oxford University Press.

Lightfoot, J.B. (1865) *St. Paul's Epistle to the Galatians.* London: Macmillan.

　(1868) *St. Paul's Epistle to the Philippians.* London: Macmillan.

Linder, A. (1987) *The Jews in Imperial Roman Legislation.* Detroit, MI: Wayne State University Press.

Lipschits, O. (2005) *The Fall and Rise of Jerusalem: Judah under Babylonian Rule.* Winona Lake, IN: Eisenbrauns.

Llewelyn, S.R. (1997) "The Prescript of James," *Novum Testamentum* 39: 385–93.

Lockett, D.K. (2011) "James," in *The Oxford Encyclopedia of the Books of the Bible,* ed. M.D. Coogan. 2 Vols. Oxford: Oxford University Press: 411–14.

Lössl, J. (2002) "Hieronymus und Epiphanius von Salamis über das judentum ihrer Zeit," *Journal for the Study of Judaism* 33: 411–36.

Lüdemann (Luedemann), G. (1989) *Opposition to Paul in Jewish Christianity*, trans. M.E. Boring. Minneapolis, MN: Fortress.

Luomanen, P. (2002) "The 'Sociology of Sectarianism' in Matthew: Modeling the Genesis of Early Jewish and Christian Communities," in *Fair Play: Diversity and Conflicts in Early Christianity, Essays in Honour of Heikki Räisänen,* ed. I. Dunderberg, C. Tuckett, and K. Syreeni. Leiden: Brill: 107–30.

(2005) "Nazarenes," in *A Companion to Second-Century Christian 'Heretics',* ed. A. Marjanen and P. Luomanen. Leiden: Brill: 279–314.

(2007) "Ebionites and Nazarenes," in *Jewish Christianity Reconsidered: Rethinking Ancient Groups and Texts,* ed. M. Jackson-McCabe. Minneapolis, MN: Fortress: 81–118.

(2012) *Recovering Jewish-Christian Sects and Gospels.* Leiden: Brill.

Luttikhuizen, G.P. (1991) "Vroeg-christelijk jodendom," in *Jodendom en vroeg christendom: continuïteit en discontinuïteit, opstellen van de leden van de Studiosorum Novi Testamenti Conventus,* ed. T. Baarda, H.J. de Jonge, and M.J.J. Menken. Kampen: Kok Pharos: 163–89.

Luz, U. (2005a) "Anti-Judaism in the Gospel of Matthew as a Historical and Theological Problem: An Outline," inU. Luz, *Studies in Matthew*, trans. R. Selle. Grand Rapids, MI: Eerdmans: 243–61.

(2005b) "Matthew the Evangelist: A Jewish Christian at the Crossroads," in U. Luz, *Studies in Matthew*, trans. R. Selle. Grand Rapids, MI: Eerdmans: 3–17.

Magness, J. (2002) "In the Footsteps of the Tenth Roman Legion in Judea," in *The First Jewish Revolt: Archaeology, History, and Ideology,* ed. A.M. Berlin and J.A. Overman. London: Routledge: 189–212.

(2012) "Sectarianism Before and After 70," in *Was 70 CE a Watershed in Jewish History? On Jews and Judaism before and after the Destruction of the Second Temple,* ed. D.R. Schwartz and Z. Weiss. Leiden: Brill: 69–89.

Maier, J. (1978) *Jesus von Nazareth in der talmudischen Überlieferung.* Darmstadt: Wissenschaftliche Buchgesellschaft.

(1982) *Jüdische Auseinandersetzung mit dem Christentum in der Antike.* Darmstadt: Wissenschaftliche Buchgesellschaft.

Mandel, P. (2006a) "The Loss of Center: Changing Attitudes Towards the Temple in Aggadic Literature," *Harvard Theological Review* 99: 17–35.

(2006b) "The Tosefta," in *The Cambridge History of Judaism, Vol. 4: The Late Roman-Rabbinic Period,* ed. S.T. Katz. Cambridge: Cambridge University Press: 316–35.

Mann, J. (1925) "Genizah Fragments of the Palestinian Order of Service," *Hebrew Union College Annual* 2: 269–388.

Marcus, J. (2006) "Jewish Christianity," in *The Cambridge History of Christianity, Vol. 1: Origins to Constantine,* ed. M.M. Mitchell and F.M. Young. Cambridge: Cambridge University Press: 87–102.

(2009) "*Birkat Ha-Minim* Revisited," *New Testament Studies* 55: 523–52.

Marguerat, D. (2013) "The Image of Paul in Acts," in D. Marguerat, *Paul in Acts and Paul in His Letters*. Tübingen: Mohr Siebeck: 22–47.

Markschies, C. (2006) "Intellectuals and Church Fathers in the Third and Fourth Centuries," in *Christians and Christianity in the Holy Land: From the Origins to the Latin Kingdoms*, ed. O. Limor and G.G. Stroumsa. Turnhout: Brepols: 239–56.

Marmorstein, A. (1924–1925) "The Amidah of the Public Fast Days," *Jewish Quarterly Review* 15: 409–18.

(1935) "Judaism and Christianity in the Middle of the Third Century," *Hebrew Union College Annual* 10: 226–63.

Martens, P.W. (2012) *Origen and Scripture: The Contours of the Exegetical Life*. Oxford: Oxford University Press.

Martin, D.B. (2001) "Paul and the Judaism/Hellenism Dichotomy: Toward a Social History of the Question," in *Paul Beyond the Judaism/Hellenism Divide*, ed. T. Engberg-Pedersen. Louisville, KY: Westminster John Knox: 29–61.

(2004) *Inventing Superstition: From the Hippocratics to the Christians*. Cambridge, MA: Harvard University Press.

Martyn, J.L. (2003) *History and Theology in the Fourth Gospel*. 3rd edn. Louisville, KY: Westminster John Knox.

Mason, S. (2007) "Jews, Judaeans, Judaizing, Judaism: Problems of Categorization in Ancient History," *Journal for the Study of Judaism* 38: 457–512.

Matsunaga, K. (1992) "Christian Self-Identification and the Twelfth Benediction," in *Eusebius, Christianity, and Judaism*, ed. H.W. Attridge and G. Hata. Detroit, MI: Wayne State University Press: 355–71.

Mayo, P.L. (2006) "The Role of the 'Birkath Haminim' in Early Jewish-Christian Relations: A Reexamination of the Evidence," *Bulletin for Biblical Research* 16: 325–44.

Mazar, B. (1973) *Beth She'arim: Report on the Excavations during 1936–1940, Vol. 1: Catacombs 1–4*. New Brunswick, NJ: Rutgers University Press.

McGuckin, J.A. (1992a) "Caesarea Maritima as Origen Knew It," in *Origeniana Quinta: Papers of the 5th International Origen Congress, Boston College, 14–18 August, 1989*, ed. R.J. Daly. Leuven: Peeters: 3–25.

(1992b) "Origen on the Jews," in *Christianity and Judaism: Papers Read at the 1991 Summer Meeting and the 1992 Winter Meeting of the Ecclesiastical History Society*, ed. D. Wood. Oxford: Blackwell: 1–13.

McLaren, J.S. (1991) *Power and Politics in Palestine: The Jews and the Governing of Their Land, 100 BC–AD 70*. Sheffield: JSOT.

Meeks, W.A. (1983) *The First Urban Christians: The Social World of the Apostle Paul*. New Haven, CT: Yale University Press.

(1985) "Breaking Away: Three New Testament Pictures of Christianity's Separation from the Jewish Communities," in *"To See Ourselves as Others See Us": Christians, Jews, "Others" in Late Antiquity*, ed. J. Neusner and E.S. Frerichs. Chico, CA: Scholars: 95–115.

Meerson, M., and P. Schäfer, eds. and trans. (2014) *Toledot Yeshu: The Life Story of Jesus*. 2 Vols. Tübingen: Mohr Siebeck.

Meier, J.P. (2009) *A Marginal Jew: Rethinking the Historical Jesus, Vol. 4: Love and Law*. New Haven, CT: Yale University Press.

Mendels, D. (1987) *The Land of Israel as a Political Concept in Hasmonean Literature: Recourse to History in Second Century B.C. Claims to the Holy Land.* Tübingen: Mohr (Siebeck).

(1992) *The Rise and Fall of Jewish Nationalism: Jewish and Christian Ethnicity in Ancient Palestine.* New York, NY: Doubleday.

Meyers, E.M., and M.A. Chancey (2012) *Alexander to Constantine: Archaeology of the Land of the Bible,* Vol. 3. New Haven, CT: Yale University Press.

Milavec, A. (2003) *The Didache: Faith, Hope, and Life of the Earliest Christian Communities, 50–70 C.E.* New York, NY: Newman.

Milikowsky, C. (1985–1986) "Gehenna and 'Sinners of Israel' in the Light of 'Seder Olam' " [Hebrew], *Tarbiz* 55: 311–43.

(1997) "Notions of Exile, Subjugation and Return in Rabbinic Literature," in *Exile: Old Testament, Jewish, and Christian Perspectives,* ed. J.M. Scott. Leiden: Brill: 265–96.

(2013) *Seder Olam: Critical Edition, Commentary, and Introduction* [Hebrew]. 2 Vols. Jerusalem: Yad Ben-Zvi.

Millar, F. (1993) *The Roman Near East, 31 BC-AD 337.* Cambridge, MA: Harvard University Press.

Miller, S.S. (1984) *Studies in the History and Traditions of Sepphoris.* Leiden: Brill.

(1993) "The *Minim* of Sepphoris Reconsidered," *Harvard Theological Review* 86: 377–402.

(2006) *Sages and Commoners in Late Antique 'Erez Israel: A Philological Inquiry into Local Traditions in Talmud Yerushalmi.* Tübingen: Mohr Siebeck.

Mimouni, S.C. (1998) "Les nazoréens: Recherche étymologique et historique," *Revue biblique* 105: 208–62.

(2012) *Early Judaeo-Christianity: Historical Essays,* trans. R. Fréchet. Leuven: Peeters.

Mitchell, S. (1999) "The Cult of Theos Hypsistos between Pagans, Jews, and Christians," in *Pagan Monotheism in Late Antiquity,* ed. P. Athanassiadi and M. Frede. Oxford: Oxford University Press: 81–148.

Modrzejewski, J.M. (1995) *The Jews of Egypt, from Rameses II to Emperor Hadrian,* trans. R. Cornman. Philadelphia, PA: Jewish Publication Society.

(2003) "'*Filios Suos Tantum*': Roman Law and Jewish Identity," in *Jews and Gentiles in the Holy Land in the Days of the Second Temple, the Mishnah and the Talmud: A Collection of Articles. Proceedings of the Conference Relations between Jews and Gentiles in the Period of the Second Temple, Mishnah, and the Talmud Held at the University of Haifa, 13–16 November 1995,* ed. M. Mor, A. Oppenheimer, J. Pastor, and D.R. Schwartz. Jerusalem: Yad Ban-Zvi: 108–36.

Moxnes, H. (2012) *Jesus and the Rise of Nationalism: A New Quest for the Nineteenth Century Historical Jesus.* London: Tauris.

Mueller, J.G. (2007) "The Ancient Church Order Literature: Genre or Tradition?," *Journal of Early Christian Studies* 15: 337–80.

Munck, J. (1959) *Paul and the Salvation of Mankind,* trans. F. Clarke. London: SCM.

Murcia, T. (2011) "Jésus adorateur d'une brique? B. Sanhedrin 107b: L'épisode talmudique du séjour de Yeshu en Égypte," *Revue des Études Juives* 170: 369–98.

Myers, D.N. (1995) *Re-Inventing the Jewish Past: European Jewish Intellectuals and the Zionist Return to History.* Oxford: Oxford University Press.

Naveh, J., and S. Shaked (1998) *Amulets and Magic Bowls: Aramaic Incantations of Late Antiquity.* 3rd edn. Jerusalem: Magnes.

Neusner, J. (1978) "Comparing Judaisms," *History of Religions* 18: 177–91.

(1980) "The Use of the Mishnah for the History of Judaism Prior to the Time of the Mishnah: A Methodological Note," *Journal for the Study of Judaism* 11: 177–85.

(1981a) *Judaism: The Evidence of the Mishnah*. Chicago, IL: University of Chicago Press.

(1981b) "The Modern Study of the Mishnah," in *The Study of Ancient Judaism, Vol. 1: Mishnah, Midrash, Siddur*, ed. J. Neusner. New York, NY: Ktav: 3–26.

(1986) *The Tosefta: Its Structure and Its Sources*. Atlanta, GA: Scholars.

(1987) *Judaism and Christianity in the Age of Constantine*. Chicago, IL: University of Chicago Press.

(1988) *The Systemic Analysis of Judaism*. Atlanta, GA: Scholars.

(1989) *Judaism and Its Social Metaphors: Israel in the History of Jewish Thought*. Cambridge: Cambridge University Press.

(1993) *Judaic Law from Jesus to the Mishnah: A Systematic Reply to Professor E. P. Sanders*. Atlanta, GA: Scholars.

(1995a) *The Documentary Foundation of Rabbinic Culture: Mopping Up after Debates with Gerald R. Bruns, S. J. D. Cohen, Arnold Maria Goldberg, Susan Handelman, Christine Hayes, James Kugel, Peter Schaefer, Eliezer Segal, E. P. Sanders, and Lawrence H. Schiffman*. Atlanta, GA: Scholars.

(1995b) "Was Rabbinic Judaism Really 'Ethnic'?," *Catholic Biblical Quarterly* 57: 281–305.

Newby, G.D. (1988) *A History of the Jews of Arabia: From Ancient Times to Their Eclipse under Islam*. Columbia, SC: University of South Carolina Press.

Newman, H.I. (1997) "Jerome and the Jews" [Hebrew]. Ph.D. Dissertation, Hebrew University of Jerusalem.

(2001) "Jerome's Judaizers," *Journal of Early Christian Studies* 9: 421–52.

Nickelsburg, G.W.E. (2003) *Ancient Judaism and Christian Origins: Diversity, Continuity, and Transformation*. Minneapolis, MN: Fortress.

Nicklas, T. (2014) *Jews and Christians? Second Century 'Christian' Perspectives on the 'Parting of the Ways' (Annual Deichmann Lectures 2013)*. Tübingen: Mohr Siebeck.

Niederwimmer, K. (1998) *The Didache: A Commentary*, trans. L.M. Maloney. Minneapolis, MN: Fortress.

Nongbri, B. (2005) "The Motivations of the Maccabees and Judean Rhetoric of Ancestral Tradition," in *Ancient Judaism in Its Hellenistic Context*, ed. C. Bakhos. Leiden: Brill: 85–111.

(2013) *Before Religion: A History of a Modern Concept*. New Haven, CT: Yale University Press.

Oppenheimer, A. (2003) "The Ban on Circumcision as a Cause of the Revolt: A Reconsideration," in *The Bar Kokhba War Reconsidered*, ed. P. Schäfer. Tübingen: Mohr Siebeck: 55–69.

(2005) "The Severan Emperors, Rabbi Judah ha-Nasi and the Cities of Palestine," in *"The Words of a Wise Man's Mouth Are Gracious" (Qoh 10,12): Festschrift for Günter Stemberger on the Occasion of His 65th Birthday*, ed. M. Perani. Berlin: De Gruyter: 171–81.

Osterloh, K.L. (2008) "Judea, Rome, and the Hellenistic *Oikoumenē*: Emulation and the Reinvention of Communal Identity," in *Heresy and Identity in Late* Antiquity, ed. E. Iricinschi and H.M. Zellentin. Tübingen: Mohr Siebeck: 168–206.

Overman, J.A. (1990) *Matthew's Gospel and Formative Judaism: The Social World of the Matthean Community*. Minneapolis, MN: Fortress.

Parkes, J.W. (1934) *The Conflict of the Church and the Synagogue: A Study in the Origins of Antisemitism*. London: Soncino.

Pearce, L.E., and C. Wunsch (2014) *Documents of Judean Exiles and West Semites in Babylonia in the Collection of Daid Sofer*. Bethesda, MD: CDL.

Peppard, M. (2007) "Personal Names and Ethnic Hybridity in Late Ancient Galilee: The Data from Beth She'arim," in *Religion, Ethnicity, and Identity in Ancient Galilee: A Region in Transition*, ed. J. Zangenberg, H.W. Attridge, and D.B. Martin. Tübingen: Mohr Siebeck: 99–113.

Petersen, A.K. (2005) "At the End of the Road: Reflections on a Popular Scholarly Metaphor," in *The Formation of the Early Church*, ed. J. Ådna. Tübingen: Mohr Siebeck: 45–72.

Petuchowski, J.J. (1974) "Das Ketzersegen," in *Das Vaterunser: Gemeinsames im Beten von Juden und Christen*, ed. M. Brocke, J.J. Petuchowski, and W. Strolz. Freiburg: Herder: 90–101.

Pines, S. (1974) "Notes on the Parallelism between Syriac Terminology and Mishnaic Hebrew" [Hebrew], in *Yaakov Friedman Memorial Volume*, ed. S. Pines. Jerusalem: Hebrew University Institute for Jewish Studies: 205–13.

Porter, S.E., and B.W.R. Pearson. (2000) "Ancient Understandings of the Christian-Jewish Split," in *Christian-Jewish Relations through the Centuries*, ed. S.E. Porter and B.W.R. Pearson. Sheffield: Sheffield Academic: 36–51.

Porton, G.G. (1988) *Goyim: Gentiles and Israelites in Mishnah-Tosefta*. Atlanta, GA: Scholars.

Price, R.M., trans. (1991) *Cyril of Scythopolis: The Lives of the Monks of Palestine*. Kalamazoo, MI: Cistercian.

Pritz, R.A. (1988) *Nazarene Jewish Christianity: From the End of the New Testament Period until Its Disappearance in the Fourth Century*. Jerusalem: Magnes.

Pucci Ben Zeev, M. (1998) *Jewish Rights in the Roman World: The Greek and Roman Documents Quoted by Josephus Flavius*. Tübingen: Mohr Siebeck.

Pyka, M. (2009) *Jüdische Identität bei Heinrich Graetz*. Göttingen: Vandenhoeck & Ruprecht.

Rabbinovicz, R.N. (1868–1897) *Diqduqe Soferim: Variae Lectiones in Mischnam et in Talmud Babylonicum*. 16 Vols. Munich and Przemyśl: Huber and Zupnik, Knoller & Wolf.

Räisänen, H. (1987) *Paul and the Law*. 2nd edn. Tübingen: Mohr (Siebeck).

Rajak, T. (1990) "The Hasmoneans and the Uses of Hellenism," in *A Tribute to Geza Vermes: Essays on Jewish and Christian Literature and History*, ed. P.R. Davies and R.T. White. Sheffield: JSOT: 261–80.

 (1996) "Hasmonean Kingship and the Invention of Tradition," in *Aspects of Hellenistic Kingship*, ed. P. Bilde, T. Engberg-Pedersen, L. Hannestad, and J. Zahle. Aarhus: Aarhus University Press: 96–116.

 (1998) "The Rabbinic Dead and the Diaspora Dead at Beth She'arim," in *The Talmud Yerushalmi and Graeco-Roman Culture*, Vol. 1, ed. P. Schäfer. Tübingen: Mohr Siebeck: 349–66.

Raz-Krakotzin, A. (2007) *The Censor, the Editor, and the Text: The Catholic Church and the Shaping of the Jewish Canon in the Sixteenth Century*, trans. J. Feldman. Philadelphia, PA: University of Pennsylvania Press.

Reed, A.Y. (2003) "'Jewish Christianity' after the 'Parting of the Ways': Approaches to Historiography and Self-Definition in the Pseudo-Clementines," in *The Ways That Never Parted*, ed. A.H. Becker and A.Y. Reed. Tübingen: Mohr Siebeck: 189–231.

(2006) "Rabbis, 'Jewish Christians', and Other Late Antique Jews: Reflections on the Fate of Judaism(s) after 70 C.E.," in *The Changing Face of Judaism, Christianity, and Other Greco-Roman Religions in Antiquity*, ed. I.H. Henderson and G.S. Oegema. Gütersloh: Gütersloher: 323–46.

(2008a) "From Judaism and Hellenism to Christianity and Paganism: Cultural Identities and Religious Polemics in the Pseudo-Clementine *Homilies*," in *Nouvelles intrigues pseudo-clémentines/Plots in the Pseudo-Clementine Romance: Actes du deuxième colloque international sur la littérature apocryphe chrétienne, Lausanne-Genève, 30 août-2 septembre 2006*, ed. F. Amsler, A. Frey, C. Touati, and R. Girardet. Prahins: Zèbre: 425–35.

(2008b) "Heresiology and the (Jewish-)Christian Novel: Narrativized Polemic in the Pseudo-Clementine *Homilies*," in *Heresy and Identity in Late Antiquity*, ed. E. Iricinschi and H.M. Zellentin. Tübingen: Mohr Siebeck: 273–98.

(2008c) "'Jewish Christianity' as Counter-History? The Apostolic Past in Eusebius' *Ecclesiastical History* and the Pseudo-Clementine *Homilies*," in *Antiquity in Antiquity: Jewish and Christian Pasts in the Greco-Roman World*, ed. G. Gardner and K.L. Osterloh. Tübingen: Mohr Siebeck: 173–216.

(2012) "Parting Ways over Blood and Water? Beyond 'Judaism' and 'Christianity' in the Roman Near East," in *La croisée des chemins revisitée: Quand l' "Église" et la "Synagogue" se sont-elles distinguées? Actes du colloques de Tours 18–19 juin 2010*, ed. S.C. Mimouni and B. Pouderon. Paris: Cerf: 227–60.

Reed, A.Y., and A.H. Becker. (2003) "Introduction: Traditional Models and New Directions," in *The Ways that Never Parted*, ed. A.H. Becker and A.Y. Reed. Tübingen: Mohr Siebeck: 1–33.

Reiner, E. (1998) "From Joshua to Jesus: The Transformation of a Biblical Story to a Local Myth, A Chapter in the Religious Life of the Galilean Jew," in *Sharing the Sacred: Religious Contacts and Conflicts in the Holy Land, First-Fifteenth Centuries CE*, ed. A. Kofsky and G.G. Stroumsa. Jerusalem: Yad Ben-Zvi: 223–71.

Reinhartz, A. (2006) "A Fork in the Road or a Multi-Lane Highway? New Perspectives on the 'Parting of the Ways' between Judaism and Christianity," in *The Changing Face of Judaism, Christianity, and Other Greco-Roman Religions in Antiquity*, ed. I.H. Henderson and G.S. Oegema. Gütersloh: Gütersloher: 280–95.

Repschinski, B. (2000) *The Controversy Stories in the Gospel of Matthew: Their Redaction, Form and Relevance for the Relationship between the Matthean Community and Formative Judaism*. Göttingen: Vandenhoeck & Ruprecht.

Reuther, R.R. (1974) *Faith and Fratricide: The Theological Roots of Anti-Semitism*. New York, NY: Seabury.

Riches, J. (2011) "Galatians," in *The Oxford Encyclopedia of the Books of the Bible*, ed. M.D. Coogan. 2 Vols. Oxford: Oxford University Press: 1.311–15.

Richmond, C. (2005) *Campaigner Against Antisemitism: James Parkes, 1896–1981*. London: Vallentine Mitchell.

Ricoeur, P. *Memory, History, Forgetting*, trans. K. Blamey and D. Pellauer. Chicago, IL: University of Chicago Press.

Ritschl, A. (1857) *Die Entstehung der altkatholischen Kirche: Eine kirchen- und dogmengeschichtliche Monographie*. 2nd edn. Bonn: Marcus.

Roemer, N.H. (2004) "Colliding Visions: Jewish Messianism and German Scholarship in the Eighteenth Century," in *Hebraica Veritas? Christian Hebraists and the Study of Judaism in Early Modern Europe*, ed. A.P. Coudert and J.S. Shoulson. Philadelphia, PA: University of Pennsylvania Press: 266–85.

Rokeah, D. (1982) *Jews, Pagans and Christians in Conflict*. Jerusalem: Magnes.

Rordorf, W. (1996) "An Aspect of the Judeo-Christian Ethic: The Two Ways," in *The Didache in Modern Research*, ed. J.A. Draper. Leiden: Brill: 148–64.

Roth-Gerson, L. (2001) *The Jews of Syria as Reflected in the Greek Inscriptions* [Hebrew]. Jerusalem: Shazar Center.

Rubenstein, J.L. (2003) *The Culture of the Babylonian Talmud*. Baltimore, MD: Johns Hopkins University Press.

(2007) "The Social and Institutional Settings of Rabbinic Literature," in *The Cambridge Companion to the Talmud and Rabbinic Literature*, ed. C.E. Fonrobert and M.S. Jaffee. Cambridge: Cambridge University Press: 58–74.

(2010) *Stories of the Babylonian Talmud*. Baltimore, MD: Johns Hopkins University Press.

Runesson, A. (2008a) "Inventing Christian Identity: Paul, Ignatius, and Theodosius I," in *Exploring Christian Identity*, ed. B. Holmberg. Tübingen: Mohr Siebeck: 59–92.

(2008b) "Rethinking Early Jewish-Christian Relations: Matthean Community History as Pharisaic Intragroup Conflict," *Journal of Biblical Literature* 127: 95–132.

(2011) "Matthew, Gospel According to," in *The Oxford Encyclopedia of the Books of the Bible*, ed. M.D. Coogan. 2 Vols. Oxford: Oxford University Press: 2.59–78.

Rürup, R. (1999) "Jewish Emancipation in Britain and Germany," in *Two Nations: British and German Jews in Comparative Perspective*, ed. M. Brenner, R. Liedtke, and D. Rechter. Tübingen: Mohr Siebeck: 49–61.

Rutgers, L.V. (2010) "The Synagogue as Foe in Early Christian Literature," in *"Follow the Wise": Studies in Jewish History and Culture in Honor of Lee I. Levine*, ed. Z. Weiss, O. Irshai, J. Magness, and S. Schwartz. Winona Lake, IN: Eisenbrauns: 449–68.

Ruzer, S. (2007) *Mapping the New Testament: Early Christian Writings as a Witness for Jewish Biblical Exegesis*. Leiden: Brill.

Saldarini, A.J. (1988) *Pharisees, Scribes and Sadducees in Palestinian Society: A Sociological Approach*. Wilmington, DE: Glazier.

(1992) "The Gospel of Matthew and Jewish-Christian Conflict in the Galilee," in *The Galilee in Late Antiquity*, ed. L.I. Levine. New York, NY: Jewish Theological Seminary of America: 23–38.

(1994) *Matthew's Christian-Jewish Community*. Chicago, IL: University of Chicago Press.

(1998) "The Social World of Christian Jews and Jewish Christians," in *Religious and Ethnic Communities in Later Roman Palestine*, ed. H. Lapin. College Park, MD: University Press of Maryland: 115–54.

Sanders, E.P. (1977) *Paul and Palestinian Judaism: A Comparison of Patterns of Religion*. Philadelphia, PA: Fortress.

(1983) *Paul, the Law, and the Jewish People*. Philadelphia, PA: Fortress.

(1985) *Jesus and Judaism*. Philadelphia, PA: Fortress.

(1992) *Judaism: Practice and Belief, 63 BCE-66 CE*. London: SCM.

Sanders, J.T. (1993) *Schismatics, Sectarians, Dissidents, Deviants: The First One Hundred Years of Jewish-Christian Relations*. London: SCM.

Sartre, M. (2005) *The Middle East under Rome*, trans. C. Porter and E. Rawlings. Cambridge, MA: Harvard University Press.

Satlow, M.L. (2006) "Defining Judaism: Accounting for 'Religions' in the Study of Religion," *Journal of the American Academy of Religion* 74: 837–60.

Schäfer, P. (1975) "Die sogenannte Synode von Jabne: Zur Trennung von Juden und Christen im ersten/zweiten Jh. n. Chr.," *Judaica* 31: 54–64, 116–24.

(1997) *Judeophobia: Attitudes toward the Jews in the Ancient World*. Cambridge, MA: Harvard University Press.

(2007) *Jesus in the Talmud*. Princeton, NJ: Princeton University Press.

(2012) *The Jewish Jesus: How Judaism and Christianity Shaped Each Other*. Princeton, NJ: Princeton University Press.

Schechter, S. (1898) "Genizah Specimens," *Jewish Quarterly Review* (old series) 10: 654–59.

Schiffman, L.H. (1985) *Who Was a Jew? Rabbinic and Halakhic Perspectives on the Jewish-Christian Schism*. Hoboken, NJ: Ktav.

Schoeps, H.-J. (1949) *Theologie und Geschichte des Judenchristentums*. Tübingen: Mohr.

Schofer, J.W. (2005) *The Making of a Sage: A Study in Rabbinic Ethics*. Madison, WI: University of Wisconsin Press.

Schofield, A., and J.C. VanderKam (2005) "Were the Hasmoneans Zadokites?," *Journal of Biblical Literature* 124: 73–87.

Schorsch, I. (1994) *From Text to Context: The Turn to History in Modern Judaism*. Hanover, NH: Brandeis University Press.

Schremer, A. (2005) "Stammaitic Historiography," in *Creation and Composition: The Contribution of the Bavli Redactors (Stammaim) to the Aggada*, ed. J.L. Rubenstein. Tübingen: Mohr Siebeck: 219–35.

(2010) *Brothers Estranged: Heresy, Christianity, and Jewish Identity in Late Antiquity*. Oxford: Oxford University Press.

(2013) "Wayward Jews: *Minim* in Early Rabbinic Literature," *Journal of Jewish Studies* 64: 242–63.

Schürer, E. (1886–1890) *Geschichte des jüdischen Volkes im zeitalter Jesu Christi*. 3 Vols. 1st edn. Leipzig: Hinrichs.

(1901–1909) *Geschichte des jüdischen Volkes im zeitalter Jesu Christi*. 3 Vols. 3rd and 4th edns. Leipzig: Hinrichs.

Schwabe, M., and B. Lifshitz (1974) *Beth She'arim, Vol. 2: The Greek Inscriptions*. New Brunswick, NJ: Rutgers University Press.

Schwartz, D.R. (1990) *Agrippa I: The Last King of Judaea*. Tübingen: Mohr (Siebeck).

(1992a) "Law and Truth: On Qumran-Sadducean and Rabbinic Views of Law," in *The Dead Sea Scrolls: Forty Years of Research*, ed. D. Dimant and U. Rappaport. Leiden: Brill: 229–40.

(1992b) "Temple and Desert: On Religion and State in Second Temple Period Judaea," in D.R. Schwartz, *Studies in the Jewish Background of Christianity*. Tübingen: Mohr (Siebeck): 29–43.

(2005) "Herodians and *Ioudaioi* in Flavian Rome," in *Flavius Josephus and Flavian Rome*, ed. J. Edmondson, S. Mason, and J. Rives, 63–78. Oxford: Oxford University Press.

(2007) "'Judaean' or 'Jew'? How Should We Translate *Ioudaios* in Josephus?," in *Jewish Identity in the Greco-Roman World/Jüdische Identität in der griechisch-römischen Welt*, ed. J. Frey, D.R. Schwartz, and S. Gripentrog. Leiden: Brill: 3–27.

(2008) 2 *Maccabees*. Berlin: De Gruyter.

(2014) *Judeans and Jews: Four Faces of Dichotomy in Ancient Jewish History*. Toronto, ON: University of Toronto Press.

Schwartz, D.R., and Z. Weiss, eds. (2012) *Was 70 CE a Watershed in Jewish History? On Jews and Judaism before and after the Destruction of the Second Temple*. Leiden: Brill.

Schwartz, J. "How Jewish to Be Jewish? Self-Identity and Jewish Christians in First Century CE Palestine," in *Judaea-Palaestina, Babylon and Rome: Jews in Antiquity*, ed. B. Isaac and Y. Shahar. Tübingen: Mohr Siebeck: 55–73.

Schwartz, S. (1990) *Josephus and Judaean Politics*. Leiden: Brill.

(2001) *Imperialism and Jewish Society, 200 B.C.E. to 640 C.E.* Princeton, NJ: Princeton University Press.

(2002) "Rabbinization in the Sixth Century," in *The Talmud Yerushalmi and Graeco-Roman Culture*, Vol. 3, ed. P. Schäfer. Tübingen: Mohr Siebeck: 55–69.

(2003) "Some Types of Jewish-Christian Interaction in Late Antiquity," in *Jewish Culture and Society under the Christian Roman Empire*, ed. R. Kalmin and S. Schwartz. Leuven: Peeters: 197–210.

(2007) "Conversion to Judaism in the Second Temple Period: A Functional Approach," in *Studies in Josephus and the Varieties of Ancient Judaism: Louis H. Feldman Jubilee Volume*, ed. S.J.D. Cohen and J.J. Schwartz. Leiden: Brill: 223–36.

(2010) *Were the Jews a Mediterranean Society? Reciprocity and Solidarity in Ancient Judaism*. Princeton, NJ: Princeton University Press.

(2011) "How Many Judaisms Were There? A Critique of Neusner and Smith on Definition and Mason and Boyarin on Categorization," *Journal of Ancient Judaism* 2: 208–38.

Schwegler, A. (1846) *Das nachapostolische Zeitalter in den Hauptmomenten seiner Entwicklung*. 2 Vols. Tübingen: Fues.

Secunda, S. (2013) *The Iranian Talmud: Reading the Bavli in Its Sasanian Context*. Philadelphia, PA: University of Pennsylvania Press.

Segal, A.F. (1977) *Two Powers in Heaven: Early Rabbinic Reports about Christianity and Gnosticism*. Leiden: Brill.

(1986) *Rebecca's Children: Judaism and Christianity in the Roman World*. Cambridge, MA: Harvard University Press.

(1990) *Paul the Convert: The Apostolate and Apostasy of Saul the Pharisee*. New Haven, CT: Yale University Press.

(1991) "Matthew's Jewish Voice," in *Social History of the Matthean Community: Cross-Disciplinary Approaches*, ed. D.L. Balch. Minneapolis, MN: Fortress: 3–37.

(1992) "Jewish Christianity," in *Eusebius, Christianity, and Judaism*, ed. H.W. Attridge and G. Hata. Detroit, MI: Wayne State University Press: 326–51.

Senior, D. (1999) "Between Two Worlds: Gentiles and Jewish Christians in Matthew's Gospel," *Catholic Biblical Quarterly* 61: 1–23.

ed. (2011) *The Gospel of Matthew at the Crossroads of Early Christianity. Papers Presented at the 58th Colloquium Lovaniense, held July 29–31, 2009, in Louvain, Belgium*. Leuven: Peeters.

Setzer, C. (1994) *Jewish Responses to Early Christians: History and Polemics, 30–150 C.E.* Minneapolis, MN: Fortress.

Shaked, S. (1995) "A Persian House of Study, a King's Secretary: Irano-Aramaic Notes," *Acta Orientalia Academiae Scientiarum Hungaricae* 48: 171–86.

Shmidman, A. (2007) "Developments within the Statutory Text of the *Birkat ha-Mazon* in Light of Its Poetic Counterparts," in *Jewish and Christian Liturgy and Worship: New Insights into Its History and Interaction*, ed. A. Gerhards and C. Leonhard. Leiden: Brill: 109–26.

Sievers, J. (1990) *The Hasmoneans and Their Supporters: From Mattathias to the Death of John Hyrcanus I*. Atlanta, GA: Scholars.

Sim, D.C. (1998) *The Gospel of Matthew and Christian Judaism: The History and Social Setting of the Matthean Community*. Edinburgh: T&T Clark.

(2005) "How Many Jews Became Christians in the First Century? The Failure of the Christian Mission to the Jews," *Hervormde Teologiese Studies* 6: 417–40.

Simon, M. (1986) *Verus Israel: A Study of the Relations between Christians and Jews in the Roman Empire (AD 135–425)*, trans. H. McKeating. Oxford: Littman Library of Jewish Civilization.

Sivertsev, A. (2002) *Private Households and Public Politics in 3rd-5th Century Jewish Palestine*. Tübingen: Mohr Siebeck.

(2011) *Judaism and Imperial Ideology in Late Antiquity*. Cambridge: Cambridge University Press.

Skarsaune, O. (2007a) "Jewish Believers in Jesus in Antiquity: Problems of Definition, Method, and Sources," in *Jewish Believers in Jesus: The Early Centuries*, ed. O. Skarsaune and R. Hvalvik. Peabody, MA: Hendrickson: 3–21.

(2007b) "The Ebionites." in *Jewish Believers in Jesus: The Early Centuries*, ed. O. Skarsaune and R. Hvalvik. Peabody, MA: Hendrickson: 419–62.

(2007c) "The History of Jewish Believers in the Early Centuries: Perspectives and Framework," in *Jewish Believers in Jesus: The Early Centuries*, ed. O. Skarsaune and R. Hvalvik. Peabody, MA: Hendrickson: 745–81.

Smallwood, E.M. (1981) *The Jews under Roman Rule from Pompey to Diocletian: A Study in Political Relations*. 2nd edn. Leiden: Brill.

Smith, J.Z. (1982) "Fences and Neighbors: Some Contours of Early Judaism," in J.Z. Smith, *Imagining Religion: From Babylon to Jonestown*. Chicago, IL: University of Chicago Press: 1–18.

(1990) *Drudgery Divine: On the Comparison of Early Christianities and the Religions of Late Antiquity*. Chicago, IL: University of Chicago Press.

Smith, M. (1971) *Palestinian Parties and Politics That Shaped the Old Testament*. New York, NY: Columbia University Press.

(1978) *Jesus the Magician*. San Francisco, CA: Harper & Row.

Spence, S. (2004) *The Parting of the Ways: The Roman Church as a Case Study*. Leuven: Peeters.

Stanton, G.N. (1992) *A Gospel for a New People: Studies in Matthew*. Edinburgh: T&T Clark.

(2007) "Jewish Christian Elements in the Pseudo-Clementine Writings," in *Jewish Believers in Jesus: The Early Centuries*, ed. O. Skarsaune and R. Hvalvik. Peabody, MA: Hendrickson: 305–24.

Stemberger, G. (1977) "Die sogenannte 'Synode von Jabne' und das frühe Christentums," *Kairos* 19: 14–21.

(1993) "Hieronymus und die Juden seiner Zeit," in *Begegnungen zwischen Christentum und Judentum in Antike und Mittelalter: Festschrift für Heinz Schreckenberg*, ed. D.-A. Koch and H. Lichtenberger. Göttingen: Vandenhoeck & Ruprecht: 347–64.

(1995) *Jewish Contemporaries of Jesus: Pharisees, Sadducees, Essenes*, trans. A.W. Mahnke. Minneapolis, MN: Fortress.

(2000) *Jews and Christians in the Holy Land: Palestine in the Fourth Century*, trans. R. Tuschling. Edinburgh: T&T Clark.

(2001) "Was There a 'Mainstream Judaism' in the Late Second Temple Period?," *Review of Rabbinic Judaism* 4: 189–208.

(2012) "*Birkat Ha-Minim* and the Separation of Christians and Jews," in *Judaea-Palaestina, Babylon and Rome: Jews in Antiquity*, ed. B. Isaac and Y. Shahar. Tübingen: Mohr Siebeck: 75–88.

Stendahl, K. (1963) "The Apostle Paul and the Introspective Consciousness of the West," *Harvard Theological Review* 56: 199–215.

(1976) *Paul among Jews and Gentiles, and Other Essays*. Philadelphia, PA: Fortress.

Stern, D. (1996) *Midrash and Theory: Ancient Jewish Exegesis and Contemporary Literary Studies*. Evanston, IL: Northwestern University Press.

Stern, S. (1994) *Jewish Identity in Early Rabbinic Writings*. Leiden: Brill.

(2003) "Rabbi and the Origins of the Patriarchate," *Journal of Jewish Studies* 54: 193–215.

(2010) "Qumran Calendars and Sectarianism," in *The Oxford Handbook of the Dead Sea Scrolls*, ed. T.H. Lim and J.J. Collins. Oxford: Oxford University Press: 232–53.

Stewart-Sykes, A. (2009) *The Didascalia Apostolorum: An English Version with Introduction and Annotation*. Turnhout: Brepols.

Stökl Ben Ezra, D. (2003) "'Christians' Observing 'Jewish' Festivals of Autumn," in *The Image of the Judaeo-Christians in Ancient Jewish and Christian Literature*, ed. P.J. Tomson and D. Lambers-Petry. Tübingen: Mohr Siebeck: 53–73.

Stone, M.E. (1981) "Reactions to Destructions of the Second Temple: Theology, Perception and Conversion," *Journal for the Study of Judaism* 12: 195–204.

(2011) *Ancient Judaism: New Visions and Views*. Grand Rapids, MI: Eerdmans.

Stowers, S.K. (1994) *A Rereading of Romans: Justice, Jews, and Gentiles*. New Haven, CT: Yale University Press.

Strack, H.L., and G. Stemberger (1996) *Introduction to the Talmud and Midrash*, trans. M. Bockmuehl. 2nd edn. Minneapolis, MN: Fortress.

Strauss, D.F. (1835–1836) *Das Leben Jesu, kritische bearbeitet*. 2 Vols. Tübingen: Osiander:

Strecker, G. (1971) "On the Problem of Jewish Christianity," in W. Bauer, *Orthodoxy and Heresy in Earliest Christianity*, trans. and ed. R.A. Kraft and G. Krodel. Philadelphia, PA: Fortress: 241–85.

(1981) *Das Judenchristentum in den Pseudoklementinen*. 2nd edn. Berlin: Akademie.

Sutcliffe, A. (2003) *Judaism and Enlightenment*. Cambridge: Cambridge University Press.

Taylor, J. (2001) "The Jerusalem Decrees (Acts 15.20, 29 and 21.25) and the Incident at Antioch (Galatians 2.11–14)," *New Testament Studies* 47: 372–80.

Taylor, J.E. (1990) "The Phenomenon of Early Jewish-Christianity: Reality or Scholarly Invention?," *Vigiliae Christianae* 44: 313–34.

(1993) *Christians and the Holy Places: The Myth of Jewish-Christian Origins*. Oxford: Oxford University Press.

Taylor, M.S. (1995) *Anti-Judaism and Early Christian Identity: A Critique of the Scholarly Consensus*. Leiden: Brill.

Tcherikover, V. (1959) *Hellenistic Civilization and the Jews*, trans. S. Applebaum. Philadelphia, PA: Jewish Publication Society of America.

Teppler, Y.Y. (2007) *Birkat haMinim: Jews and Christians in Conflict in the Ancient World*, trans. S. Weingarten. Tübingen: Mohr Siebeck.

Thiel, N. (2014) "'Israel' and 'Jew' as Markers of Jewish Identity in Antiquity: The Problems of Insider/Outsider Classification," *Journal for the Study of Judaism* 45: 85–91.

Thornton, T.C.G. (1987) "Christian Understandings of the *Birkath ha-Minim* in the Eastern Roman Empire," *Journal of Theological Studies* 38: 419–31.

Tomson, P.J. (1986) "The Names Israel and Jew in Ancient Judaism and in the New Testament," *Bijdragen: Tijdschrift voor filosofie en theologie* 47: 120–40, 266–89.

 (1990) *Paul and the Jewish Law: Halakha in the Letters of the Apostle to the Gentiles*. Assen: Van Gorcum.

 (2003) "The Wars against Rome, the Rise of Rabbinic Judaism and of Apostolic Gentile Christianity, and the Judaeo-Christians: Elements for a Synthesis," in *The Image of the Judaeo-Christians in Ancient Jewish and Christian Literature*, ed. P.J. Tomson and D. Lambers-Petry. Tübingen: Mohr Siebeck: 1–31.

 (2005) "The Halakhic Evidence of Didache 8 and Matthew 6 and the Didache Community's Relationship to Judaism," in *Matthew and the Didache: Two Documents from the Same Jewish-Christian Milieu?*, ed. H. van de Sandt. Assen: Van Gorcum: 131–41.

Townsend, P. (2008) "Who Were the First Christians? Jews, Gentiles and the *Christianoi*," in *Heresy and Identity in Late Antiquity*, ed. E. Iricinschi and H.M. Zellentin. Tübingen: Mohr Siebeck: 212–30.

Trebilco, P. (1991) *Jewish Communities in Asia Minor*. Cambridge: Cambridge University Press.

Urbach, E.E. (1981) "Self-Isolation or Self-Affirmation in Judaism in the First Three Centuries: Theory and Practice," in *Jewish and Christian Self-Definition, Vol. 2: Aspects of Judaism in the Graeco-Roman Period*, ed. E.P. Sanders, A.I. Baumgarten, and A. Mendelson. Philadelphia, PA: Fortress: 269–98.

Urbano, R.C. (2012) "Levinas and Interfaith Dialogue," *Heythrop Journal* 53: 148–61.

Vahrenhorst, M. (2002) *"Ihr sollt überhaupt nicht schwören": Matthäus im halachischen Diskurs*. Neukirchen-Vluyn: Neukirchener.

Van de Sandt, H., ed. (2005) *Matthew and the Didache: Two Documents from the Same Jewish-Christian Milieu?* Assen: Van Gorcum.

Van de Sandt, H., and D. Flusser. (2002) *The Didache: Its Jewish Sources and Its Place in Early Judaism and Christianity*. Assen: Van Gorcum.

Van de Sandt, H., and J.K. Zangenberg, eds. (2008) *Matthew, James, and Didache: Three Related Documents in Their Jewish and Christian Settings*. Atlanta, GA: Society of Biblical Literature.

Van der Horst, P.W. (1998) "The Birkat Ha-Minim in Recent Research," in P.W. Van der Horst, *Hellenism-Judaism-Christianity: Essays on Their Interaction*. 2nd edn. Leuven: Peeters: 113–24.

Van Henten, J.W. (2011) "2 Maccabees," in *The Oxford Encyclopedia of the Books of the Bible*, ed. M.D. Coogan. 2 Vols. Oxford: Oxford University Press: 2.15–26.

Vana, L. (2001) "La *birkat ha-minim* è una preghiera contro i giudeocristiani?," in *Verus Israel: Nuove prospettive sul giudeocristianesimo, Atti del Colloquio di Torino (4–5 Novembre 1999)*, ed. G. Filorama and C. Gianotto. Brescia: Paideia: 147–89.

VanderKam, J.C. (2004) *From Joshua to Caiaphas: High Priests after the Exile.* Minneapolis, MN: Fortress.

(2010) *The Dead Sea Scrolls Today.* 2nd edn. Grand Rapids, MI: Eerdmans.

Verheyden, J. (1990) "The Flight of the Christians to Pella," *Ephemerides Theologicae Lovanienses* 66: 368–84.

Vermes, G. (1973) *Jesus the Jew: A Historian's Reading of the Gospels.* London: Collins.

Visotzky, B.L. (1988a) "Jots and Tittles: On Scriptural Interpretation in Rabbinic and Patristic Literatures," *Prooftexts* 8:257–69.

(1988b) "Trinitarian Testimonies," *Union Seminary Quarterly Review* 42: 73–85.

(1989) "Prolegomenon to the Study of Jewish-Christianities in Rabbinic Literature," *AJS Review* 14: 47–70.

(2003) *Golden Bells and Pomegranates: Studies in Midrash Leviticus Rabbah.* Tübingen: Mohr Siebeck.

(2008) "Goys 'Я'n't Us: Rabbinic Anti-Gentile Polemic in Yerushalmi Berachot 9:1," in *Heresy and Identity in Late Antiquity*, ed. E. Iricinschi and H.M. Zellentin. Tübingen: Mohr Siebeck: 299–313.

Vööbus, A., ed. (1979) *The Didascalia Apostolorum in Syriac.* 2 Vols. Leuven: Secrétariat du CorpusSCO.

Weber, F. (1880) *System der altsynagogalen palästinischen Theologie aus Targum, Midrasch und Talmud*, ed. F. Delitzsch and G. Schnedermann. Leipzig: Dörffling & Franke.

Weinberg, J. (1992) *The Citizen-Temple Community*, trans. D.L. Smith-Christopher. Sheffield: JSOT.

Weinfeld, M. (2005a) "The Crystallization of the 'Congregation of the Exile' (*kehal ha-golah*) and the Sectarian Nature of Post-Exilic Judaism," in M. Weinfeld, *Normative and Sectarian Judaism in the Second Temple Period.* London: T&T Clark: 232–38.

(2005b) "Universalistic and Particularistic Trends During the Exile and Restoration," in M. Weinfeld, *Normative and Sectarian Judaism in the Second Temple Period.* London: T&T Clark: 251–66.

Weitzman, S. (2004) "Plotting Antiochus' Persecution," *Journal of Biblical Literature* 123: 219–34.

(2005) *Surviving Sacrilege: Cultural Persistence in Jewish Antiquity.* Cambridge, MA: Harvard University Press.

(2008) "On the Political Relevance of Antiquity: A Response to David Goodblatt's *Elements of Ancient Jewish Nationalism*," *Jewish Social Studies* 14:165–72.

White, H. (1978) *Tropics of Discourse: Essays in Cultural Criticism.* Baltimore, MD: Johns Hopkins University Press.

White, L.M. (1991) "Crisis Management and Boundary Maintenance: The Social Location of the Matthean Community," in *Social History of the Matthean Community: Cross-Disciplinary Approaches*, ed. D.L. Balch. Minneapolis, MN: Fortress: 211–47.

Wiese, C. (2005) *Challenging Colonial Discourse: Jewish Studies and Protestant Theology in Wilhelmine Germany*, trans. B. Harshav and C. Wiese. Leiden: Brill.

Williams, M.H. (2008) *The Monk and the Book: Jerome and the Making of Christian Scholarship.* Chicago, IL: University of Chicago Press.

(2009) "No More Clever Titles: Observations on Some Recent Studies of Jewish-Christian Relations in the Roman World," *Jewish Quarterly Review* 99: 37–55.

Wilken, R.L. (1983) *John Chrysostom and the Jews: Rhetoric and Reality in the Late 4th Century*. Berkeley, CA: University of California Press
    (1984) *The Christians as the Romans Saw Them*. New Haven, CT: Yale University Press.
Wilson, S.G. (1995) *Related Strangers: Jews and Christians, 70–170 C.E.* Minneapolis, MN: Fortress.
    (2004a) "'Jew' and Related Terms in the Ancient World," *Studies in Religion* 33: 157–71.
    (2004b) *Leaving the Fold: Apostates and Defectors in Antiquity*. Minneapolis, MN: Fortress.
Yerushalmi, Y.H. (1982) *Zakhor: Jewish History and Jewish Memory*. Seattle, WA: University of Washington Press.
Yoder, J.H. (2003) *The Jewish-Christian Schism Revisited*, ed. M.G. Cartwright and P. Ochs. Grand Rapids, MI: Eerdmans.
Yuval, I.J. (2006) *Two Nations in Your Womb: Perceptions of Jews and Christians in Late Antiquity and the Middle Ages*, trans. B. Harshav and J. Chipman. Berkeley, CA: University of California Press.
Zellentin, H.M. (2011) *Rabbinic Parodies of Jewish and Christian Literature*. Tübingen: Mohr Siebeck.
Zetterholm, M. (2003) *The Formation of Christianity in Antioch: A Social-Scientific Approach to the Separation between Judaism and Christianity*. London: Routledge.
    (2009) *Approaches to Paul: A Student's Guide to Recent Scholarship*. Minneapolis, MN: Fortress.
Zsengellér, J. (2007) "Maccabees and Temple Propaganda," in *The Books of the Maccabees: History, Theology, Ideology. Proceedings of the Second International Conference on the Deuterocanonical Books, Pápa, Hungary, 9–11 June, 2005*, ed. G.G. Xeravits and J. Zsengellér. Leiden: Brill: 181–95.

Index